JOHN MALLET,

The Huguenot,

AND HIS DESCENDANTS.

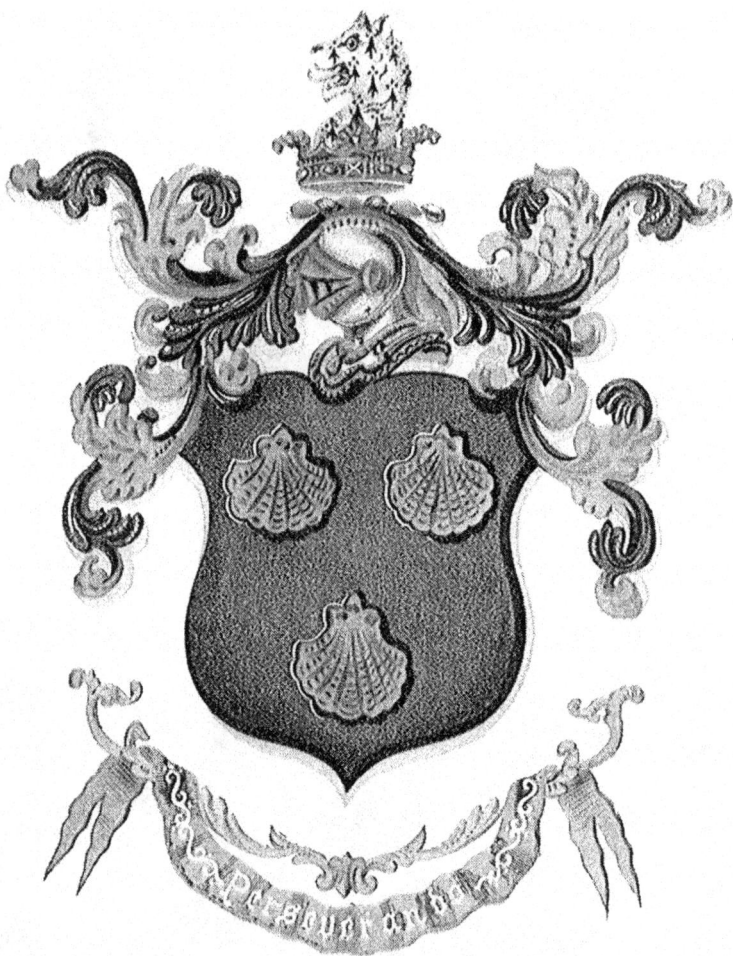

Pres tour en bel

Mallett.

JOHN MALLET
THE HUGUENOT
and
His Descendants, 1694-1894

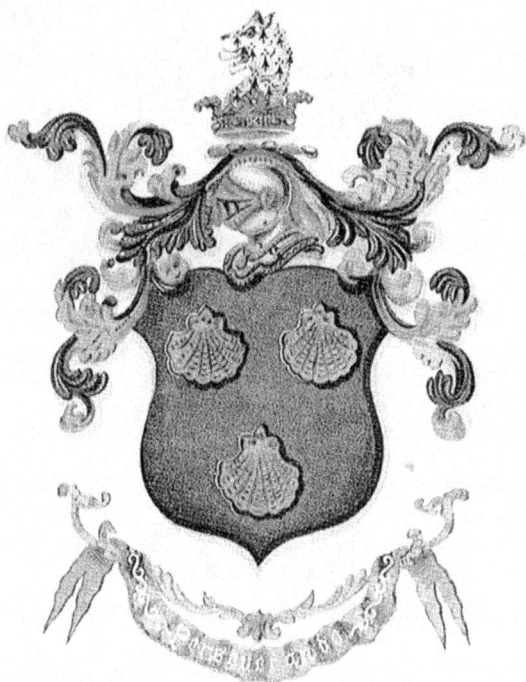

Compiled by
Anna S. Mallett

HERITAGE BOOKS
2010

HERITAGE BOOKS

AN IMPRINT OF HERITAGE BOOKS, INC.

Books, CDs, and more—Worldwide

For our listing of thousands of titles see our website
at
www.HeritageBooks.com

A Facsimile Reprint
Published 2010 by
HERITAGE BOOKS, INC.
Publishing Division
100 Railroad Ave. #104
Westminster, Maryland 21157

Originally published

Harrisburg, Pennsylvania
Harrisburg Publishing Company
1895

International Standard Book Numbers
Paperbound: 978-0-7884-1589-0
Clothbound: 978-0-7884-8514-5

PREFACE.

AMONG the faces pictured in the memories of my early childhood is that of Esquire Isaac Sherman, a gentleman well versed in the history of his native town. It was from him that my father learned that the ancestors of our family were still resting in old Stratfield burying-ground. This information resulted in a family expedition to the designated place and a search for the grave-marks. These were found lying on the ground covered with moss; they were afterwards re-set, and are still standing in a good state of preservation.

This incident, and the fact which I soon learned, that this John and Joanna Mallet were Huguenots, driven from their home in France during times of religious persecution, fired my childish imagination and inspired a strong desire to know more of the family history—and has, after many years, resulted in the following sketch and record of names and dates. Mrs. Mary L. Shelton Fairchild became equally interested in the subject, and for the past six years has been most indefatigable in her search for additional facts. Indeed, to her industry is due a very large part of the data which has made this record possible, and only her own modesty is answerable for the fact that her name does not appear upon the title page. The town and county records of Fairfield County, Conn., the almost obliterated inscriptions on old tombstones in most out-of-the-way places, and no end of living descendants of our Huguenot great-grandfather, have each and all yielded their quota of information to her pertinacity, and to her living illustration of the family motto.

We are indebted to Miss Martha E. Beach for the drawings of the old grave-marks, as well as for various items of family history. Others who have rendered most efficient aid are Mr. Percy S. Mallett, of New York city; Miss Caroline G. Mallett and Mrs. Spier Whitaker, of North Carolina; Mrs. Smith Mallett, of Elmira; Miss Margaret A. Mallett and Mr. James Mallett, of Stratford, Ct., besides many other persons. To them all, I am most grateful for their interest and their assistance. There is still lacking much which we would gladly know of the *personelle* and the manner of life of the early representatives of our family. I trust that this effort to rescue part of the history from oblivion will bring to light many more scattered facts and traditions. I shall consider it a favor if any one having such knowledge will communicate with me upon the subject.

Since the earlier pages of this volume were put in print, various interesting items have been received, which, as far as possible, have been worked into their proper places in the record, hence has come the delay in publication ; and also the necessity of putting into an Addenda, much which was received too late for other treatment.

We have had many puzzles ; some of them still remain puzzles. One, the family name of Mary Mallett, wife of (7) Peter, is only partially solved. (490) Mrs. Dexter Horton quotes (163) Mrs. Wm. Carpenter, as saying of her grandmother, this same Mary, " Her name was Booth, which made my parents ;'' (37) Naomia Mallett and Solomon Booth "cousins, and their marriage was opposed, on that account.''

The family name of (4) John's wife Martha, is also unknown. All trace of the descendants of (6) Johannah Angevine is entirely lost, beyond one grandchild, Huldah, who was mentioned in a deed of land from (32) Lewis Angevine, drawn June 18, 1771. Neither can we follow (9) Hannah Porter's family beyond her own four children. We know nothing further than is given of (13) Prudence, (15) Sarah, (20) Mercy, (21) Ruth, (22) Olive, (23) Edmund, (24) Henry, (36) Phebe. (58) Hannah, (59) Zachariah. We have been unable to get any clue to (44) Benjamin ; (43) Benjamin doubtless died in infancy. Another nearly lost link is the family of (51) Joseph ; (57) Benjamin had no descendants ; (61, 62) Rhoda and Bethiah we have been unable to follow ; (63) Huldah's children appear in the Addenda ; (71) Ebenezer Wheeler, (76) Anna Beardsley, (90) Abigail Haines, (95) Lewis Beardsley, (239) Elizabeth Beardsley, (243) Ephraim Middlebrook, and (246) Josiah Mallett had no children.

For 110, 112, 114, 116, 119 and 120, see Addenda.

The descendants of Eben Booth, given by Rev. Mr. Orcutt, in his "History of Stratford," are wrongly attributed to Eben, son of Solomon. I know nothing of (157) Eben's wife or family.

Possibly some interested reader may be able to solve some of these enigmas ; and also these others, taken from various marriage-records :

In Roxbury, Ct., Sept. 30, 1798, Abraham Summers was married to Abigail Mallett.

In Stratford, Nov. 10, 1833, David Mallett to Maria Pendleton.

Nov. 15, 1846, Isaac E. Dart to Eliza Ann Mallett.

In the will of a relative are mentioned Stephen (s. of Nehemiah) Beach, and his wife Huldah (d. of David) Mallett.

From Hubbell Genealogy, "Amarilla, d. of David Hubbell, m. William Mallett, and had issue, Jennette, who m. Chas. Benedict."

Lena Mallette m. James Mitchell. Their son, John Mitchell, of Ithaca, N. Y., was born Oct. 17, 1798. Samuel Mitchell born Oct. 5, 1803.

Fairfield, Ct., Wills, Jan. 1, 1774. Will of Daniel Middlebrook mentions wife Lydia (Mallet) and children Moses, Hannah and Sarah.

The Genealogical Record is an attempt to gather into a continuous whole, the names and dates of all the descendants of John the Huguenot: obviously, the result is very incomplete. Care has been taken to verify names and dates in every instance, still errors have doubtless crept in and verified corrections will be gladly received.

As several points of historical interest have been brought to my notice during the past year, I venture to insert them in this place.

The notes of the late Nathan G. Pond, of Milford, Ct., contain this— "John Mallet, the Huguenot, born in France 1660, died 1750. Married Jane or Joan Liron, sister to Louis Liron, merchant, of Milford." (Other notes of Mr. Pond will be found in the Errata. They are also the source of names and dates given in Addenda, page 256, children of (25) Lewis)

A recent search in the old cemetery at Milford was rewarded by finding two grave-marks with the following inscription : "Mr. Louis Liron, Merchant departed this Life September ye 18th 1738 in ye 88th year of his age." "Mrs. Katharine Liron wife to Mr. Louis Liron departed this Life Novr the 26th 1727 in the 58th year of her age."

Baird, in his Huguenot emigration to America, says : II. § 32, "Louis Lairon, a French Protestant refugee, from Nismes, in Languedoc, established himself in Milford, as early as the year 1695. He lived to become wealthy, and, dying at a good old age, made generous bequests to the French churches of Boston and New Rochelle, to the poor of Boston and to Yale College." Probate Records, New Heven.

II. 132. " Louis Liron, another fugitive from the same city (Nismes, in the lower Languedoc), established himself in trade at Milford, Conn."

" Denization (registration of names as naturalized subjects of Great

Britain) was granted, Oct. 28, 1696, to Lewis Lyron, a French Protestant." " He was naturalized September 9, 1698. He was asso-
ciated in business with Bongrand.   By his will, dated Oct. 9, 1736, he
left £200 to the French church in Boston, and £100 to the French
church in New Rochelle, ' whereof Mons. Mulinor is or lately was the
pastor or minister.'   Liron left no children—he married late in life, the
widow of Alexander Bryan."

(163) Mrs. Carpenter, before quoted, also related this tradition : " In
the days of persecution in France, one 'Mary Nymen' (the name is
spelled from memory of its sound, may it not have been Lyon or
Lyron ; and the Christian name of the grandmother, Mary, have been
ascribed to the great-grandmother ?) and her brother was secretly
helped on board a vessel by their father to flee the country and save
their lives.   This Mary Nymen married a Mallett and settled in Connecticut."

The title of ' Mr.,' which is found on these old grave-marks, was, I
learn, a record of the aristocracy of the time, and the title ' servant,'
applied to Johannah Lyon or Lyron, had no signification of degradation
or servitude.

Deeds and surveys of land, to be found among the Land Records of
Stratford, Conn., tell us of many land transactions in Tashua and other
districts of Stratford, made by different descendants of John Mallett,
from 1736 to 1794.   One, a Warrantee Deed, dated July 21, 1762, given
by Theophilus Nichols, of Stratford, recites : " Having formerly given
to Peter Mallett of ye Town, County & Colony above said, a Deed of
one acre Land joyning to his Father's heirs Land, including his grave,
dated March, 1761 ;" that deed having been lost, sd. Nichols hereby
gives a new one.

May 11, 1765, is the date of the last deed bearing the name of Peter
Mallett ; this deed also bears the name of Peter's mother, Mary Mallett.

A quit claim deed dated June 30, 1794, is given by Mary Mallett
(relict of Peter), Zachariah Mallett and Philip Mallett to Samuel Mallett, their brother.

Among the old Town and Probate Records of Fairfield, Ct., I found
these documents recorded :

" Bill brought in by David Mallet to estate of Mrs. Joanna Mallet,
May, 1758–Sept., 1764.

Sundries, amounting to, ...£11 : 15 : 4

To my Mother's Bord and taking care of her from the 7th
    day of April, 1758, to the 16th of Sept., 1764, being 335
    weeks at 5 s. pr week being for the whole, ... 83 : 15 : 0

pd to Doctr Allen, ... 0 : 2 : 0

to tendence on my mother in her Last Sickness, ... 1 : 4 : 0
    Paid by David Mallett, Exec.

To Debts and Charges after my Mother's Decease :

To digging the grave, ... 0 : 6 : 0

To going to Fairfield to settle sd. Will and Expenses, . . . 0 : 6 : 0

pd. to Timothy Sheehan for witnessing to the will, ... 3 : 0

pd. to the Court of Probate, ... 6 : 0

pd. to the Appraiser, ... 5 : 4

to my own time with ye prisers, ... 2 : 6

To going to fairfield to carry ye Inventory, ... 5 : 0

pd the Court of Probate, ... 0 : 4

paid to Zach. Angevine, ... 12 : 12 : 9

to going to ye probate to exhibit of acct, ... 5 : 0

July, 1764, pd. for 3 writs and serving on Peter Mallett and
    his mother, ... 10 : 0

Letter, apparently signed by Mary Mallet herself :

STRATFORD, May 1, 1765.

HONOUR'D SIR.

Sence I was at Fairfield, I have examined into the Afairs of the
Estate and Find that their aught to be Land Sold According to the Act
of the Assembly and therefore give my consent to have Land sold where
yourself and my Son shall thing most for the Intriss of my children

Sir I am Your to serve

MARY MALLET.

Another paper filed by Peter Mallet, Jr., is this :

The Estate of Peter Mallet Late of Stratford, Dec'd, Dr.

1760.

Jany. To coming to Court of Probate, ... 4 : 0

    " cash to " " " . . . . 6 : 0

    To cash to Doct'r Wheeler cleansing the house my
        father died in, ... 2 : 15 : 0

To Do Doctors Accts Beebe & Willoughby, ... 1 : 0 : 0

" probate of Inventory, ... 1 : 8 : 6

Feb. " Expense to Hartford, ...   12 : 0

" my Time to do & Horse 4 days, ... 1 : 06 : 0

Mar. " Dr. Christian Foot acc't tending sd. Decd. in his

small-pox, ... 5 : 11 : 6

June " funeral charges, ... 2 : 12 : 0

" Cash pd. Summers & Hawley for boarding the

children of sd. Decd. in his sickness, ... 1 : 4 : 0

" Cash pd. W. S. Johnson, ... 38 : 0 : 0

Sept. " Dr. Jonas Curtis, acct, ...   9 : 8

"   " Edmd   "   . . . .   6 : 0

1762.

Feb. " Int. Money to pd. Joanna Mallet, ... 11 : 0 : 0

To Sundry Journeys to New York and to many places

in this Government, and my Time & Expence

and to much Time & Expence & Trouble in set-

tling Accts with people & exchanging great

sums of money, &c., ... 72 : 11 : 6

Total, . 199 : 6 : 0 (?)

I am often asked about family silver: the only pieces of which I know anything are in the possession of different descendants of (38) Peter, of North Carolina; a coffee pot and two mugs or cups, all bearing the family crest and motto.

On page 26, when the death of this same Peter's wife and little boy are recorded, no mention is made of the fate of the little daughter whose baptism is noted in Stratford church record, Sept. 14, 1773, and who was doubtless on her way to North Carolina with her mother and brother. From another source I learn that this little motherless girl Mary, who also was ill with the small-pox, was left by her mother in charge of Mrs. Emmet, the wife of Col. Emmet, who was in command at Harper's Ferry—to whom she became devotedly attached, calling her "Ma Emmet," and being herself known as "the child of the Regmient."

"When Mary was seventeen, she yielded to her love for the brilliant and handsome young Irishman, Edward Jones, and sailed away with him. Peter fired at the boat as it shot from under the window of the room in which he had confined his daughter, happily doing no damage.

He, however, soon became reconciled to her, and bestowed upon her, a residence and tract of land in Chatham County, North Carolina, long the homestead of the family, and known as Rock Rest in their annals."

" Edward Jones, the second son of Dr. Conway Jones, and Mary Wray Todd, his wife, was born at Lisburn, Ireland; but came to the United States in 1783. He attained high distinction as a lawyer and statesman, and in 1791 became Solicitor General of the State." A younger son of (38) Peter was named for this Edward Jones, and became himself, a man of considerable prominence.

Of the children of Edward and Mary Jones, the youngest son was sent to Paris for a medical education, and became a distinguished physician of North Carolina, the eldest daughter married Rev. William Hooper, D. D., a scholar and literateur, and descendant of the signer of the Declaration of Independence ; the next two, lawyers of North Carolina, and the youngest, Louisa, who is still living, married Abraham Renchor, a lawyer, member of Congress and Governor of New Mexico.

Mrs. Hooper's granddaughter is the wife of Hon. Spier Whitaker, until very recently Judge of the Superior Court of North Carolina, and youngest son of Spier Whiteker, the Attorney General, North Carolina, 1842–1846.

It seems that the military record of the family is not quite complete, for I find that

Philo[5] Mallet was a Drum-Major during the Revolution.

David Mallett was in service in the War of 1812.

Peter's son, Charles Peter, was the father of seven sons who served faithfully in the Confederate Army.

Wm. Mallett, of Western New York, was in the Union Army, also (728) Henry Wm. M., of New Milford, Ct.

Of men who have married daughters of John the Huguenot :

In the Revolution : Hezekiah Edwards.

In the Civil War, Union Army: Levi Lyon, Homer F. Tilford, Henry Jenkins, David Smith, Edward Hall, Daniel Compton.

The latter was one of five brothers who served from Pennsylvania. He was wounded, promoted to be Second Lieutenant and served till the close of the war.

Doubtless other names have been omitted, which should be included in the Honor Roll.

Washington, D. C., June 1, 1895.

CONTENTS.

EXPLANATIONS.

In the tabulated portion of the Genealogical Record, commencing on page 44—the first column contains the number of each individual descendant of John Mallet, No. 3 to No. 3577, consecutively. The second column gives the name of each descendant (quotation marks indicating the name commonly used), and under that name, and a little to the right, the name of wife or husband in italics. If the wife of any descendant has been previously married, her name, by that marriage, follows in brackets, her maiden name. The small number following the name of each descendant, is the generation number, ten generations being represented. In the third column is given the date of birth, or in some instances of baptism; in the fourth, the date of marriage; in the fifth, the place of residence, (where possible, I have followed this plan, of chiidren of all who died young, and of wives who have died before their husbands, I have given their places of birth—of those of maturer years, including widows, their place of actual residence); the sixth column gives the date of death—the seventh, the place of burial.

To find any name, refer to index, which gives record number and page number.

To find the ancestor of any person trace back—for instance page 240, take No. 3315, the child of No. 2207; page 179—No. 2207 is the child of No. 987; page 106—No. 987 is the child of No. 392; page 66—No. 392 is the child of No. 129; page 51—No. 129, is the child of No. 35; page 46—No. 35 is the child of No. 7; page 44—No. 7 is the child of No. 2; No. 2 is the child of No. 1.

On the other hand, to find the descendants of any person mentioned, trace down—for instance, take No. 5, page 44, his children occur on page 45, Nos. 25, 26, 27; grandchildren page 50 and 51, No. 108 to 127; next generation, page 63 to 65, No. 340 to 390; together with others to be found in the Addenda; next generation, page 97 to 105, No. 852 to 979; next generation, page 168 to 179, No. 2010 to 2197; next generation, page 233 to 239, No. 3188 to 3301; next generation, page 253, No. 3524 and 3525.

PLACES OF BURIAL.

The old "Stratfield Burying Ground" formerly lay in the town of Fairfield, but is now within the city limits of Bridgeport, Conn. The principal cemetery of Bridgeport is Mountain Grove, for which the abbreviation M. G. C. B. C. has been used.

In the town of Trumbull, formerly a part of Stratford, are cemeteries at Tashua, Long Hill (L. H. Tr.), Unity and Trumbull.

At Fayetville, N. C., 1. Fayetteville distinguishes the private burial-place of General Peter Mallett and his family from the public cemetery of the city.

At Catharine, N. Y., is a cemetery in the village itself, and also one at North Settlement. At Montour, the adjoining settlement west of Catharine, and near to each other, are the Highland (H), and the old Coe cemeteries. Havana is also in Montour.

ABBREVIATIONS.

Page 111, Col. c., College Cemetery.
" 54, N. Cem., New Cemetery.
" 65, O. C., Old Cemetery.
" 68, O. C., Oakwood Cemetery.
" 69, P. P., Pine Park. (Plantation).
" 62, St. Oloff, a Cemetery in Minnesota.
" 264, F. L., Forest Lawn Cemetery.

OTHER ABBREVIATIONS.

ae.   signifies aged.
B.   "   Brook.
bap.   "   baptized.
d.   "   (in 2d column) daughter : (in 6th) died.
dec.   "   deceased.
E. B.   "   East Bridgeport, p. 78.
Eng.   "   England.
Gr. and Gd. signifies Grand Rapids.
inf.   signifies infancy.
Lt.   "   lieutenant.
m.   "   married.
Mt.   "   mount.
N. E.   "   North Elmira.
N. M.   "   near Monroe, p. 53, 70.

Rev.   "   Revolutionary, p. 51.
s.   "   son.
Spr. Spgs. signifies Springs.
Tp. signifies township.
unm.   "   unmarried.
Val.   "   valley.
W. T.   "   West Toledo, p. 56.

ERRATA.

NOTE.—Items due to Town Records of Orange, Ct., marked (O).
Items due to manuscript of Nathan G. Pond, marked (P).

Page 7, line 25, insert "30."

" 10, " 27, for 1775 read 1755.

" 15, " 5, for "father's," read "grandfather's."

" 15, " 10, for "is," read "stood on the site of."

" 15, lines 18, 20, and 22, for (448) read (456).

" 15, last line, for (516) read (524).

" 44, second column, title, read "Name, and that of Wife (or Husband).

" 44, (2) wife was Jane or Joan Liron. (P).

" 44, (4) John lived in Tashua; his wife, Sarah's mother, was Abigail Hubbell.

" 44, (5) Lewis' wife's mother was Abigail, (d. Nathaniel and Mary Camp) Briscoe.

" 45, (25) Lewis' wife's father was Miles Merwin.

" 45, (25) children (P), see Addenda.

" 45, (26) husband Nathan born 12–24, 1721 (P) for children (P), see Addenda.

" 45, (27) husband David died 1784. (P).

" 48, (72) wife, Patience (d. Eliakim) Walker.

" 49, (102) bap. for 5–25, read 6–25.

" 50, (106, 107) dates given are for baptism, not birth.

" 50, (111) born 11–6, 1762; d. 6–25, 1844; wife born 1–9, 1767. (O).

" 51, (126, 127) for marriages (P), see Addenda.

" 52, (163) husband Wm. B. Carpenter.

" 53, (173) second wife, for "de Berniene," read "de Berniere."

" 53, (174) second wife, Abigail Jane, (d. David L. Haight.)

" 55, (215) marriage to Sarah, not Eunice, 1804.

" 57, for children of (63) see Addenda, p. 257.

" 57, (238) husband born 1808.

Page 57, (243) wife, for 9-11 read 9-17.
" 58, (250) death, for 12-24 read 12-29.
" 59, (265) death, for 1885 read 1855.
" 59, (269) wife's mother was Susannah Mead.
" 62, (326) for Shuman read Sluman.
·" 63, (340) husband, born 1774; died 10-3, 1830.
" 63, (342) for Sibbe read Sibyl ; m. 2-12, 1818. (O).
" 63, (350) m. Jan. 3. (P).
" 63, (353) died 10- , 1823 ; husband died at Darien, Ga. (P).
" 63, (354) husband, b. 3-17 ; m. 1819 ; d. 6-9, 1819. (P).
" 63, for children of (110) see Addenda, p. 258.
" 64, (357) died 3-3, 1810, at Orange, unmarried (P), consumption.
    (O).
" 64, (361) husband, add grandson Capt. Bradford and Sarah Bald-
    win Steele.
" 64, (361) m. Burr Steel, of Derby, 11-8, 1821. (O) (P).
" 64, (363) m. Zalina Bristol, and d. 12-21, 1828. (P).
" 64, for children of (112) see Addenda, p. 259.
" 64, (364) d. in Milford, 3-28, 1881, unm. (O).
" 64, (365) Falla. (O).
" 64, (366 and 362) Fowler and Phebe, b. 9-2, 1808. Fowler lived
    in Orange. (O).
" 65, for children of (114, 116, 119, 120) see Addenda, p. 259, 260.
" 65, (373) second wife, Sarah Staley. (P).
" 65, (374) husband died 1868. (P).
" 66, for children of (126, 127) see Addenda, p. 261.
" 67, (409) h. b. for 12-4, read 12-24.
" 67, children of 157, for reason of blank numbers, see Preface, under
    Eben Booth.
" 68, children of 159, for correct list see Addenda, p. 262.
" 69, (441) husband ; burial, for Wilmington read Chapel Hill.
" 70, (450) birthplace, Fayetteville, N. C.; husband lived at Mobile,
    Ala.
" 70, (459) wife, b., for 5-18 read 5-8.
" 72, (495) death, for 12-13 read 12-31.
" 72, (497) burial, for Ia., read Ill.
" 73, (515) wife, b. Canisteo, N. Y.; 2d wife, b. in Millport.

" 73, (518) husband, b. 6–24, 1818.

" 75, (537) husband, for 1295 read 1282.

" 79, (600) death, for 6–16 read 1–16.

" 79, (601) second wife, birth, for 3–19 read 11–19.

" 79, (604) m., for 2–25 read 2–5.

" 80, (612) for Dey read Day.

" 80, (613) for Delason read Davis.

" 80, (615 b, 615 d, 615 g) see Addenda, p. 263.

" 80, for 515 j read 615 j.

" 81, 615 o and 615 oo, see Addenda, p. 263.

" 83, (643) husband, for 1403, read 1390.

" 84, (657) entirely wrong, number vacant.

" 86, for children of 261, see Addenda, p. 264.

" 87, (702) for Lyman read Lynson.

" 88, (712) wrong, number vacant.

" 88, (713) Salmon Dewitt.

" 89, (737) column 5, for Booklyn read Brooklyn.

" 89, (738) m., for 5 read 3; burial, for Trumbull read Pembroke
        Cemetery, Bridgeport, Ct.

" 90, (753) deceased.

" 92, for children of (315) see Addenda, p. 265.

" 93, (806) husband, for 9–6 read 7–6.

" 100, for 364 read 354.

" 102, (919a) for Newton read Norton.

" 103, (928) b., for 1855 read 1835.

" 104, (954) for Ball read Bull.

" 107, (1009) death, for 3 read 5.

" 108, (1023) husband, George N.

" 114, (1102) wife, for J. read I.

" 119, (1206) for Millport read West Virginia.

" 120, (1224) for N. J. read N. Y.

" 124, (1287) husband, for (2190) read (2202).

" 125, (1298) wife, for Emeline read Emeline A.

" 128, (1345) husband, for (2574) read (2586).

" 141, line 28, for 615 p read 615 oo.

" 142, for children of 620 see Addenda, p. 267.

" 142, for children of (624) see Addenda, p. 268.

" 142, (1575) wife, for Godfreg read Godfrey.

" 150, for children of 694 see Addenda, p. 268.

" 152, (1745) wife, for Bond read Baun; for 5——, read 5–23.

" 156, (1808) m. Georgia A. Field; he died in Texas, probably in
      1885, leaving one son, name unknown.

" 156, (1809) did not marry G. A. Field.

" 161, line 28, for Frelich read Freeling.

" 173, (2111) husband, (s. David B.).

" 184, for children of (1028 d) see Addenda, p. 268.

" 184, "   "   " (1041 a, b, c, d, e, f, h) see Addenda, p. 269.

MALLETT.

Many persons now living in the United States bear the name of Mallett. The word is sometimes accented on the first syllable, precisely like the implement of labor of similar name; and in other cases, with more euphony, the accent is thrown on the last syllable; possibly it might be still better if all could return to the French pronunciation, with the *e* sounded like *a* in gain.

Some of the Malletts scattered through the Western and Southwestern States, and on the Pacific slope, came there directly from England; others of them trace their ancestry to one, of the Roman Catholic faith, who came from France to Canada in 1640.

Most of those living in the Atlantic States, who bear the name, trace back to (2) John[2] Mallet, a Huguenot, who escaped from France after the Revocation of the Edict of Nantes, and came first to South Carolina. After one or two voyages between England and America, he came to New Rochelle, and finally settled in Fairfield, Conn., about 1700.

All of these scattered representatives can trace their origin back to a Norman tribe, which invaded France from Scandinavia, early in the eighth century.

Hume thus gives the origin of the Normans: * "The Emperor Charlemagne, though naturally generous and humane, had been induced by bigotry to exercise great severities upon the pagan Saxons in Germany, and had obliged them, by the most rigorous edicts, to make a seeming compliance with the Christian doctrine. That religion which had easily made its way among the British Saxons, appeared shocking to their German brethren when imposed on them by the violence of Charlemagne; many of them fled northward into Jutland, in order to escape his persecutions.

"Meeting there with a people of similar manners, they were readily received among them, and they soon stimulated the natives to concur in enterprises which promised revenge on the haughty conqueror."

---

* Hist. of Eng., Vol. I., Chap. 2.

"They invaded the provinces of France, which were exposed by the degeneracy and dissensions of Charlemagne's posterity ; and being there known under the general name of Normans, which they received from their northern situation, they became the terror of all the maritime, and even of the inland countries."

One member of our wide-spread family, the Genevese, Paul Henri Mallet, was called, in 1752, to a professorship of Belles-lettres, in the city of Copenhagen.

Some of his leisure time he occupied in studying and writing the history of Scandinavia.

* "He first clearly showed the Scandinavian element in the civilization of the French, the English, the Spanish, the Italians, and all the people generally, who are formed from the mixture of the degenerate descendants of the Romans with the vigorous children of the North."

† In 1066, William, duke of Normandy, took the first step toward the conquest of all England, when he won the battle of Hastings.

In 1069, one of William's followers, William Mallet, was *second* in command of the castle of York ; *first*, after Robert Fitz-Richard was slain. William Mallet was himself killed, with 3,000 men, in the assault upon the castle of the Danes.

Again, Robert de Mallet is cited among the Norman nobles in England, who influenced Robert, duke of Normandy, to attempt to wrest the English throne from his brother, Henry I. And still again, allusion is made to "the great estates of Robert Mallet," from which he had been excluded, and which were bestowed upon Stephen, afterwards king of England.

All of which only goes to show that there have been representatives of this Norman tribe, or family, living in England certainly ever since the conquest.

In a letter written from Southampton, England, in September, 1882, General, the Baron de Mallet Molesworth, says that "The family of Mallets, or Malets, an ancient Norman tribe, came from Scandanavia about 700 or 750 A. D." It was distinguished by a terrible weapon, which did great execution, "a long hammer, with a *point* at the other end"—a *mallet* with one side pointed.

Later, the word was Latinized, and became Maillet, or Mallet, as in English.

---

* Weiss. Hist. of the French Prot. Refugees.   † See Hume.

"In France there are Mallets nearly everywhere, east and west. It is probable that the name was written *Malet*, as better Latin; then Mallet, but never Mallett, that is an embellishment entirely Anglo-Saxon. In England there is Sir Alexander Malet and Sir Louis Mallet. The chief of all the Mallets, Malets, is the Marquis Malet de Graville of Normandy."

At least *one* of the earlier Mallets joined the Crusaders led by Baldwin, Count of Flanders; he did not return to France, but settled in Antioch; his descendants however eventually returned to Normandy.

In 1530, one of the chiefs of the Norman family, Malet de Graville, Jacques Mallet, of Rouen, a Huguenot, was compelled to hurriedly leave his fatherland, on account of his religious convictions; he settled in Geneva, then ruled by Calvin. Some of his descendants still reside in that city.

Both in France and Switzerland many of the name have been distinguished in literature, as well as in the army and navy.

Exile to America.

After the Revocation of the Edict of Nantes by Louis XIV., in 1680, which caused such great distress to the Huguenots of France, numbers of them escaped from their fatherland, some of the refugees finding a home in America.

Very early in that period, a colony of them, about one hundred and fifty families, settled New Oxford, Mass; and in the early records of Charlestown, Mass.; of Warren, Maine; and of Rhode Island; I find different notices of the name of Mallett, but whether or not connected with our branch, I am unable to decide. Certainly they were not descendants of (2) John² Mallet, of Fairfield, Conn., although in one instance it is recorded that a "notice be sent to the (14) Matthew⁴ Mallets, of North Stratford, Conn.," which would point to some knowledge of each other.

☐ Previous to the Revocation, (1) David¹ Mallet, a Huguenot, held some position of prominence in the army of Louis XIV.; his five sons were also in that army.

After the Revocation, persecution ensued; one of the sons was broken on the wheel; the father and the other four sons escaped. (1) David¹ fled to England; one son had already established himself in Yorkshire as a physician; one son went to Germany; the third son (2) John² came

to America, bringing with him a brother, and a nephew, Peter.[3]
(2) John[2] was apparently a man of wealth, and succeeded in bringing
some of his property with him in his escape from France; although
among his descendants in Connecticut and western New York, the
story has always been current that our ancestor was a ship carpenter,
and that he escaped from France, probably Lyons, with only his broad-
axe and his Bible.   A further version tells of his being secreted in a
carpenter's chest by his young wife and thus carried on board ship,
and that his Bible was hidden in a block of wood shaped like a foot-
stool.   We have searched in vain for that Bible, which was probably
a copy of the edition of 1643, which bore this title-page:

LA SAINTE

BIBLE

INTERPRETEE PAR JEAN DIODATI

MDCXLIII

Imprimee a Geneve.

The letter, to be found later on, written by John's grandson,
(38) Peter,[4] (Gen. Peter Mallett, of Wilmington and Fayetteville, N. C.,)
gives a somewhat different coloring to his antecedents.   According to
this (2) John[2] purchased lands on the Santee river, in South Carolina,
and settled his nephew Peter[3] there; he also bought land in Boston,
Mass., and settled his brother in that place.   For himself he bought
land at New Rochelle, N. Y., but soon exchanged it for other land at
Fairfield, Conn., and was living there as early as 1710.   The young
wife, whose name we do not know, who came with (2) John[2] from France,
died in South Carolina, and also her two boys;[3] the third and only
remaining child[3] died at the North.   About 1699 (2) John[2] married his
servant, Johannah Lyon, who also had come with him from France.
She could neither read nor write, and was perhaps a peasant woman.
It is told of her, in illustration of her physical strength, that upon one
occasion she took up a wooden plough and carried it on her shoulder
to her husband, who was at the time on Toilsome Hill, some three or
four miles north of his home.

LIFE IN CONNECTICUT.

We are now getting down to the time of actual record.   After search-
ing the Town Records of Fairfield, Bridgeport and Stratford; the Church

Records of these towns, and of Trumbull and Huntington, Conn.; as well as of Wilmington and Fayetteville, N. C.; records in family Bibles innumerable, and upon countless tombstones, in widely scattered cemeteries—there has been compiled the accompanying Genealogy of the Mallett family, for nearly two hundred years, and this brief sketch of the life of some of its members in the United States.

Stratford, Connecticut, was settled in 1639; Fairfield, its adjoining neighbor on the West, at about the same time; Bridgeport, the intervening town, whose territory has been carved from that of Stratford and Fairfield, counted a few settlers in 1665. *"The first hundred years produced only a farming community with beautiful fields, comely residences and a numerous, toiling, happy people, with now and then a vessel sailing out of the harbor. The farmer in his manly frock of tow, plowed the smooth fields, and gathered in the abundant harvest from year to year, with increasing pleasure and gain—while his womanly wife spun the tow to make the frock, and provided the frugal, healthful repast, by the strength of which, the harvests were gathered, and the homes made comfortable."

The settlement flourished under the names of Pequonnock, Fairfield village, Stratfield, and Newfield, until in October, 1800, it was incorporated as the Borough of Bridgeport, the first incorporated Borough in Connecticut. The fine street in that town, now known as Park avenue, was in earlier years known as Division street, and served as the Division line between Bridgeport and Fairfield, or in the earlier part of the eighteenth century, between Stratford and Fairfield.

On the west side of the lower part of this Division street (or Mutton Lane), has stood until this year (1893) a plain frame dwelling, known for many years as the Mallett homestead. Whether or not this identical house is the same alluded to by Gen. (38) Peter⁴ Mallett, as "the elegant mansion built by his grandfather, in the French style," I am not prepared to affirm; but that the particular tract of land (forty acres) occupied in part, by that house, and by many of the fine residences in the neighborhood, and by some portion of Seaside Park, was the homestead of the first (2) John² Mallett, is proved by several deeds, still preserved in the old land records of Fairfield and Stratford.

This farm, bounded north by the highway, south by the Sound, east and west by the lands of Timothy Wheeler and Isaac Hall; was sold in

---

* Orcutt's History of Stratford and Bridgeport.

1700 by Ephraim Wheeler of Stratfield, to "Johanest Courtlandt of New York city, marchant."

Said Courtlandt sold the forty acres, July 3, 1701, for "one hundred and fifty pounds, current money of N. Y.," to Lewis Lyon of Milford, Ct., marchant." Lewis Lyon was the brother of Johannah Lyon, wife of (2) Mr. John[2] Mallett, and March 20, 1710, he deeded this same farm to (3) David,[3] (4) John,[3] and (5) Lewis[3] Mallett, in consideration of two hundred pounds paid to him by their father, (2) John[2] Mallett; with the proviso that Jane (or Joanna) Mallett, their mother, "shall have the full use of ye above said farm and 'bulding' during her natural life."

A lease of this same homestead was given Sept. 10, 1736, by (5) Lewis[3] Mallett, of Milford, to his father and mother (2) John[2] and Jane; consideration, one bushil of apples yearly, also a quit-claim of same date, by (5) Lewis[3] to (3) David[3] and (4) John[3] of the "aforesaid homestead on which my father now dwells." All these records make it seem very probable that (2) John[2] Mallet resided on this homestead, on the west side of what is now Park Avenue, Bridgeport, from before 1710, until his death in 1745. One of his descendants tells me, that when her ancestor built upon this land, there were but four houses on the street.

It would be most interesting, if any of the belongings of (2) John[2] or Joanna had been preserved to the present time, but none have as yet come to light. The nearest approach is the description given by the late Mrs. Brothwell of (2) John's[2] coach or carriage which she remembered. In the Parish Records of the Church of Christ, of Stratfield, which was the predecessor of the present North Congregational Church of Bridgeport, appear these entries :

Renewed covenant, Mallet, Mr., Apr. 29, 1705.
"   David, Mch. 5, 1731–2.
Baptism, David, son of Mr. Mallett, bap. Apr. 29, 1705.

Apparently (5) Lewis[3] Mallett, of Milford, became the owner of the Division St. homestead, after the death of his mother in 1764 ; but both he and his son (25) Lewis[4] continued to live in Milford. In 1781 and in 1787, we find (108) Lewis, grandson of the first (5) Lewis[3] buying lands contiguous to the old homestead, and in 1790, (5) Lewis[3] deeds this same thirty acres, house, barn, etc., to his son (25) Lewis[4] of Milford, and his grandson (108) Lewis[5] of Fairfield.

Mrs. Stephen Hawley, a lineal descendant of (25) Lewis⁴ told me that he bought this land, but preferring to live in Milford, he told his son (108) Lewis⁵ that if he would marry, he should have the property; accordingly this (108) Lewis⁵ married Anna Beach, came to live upon the Fairfield homestead in 1778 or 1779, (so Anna says in her Pension Application,) and it has belonged to him and to his descendants in a direct line to the present time.

In addition to this land on the Sound, John Mallett bought of Agur Tomlinson, May 5, 1710, 32 acres at Tawtashua hill, for 32 pounds. Nov. 20, 1710, Lewis Lyon sold to "John Mallet, shipwright," "eighty acres of woodland lying in ye county of Stratford, being of ye six miles division so called according to ye grant of said towne of Stratford;" that also being in Tashua. In 1739, and 1740, deeds are recorded, showing gifts from (2) John² to his sons (3) David³, and (4) John³ of 230 acres of land at Tashua, and one to his daughter (6) Joanna³ Angevine, of land in Stratford, which I think was situated on the north side of the King's highway, (now North Ave.) near its intersection with Park Avenue.

The Tashua lands, or portions of them, are still in possession of (2) John's² descendants of the same name; mostly, I think, in the line of (3) David³, his eldest son. Two slate-stone grave marks, sacred to the memory of (2) John², and Joanna Mallet are still in existence, in the old Stratfield burying ground, corner North and Clinton avenues, Bridgeport, Conn., drawings of which are given elsewhere. On page will be found the will of (2) John² Mallet in full—the inventory of his estate amounted to £2,039, but he had given the most of his landed property to his five children before his death.

FAMILY OF (2) JOHN² AND JOANNAH MALLET.

There is still in existence an old worm-eaten paper once in the possession of Rev. James Kant, who was the pastor of Trumbull Congregational Church, until 1835, which bears this record;

"The heirs of John and Johannah Lyon Mallet are as follows :

David, born in Stratfield, Conn., ... 1701

John, jr., born in Stratfield, Conn., ... 1703

Lewis, born in Stratfield, Conn., ... 1706

Johannah, born in Stratfield, Conn., ... 1710

Peter, born in Stratfield, Conn., ... 1712

The heirs of John Mallet, jr., were 4 sons, 8 daughters; the heirs of Lewis were 1 son, 2 daughters; Johannah Mallett married Leah Angevine, her heirs were 3 sons and 4 daughters; the heirs of Peter were six sons and 3 daughters.''

Of these five children (5) Lewis[3] was taken by his uncle Lewis Lyon, of Milford, whose namesake he was; lived with him in Milford and became his heir. The other three sons, (3) David[3], (4) John[3] and (7) Peter[3] settled on the Tashua lands; although it seems probable that David and John spent part of their lives on the homestead on the Sound. (6) Johannah[3] Angevine (whose husband's name is given in deeds as Zechariah) was given a home in the upper part of Stratfield; her son (29) Zechariah[4] afterward owning an adjoining farm. It is said of (6) Johannah[3] Mallet that she was '' the handsomest girl who ever crossed the water;'' that she was engaged to be married to some gentleman who left her for a journey to the old world. He was away for such a long time that she wearied of waiting for him, and instead married Mr. Angevine. (3) David[3] married Esther Angevine, a French lady, then living at New Rochelle. He died at Tashua Aug. 22, 1777. His will, dated March 15, 1775, mentions his wife, his daughter (12) Esther[4] Wheeler, and his three sons, (8) John[4], (10) David[4] and (11) Joseph[4], but does not mention his daughter (9) Hannah[4] Porter—she may have died before her father.

(3) David's[3] second son (10) David[4] kept an inn at The Old Landlord House, north of Chubb brook on Tashua street. His family were sometimes called the Nepucket Malletts, in allusion to a story connecting him with the Indians. An Indian squaw lived on the west side of Tashua street, between Chubb brook and the place now owned by (228) George A. Mallett's[6] heirs. Upon one occasion, before going to '' The Salts '' (which was the shore of Long Island Sound), she turned her spotted pig, '' Nepucket,'' into the woods near by, to feed upon the nuts while she was away. Her absence was so prolonged that (10) David[4] Mallett, thinking that she must be dead, caught and killed the pig. Sometime afterward the squaw returned, and brought suit against (10) David[4] for her pig. A piece of pork was all that remained of poor '' Nepucket.'' An interesting relic of this same (10) David[4], is a valentine, sent by him, in 1780, to his third wife, Polly Youngs, a Jewess. It must be seen to be appreciated. When folded, it is about four inches square, and has a pansy painted on the cover; it has four other illustra-

tions in colors, and twelve verses, and is so curiously folded that upon unfolding, each illustration develops into two more. These are the verses :

> Adam comes first upon the stage
> And Eve out of his side
> Was given to him in Mariage
> Turn up and see his Bride.
>
> Eve Inocent You may behold
> From pride & afectation Free
> The under leaf you may Unfold
> Another Sight To See
>
> View not the mairmaid if you do
> her Sweet Aluring Song
> will lead you into further Woe
> with her Deluding Tongue
>
> A Lion Roaring from his Den
> Created was To Range
> He'se Turned into another Shape
> Turn up & See how Strange
>
> A Griffen here you may behold
> half bird half beast is he
> Do but the under leaf unfold
> A Stranger Sight Youle See
>
> See here within an Eagles Claws
> A little Infant Lies
> which he has Siez'd on as a Pray
> with Expanded wings to Fly
>
> Now I've escaped the eagles claws
> And am from Danger Free
> I'le set myself to gathering Gold
> Turn down the leaf & See.
>
> My heart here is Oppresst with Care
> What Salve can Cure the Same
> Under the leaf there is a Cure
> Lift up & See it Plain
>
> A piece of gold & Silver Store
> has Cur'd my heart tis Sick no more
> but is from cares & Troubles Free
> no Worldly fears shall Trouble me

Now I have gold enough in Store
bribe from the ritch Work from the poor
what worldly cares Can Trouble me
Turn down the leaf & there youle See

Sickness comes on & death draws nigh
Help gold & silver elce I Die
Allas tis vain it is but Dross
Turn up and see my end at last.

See now poor man thou art but Dust
Thy gold & silver is but dust
thy Time is Done thy glass is Spent
Thy Cares nor fears can't Death prevent

The family of (4) John[3] has long been an enigma ; but the discovery
of his will has given us indisputably the names of his twelve children.
*His son (14) Matthew[4] was in 1773 "established by the Connecticut
Assembly to be Lieutenant of the company or train-band in the north-
western part of the town of Stratford," which company had been formed
in 1772 upon the "memorial of Matthew Mallett and others." Later,
this same (14) Matthew[4] proved a turncoat and became a Tory, dying
in the English service, in 1775 or later. His son (74) Stephen[5] also
joined the British, and in 1780 part of his estate was confiscated.
(7) Peter,[3] the youngest child of (2) John,[2] lived at thefoot of Tashua
hill, on the west side of the road. He was a blacksmith by trade,
but increased his means by carrying on a barter in negro slaves. Both
(2) John,[2] and (7) Peter[3] mention negro slaves in their wills. (7) Peter[3]
was also a Commissary in the army during the French and Indian
wars in 1775-6. He died of small-pox, contracted during a visit
to New York, in connection with his business of trading in slaves
and cattle ; and was buried in the field back of the saw mill ; the
burial being made at night, by his wife and children ; his grave-
mark is still standing. The inventory of (7) Peter's[3] estate amounted
to £7,046 ; his property consisting of personal effects, live stock,
real estate, notes, and bonds. His wife Mary, and eldest son (38)
Peter[4] were appointed executors of the estate, and in the Colonial Records, as well as in the Town Records, are several notices of facts relating to the fulfilling of these duties. Also Records are still extant of
appointment of guardians to the younger children. This son (38)

---

* Colonial Records, Conn.

Peter[4] seemed to succeed, in a measure, to his father's business of Commissary in the Colonial army, and later occupied a similar position to the Continental troops of North Carolina, during the earlier part of the Revolution.

The will of Mary Mallett (widow of (7) Peter[3]) was dated Feb. 23, 1778; probated May 23, 1779. In this she gives to her "beloved son Peter, ten shillings, who has nearly had his proportion before." Her son Philip is to have " my dwelling house where he now lives, and what land under it and adjoining to it, in that town. Moreover, I give unto him my great Bible." Other children mentioned are Samuel and Zachariah, Daniel, Mary Summers, Phebe Hawley, and Naomi Booth.

From all this we learn that the father of the Malletts, and his own immediate family, lived for the greater part of their lives in the southwestern corner of little Connecticut, and died in their own homes. The next generation began to wander, and now the homes of the twenty-one hundred descendants are scattered over the entire globe.

Of the grandchildren of (2) John,[2] (3) David's[3] sons and daughters, settled within a few miles of their father's home; most of (4) John's[3] twelve children did likewise, but his two daughters (half sisters), Mehitable and Eunice, who married two brothers, Isaac and Michael Beardsley, moved to Catharine, Schuyler co., N. Y., in 1800. Mehitable and Isaac, however, must have returned to Connecticut, and are buried in Huntington.*

(7) Peter's[3] eldest son (38) Peter,[4] and the next to the youngest son, (42) Daniel,[4] migrated from the rocks of Connecticut to the sands of North Carolina.

In Fayetteville, N. C., there is a beautiful sheet of water which still bears the name of " Mallett Pond," taking the name in honor of Gen. (38) Peter.[4]

Hundreds of miles north of this point, on the Vermont side of Lake Champlain, there is an inlet of the lake, a few miles north of the city of Burlington, known as Mallett Bay. Tradition derives the title from one Stephen Mallett, a Frenchman, who settled there probably some time before the Revolution; he was a sort of hermit, and had neither wife nor children.

(4) John[3] had a son, (14) Matthew,[4] whose eldest son was named (74) Stephen,[5] and might possibly have been the Vermont hermit; but I

---

* See Orcutt, p. 968.

am more inclined to believe that this man was a descendant of the family mentioned on page 1, who came to Canada in 1640. Some of the Vermont records say that the first raft of oak timber taken to Quebec was owned by Stephen Mallett, of Colchester. "Mallett, as he was called by every one, was one of the first settlers in town. No one knows where he came from, but he had built a log cabin on the shore of the bay which bears his name, long before the Revolution, and the clearing about the house had the appearance of being very ancient; he died a very old man in 1789 or '90." "His improvements must have been earlier than those under the charter, but all that remains of him is the old cellar and the name he left to the point and the bay where he lived, Mallett Head, Mallett Bay, and Mallett Creek."

THE REVOLUTION.

No history of any family in existence since Colonial times would be complete without the story of the part taken by that family in the Revolutionary struggle.

I have frequently been told in Connecticut that the only interest taken by the Malletts in the War for the Independence was on the Tory side, and I am most happy to refute that slander. Two names are on record as taking the side of the British, (14) Matthew[4], son of (4) John[3], who lost his life in the English army, and his son (74) Stephen[5], whose estate was confiscated "because he had joined the enemy of the United States."

Over against these two names, is this Roll of Honor: (25) Capt. Lewis[4] Mallett; (108) Corp. Lewis[5]; (111) Miles[5]; (109) John[5]; (38) Gen. Peter[4]; (40) Corp. Philip[4]; (42) Daniel[4]; and (48) John P. Mallett[5].

In the Pension Office at Washington, D. C., is this record: "United States, debtor to the State of Connecticut for the service of State troops, etc., 1756-1825;" and "Capt. Lewis Mallett served from April to November, 1780."

Capt. (25) Lewis[4] Mallett's son (108) Lewis[5] served as private, then as corporal. His widow, Anna, applied for a pension May 22, 1839. "Her statement, relative to the soldier's service, which was rendered entirely with the Connecticut troops," shows "three month's service in 1775, two and a half months in 1776, one month in 1777, three months in 1778, one half month in 1779, three months in 1780, and four months in 1782."

(108) Lewis'[5] brothers (111) Miles[5] and (109) John[5] were themselves pensioners in 1832 and 1840, respectively.

(48) John (Porter) Mallett[5] was in Capt. Jabez Wheeler's Co., Col. Whiting's Regiment, commanded by Lt.-Col. Jonathan Dimon, at Peekskill, Oct. 5–30, 1777. He was also in service with rank of corporal at Green's Farms, March 15, 1781, in the company of Capt. Najah Bennett, Gen. Waterbury's State Brigade. (See Conn. Men in the Rev.)

*(38) Peter[4] Mallett was appointed Commissary of the Fifth Regiment, North Carolina troops, in Continental line, April 23, 1776. His brother (42) Daniel[4] was appointed Commissary of the Fourth Regiment, N. C. troops, Dec. 16, 1776.

† In the War Records on file at the State Department in Washington, (38) Peter Mallett[4] appears as a Deputy Commissary of Purchases in a list of accounts in the Register's office. The amount appears in column headed "Old Emiss," 1,020,000.

‡ Among the Reports of the Board of Treasury is the following:

TREASURY OFFICE,

PHILADA., *Augt. 22nd, 1777.*

The Commissioners for adjusting accounts to be presented to Congress for Payment having rendered the sums due on the following account to the Auditor General, he begs leave to Report—

drs pts (parts)
3421,77   That there is due to Peter & Daniel Mallett a balance of their accounts for supplying & paying the nine Regiments from North Carolina their Rations from the time of leaving that State to the 1st Aug. ins. amounting to £5400 0 9
of which they Credit 10000 Dollars received from Benj. Harrison P. MrG'l in Virginia   3750
for Rations drawn out of the Public Stores 382 14 2
or the difference between Carolina C. T Dollrs. a 8 | & dollrs. 7 | 6, on 24326 Rations charged at 10d Dollrs. at 7 | 6 instead of 10d Dollrs. at 8 | £64 2 8

                                                        4196 16 10

        balance £1203 3 11
equal to 3421⁷⁷⁄₉₀ths Dollars

---

* Dr. D. Schenck's Hist. of N. C.   † Cong. Papers, 143, p. 131.   ‡ C. P. 136-1-375.

(38) Peter[4] and (42) Daniel[4] Mallett also received each a bounty of five thousand acres of land in Tennessee.

That the fighting element, which had been inherited from (1) David[1] Mallet, as shown in the service of the army of Louis XIV., had not entirely died out, even with the close of the Revolutionary War, is proved by the fact that the Records of the Connecticut men in the War of 1812 give these names : Under Commander Philip Walker, at Bridgeport, in 1814, (215?) William Mallett, April 15 to 17 ; (64?) David Mallett, Sept. 30 to Oct. 3 ; under Commander Charles Parks, (210) Jesse Mallett[6], July 12–Sept. 17.

Also (189) Isaac[5] Mallett, son of (40) Philip[4], enlisted in 1812, from Catharine, N. Y., became ill and died in the service near Buffalo.

In the Muster Roll of Connecticut Militia from 1817 on, the name of (192) Joseph E.[5] Mallett appears as private in Fifth Co. First Regiment Light Artillery.

During the recent Civil War, representatives of our family, from both sides of Mason and Dixon's line, fought bravely for that which each believed to be the right principle, but in deadly opposition to each other.

God grant that there may never again be need for actual assertion of the fighting element by members of our clan.

CHURCH AND STATE.

But it is not only on the field of battle that the name of Mallett has been known. In the early history of Connecticut, the church and the common school occupied prominent places in the lives of the people. In this connection we find in Orcutt's History, in 1768, the names of (39) Samuel[4] and (40) Philip[4] Mallett, in 1773, of (14) Matthew[4] Mallett, of Daniel Hawley, Jonathan Nichols and Benjamin Sears, whose wives were all granddaughters of (2) John[2] Mallett; in 1778, on the school committee, Solomon Booth husband of (37) Naomi Mallett[4]; John Wheeler, husband of (12) Esther Mallett[4]; and (11) Joseph Mallett.

All of the houses on Tashua street were in those early times occupied by members of this family, and about 1760 Christ (Episcopal) church was organized, and a small building 36x26 built, near the north gate of the present churchyard, at the upper end of the street.

The larger part of the parishioners must then have belonged to the Mallett family. A similar state of things exists even now; in 1880, out of the whole number, eleven, on the roll of wardens and vestrymen, four bear the name of Mallett, and four others are connected with the family by marriage.

A son of (199) Daniel[5] Mallett, tells me that in his boyhood, it was the custom for the minister to spend the Sunday "nooning;" or the hour between morning and afternoon services, at his father's house, where he was joined by many members of the congregation, making a half-circle in front of the wood fire in the great open fire-place. The clergyman at that time was Rev. Ashbel Baldwin, whose ministrations were shared by Christ Church, Stratford, and Christ Church, Tashua, and the house then occupied by Daniel Mallett, is the one now used as the Rectory of the church in Tashua.

Col. (38) Peter[4] Mallett, who settled in North Carolina, married for his second wife, "pretty Sally Mumford," of New London, Conn.; she was one of the two people in Fayetteville who were Episcopalians, and who owned prayer-books ; and many of the occasional services of the church, which could be enjoyed in those days, were held in her house.

The sons and daughters of (38) Peter[4] and Sally carried on the same devotion to the church in Fayetteville. (172) Charles Peter[5], being vestryman for many years, and his son (448) Charles Beatty[6], also vestryman and senior warden until his death.

Prior to the Civil war (172) Charles Peter[5] Mallett and (448) Charles Beatty[6] Mallett were large cotton manufacturers in Fayetteville, and their losses at that time were correspondingly heavy. (448) Charles Beatty was largely instrumental in building the first railroad to Fayetteville, now known as the Cape Fear and Yadkin Valley R. R., and he was its first president.

Another son of Col. (38) Peter[4] was Gen. (174) Edward Jones Mallett. In his early manhood he moved to Providence, R. I., where he married the daughter of Gov. James Fenner. He lived there until 1845, when he removed to New York. In 1858, he accepted the appointment of United States Consul General to Italy, and upon his return to America in 1862, was appointed by President Lincoln, paymaster in the U. S. Army.

Returning again to Connecticut, we find that in 1764, (5) Lewis[3] Mallett was one of the three who gave the land where the (stone) (Episcopal) Church of Milford, now stands, and in 1778, his son (25) Lewis[4] gave a lease of land to pay a church debt.

My father (516) Charles[6] Mallett, after spending his early years on his father's farm, gaining as much education as the district school and the higher grade academy could give him, journeyed to what was then the far west, Niagara co., N. Y., and engaged for a time in school teaching. Yielding to the earnest solicitations of his sisters, he returned to Connecticut and located in Bridgeport.

In 1834, he erected the "first store on Main st. and was the first to conduct a purely mercantile business on that street." His influence was always exerted for the good of the town, but he would never accept any official position. He was a constant attendant at old St. John's Church, and many times a member of her vestry.

(40) Philip[4], son of (7) Peter[3], and brother of Col. (38) Peter[4], moved with his family to Catharine, Schuyler co., N. Y., in the autumn of 1802—his sons (183) Dimon[5] and (184) Daniel[5] having preceded him the Spring of the same year ; a third son (187) Levi[5] bought new land in the same vicinity, cleared it, lived, and died on the farm that he had thus rescued from the wilds, one half mile S. W. of Johnson's settlement, (now Catharine,) and still known as the Malette farm.

(40) Philip[4] prospected for iron, and silver ore in the hills of N. Y., but was unsuccessful, and died much in debt. Numerous descendants of (40) Philip[4], and of (16) Mehitable[4], and (19) Eunice[4] (Mallett) Beardsley still live in Schuyler, and adjoining counties, and others have scattered from there, through the Western States.

Of (2) John Mallet's[2] thirty-seven grandchildren ; (3) David's[3] five children settled in Tashua, or the town of Trumbull, Fairfield county, Conn. (of which Tashua is a school district)—part of (4) John's[3] twelve, remained in Conn., part went to Central New York—(5) Lewis's[3] three lived in Milford, New Haven co., Conn.—(6) Joanna's[3] seven, are partly undiscovered—(7) Peter's[3] ten, were fairly divided between Trumbull, Conn., Catharine, N. Y., and Fayetteville, N. Carolina.

The descendants of these thirty-seven, down to the tenth generation, to the number of twenty-three hundred, are, or have been, found in almost every State in the Union, and quarter of the globe. And their occupations have been equally diverse—farmers, artisans, merchants, printers, publishers, soldiers, dentists, physicians, lawyers, clergymen of various denominations—all classes are represented in our clan—the poor and the rich ; the high and the low ; the learned and the ignorant.

And all can trace their ancestry back to John the Huguenot, and

Johannah Lyon his wife—and thence to David, the Commissary in the army of the great French king.

What would be the astonishment of that same John the Huguenot, could he rise from his grave in quaint, old Stratfield burying-ground! Think you he could easily find his way to his old home on Park avenue —even if the street cars (electric perhaps), were ready to carry him to his very door?

These past two hundred years have wrought mighty changes even in Bridgeport.   A. S. M.

LETTER OF GEN'L (38) PETER MALLETT[4].

As it may give some pleasure and satisfaction to my family that follow me to know whence the family and name arise, and the manner of our forefather's first coming to America, as well as to be acquainted with their situation, manner of living and hardships and dangers of their predecessors to my children and to them only I address this. In order to lead you into the knowledge I have myself of my family I must first inform you that when I was a child, perhaps not more than two or three years of age, I was taken home by my grandmother, who, I believe, meant to bring me up at this time. My grandfather was living when I was between five and six years old, and died at his farm, three miles from Fairfield, Conn., aged ninety and upwards. I continued with my grandmother about two years after. She was a good, old French woman and could not speak a word in English, and from my living with her, I could not speak nor understand the English language as all the servants and every person in the house, my grandfather and grandmother knew nothing than French. At this time, my grandmother and my uncle David had some dispute with my father about a farm which my uncle found means to withhold which so much displeased my father that he took me away from my grandmother. Notwithstanding I was taken away from her, she ever spoke of me with tenderness and affection ; often supplied me with money and other articles.

I believe I never but once saw her before my father's death which occurred nine years after. After his death, my grandmother renewed all her former fondness for me, and I am sure had she not disposed of what was in her power in the course of my absence, it would have come to me. About a month before she died, in 1763, she sent for me, and gave me a number of French books. Among them was a handsomely bound book, which she handed me, and told me that it was my great-grandfather's and grandfather's journal and that it was highly worth my notice and attention, and that her then last prayer was that I should never feel or know such hardships, distress, disappointments, fatigues, dangers, difficulties, &c., &c.

At this time I was about nineteen, and having a command of money and company, paid very little regard to the injunctions of my good grandmother or the books, although I took particular care of them, until I came to settle in Wilmington in 1769.

The age of my grandmother I do not recollect, more than hearing the family frequently say that she was two or three years older than my grandfather, tho' she would have it that she was some years over one hundred. In 1769–70, an Irish gentleman, Mr. Bennis (?) stayed with me, who read the French language better than English, as he received his education in that country. It so happened that he got a sight of the French books given me by my grandmother, among them a great deal of the laws, trials, disputes, &c., and often the name of my grandfather mentioned. Mr. Bennis enquired of me if I knew the history of my forefathers. I told him not, but my grandmother had given me what she called a journal, written by my greatgrandfather. I told Bennis of what my good grandmother had given me, but I was never taught to write or read French, although I could speak no other language, but had now almost forgot to speak it ; upon which Bennis undertook to translate it into English. If I recollect right, there were 180 pages or more, written in a large book, and neatly in the style, and often the custom with the General and Field officers in the army. This book and the English of it, I had laid up carefully at Cross Creek, now Fayetteville, until 1781, when a Colonel Fannen and his troop of horse came there and took the town, broke open the trunks and this, with other books and papers, was destroyed, which, of course, deprives me of giving you a full account ; but as I went over the translation of Bennis frequently, and have still in remembrance the substance of what related to my two grandfathers, the first part of which was written by the hand of the elder, (whose name was David,) the latter part by his son John, my grandfather.

My great-grandfather, and his family, lived in Rochelle, France. He had considerable command there, either in the army, or civil department, in Louis the 14th time. This is clear—because in his book were copies of several letters from Le Tellier, who was, it seems, a judge appointed by the King, probably for the purpose only to try the Calvinists. Bennis read me of a proclamation, directed to David Mallett, Commissary of the 4th Division. Le Tellier writes at the bottom of this proclamation, a note in very respectful terms, inviting my great-grandfather to recant, and draw his followers over ; advises by no means to suffer his family, or those who relied on him, to go near those

Preachers, then about, nor to depend too much on a Mr. Colbrit, tells him his son the Marquis de Louvois shall meet him at some private place, &c. However, it seems my great-grandfather would not listen to him ; that he, and his five sons led many thousands.

At last the King's troops turned out, took Rochelle, put to death all before them—indeed the cruelties committed among the women and children, by the soldiers, is beyond expression. My great-grandfather, with his sons, and such of the family as were spared, made a good retreat into the country, where they made a stand for some time.

In 1686 there were four hundred officers broken on the wheel, among them my grandfather's brother, brother-in-law, and their wives and children, either burned, or put to death other ways, for signing some text to a Rev'd ——— Protestant. My great-grandfather, and grandfather, with many thousands, forced their way to some shipping, and landed in England in 1687. From every appearance they brought with them a great deal of money and many servants. In 1691 my great-grandfather died ; his age I do not recollect. My grandfather returned to France privately, got away his wife, two children, some money, and two ships, which had either been concealed for him or given in payment for some property. These ships came to England. There my grandfather takes in a number of passengers of his own country, and with three other ships sailed for S. Carolina. Three of the ships arrived off Santee, two, to the South. At Santee my grandfather and family arrived. The other two of the ships landed their passengers at Bufort, and then went around to the Savannah river. A settlement was made on the Santee by these people, great land purchases were made, the families of Linet, Horner, Hague, and a number of French names remain there yet. My grandfather sent his ships some voyages, and remained himself, either to form a settlement, or some other plan.

Before they returned, he lost his wife and one child; he had two children left. This distressed him so much that he returned to some part of Germany, where his brother had gone, but left behind him Johanna Lyon, his two children, and a nephew named Peter, whom he sent back, as his journal says, to the highlands he had purchased for him. This must be the high hills of Santee, as some of Peter's family are there still.

My grandfather went into some army against his country for nearly two years, when he returned by way of New York to Santee. He found Hannah Lyon (his servant), one child, and nephew alive. He takes with him Hannah and his child, leaves his nephew, and goes to New York, where he and the Angevines, Alias, Febels, and a number of French that had been to Germany, purchased five square miles and called it New Rochelle, twenty miles eastward of New York. This was about the year 1695. One of my grandfather's brothers was a physician and settled in Yorkshire, England, another settled in Germany, and a third came out with his ships.

He kept him with him ; it seems he turned out badly by being a drunkard. My grandfather gave him some property, and settled him in Boston. I have found some of the same name there, and found them to be of the family ; they are mostly worthy tradesmen.

In 1695 my grandfather married his faithful servant, Hannah Lyon, and sent a brother of hers to his brother in Yorkshire, who had before been his servant boy, to study under his brother, the doctor ; and to exchange with Louis Angevine his portion of the New Rochelle purchase for lands near Fairfield, where he lived in the greatest plenty, had an elegant house, built in the French style, a handsome little farm, and two others six miles distant. He kept eight or ten French servants, and when my uncle David and John were settled, Louis Lyon returned and settled as a doctor in Milford, Conn., where in a few years he made a handsome fortune, and took with him, as his own son, in 1721, my uncle Lewis Mallett. They lived together in great harmony for many years, and made a handsome fortune. Doctor Lyon having no other family than my uncle and three children. Doctor Lyon died, and soon after my grandfather left all his fortune to my uncle Lewis, his son, and my cousin.

My grandfather returned twice to Europe after he settled in America ; once he took with him his eldest son, David, having lost his son at Rochelle, that he brought from Santee. The last time he went to Surrey (?) and sent my father over to France, to negotiate some money matters, which he and my father complained hardly against some relations cheating them, so they must have failed mostly in their expectation. From the small idea I have of him myself, and from what I have generally understood from his friends and neighbors, he was an officer-like man, been used to hardships of war, and others, with a remarkable constitution ; never slept in a bed, nor would he suffer his sons until they were settled in their mode of living ; calm in his temper, but revengeful when displeased, his neighbors generally feared and loved him. His countrymen he treated haughtily. I recollect when he died. He lett five sons, David, Zackarie, John, Louis and Peter. The youngest was my father. None of them equaled their father in any degree whatever.

David and John, soon after the death of their father, persuaded their mother to sign a lease of her property, but as she always said, so sayeth my father, that this property was meant for my father, or myself at her death. On examining the conveyance it was found to be a real bill of sale forever. This brought on a quarrel that was never settled during the three brothers lifetime. Though my uncles had then valuable lands, large stocks and many servants as are necessary in that country, and considerable in cash, yet they and their families, except one son of John, came almost to nothing, at least they were forced to work. Matthew, the son of John, seemed very fortunate at his first beginning. Unluckily, in 1776, he raised two armies, joined the British, had a major's commission, and was killed in 1777. My Uncle Lewis, who was an easy, well meant man, and one who had no desire for more property than would afford him an easy living and a plentiful table. He lived in Milford, in this easy, honest way, until his death. Lewis, his son, followed nearly the steps of his father, enjoying nearly the same, not more, nor less than he did.

At the death of Dr. Lyon, Peter, my father, was of a lively, gay turn, fond of company and traveling, and was in trade, seemingly with success, too. When the war broke out in 1755 he engaged either with the quartermaster's department or commissary, perhaps both. In 1757 he took me with him, and in 1759 I had become so well acquainted with the business that I was relied on for almost all purchases of cattle, horses and stock, and wet provision for 12,000 men.

I was born November 14, 1744, of course but little over sixteen, when the settlement of my father's estate came to me. This business was too much for any such boy to undertake. The inventory of my father's estate, notes and lands amounted to over £30,000, including the value of lands, and it was expected the estate was worth at least half that sum, clear, which I doubt not, was it possible to have justice done.

After the death of my father, I continued on my own account to purchase cattle and beaves for several garrisons, and by the time the troops were called home, on peace being made, I had cleared to myself 8 or

£10,000. This, and the handling of such a property, rather raised my ideas too high, together with the great change between peace, and war, of which I was not a proper judge at that age. Shortly after, the creditors brought suit against my father's estate, I acted as executor for all who owed money, but being so sure of a large property out of the estate left, I made no guard in pleas to those actions for the insolvence of the estate. I succeeded shortly with the assistance of William Samuel Johnson, the first lawyer in the country, to obtain judgments against the debtors of the estate, for upwards of £20,000, and had suffered judgments against the estate nearly half that sum, had not the least fears of money. In 1764 debtors to the estate failed, and the money never recovered to amount more than half. Then all went wrong, and of course I was pressed from every quarter, and from not making proper pleas, became myself liable, tho' in fact, by this time I had more than spent all my own money, and had (illegible) run in something what I expected my own share of the estate. At this time I was engaged to be married to Miss Eunice Curtice. Her father had promised me some money and other property, which would in value have been $6,000. However he shortly turned against the match, and finally gave not a shilling. Everything seemed to run to my destruction, particularly to one so young, and had never known the want of money, nor the necessity of such industry and care, in that country which above all others in America it requires. In November, 1764, I was married, and in 1765 was resolved on travel and trying again my fortunes.

Accordingly I waited on Dr. Johnson, my friend who had known all the business, and told him without much ceremony that I felt myself in a bad situation, and asked his advice what to do; and after relating to him the disappointments I had met with on my part, even my father-in-law, who was able but entirely indifferent; and pointing out to Dr. Johnson the true statement of my father's personal property—the real estate I had given up to the heirs—and that my own property would nearly pay what befel me to do, we both concluded that in honesty I could do no more than leave and otherwise seek my fortune.

Thus far was all I intended when I first sat down, but as my own life and fortune has been rather extraordinary and uncommon, I thought I would amuse my sons with a short account.

At the winding up of affairs as mentioned, and lodging an account with the Probate, mortgaged all my own property to pay the debts of my father, as I had perhaps made use of some of the estate's money, and about leaving my country for what place I knew not, except the calling at *Hispanola* (?) in hopes of receiving $2,000 due me by a Col. Hopkins of the French army, I left my wife towards the end of June, 1765, then not twenty-one as to years, tho' I had seen more life than most men of forty. With the value of $200 and an order on some persons in New York for about $800 more, this all arose from an aunt of my wife's. With this sum I went to Canobay (?) purchased half of two vessels, went with one after Col. Hopkins, to whom I had lent money in 1760, in Canada, but succeeded poorly, received to the value of $500, handsome treatment and fair promises. From thence I came to Charleston, in Virginia. By this time, in the Fall of 1765, I undertook the command of my own vessel, went to Spain, part of Portugal, Denmark and England. From thence to the coast of Guinea, thence to the Barbadoes, Jamaica, thence to the Spanish Bay of Honduras, to Virginia, thence returned to Charleston. Various were the hardships in those voyages, almost too much to enter upon, both by sickness and want, especially from Senegal to the West Indies, where part of the crew preserved their lives by the flesh of the negroes, sickness which carried off all the crew except one man and boy on the South Main. I continued master of my own vessel and had made very considerable gain, so as to suppose myself worth $10,000 or $12,000; went to Connecticut for my family early in 1768, who had never heard of me after my departure. In June I lost my vessel and cargo to the full value of my worth on Cape Hatteras, went on shore about 2½ leagues on the foreyard, lost seven seamen out of thirteen. After some difficulties we got to Newbern, a stranger without a hat or a shoe.

I was then bound to London, but now found myself reduced to nothing, worn down with hardship and fatigue. However, I found a friend to clothe me, lent me money to carry me back to Charleston. I wrote my wife advising her to remain where she was, until I recovered my fortune, which I should again try. The sixth day after I arrived in Charleston, I again sailed for Liverpool, with a cargo half mine, on credit, and a chartered vessel at a low rate.

I made a very short passage and came to a good market. I got a freight of King's provisions, for Port Royal, Jamaica, and Pensacola. At the same time an Irish lady took her passage with me for Jamaica, and a number of servants. Before we reached our intended port I found she was the intended wife of the Governor of Campeche. She offered me a handsome sum to land her in the Bay of Campeche, and after further arguments promised to assist me to trade with the Spaniards there. At Kingston I readily obtained some freight belonging to myself and those concerned with me in Charleston, in negroes, rum, and printed linens, which articles were suitable to that country, double manned my crew—added two more guns, proceeded first to land my Kingston stores, and other freight at Pensacola, crossed the bay of Mexico with the lady and her servants, landed her in Campeachy with some difficulty.

We first made our trade peaceably, to about one-half, the Governor being very friendly as far as he dared, but at last about the middle of the night, about the sixth day we had been at anchor he privately ordered, or she did, that several Spanish boats should take my vessel and cargo that night. In that country, the last of the night, and all of the morning is calm, so had no other way but to defend with our guns. Accordingly we made ready. At daybreak I believe from 300 to 400 men in six boats came boldly alongside.

When within speaking distance I desired them to come no nearer, or I would sink them. They, however, continued with all force of oars, when I brought alongside on them, sunk two boats at once, and, as I heard afterwards, up the Mississippi, that I killed and drowned near thirty. The rest made off as fast as they had before come toward me. As soon as the wind changed, about nine o'clock, I departed for New Orleans, where a Spanish fleet had just arrived in order to take possession of the place from the French according to the treaty of 1763. I got permission from the French officers to deal with the French about 180 miles up the river.

I shortly made sale of the remainder of my cargo, purchased pork, and other articles, sent my vessel to Pensacola, crossed by land myself, sold part there, and returned from thence to Charleston. This voyage was performed in less than eight months, my share of the profits exceeded $3,000.

On my arrival I found a letter in the postoffice, informing me that a friend of mine had made insurance on my account, unknown to me, on the new vessel and cargo lost the year before, on Cape Hattras, to amount of 1,000 guineas. These two sums enabled me to get credit in

England, in the West Indies, and in Charleston. I then left the sea—
went to Edenton commissioned by Wilcox, Cram & Co., to fill up two
cargo ships belonging to Handly and Edom, London, that was in a way
of laying on demurrage. During my stay there, Maurice Moore, Esqre.,
one of the circuit judges, invited me to come to Wilmington and go
into trade. I came along with Mr. Moore, and accordingly entered into
business. That, together with having half the agency of victualling
the North Lowland, yielded me a handsome profit. In 1770 I sent a
vessel for my wife and child. Her father refused her coming and my
wife did not urge it with that warmth I expected. I was so vexed that
—for more than a year. At last being uneasy to know I had a wife and
child and to treat her coldly without being sure she was to blame I sent
a Capt. Magill to her. She wrote me she could not come away unless it
was unknown to her father—in that situation with strangers—that she
could come with myself anyhow. I accordingly in July, 1772, took a
pilot boat, went to the mouth of Fairfield harbor, met her, she came to
the water side with her son, took her in our boat, and after spending a
few months in Rhode Island, Boston and New York I brought her to
Wilmington. We lived happily about a year together, when I found
it necessary to preserve her life as well as the child's that she should return northwardly, she being sickly and then pregnant with my daughter
Mrs. Jones. A number of difficulties befell us both at this time, too
tedious to mention, and some not proper. She remained to the northward until October, 1776, when I sent a lad, an apprentice to me, Mr.
Potafida, with a wagon and money to purchase a carriage and horses.
She came off with Portafield and her two children and servants.

My little boy who I had inocculated in 1772, went with Portafield
through the city of Philadelphia, where his mother kept close for fear
of the smallpox. It had happened we had been deceived, and the little
boy had not taken the disorder when he was inocculated.

In Virginia he was taken ill with it, when he and his mother both
died with it, two miles from Nowlands Ferry, and not far from the present great city.

By this time the war between England and America became warm and
general. I myself stood high in esteem of the Americans, my knowledge of the army and commissary department raised my credit through-
out the States, and at the time of Portafield's returning, in 1776, I had
the victualing of a large army, which was profitable until the money

then in circulation depreciated. I continued with the army as commissary until October, 1786, and was from North to South; sometimes one way, sometimes another. Was in all the great engagements to the northward until 1778, afterwards to the southward.

After General Gates' defeat at Camden, August, 1780, the paper in value fell almost to nothing, provisions for the troops in Hillsborough and other places were not to be had on public credit, and I became liable in person for a number of purchases. This hurt me much, my loss in three months was not less than $80,000, by depreciation in paper money.

At the General Assembly in Hillsborough, 1780, September, I resigned my office as Commissary General to the State and to General Gates as Commissary to his division, yet proposed to remain under pay, provided funds would be found me to purchase, but absolutely refused supplying by impressing and taking provisions on my own account, and certificates. Generals Burke and Nash were my enemies; they immediately did all against me in their power. However, I remained firm, and removed to my plantation, Council Hall, near Campbellton, where during the winter, I was in large trade at Wilmington, Cross Creek and Pedee; had a large value in goods. During that time I was much suspected as a Tory, an enemy to the Americans; of course watched, threatened, and vexed every day and night. About February, 1781, the English took Wilmington. Daniel Mallett left them all my goods. About the same time they surrounded Portafield at Pedee; took all my property there also. Upon this it was reported and believed that I had a correspondence with the British, and had my property put in their way on purpose. I was obliged to arm my house every night with twelve or fourteen men, and always kept about that many armed with bayonets, &c.

About the last of March the engagement at Guilford happened between Lord Cornwallis and General Greene, the latter rather had the best; the former then moved toward the nearest shipping, say Wilmington. A few days after, a Mr. Swain (?) with about 40 men, for the third or fourth time, attacked me at Council Hall, under pretense of being on the side of the English, wanted provisions as they said, laid up for Lord Cornwallis' army. I refused them admittance. As it happened my men were all out except one black man, Johny. After an hour or two parley they forced into the lower part of the house, and my wife, myself,

Johny, and a negro woman defended ourselves with arms, not only forced them from the stairway, but out of the house. One gun only was fired. My wife and servant Hannah were noble soldiers. A few days after Lord Cornwallis' army came along. A great many of his officers were old acquaintances of mine; some had been tent-mates with me in the Canada war. I went over the river out of the way, and not the least idea of joining them; but after a day or two, a Mrs. Southerland and Miss Coit, an aunt of my wife's, sent me word to come in, that Lord Cornwallis and a number of officers had been at the house, that I should have all my goods at Wilmington and Pedee. I went in, of course, and with them to Wilmington, but my goods had all been sold and distributed among the soldiers and officers, with other prized goods. I was then pressed to go with Lord Cornwallis, as his Commissary, to Virginia. This I absolutely refused. Having been for years in the American ermy, I could not think of acting against them that in principle I felt for.

However, of this I repented, for I never could be reinstated again, and was obliged to suffer beyond expression, both in hardships, money, by the printed Act of Assembly, directions to the court, trials, and indeed everything—mob, after mob.

However, upon the whole, I always succeeded either in one way or the other, that during my passage through life. I was wounded twice before I was sixteen years old. Had one horse killed under me at Halfway brook, above Fort Edward, 1758. A ball partly through the calf of my leg at Fort George, 1759, wounded slightly in the other.

At Edenton a ball just broke the crown of my head, this was in an affair called honor. At ———, in Jersey, 1777, a wound in the ankle. 1780, at Cotton's house in ———, a Lt. Gen. and myself, with about eighteen men, were surrounded and attacked by about 80 tories. We defended ourselves wonderfully through a log house, and even saved all our horses, except one lost, and two wounded. We killed, and wounded 8, some say 12. We had two men slightly wounded. I had two buckshot enter my left side—one I cut out the next day, the other was too deep, and remained working its way, sometimes giving me great pain, until after living seventeen years and a few days it got down to my hip and gave me two months of the greatest pain in Chatham, where I was so fortunate as to have it cut out.

END.

LETTER FROM ISAAC MALETT TO HIS PARENTS.

Dear Honored Parents this ma inform you I am well hoping this ma find you so we are now at Youngstown in sight of the enemy altho there is no signs of actual hostility there is several deserters from the British camp the Royal George is taken By the American Brg Oneida a Raft of Boards was taken by our men from the British Valued at 1000 Dollars we have moved from Black Rock where we first arrived to Youngstown 30 miles Below 1 mile from Fort Niagara it is a general time of health in our camp ; I wish you to write to me as soon as possible I have heard from you by Mr. Fossit but I want a letter from you the people are moving from the line on Both sides this is a beautiful place on this side of the River is Fort Niagara on the other side is Fort George in the Village of Neveare the River is about three-quarters of a mile wide here between the two is where the River empty itself into Lake Ontario we do not apprehend any danger at present from the enemy in the engagements between the George and Oneida there was killed & wounded of our men 60 on the side of the enemy 130, 14 only escaped unhurt of the British and were taken I have seen this River from one end to the other that is from Black Rock to Fort Niagara the Niagara Falls is great natural curiosity I ever saw if you have anything Phillip I want you to inform me of it no more at present but I remain your most dutiful son

Youngstown July 8th 1812.   ISAAC MALETT.

PHILLIP MALETT

N B.—I wish to be remembered to all enquiring friends Neighbors and acquaintances.

To   Mr

Phillip Malett

of

Catharine

County of Tioga

EXTRACTS FROM THE RECORD OF ELAM BEARDSLEY[6].

" There is a difference of opinion in regard to the orthography of the name (Beardsley). Some terminate with *ey*, others with *ee*. I am among the latter. I bring in support of my opinion, Jared Beardsley, whom I knew in my early days. He asserted that the name was compounded of Beard and Lee. It is well known that names were formed in that way anciently. For instance, from John's son, we have Johnson ; David's son, we have Davidson. So Beard had a son Lee, of course he was Beard's Lee, as in the example given above—in like manner the two became Beardslee, by throwing away the apostrophe denoting possession, but retaining the s.''

" My maternal grandmother was Mehetable Mallett. Her grandparents fled from Erance on account of religious persecution in that country. They settled a few miles north of what is now the city of Bridgeport, Ct., at some period during the 16th (17th ?) century. They were Huguenots.''

" My grandparents Isaac and Mehetable were strongly wedded to the English or Prot. Epis. Church, and as a matter of course, adhered to Geo. the 3rd, and consequently he refused to take up arms against him in the Revolutionary struggle which he always *demonstrated* the Rebellion.''

" He had taken the oath of allegiance to the British Crown and held that no man, or number of men, had power to absolve him from that oath. He was not a Tory in the meaning of the term as understood and applied but simply a noncombatant.''

WILL OF (2) JOHN MALLET.[2]

Recorded at Fairfield. Probate Record Dec. 3d. 1744. Book 1741-1748, page 290.

In ye name of God. Amen. I John Mallet of ye town of Fairfield and county of Fairfield being in health of body and of sound mind and memory Calling to mind my mortal State Doe make and Or Dain this my Last Will and Testament : first and Chiefly I Commend my Soul to God who gave me being firmly Trusting in his mercy thro Christ my Redeemer, my Body I bequeath to ye Dust to be Decently Enterred att ye Discretion of my Christian Friend, My Worldly goods after my Debts and funeral Charges are defrayed and payed : I give and Bequeath them in manner following—

Item to my Eldest Son David Mallett I give twenty Shillings in money having heretofore had a Large tract of Land which I paid ye purchase of, that with ye twenty shillings I now give him makes ye whole of his Portion Except ye Revertion of Lands hereafter mentioned.

Item to my Son John Mallet: I having heretofore purchased Lands which I Caused ye aliances to vest ye tittle of in him my sd Son John and his heirs &c. I now give him five shillings in money which makes ye whole of his portion.

Item to my Son Lewis Mallet I having heretofore purchased Land which I *prosered* ye Grantors to vest ye title in my sd Son Lewis. I now give him fifteen Shillings in money which makes ye whole of his portion.

Item to my Son Peter Mallet having heretofore given him Lands of considerable value I now give him fifteen Shillings in Money which makes ye whole of his portion.

Item to my Daughter Joannah Angevine having already given her above three hundred Pounds: I now give her fifteen Shillings in money which makes ye whole of her portion.

Item to my beloved wife Joanah Mallet I give and bequeath all my Estate not above given yt is all my Land, housing and moveables Estate in ye bounds of Stratford or Fairfield to her and heirs forever to use and Dispose of as She Shall think fitt, and further it is my Will if my Wife Shall Die Seized of ye Estate I now give her that then and in Such Case my Eldest Son David Shall have all ye Land: I have given to my sd Wife to him and to his heirs in fee and also my black negro man James —and my Son Peter Mallet shall have my negro man Mingo, and further yt in Such Case as above mentioned then my Daughter Joannah Anjevine Children Shall have my mollto Wench Dinah and her Children, and I do hereby Constitute and ordain my beloved Wife Joanah Mallet to be my sole Executrix of this my Last Will Declaring this and this only to be my Last Will and Testament to Confirm which I have hereunto Set my hand and Seal this third Day of December Anno Dom: 1744.

Signed, sealed pronounced and declared to be ye Last Will of Testator

JOHN MALLET [Seal.]

in presence of us

THEOPHILUS NICHOLS, ⎫
DAVID LACY, ⎬ A true Copy of ye Orig'l.
DAVID WELLS, ⎭ Recorded pr DAVID BURR,

Regis'or.

Att a Court of Probate held in Fairfield, Oct. 8, 1745, then personally appeared Theophilus Nicholas, David Lacy, and David Wells, witnesses to ye forgoing will and made Solemn Oath yt they saw John Mallet signer and sealer to ye sd will sign and seal ye same and heard him declare it to be his Last will and yt they signed in ye presence of ye Testator as witnesses and yt they judged him to be of sound mind and Disposing memory: at sd Court personally appeared Joanah Mallet sole executrix to sd will and accepted ye trust committed to her as Executrix and exhibited at ye sd Court ye foregoing will in order for probation sd will being proved is by sd Court approved and ordered to be recorded.

Test., DAVID BURR, *Clerk.*

JOANNA MALLET'S WILL.

March 18, 1763. Fairfield Probate Records. Book 1754 to '64.

In ye name of God, Amen. I Joanna Mallet of Stratford in ye county of Fairfield being far advanced in age and knowing yt ye time of my departure draws near but thro ye goodness of God I am of sound mind and memory think it best to make this my Last Will and Testament, and first I give my soul into ye hands of God who gave it and my body to Return to ye dust to a decent burial and as to what worldly goods and estate it hath pleased God to bless me with I freely dispose of ye same as followeth—

And first my Will is all my just Debts and Funeral Expenses being first paid and satisfied out of my estate.

Item—I freely give unto my Loveing son John Mallet ye whole of what shall be due and unpaid at ye Time of my death on one Certain Bond given to me by my Son Peter Mallet now dec'd said bond is for four hundred pounds old Tenor conditioned for Two hundred pounds old Tenor to be to him forever.

Item, all the rest of my estate of what nature or kindsoever I freely give unto my two Sons namely David Mallet and John Mallet in ye Proportion as followeth to say Two Third parts thereof to my sd son David and one third part thereof to my said son John Mallet they haveing done considerable for me toward taking care of me and providing for my support.

The rest of my Children haveing had already ye full of what I think they ought to have, therefore I do not give them anything more at this time, and I do hereby constitute and appoint my said Two Sons David and John Mallet to be Executors of this my last Will and Testament, in witness whereof I have set my hand & Seal this 18th day of March, A. D. 1763

her

JOANNA ✕ MALLET   [SEAL]

mark.

Signed, Sealed, Published & declared by Joanna Mallet to be her last Will & Testament in presence of Witnesses

TIMOTHY SHEEHEN

SAMUEL ADAMS

At a Court of Probate held at Fairfield Octob 9th 1764 personally appeared John & David Mallet Esqrs to ye foregoing Will and exhibited ye same for Probation—ye same being proved by said Court approved and ordered to be Recorded at ye same time Sd Executors accepted ye trust committed them by ye Testator——

Test—   ANDR ROWLAND, *Clerk*

A true copy &

ANDR ROWLAND *Regr*

A. R. I

WILL OF (3) DAVID MALLITT[3].

Recorded at Fairfield. Probate Records March 15th, 1775. Book 1775 to 1778, page 196.

In the Name of God Amen. I David Mallitt of Stratford in ye County of Fairfield being of Sound Memory & Mind Do hereby Make & ordain this my Last Will and Testament—

Imprimis Bequeath my Soul to God in Humble hopes of Mercy Through Jesus Christ & my Body to ye Earth to be Buried in a Decent Christian Manner at ye Discretion of my Executors & as Touching Such worldly Goods & estate as it has Pleased God to Bless me with in this Life I dispose tharof in manner following (viz) To my Beloved wife Esther Mallitt I give & Bequeath all my moveable Estate that I shall die Possest of (Excepting Such articles as I shall hereafter otherwise Dispose of) to be her own forever also the use and Improvement of all my meadow Called the Boggy meadow near to where my Son David Mallitt now lives During the Term She Shall Remain my Widow & also the use and Improvement of all the other Land I shall Die Possest of after my Debts and Legacies Shall be paid out of them as I shall hereafter order During her Natural Life.

Item To my Son Joseph Mallitt I give my Carpenter Tools to be his own forever.

Item To my Son John Mallitt I give my Best Bever hat & two Stub Sythes.

Item To my Son David Mallitt I give my Best Spade and Twenty Shillings in money to be paid as I shall hereafter order.

Item To my Daughter Esther Wheeler the wife of John I give Four pounds Lawfull money to be paid her out of my Lands in Two years after my Decease.

And my Will is that my Executors Shall Sell so much of my Land at the Long Beach & Black Banks so-called as shall be Sufficient to pay all my Debts Funeral Charges & Legacies & if they Shall not be Sufficient, then my Will is that they Shall Sell any Other piece or parcel of my Land as Shall make up such Deficiency.

And my Will is if any of my Lands Shall Remain unsold after my Just Debts & funeral Charges & Legacies are all Paid that the same shall be Equally Divided between my three Sons John Mallitt, David Mallitt & Joseph Mallitt after the Death of my wife and I Do hereby give & Bequeath the Same Accordingly & also I give them all my wearing Apparrel that I shall Die Possest of.

And I do hereby appoint my Loveing wife Esther Mallitt & my Son Joseph Mallitt to be my Executors of this my Last Will and Testament and my Will further is that if Either of my Executors Should Die before my Estate is Settled that ye Survivors may Sell and Convey my Lands According as I have above ordered & in Witness whereof I have Hereunto Set my Hand and Seal this 15th day of March A. D. 1775

DAVID MALLITT   [Seal]

Signed, Sealed Published and Declared to be the Last Will and Testament of David Mallitt in Presence of

ABIJAH SEELEY
ABIJAH GREGORY
ISAAC NICHOLS

At a Court of Probate Held in Fairfield Octr. 16th, 1777 Then ye above & foregoing Will was Exhibited to this Court for Probation by me of ye Executors therein
mentioned whi accepted the Trust & said Will being proved was by sd Court accepted and ordered to be Recorded as may appear by ye Origl on file

Test—   HEZEK SILLIMAN, *Clerk*

WILL OF (4) JOHN MALLET.[3]

Recorded at Fairfield. Probate Records June 26th, 1767. Book 1775 and 76, Page 545.

In the name of God, Amen. I John Mallit of Stratford being at this Time through
the Goodness of God of Sound Mind and memory think best to make this my Last
Will and Testament.

And first of all I freely Resign my Soul into ye Hands of God who Gave it and
my Body to Return to ye Dust from whence it was taken. Hopeing for a Blessed
Resurrection to Immortal Glory and as for what Worldly Goods and Estate it hath
pleased ye Lord to Bless me with in this Life—

I freely Dispose of ye same in ye following manner (viz) My Will is that all my just
Debts and funeral expences be first paid and satisfyed out of my moveable estate—
Imprimis—I freely Give unto my beloved Wife Martha Mallit one third part of all
my moveable estate after Debts and charges paid to be her own forever and also ye
use and Improvement of one half on my Dwelling House and one half my Barn and
one third part of my Land, Dure the time She Shall Remain my Widow ; and also I
give my said Wife one years provision out of my Estate—

Item I give unto my Daughter Prudence, Daug, the Sum of five Shillings, Lawfull
money besides what she hath already had and that to be ye whole of her portion—

Item I freely give unto my Son Matthew Mallit ye sum of five Shillings besides
what he hath already had and yt to be ye whole of his portion—

Item I give to my Daughter Sarah Sears besides what she hath already had ye sum
of five shillings and that to make ye whole of her portion—

Item I freely give to my Daughter Mehitable Beardslee besides what she has heretofore had ye sum of five Shillings and yt to be ye full of her portion.

Item I Give unto my Daughter Eunice Beardslee besides what she has before had
ye sum of five Shillings and yt to make her portion.

Item I Give to my Daughter Hannah Bennit besides what I have already given her
ye Sum of Twenty pounds Lawfull money to be paid as is hereafter provided and yt
to be ye whole of her portion—

Item I Give unto my Daughter Mercy Mallit ye Sum of Thirty pounds Lawfull
Money to be paid as heretofore provided and yt to be the whole of her portion

Item I give unto my Daughter Ruth Mallit ye Sum of Thirty pounds Lawfull
Money to be paid as hereafter provided and yt to be ye whole of her portion

Item I freely give unto my Daughter Olive Mallit ye Sum of Thirty pounds Lawfull Money to be paid as Hereafter provided and that to be ye full of her portion

Item I freely give and Bequeath unto my three Sons namely John Malit & Edmund Mallit and Henry Mallit and to their Heirs forever all my Land and Building
after my Wife's use is End in ye Same and to be Equally Divided between them

they to Receive what is not Given ye use of to my Wife Imediately after my Decease and also my moveable Estate that is not Disposed of to my said three Sons in Equal proportion to be Divided between them.

And it is to be understood that what I have given to my Abovesd three Sons is on this Condition that they Shall pay unto my four Daughters namely Hannah, Mercy, Ruth and Olive what I have given to them in this Will and to be paid by said three Sons in Equal Proportion at ye End of Twelve years from my Decease and not Sooner Except they my Said Sons Shall see Cause.

And I do hereby Appoint my two Sons namely John Mallit and Edmund Mallit to be my Executors of this my Last Will and Testament and I Do hereby Revoke and make null and void all other and former Wills by me Heretofore made, Ratifying and Confirming this and Only this to be my Last Will and Testament in Witness whereof I have Hereunto Set my Hand and Seal this 26th Day June 1767.

JOHN MALLIT   [Seal]

Signed, Sealed, published & Declared by
Mr John Mallit to be his Last Will &
Testament in presence of us Witnesses

    AGUR JUDSON
    TIMOTHY HUBBELL
    SAMUEL ADAMS

FAIRFIELD }
COUNTY ss }   STRATFORD, *July ye 2d Ad 1776.*

Personally appeared Samuel Adams Esqr and Messrs Agur Judson and Mr. Timothy Wheeler Witnesses to ye within and foregoing will and made Solomn Oath that they Saw the Testator Sign and Seal ye foregoing Will and heard him Publish pronounce and Declare the Same to be his Last Will and Testament and yt they signed as Witnesses in presence of ye Testator and that they see Each Other Sign and Judged him the Testator to be of a Sound Disposine Mind and Memory.

Sworn by me DANIEL JUDSON,

Justice of Peace

At a Court of Probate Held in Fairfield July ye 4th 1776 Then ye above and foregoing, being by John Mallit and Edmund Mallit named Executors in sd Will Presented to this Court for Probation. And ye same being proved was by said Court Approved and Ordered to be Recorded and ye same Time said Exes. accepted ye Trust Reposed in them by ye Testator.

Test. HEZEKIAH STILLMAN, *Clerk.*

WILL OF (7) PETER MALLET.[3]

Recorded at Fairfield. Probate Records Dec. 10, 1759. Book 1747 to 1761, Page 456,

In the Name of God amen. I Peter Mallett of Stratford in ye County of Fairfield and the Colony of Connecticut in New England being in Health of Body and Sound Memory do make and ordain this my last Will and Testament.

First and chiefly I recommend my soul to ye Hand of God My Creator firmly trusting in his infinite Mercy Thro' Christ my Redeemer, My Body I bequeath to the Dust to be decently buried at the Discretion of my Christian friends. My worldly Goods after my just Debts and funeral Charges are Paid I will & bequeath them in Manner following—

Item To my beloved Wife Mary Mallett I give and bequeath Sixty pounds Lawfull Money to be paid in Thest of my movable Estate—also the use of One third part of my Real Estate so long as she shall continue my widow and in Case she shall marry after my Death then she shall have the use only of so much of my Estate as shall be valued to be worth one hundred and forty pounds & that during her natural Life—

Item To my Daughter Mary Summers haveing already given her about one hundred pounds, I now give ten pounds which makes the whole of her Portion.

Item To my Daughter Phebe Hawley haveing already given her about one hundred pounds, I now give her ten pounds which makes the whole of her Portion.

Item To my Six Sons Peter Mallett & Sam'el Mallett & Philip Mallett & Zachariah Mallett & Dan'el Mallett & Benj'n Mallett to them & their Heirs and Assigns forever I give and bequeath all my Estate in Lands Housing and Movable not above given to my Wife and Daughters to be equally Divided between my s'd Six Sons in Equal Shares and if either of them should die Childless then his Part to be equally Divided between his Surviving Brethren and in Case my wife should bear me another son My Will is he shall Divide Equal with his Brethren and in Case she bear me a Daughter she to have an hundred pounds and further it is my will all my Negroes shall be sold ; and I hereby Constitute and appoint my beloved Wife Mary and my Eldest Son Peter Mallet to be my Exec'r of this my Last Will and Testament hereby Declaring this and this only to be my Last Will and Testament which to confirm I have hereunto Set my Hand and Seal this 10th day of Decem'r A. D. 1759.

PETER MALLET   [Seal.]

Signed, Sealed pronounced
& Declared to be ye Last Will
and Testament of the Testator
in presence of us
    THOP'S
    JOSEPH HILL
    SAM'EL GREGORY

Know all whom this May Concern that I Mary Mallett wife to the above Signing Testator do hereby Declare that I do accept of and am perfectly satisfied with ye Dower my s'd Husband has given me by his within Will which to Confirm I have herto Set my Hand ye date above.

MARY MALLETT.

Signed in Presence of
    JOSEPH HIDE,
    SAM'EL GREGORY.

At a Court of Probate held in Fairfield.

Janry 24th 1760

Personally appeared Thops (Nichols) and Samel Gregory two of the Witnesses to the foregoing Will and made Solemn Oath yt they Saw Peter Mallett ye above Testator sign and seal and heard him declare the Same to be his Last Will & Testament & that they then Judge him to be Sound Disposing mind & memory and that Joseph Hide signed the same as Witnesses to the Same in Presence of the Testator and of each other

Sworn Before the Court Test

At the aforesd also Personally appeared Peter Mallett One of the Execr named in sd Will accepted the Trust committed to him by ye Testator and at the same Time exhibited sd will to sd Court for Probation which being proved is by sd Court approved and ordered to be Recorded Test.

A True Copy of the Original Recorded.

WILL OF MARY MALLETT.

At a Court of Probate held at Stratford, this 23rd day of September, 1797. Robert Walker, Esq., Judge; Joseph Walker, Esq., Clerk.

In the name of God, Amen.

This 23rd day of February, 1778 I, Mary Mallett of the town of Stratford, and Parish of North Stratford, and County of Fairfield, being under bodily illness but of sound mind and memory considering my mortality, do make and ordain this my last will and testament.

First. I recommend my soul to God through Jesus Christ in hope of eternal life through his merits, and my body to the earth to be decently buried at the discretion of my executor hereafter named, believing its redemption at the last day, and as to such worldly estate wherewith it has pleased God to bless me with in this life, I give and dispose of the same in manner and form as followeth, viz:—First, I order and will that all my just debts and funeral charges be paid out of my movable estate.

Then I give and bequeath to my beloved son Peter, ten shillings, who has nearly had his proportion before.

Then I order and will that my three beloved sons Samuel, Philip and Zachariah should not pay what they owe me on book or note if I do not call for it while I live.

Then I give my beloved son Philip my dwelling house where he now lives, and what land under it and adjoining to it in that town, to be his and his heirs forever, moreover I give unto him my great Bible.

Then I give my beloved daughter Mary Summers, my black quilt, and as to the rest of my movable estate, I order and will that my beloved children Samuel, Philip, Zachariah, Daniel, Mary Summers, Phebe Hawley and Naomi Booth should share equally and alike, and also that my daughters above mentioned should have their choice in my clothes.

Finally I hereby constitute and ordain Daniel Hawley, my son-in-law, to be my executor on this my last will and testament hereby revoking all other wills, declaring this to be my last will and testament.

In Witness Hereof, I set my hand and seal the day and date above written.

    In presence of   MARY MALLEIT. [Seal.]

SETH HIGBY,

JONATHAN TYRRELL,

PATTY TYRELL.

LITCHFIELD COUNTY, *ss.*·   WATERTOWN, *Sept. 21st, 1797.*

Personally appeared Jonathan Tyrrell, Patty Tyrrell, both of Woodbury in said county and made solemn oath that the date of the foregoing will; they were personally present and saw Mary Mallett sign and seal the said will and testament, and heard her declare the same to be her last will and testament, and that they each of them were requested by the said Mary Mallett to subscribe their names as witnesses to the same, and as they looked upon her of sound disposing mind and memory, they then in the presence of said testator and in presence of each other and of Seth Higby, the other subscribing witness, subscribed their names to the same as above, and that they both saw the said Seth Higby subscribe his name as a witness to the same.

                    Sworn before me,

                      ELI CURTISS,

                      Justice of the Peace.

Personally appeared Daniel Hawley and Abijah Hawley and made oath to the foregoing will before said court and gave bond, the same is approved and ordered to be recorded.

                ROBERT WALKER, *Judge of Probate.*

    At a Court of Probate held at Stratford, Dec. 4th, 1797.

                ROBERT WALKER, *Judge.*

                JOSEPH WALKER, *Clerk Present.*

WHEREAS, Daniel Hawley and Abijah Hawley executors of the estate of Daniel Hawley, late of Stratford, deceased, who was in his lifetime executor on the last will and testament of Mary Mallett, late of said Stratford, deceased, have this day represented to this court that the estate of said Mary is insolvent and insufficient to pay discharge debts due, therefore whereupon this court appoint, empower and fully authorize Abraham Brinsmade Esq. of Trumbull and David Nichols of Huntington, Commissioners to receive, examine and adjust the several claims against said estate and report make to this court in six months.

                Attest :

                JOSEPH WALKER, *Clerk.*

The Estate of Mary Mallett Inventoried and appraised this 23 day of Sept 1797.

INVENTORY OF ESTATE OF JOHN MALLET, DEC. 30,1745.

Fairfield Ct. Probate Records. Book 1741-48. P. 304.

An Inventory of ye Estate of John Mallet Late of Stratfield Dec'd taken by us ye Subscrbers hereunto being appointed, therefore and sworn thereto as ye Law Directs Nov 12 A. D. 1745.

One old beaver hatt 1 lb | 10 s 1 broad cloth 3 lb 1 Coat 3 lb | 10 . . . . . 8 0 0
One Drugget Coat 4 lb 10 s—1 hollen Shirt 1 lb 5 s—home spun Do 1 : 5 . 7 0 0
one handkerchief 18 s | 1 pr. of Old boots 10 s | 1 Gun 6 lb—2 Sermon Books
   1 lb 8 8 0
two bolsters 2 lb —1 feather bed —55 lb £12. 1 Do tow tuking wt 44— . . 25 0 0
1 other bed in ye Chamber wt 45 lbs—14 lb 14 0 0
one old Leather Bed wt 48 lbs—8 lb 1 Bedstead & Cord 1 lb—10 s 9 10 0
1 bedstead Cord & under Bed all 1 lb 10 s | 1 set of Cailico Curtains 7 lb—10 s 9 0 0
1 Rugg 4 lbs—10 s 1 Coverlid 3 lb | 1 old Do 1 lb 8 10 0
two Coverlids at 3 lbs | 2 Coverlids at 3 lb—15 s 6 15 0
1 lb feathers 7 s | 1 old pillow 3 s | two Coverlids 15 lbs | 27 Sheets 20 lbs . 25 10 0
to Coverlids 1 lb & 4 pillow cases 1 lb—8 s 2 8 0
4 table Cloaths 1 lb 5 s & 1 bedstead & Cord 1 lb 18 s 3 0 0
to 1 Sheet 12 s | 1 tankard 10 s | 1 qurt Pot 14 s | 1 pint pot 10 s | 2 6 0
to 15 plates 4 lbs 3 plates 2 lb 4 platters 6 lb 12 0 0
1 bason 12 s 2 porrengers 10 s & 7 Spoons 4 s | 1 6 0
6 knives & 10 forks 1 lb and warming pan 2 lb 10 s 3 10 0
3 Candlesticks brass 1 lb 10 s & a Stand Candlestick 3 lb 10 s 5 0 0
1 Copper Kettle 20 lb Do brass 10 lb Do 3 lb 33 0 0
Large Ironpot 5 lb Do 1 lb 10 s Do 10 s Ironpot 1 lb 5 s Do 11 s | 8 16 0
frying pan 1 lb 8 s & brass things 12 s & flesh fork 3 s | tongs 10 s | . . . 2 13 0
a Lamp 5 s Stilyards 15 s | 2 trammels 2 lb | 1 broken hand Iron 4 s . . . 3 4 0
Peal 5 s | hand Irons 1 lb 15 s | hetchel 1 lb | 5 s do 10 s 3 15 0
A spade 1 lb | and 2 broad axes 1 lb | & 4 ring bolts 1 lb 10 s 3 10 0
timber chain wt 25 lb at 2 lb 10 s | teatable 2 lb 10 s do 2 lb 7 0 0
6 black chairs 3 lb | 2 Chws ma 1 lb and looking Glass, 5 lb 9 0 0
Bread tray 7 s & black Chair 10 s | 1 trunk 5 s | basket & 5 bushels malt
   3 lb 4 2 0
Old Cask oat malt 6 s old Chest & bushel & ½ beans 1 lb 4 s 1 10 0
whip saw 1 lb | an auger 5 s | & reel 7 s | 3 sythes 10 s old Iron 1 lb . . . 3 2 0
2 basketts 10 s | old nails 10 s   25 lb wool 6 lb | 5 lb Coarse wool 1 lb . . . 8 0 0
9 chairs 2 lb 12 s | one table 1 lb 5 s | do 1 lb 10 s | an adds & Chisel 3 s | . 5 10 0
2 chests 2 lb | & a drawing knife 6s | a square 7 s | 3 gimblets 3 s | 3 6 0
a Cradle 15 s | a rule 5 s | a mallet 2 s | old Iron 15 s | 1 17 0
1 hide 2 lb | hammer 2 s pully block 1 s | 6 d honey pot 7 s | 2 10 6
leather 9 lb at 1 lb | 10 s | 7 boles 7 s | a brush 5 s 2 2 0

Earthen ware 12 s | a mortar 3 s | a sieve 4 s & a Riddle 6 s | 5   5   0

a wooden bowl 6 s | 2 pails 3 s | 6 d 2 Cupboards 2 lb 10 s 2 15   0

a saddle 5 lb & 3 bridles 10 s a basket 3 s | a little wheel 10 s | 6   3   0

a great wheel 10 s | 2 rakes 4 s | a pitchfork 7 s | 1   1   0

4 hogsheads of Cyder 12 lb | 1 barrel of Cyder 1 lb | one barrel of mytheg-
lin 7 lb 20   0   0

Old Cask 5 lb | Earthenware 5 s | padlock 12 s | pitch tunnel 2 s   6   0   0

box and heaters 5 s | a sow and 7 pigs 5 lb 10 s | 60 bushels of Corn at home
21 lb | 26 15   0

3 Cows, 36 lb | 1 black steer 18 lb | 1 red steer 11 lb 65   0   0

4 yearling 22 lb | 1 bay mare 50 lb | 1   Iron fetters 1 lb | barley in ye sheaf
1 lb 74   0   0

Oats in ye sheaf 32 lb | Eleven Loads of Rye 40 lb 72   0   0

to corn at Tautashua 22 lb flax in ye barn 15 lb 10 bushels flax seed 4 lb . 41   0   0

to negro man James 170 lb do red head Mingo negro 170 lb 340   0   0

to 1 negro Woman Dinah 130 lb | negro child 30 lb 160   0   0

a grindstone 10 s & 10 small swine 12 lb | 2 sythes 1 lb 10 s 14   0   0

a hand saw 2 lb | 3 augers 16 s | 5 old Baules 1..5 | Cart Rope 5 s   4   6   0

Broken chain 15 s | old Iron 2 s | a beetle 6 s | 1 trammel 1 lb | Iron pot
17 s   3   0   0

a bed & bedstead & cord 3 lb | 1 hold fast 15 s | old pewter 3 s | 3 18   0

8 swine 32 lb | 2 narrow axes 1 lb 10 s a rone horse 45 lb 78 14   0

a bay mare old one 50 lb a black 2 yr old horse 30 lb | Colt 15 lb 95   0   0

21 sheep 28 lb | plow and Irons 2 lb 5 s | 8 acres of Wheat and Rye 20 lb . 50   0   0

8 acres of Wheat & Rye on David's Land 20 lb : 4 oxen 80 lb 100   0   0

a white mare 12 lb | an Iron bound Cart & Clevis 16 lb 28   0   0

two yokes and Irons 17 s | horse Gears 1 lb 5 s | 1 chain 1 lb   3   2   0

one chain 1 lb | Iron kettle 8 s | a sadle 2 lb | 2 stubine axes 10 s 3 18   0

a stone jarr 6 s | an inch auger 4 s | a fan 10 s | & 2 sickles 10 s 1 10   0

an Iron Crow barr and 2 rings & bolts 1 lb 10 s 1 10   0

a pide steer 14 lb | 3 : two yr olds 30 lb white steer 15 lb & Cow 10 lb . . 69   0   0

two 2 yr old heifers, 19 lb | a brown heifer 13 lb 32   0   0

five Calves 16 lb 16   0   0

2 Chairs 12 s | 2 baggs 10 s | 1   2   0

to eighteen acres of Land at Tautashaway Hill 250 lb 250   0   0

35 acres of Land north of Tautashaway Meadow 200 lb 200   0   0

a true Copy of ye Orig'el on file Record'd

     Test— DAVID BURR,   JOSEPH BOOTH   ⎫
             Regis'r   DAVID SHERMAN, ⎬ *apprisers under oath*
                       THEOP'S NICHOLS, ⎭

Att a Court of Probate held at Fairñeld Decem'r 30th 1745 Eben'r Stillman Esqr Judge personally appeared Joanah Mallet Executrix of ye Last Will of her husband John Mallet Late of Stratfield Dec'd and Exhibited ye foregoing Inventory to sd Court made Oath yt ye same is a true and perfect Inventory of all ye Estate of sd

Dec'd yt she knows of and if anything hereafter appears belonging to sd Estate she will Cause ye same to be Inserted ; said Inventory being proved is by sd Court approved and Ordered to be Recorded.

Test,   DAVID BURR, *Clerk.*

[*Copy.*]

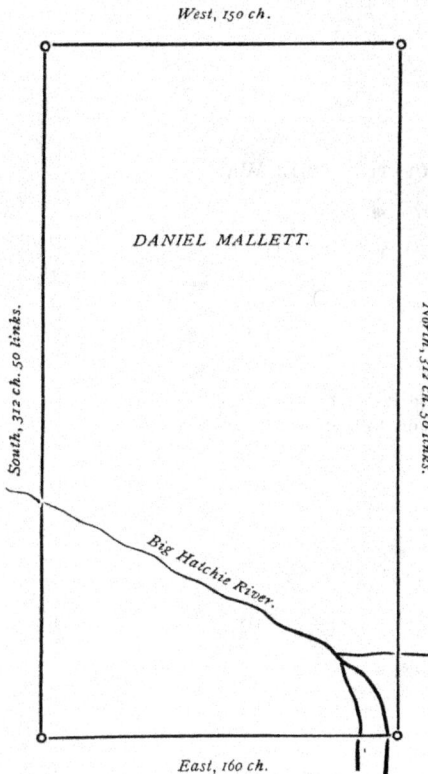

West, *150 ch.*

DANIEL MALLETT.

South, *312 ch. 50 links.*

North, *312 ch. 50 links.*

Big Hatchie River.

East, *160 ch.*

WARRANT No 1760

Scale 80 chs pr Inch.

STATE OF NORTH CAROLINA, WESTERN DISTRICT.

By virtue of a warrant from the State Entry takes No 1760 dated 12 January 1785 I have surveyed for Daniel Mallett 5000 acres of land lying on both sides of Big Hatchie river. Beginning at the north East corner of John Estes's Entry No 1253 at a black walnut tree marked I R. running east 160 chs, to a white oak, thence north 312 chs. 50 links to a black oak tree west 160 chains to a stake thence South 312 chs 50 links to the Beginning.

Surveyed Nov. 12. 1786

ISAAC ROBERTS.

WM BUSH
THO. JAMISON   } C. C.

Grant No 276 dated 25 April 1789

HEROES OF THE REVOLUTIONAY WAR.

Captain Lewis[4] Mallett.
Corporal Lewis[5] Mallett.
Private Miles[5] Mallett.
Private John[5] Mallett.
General Peter[4] Mallett.
Corporal Philip[4] Mallett.

Commissary Daniel[4] Mallett.

Corporal John P.[5] Mallett.

David[5] Baldwin, died in the prison-ship.

Lewis[5] Baldwin,   "   "   "

Tories.

Matthew[4] Mallet.

Stephen[5] Mallet.

SOLDIERS OF THE WAR OF 1812.

William Mallett.

Jesse[6] Mallett.

Isaac[5] Mallett, died in the service.

HEROES OF THE CIVIL WAR.

Union Army.

Sergeant Sylvester T. Malette, Co. G. 50th Engineers, N. Y.

      Ephraim Malette,   "   "

      Henry Wisner Malette,   "   "

      William Smith Malette,   "   "

      John Fiddler Malette,   "   "

      Huson W. Malette, died in prison at Salisbury, N. C.

      George Abel Mallette, Conn. Volunteers.

      William Averill, killed.

      Myron Couch,   "

      Joel Guild,   "

      Charles Bacon,   "

      Eli John Beardsley, 50th Reg't, N. Y. V.

      Eli Plumb Burton.

      Rollin Stiles Burton, died June 30, 1863.

      Jerome M. Esney,   " Sept. 12, 1862.

Confederate Army.

Colonel Peter Mallett, 3rd Reg. N. C.

      A. Fridge Mallett,   "   "

Lt. Col. Edward Mallett, 41 "   " killed.

Adj. Richardson Mallett,   " "   "   "

      Cecil Mallett,   1 "   "

      Jno. W. Mallett,   1 "   "

Lieut. C. P. Mallett,   3 "   "

Surgeon Du Ponceau Jones, died.

      Edward Jones.

      Edward Jones Eccles.

      Geo. D. Hooper.

      Chas. M. Hooper.

Here lyes Buried
the Body of Mr.
PETER MALLET
who Departed this life
Jan y 10 1760
Aged 48 Years

Here lyes y Body of
Mrs. JOANNA MALLIT
Widow to Mr.
JOHN MALLIT
Who departed this life
Sep y 16 1764 in y
101t Year of Her Age

Here lyes Buried
y Body of Mr.
JOHN MALLET
Who departed this
Life September 28
Anno Dom 1745 in y
72 Year of his Age

FAC-SIMILE OF GRAVE MARKS.

GENEALOGICAL RECORD.

No.	Name of Wife (or Husband).		Date of Birth.	Date of Marriage.	Residence.	Date of Death.	Place of Burial.
1	DAVID MALLET,	1			France,	1691	England.
2	*Third son of 1 DAVID MALLET,*[1] John Mallet,	2	1673	1695	Fairfield, Ct.,	9-23, 1745	Stratfield, Ct.
	Johannah Lyon,		1663		"	9-16, 1764	"
	Children of 2 JOHN MALLET,[2]						
3	David Mallet,	3	1-10, 1701			8-22, 1777	Tashua, Ct.
	Esther Angevine,		1711		Tashua, Ct.,	1-16, 1787	"
4	(Capt.) John, jr.;	3	10-16, 1703		New Rochelle, N.Y.		
	Sarah (d. of Sam.) French,		1716		Tashua,	12-5, 1742	Stratfield, Ct.
	Martha,				"		
5	Lewis,	3	8-14, 1706		Milford, Ct.,	9-7, 1790	Milford, Ct.
	Eunice (d. of Ezek.) Newton,		1712			10-19, 1789	"
6	Johannah,	3	3-10, 1710		Stratfield,	living, 1783	
	Zachariah Angevine,					1760	
7	Peter,	3	3-31, 1712		Tashua,	1-10, 1760	Tashua, Ct.
	Mary (Booth?),				"	living, 1794	
	Children of 3 DAVID MALLETT,[3]						
8	John Mallett ye 3d,	4	10-28, 1731	9-25, 1754	Tashua,	5-28, 1784	Tashua, Ct.
	Rebecca Porter,				Trumbull,	9-28, 1784	
9	Hannah,	4	9-10, 1733	12-27, 1750			
	Seth Porter,						
10	David, jr.,	4	11-15, 1735		Tashua,	7-16, 1822	Tashua, Ct.
	Rhoda (d. of Gamaliel) French,		1740			3-5, 1777	"
	Bethia (d. of Gideon) Bennett,		1749			10-14, 1788	"
	Polly Young,		1747			5-13, 1835	"
11	Joseph,	4	3-25, 1740	2-4, 1768		9-15, 1818	"
	Mrs. Jerusha Middlebrook,		8-31, 1742			8-31, 1819	"
12	Esther,	4	1-1, 1745	11-26, 1761	Trumbull,	5-9, 1818	L. H. Trumbull.
	John Wheeler,		1738		"	3-15, 1801	"
	David Summers,		1738			2-26, 1818	"

No.	Name		Born / bap.	Married	Place		Died / Living	Buried
13	*Children of 4 John Mallett, jr.,*[3]	4						
	Prudence Mallett,	4		5-13, 1752				
	Isaac Daw,							
14	Matthew,	4	bap. 1-7, 1733	12-23, 1751	Tashua,		1777	
	Abigail Morris,	4						
15	Sarah,	4	bap. 4-6, 1735	12-25, 1755				
	Benjamin Sears,							
16	Mehitable,	4	bap. 3-4, 1737		Catharine, N. Y., & Huntington, Ct.		3-25, 1820	Huntington, Ct.
	Isaac Beardsley,	4	bap. 3-4, 1734				4-16, 1820	"
17	Hannah,	4	bap. 5- , 1739	12-30, 1762				
	Gideon (s. of Isaac) Bennett,							
18	John,	4	1740		Tashua,		4-18, 1826	Tashua.
	Sarah (Beach?)	4	1786				5-20, 1786	
19	Eunice,	4	1744	4-7, 1763	Catharine,		3-25, 1820	Catharine.
	Michael Beardsley,	4	1740					
20	Mercy,	4	bap. 9-14, 1740				living 1767	
21	Ruth,	4					living 1782	
22	Olive,	4						
	Lewis Nevisshee,							
23	Edmund,	4						
24	Henry E., ————,	4	bap. 2-13, 1763	12-11, 1783				
	Susannah Haines,							
25	*Children of 5 Lewis Mallett,*[3]							
	Lewis Mallett,	4	3-19, 1734	9-4, 17—	Milford,		4-1, 1804	Milford.
	Mary Mervin,	4	5-21, 1734				5-27, 1802	"
26	Eunice,	4	bap. 11- , 1735		Milford,		1824	"
	Nathan (s. of Nathan) Baldwin,	4	" 9-24, 1721					
27	Avis (Olive ?),	4	" 4- , 1737		"		5-9, 1804?	"
	Major David (s. of Nat.) Baldwin,	4	" 3-1, 1724	2-2, 1764			1813	
28	*Children of 6 Johannah Mallett Angevine,*[3]							
	Mary Angevine,	4		6-25, 1754	Stratfield, before		10-21, 1766	
	Andrew Sherwood,							
29	Zachariah,	4	bap. 4-18, 1736		"		living 1763	
30	Sarah,	4					living 1768	
31	Antony,	4					living 1768	
32	Lewis,	4			Trumbull,		(5- , 1802?)	

No.	Name of Wife (or Husband).	Date of Birth.	Date of Marriage.	Residence.	Date of Death.	Place of Burial.
33	——— , [4]					
34	——— , [4]					
	Children of 7 PETER MALLETT,[3]					
35	Mary Mallett, [4]	1738	1–13, 1756	Tashua,	10–17, 1801	L. H. Trumbull.
	David Summers,	1731		Trumbull,	2–28, 1818	"
36	Phebe, [4]		3–26, 1758	Tashua,		Catharine.
	Daniel (s. of Oliver) Hawley, [4]	8–, 1734		Trumbull, ...	before 12, 1797	"
37	Naomia, [4]	11–28, 1742	8–30, 1764	Tashua,	5–23, 1817	"
	Solomon (s. of Nathaniel) Booth, [4]	10–27, 1740		Catharine, N. Y.,	1–12, 1821	1 Fayett'ville, N. C.
38	Peter, [4]	11–14, 1744	3–7, 1765	N. Carolina,	2–2, 1805	Nowland's Ferry, Va
	Eunice (d. of J. Judson) Curtis,	bap. 7–, 1744	11–24, 1780	Stratford,	1776	1 Fayetteville.
	Sarah Mumford,	9–10, 1765		New London, Ct.,	4–2, 1886	Stanford.
39	Samuel, [4]	5–15, 1747		Stamford, N. Y.,	1823	"
	Kate (d. of Benj.) De Forest, [4]	3–18, 1753	1785	Stratford, Ct.,	1810?	Catharine.
40	Philip, [4]	5–20, 1756?	1778?	Catharine,	3–7, 1819	"
	Sarah (d. of Joseph) Frost, [4]			Danbury, Ct.,	1824?	Tashua.
41	Zachariah, [4]	2–28, 1752	10–26, 1775	Tashua,	1–4, 1813	"
	Rhoda (d. of Joseph) Edwards, [4]	2–17, 1753			5–8, 1834	
42	Daniel, [4]	1–15, 1755	About 1795	Wilmington, N. C.		
	Mary Lillington, [4]			"	1808	
43	Benjamin, [4]	1–5, 1755				
44	Benjamin, [4]	bap. 10–16, 1757				
	Children of 8 JOHN MALLETT YE 3D[4]					
45	David Mallett ye 3d, [5]	8–19, 1755	10–23, 1777	Tashua,	9–19, 1830	Tashua.
	91 Polly Bennett,[5]	3–15, 1760			12–14, 1843	"
46	Huldah, [5]	1756		Tashua,	10–29, 1758	Stratfield.
47	Seth, [5]	7–27, 1759	3–31, 1785	"	4–14, 1802	Tashua.
	Olive Hall, [5]	8–26, 1758			2–2, 1828	"
48	John Porter, [5]	4–14, 1762	unm.	Tashua,	2–16, 1769	L. H. Trumbull.
49	Ephraim, [5]	7–24, 1765		Tashua,	7–27, 1838	"
50	Ebenezer, [5]	bap. 4–5, 1771			1–20, 1863	Tashua.
	Grisselda Burr, [5]	1776				

No.	Name		Baptism / Birth	Marriage	Place	Death	Place
61	Joseph,				Emmetsburg, Herkimer co., N.Y.	5– , 1818	
	Loretta Porter,						
	Children of 9 HANNAH MALLETT PORTER, [4]						
52	Samuel Porter,	5	bap. 7-18, 1752				
53	John,	5	7– , 1756				
54	Esther,	5	4– , 1763				
55	Sarah,	5	6– , 1767				
	Children of 10 DAVID MALLETT, jr., [4]						
56	Philo Mallett,	5	bap. 5-22, 1782	7-6, 1780	Canojoharie, N.Y.,	4-2, 1820	Canojoharie.
	Eunice Wheeler,	5	4– , 1762			10-10, 1848	Tashua.
57	Benjamin,	5	bap. 12-18, 1763	1-6, 1785		11-6, 1798	
	Olive French,						
58	Hannah,	5	bap. 6-28, 1761	2-3, 1777	Waterville, N.Y.	before 1848	
	Isaac Edwards,						
59	Zachariah,	5		5-18, 1790	Paris, Oneida co., N.Y.		
	Abigail Osborne,						
60	Aaron,	5	bap. 6-30, 1771	2-24, 1805	Tashua,	12-31, 1855	Tashua.
	Eunice Beach,	5	7-1, 1783			11-27, 1860	"
61	Rhoda,	5	5-12, 1765		Illinois,	before 1848	
	— *Sanford.*						
62	Bethiah,	5	bap. 9-30, 1781	1801	Mt. Pleasant, Pa.		
	Jonathan Nichols,		2-6, 1777				
	James Hall,						
63	Huldah,	5	bap. 1-19, 1783	1807	Bridgeport.	2-23, 1834	Tashua.
	Amos Hawley Wheeler,						
64	David,	5	bap. 8-15, 1784	unm.	Tashua,	6-3, 1848	Tashua.
65	Charity,	5	9-20, 1788	12-25, 1811	"	12-16, 1832	L. H. T.
	Stephen (s. of Nehemiah) Beach,		5-8, 1769		Trumbull,	2-8, 1835	"
	Children of 11 JOSEPH MALLETT, [4]						
66	Elizabeth Mallett,	5	2-7, 1769		Tashua,	4-16, 1852	"
	David (s. of Lt. Ephraim) Middlebrook		4– , 1768		Trumbull,	11-27, 1819	"
67	Ephraim,	5	2-18, 1772		Tashua.	12-1, 1772	L. H. T.
68	Elijah,	5	8-31, 1773		Tashua,	7-6, 1806	Tashua.
	Sarah Sanford,	5	1-11, 1777	12-1, 1795		2-27, 1834	"
69	Robert,	5	6-15, 1778		"	12-17, 1852	"
	Sally C. (d. of Philo) Nichols,	5	1-10, 1782	12-15, 1804	"	1-10, 1850	"

No.	Name of Wife (or Husband).	Date of Birth.	Date of Marriage.	Residence.	Date of Death.	Place of Burial.
70	Esther, [5]	4–8, 1781		Tashua, Ct.,	7–16, 1824	Easton, Ct.
	Arron Seeley,	6–10, 1776		Easton, Ct.,	5–3, 1864	"
	Children of 12 Esther Mallett Wheeler,[4]					
71	Ebenezer Wheeler, [5]	2–11, 1765		Trumbull,	11–11, 1823	L. H. T.
	Naomi Lewis,	8–29, 1770			8–29, 1840	"
72	David, [5]	7–, 1767		Trumbull,	9–22, 1822	"
	Patience (d. of Nichols) Walker, [5]	1–1, 1772			3–8, 1862	"
73	John Mallett, [5]	1–7, 1769		Trumbull,	2–21, 1851	"
	Ann (d. of Eliakim) Walker,	7–11, 1774			5–24, 1855	"
	Children of 14 Matthew Mallett,[4]					
74	Steaven Mallett, [5]	bap. 9–5, 1779			before 9–, 1784	
75	Abel, [5]	bap. 7–25, 1762			11–7, 1812	Tashua.
76	Anna, [5]	bap. 4–, 1761			8–29, 1809	"
	Henry Beardsley,					
77	Salmon, [5]	bap. 6–10, 1764	5–6, 1787	Pittsfield, N. Y.,	4–7, 1825	Fairport, N. Y.
	Phebe Bennett,	11–14, 1767		"	4–11, 1803?	Pittsfield.
78	Matthew, [5]	bap. 11–18, 1770	7–5, 1795	New Milford,	10–14, 1822	Northville.
	Anna Morehouse,	1764		"	10–19, 1822	
	Children of 15 Sarah Mallett Sears[4]					
79	Mehitable Sears, [5]	bap. 9–19, 1756				
80	Hannah, [5]	bap. 6–18, 1758				
81	Elizabeth, [5]	bap. 2–19, 1760				
82	Alathea, [5]	bap. 6–, 1762				
83	Bartholome, [5]	bap. 6–16, 1768				
84	Benjamin, [5]	bap. 1–, 1771				
85	Gideon, [5]	bap. 2–23, 1773				
	Children of 16 Mehitable Mallett Beardsley,[4]					
86	Eli Beardsley, [5]	12–11, 1764	1–21, 1786	Catharine,	7–15, 1845	Catharine.
	Rhoda (d. of Othniel French),	11–25, 1767		New Stratford, Ct.,	3–25, 1841	"

No.	Name	Gen.	Born / Baptized	Married	Residence	Died	Place
87	Hannah,	5	bap. 4-27, 1765		(Corn Hill,) ? Ct.		
	Josiah Walker,				" "		
88	Esther,	5	bap. 11-2, 1766		New Stratford. Ct.,		
89	*Abner French,*	5			" "		
90	Isaac,	5			Zoar, Ct.		
	Polly Clark,		1770		Chestnut Hill. Ct.,	9-10, 1832	L. H. T.
	Abigail,	5	1758		Trumbull.	10-15, 1834	" "
	William Haines,						
	Children of 17 HANNAH MALLETT BENNETT.[4]						
91	Polly Bennett,	5	3-15, 1760	10-23, 1777	Tashua,	12-14, 1843	Tashua.
	45 David Mallett,[5]		3-19, 1755		"	9-19, 1830	"
	Children of 18 JOHN MALLETT,[4]						
92	Sarah Mallett,	5	bap. 4-12, 1767	unm.,	Tashua,	1790	Tashua.
93	Lucy,	5	bap. 9-5, 1772	"	"	3-22, 1852	"
94	*John Lewis,*	5	bap. 4-30, 1775		"	4-4, 1852	"
	Hannah Hubbell,		1777			9-19, 1884	"
	Children of 19 EUNICE MALLETT BEARDSLEY,[4]						
95	Lewis Beardsley,	5	1-22, 1764		Catharine,	5-26, 1802	Catharine.
96	*Pattie Hyde (Lane),*	5	10-14, 1765	about 1790	Huntington,	2-19, 1854	Huntington.
	Luke,		9-22, 1754			11-22, 1889	"
97	*Sarah Laborie (Lane),*	5	6-3, 1769	5-5, 1794	Catharine,	6-30, 1846	Catharine.
	David,		5-4, 1775			2-9, 1858	"
98	*Pamela Clark,*	5	6 5, 1771	9-13, 1795	Catharine,	12-4, 1851	Catharine.
	James,		4-20, 1778			9-26, 1851	"
99	*Hannah (d. of Nehemiah) Beach,*	5	5-5, 1778		Catharine and Illinois,	8-6, 1852	Winnebago co., Ill.
	Elias (Rev.),						
	Amy Somers,						
100	Pallina,	5	11-21, 1786		Catharine and Illinois.	1859	Wisconsin.
	Amos Bonney,						
	Children of 23 EDMUND MALLETT,[4]						
101	Eli Mallett,	5	bap. 2-27, 1773				
102	Avis,	5	bap. 5-25, 1775				
103	Eastman,	5	bap. 6-10, 1778				
104	Abraham,	5	bap. 3-19, 1781				

No.	Name of Wife (or Husband).	Date of Birth.	Date of Marriage.	Residence.	Date of Death.	Place of Burial.
105	Sally Nichols, ... 5	bap. 9-27, 1782				
	Children of 24 HENRY E. MALLETT,[4]					
106	Henry Mallett, ... 5	1-28, 1787				
107	John Goldsmith, ... 5	6-21, 1789				
	Children of 25 LEWIS MALLETT,[4]					
108	Lewis Mallett, ... 5	5-31, 1756	2-1, 1778	Bridgeport,	1-14, 1825	M. G. C. B. C.
	Anna (d. of Orlando) Beach,	3-5, 1758			7-8, 1843	"
109	John, ... 5	1-8, 1759	1789		1-8, 1835	"
	Mehitable (d. of Duncan) Weir,	10-10, 1768			1-8, 1835	
110	Eunice, ... 5	1761		Milford,	1837	
	Coggeshall,					
111	Miles, ... 5	1762	1-2, 1788		1844	
	Mary Ann (d. of Samuel) Mile,					
112	Lucy, —— *Fowler,* 5	3-6, 1765			1829	
113	Ann, —— *Fowler,* 5	3-6, 1765		Stratfield,	4-22, 1846	M. G. C. B. C.
	Samuel Wordin,	1-20, 1757			8-30, 1833	"
114	Mary, ... 5	17—			11-, 1799	
115	Peter; 5	1778			1855	Milford.
	Eliza (d. of Samuel) Terrell,	1773			9-17, 1828	"
116	Avis, —— *Turner,* 5					
117	Isaac, ... 5		6-2, 1796		1802	lost at sea.
	Sarah Brintnall,					
	Children of 26 EUNICE MALLETT BALDWIN,[4]					
118	Avis Baldwin, ... 5		unm.,	Milford,	dec.,	Milford.
119	Content, ... 5				before 1802	
	Elias Carrington.					
120	Mary, ... 5					
	William Durand.					

No.	Name		Born	Married	Place	Died	Place
121	Nathan,	5	11–8, 1755 }	2–16, 1784	Milford,	3–25, 1805	Milford.
	Avis Durand,		11–26, 1765 }		Milford,	2–8, 1851	"
122	David,	5	bap. 1–15, 1765			1779	Rev. Prison Ship.
123	Lewis,	5				1779	Milford.
124	Richard,	5	bap. 3–27, 1768	unm.,		4–3, 1834	
125	Abel,	5	bap. 2–24, 1772	"		9–1, 1802	
	Children of 27 AVIS MALLETT BALDWIN,[4]						
126	Elihu Baldwin,[4]	5	11–28, 1764			9–3, 1831	Milford.
127	Elizabeth,	5	10–20, 1768				
	Children of 32 LEWIS ANGEVINE,[4]						
128	Huldah Angevine,	5				living 1771	
	Children of 35 MARY MALLETT SUMMERS,[4]						
129	Abiah Summers,	5	10–7, 1756 }	2–1, 1776	Trumbull,	10–31, 1842	Trumbull.
	Eliakim (s. of Samuel) Beach,		7–13, 1751 }		Trumbull,	1–16, 1821	"
130	Ruth,	5	3–31, 1758		"	4–10, 1765	"
131	David,	5	11–1, 1760		"		
132	Peter,	5	6–16, 1762		"	4–2, 1765	"
133	Mary,	5	3–22, 1764				
	John French,		bap. 12–23, 1746				
134	Martha,	5	7–25, 1765		Trumbull,	3–8, 1852	L. H. T.
	Hezekiah Edwards,		1–4, 1761		Trumbull,	3–5, 1854	"
135	Ruth,	5	2–13, 1767	1796	Trumbull,	2–7, 1860	"
	James Beardsley,		1757		Trumbull.	6–6, 1843	"
136	Peter,	5	6–7, 1768		Trumbull.		
137	Ephraim,	5	12–28, 1769		"		
138	Phebe,	5	3–15, 1772				
	Elijah Beach,						
139	Hepzibah,	5	8–16, 1773		Trumbull,	7–18, 1852	Trumbull.
140	Seliok.	5	2–2, 1775		Catharine,	11–1, 1817	L. H. T.
			4–7, 1773			12–20, 1791	Catharine.
141	Eli,	5	9–9, 1776		Trumbull,	10–18, 1825	Trumbull.
142	Levi,	5	1–22, 1778		"	11–2, 1777	"
143	Naomia,	5	3–26, 1780 }	3–25, 1798		6–25, 1843	Trumbull.
	Ely (s. of Benjamin) Burton,		1–18, 1773 }			5–26, 1819	"

No.	Name of Wife (or Husband).	Date of Birth.	Date of Marriage.	Residence.	Date of Death.	Place of Burial.
144	Ira,	9-18, 1781	1800	N. Y. State,	2-7, 1862	Birmingham, Ct.
	Abigail (d. of James) Nichols,	1782				
	Children of 36 PHEBE MALLETT HAWLEY,[4]					
145	Naomi Hawley;	3-30, 1759	5-18, 1785	Trumbull.		
	Samuel Wakeley,					
146	Ruth,	3-1, 1761		"	d. young.	
147	David,	5-8, 1763		"		
148	Joseph,	7-11, 1765		"		
149	Benjamin,	7- , 1767		"		
150	Daniel,	10- , 1770		"		
151	Mary,	bap. 8-16, 1772				
152	Hannah,	bap. 5-7, 1775				
153	Abijah,	bap. 7-13, 1777				
154	Ruth,	10-21, 1779				
155	Edward,	4- , 1782				
	Children of 37 NAOMIA MALLETT BOOTH,[4]					
156	Aaron Booth,	2-2, 1766				
157	Eben,	4-9, 1768				
158	Reuben,	4-10, 1770		Catharine.		
159	Elijah,	bap. 5-6, 1773				
160	Mary,	8-7, 1776				
161	Isaac,	7-2, 1781	unm.,	Catharine.		
162	Daniel Mallett,	5-11, 1784				
163	Nancy,	11-5, 1788	1-21, 1815			
	William Carpenter,					
	Children of 38 PETER MALLETT,[4]					
164	Judson Curtis Mallett,	1766?		Stratford,	11-?, 1776	Nowland's Ferry, Va.

No.	Name		Born	Married	Married where	Died	Where
165	Mary Elizabeth Mallett, ...	5	6-15, 1773	6-20, 1790	Stratford, N. C., . .	1-26, 1837	Pittsboro.
	Col. *Edward Jones*, . . .		3-10, 1762	1-27, 1799	Pittsboro, N. C., .	7-8, 1841	1 Fayetteville.
166	Sarah Jane, ...	5	3-8, 1782		Fayetteville,	7-8, 1801	
	William Smith, . .		4-14, 1775		"	9-6, 1801	
167	Elizabeth Hetty, . .	5	5-29, 1784	2-10, 1806	"	4-22, 1808	
	Dr. Andrew Scott, .				"		
168	Charles Robinson, . .	5	1-20, 1786		"	2-8, 1789	1 Fayetteville.
169	Peter Francis, . .	5	8-15, 1787		"	8-20, 1791	
170	Caroline Mary, . .	5	3-5, 1789	6-10, 1807	"	11-20, 1862	1 Fayetteville.
	Carleton Walker, .		1-5, 1777		near Wilmington,	10-10, 1840	Hillsboro. N. C.
171	Henrietta Ann, . .	5	10-26, 1790	2-14, 1809	Wilmington.	1-4, 1851	Fayetteville.
	Hugh Campbell, .		8-14, 1774		Fayetteville,	8-15, 1824	
172	Charles Peter, . .	5	2-14, 1792	5-6, 1809	"	8-23, 1874	N. Monroe, La.
	Sophia Sarah Beatty,		5-4, 1796	about 1839		2-20, 1829	1 Fayetteville.
	Sarah Greene, .					10-12, 1884	Bastrop, La.
173	Peter James, . .	5	6-14, 1795	9-12, 1816	Fayetteville,	4-26, 1830	1 Fayetteville.
	Margaret Isabella Gibbs,		11-23, 1797			3-1, 1824	1 "
	Ellen Madeline de Berniene,		1-8, 1801	4-19, 1827	Charleston, S. C.,	3-6, 1828	1 "
174	Edward Jones, . .	5	5-1, 1797	9-11, 1820	New York,	8-20, 1883	New York.
	Sara (d. of Gov.) Fenner,		5-13, 1797		Providence, R. I.,	5-17, 1841	Providence.
	Jane Haight (Granger),			1844	N. Y.,		N.Y.
175	William Smith, . .	5	8-29, 1798		Fayetteville,	7-3, 1799	1 Fayetteville.
176	Lallerstedt Dunlap, .	5	9-7, 1800	7-19, 1826	"	11-11, 1858	Texas.
	Jane Smith, .		12-12, 1807		"		Cumberl'd co., N.C.
	Frances London, .		2-13, 1806	5- , 1835	"	6-5, 1880	1 Fayetteville.
177	Sara Smith, . .	5	11-7, 1801			2-3, 1871	1 "
178	Giles Mumford, . .	5	1-24, 1804	5-31, 1827	Osyka, Miss.,	6-30, 1875	Osyka.
	Sarah Howard, .		9-29, 1810				"
	Children of 39 SAMUEL MALLETT,[4]						
179	Catharine Mallett, .	5			Stratford, Ct.,	before 1788	Catharine.
180	Catharine, . .	5	7- , 1788	1816	Catharine,	1877	"
	Eaton Agard, .		1790		Litchfield, Ct.,	10-7, 1863	
181	Samuel, . .	5	1792	181-	BloomingGrove,NY	1826	Blooming Grove,
	Mary Cannon, .		1795		New York,	1829	N. Y.
182	Daniel, . .			unm.,	Catharine,	died ae. 40	Kentucky.
	Children of 40 PHILIP MALLETT,[4]						
188	Dimon Mallett, .	5	1780	1798?	Catharine,	3-20, 1828	Catharine.
	Eunice (d. of Jonathan) Couch,		6-29, 1775		Danbury, Ct., ?	7-23, 1856	"

No.	Name of Wife (or Husband).	Date of Birth.	Date of Marriage.	Residence.	Date of Death.	Place of Burial.
184	Daniel, .5	12-3, 1781	} 1808	Danbury,	4-1, 1851	Redding, Ct.
	Mary (d. of Tom.) Sanford (w. of Thom.) Couch, .5	11-13, 1779		"	10-27, 1828	"
	Mabel Hill, .5	12-17, 1791	11-8, 1829		12-17, 1845	Durhamville, Tenn.
185	Esther, .5	1782	unm.,	Catharine,	9-17, 1840	Chemung, N. Y.
186	Naomi, .5	1784		"	1855	
	Rhositer (s. of Dr. Thom.) Averill, .5	1777	1810		1873	
187	Levi, .5	12-14, 1786	5-21, 1809	Danbury,	2-21, 1853	Catharine.
	Rebecca (d. of Thomas) Stocker, . .5	6-30, 1785		Catharine,	1-13, 1864	"
188	Philip, . . .5	5-13, 1789	11- , 1830	Danbury,	4-27, 1856	"
				Catharine,		
				Tennessee.		
189	Isaac, . .5	1790	unm.,	Catharine,	1813	Buffalo, N. Y.

Children of 41 ZACHARIAH MALLETT.[4]

No.	Name of Wife (or Husband).	Date of Birth.	Date of Marriage.	Residence.	Date of Death.	Place of Burial.
190	Mary Mallett. .5	9-6, 1776		Tashua.		
	Daniel Hubbell, .5				9-20, 1833	Easton.
191	Eunice, .5	12-2, 1777	12-24, 1795	Tashua,	11-6, 1847	"
	Justus Bennett, .5	8-17, 1773		Easton,	2-12, 1829	Tashua.
192	Joseph Edwards, .5	8-1, 1779	4-19, 1805	Tashua,	12-29, 1828	"
	Hannah (d. of Wm.) Haines, .5	7-25, 1782		Chestnut Hill,	9-1, 1867	"
193	Samuel, .5	11-2, 1782	1-1, 1810	Monroe, Ct.,	12-21, 1862	M. G. C. B. C.
	Betsey Sherman, .5	9-23, 1784			4-28, 1821	"
194	Charity, .5	10-15, 1786	5-8, 1814	Bridgeport,	4-2, 1822	Grand Rapids.
	Daniel Edwards, .5	4-2, 1784		"	4-2, 1857	N. Y. State.
195	Phebe, . .5	10-22, 1788		N. Y. and Mich.,	8 or 9, 1831	Tashua.
	David Leavitt, .5				9-2, 1793	"
196	Zachariah Curtis, .5	1790			9-, 1831	
197	Daniel, .5	11-22, 1794		Tashua,	8-20, 1832	
	303 Sally (d. of Jn. Lewis) Mallett,[6] .	7-14, 1795			7-14, 1837	

Children of 45 DAVID MALLETT.[5] (and 91).

No.	Name of Wife (or Husband).	Date of Birth.	Date of Marriage.	Residence.	Date of Death.	Place of Burial.
198	Ephraim Mallett, .6	3-23, 1778				
	Esther ———, .6					
199	Daniel, .6	1-17, 1780	2-8, 1806	Roxbury,	3-26, 1867	} N. Cem., Bridge-
	Eunice (d. of Naamiah) Beach, . .6	7-1, 1787			12-2, 1843	} water, Ct.

No.	Name		Birth	Marriage	Residence	Death	Burial
200	Huldah Hannah,	6	3–31, 1782	8–16, 1800	Tashua,	10–10, 1805	Easton.
	Samuel Lyon,		8–27, 1780		Easton,	1872	"
201	Polly,	6	8–31, 1785	unm.,	Tashua,	5–25, 1868	Tashua.
202	Gideon,	6	3–14, 1788		Trumbull,	10–13, 1879	L. H. T.
	Parthenia (d. of Nath'l) Sherman,		10–8, 1793	3–31, 1812		5–9, 1866	"
203	Esther,	6	6–9, 1793	unm.,	Tashua,	2–3, 1867	Tashua.
204	Anna Asenath,	6	7–20, 1797	"		6–8, 1846	"
	Children of 47 Seth Mallett,[5]						
205	Rebecca Mallett,	6	11–14, 1785				
	Burr Turney,		12–20, 1796				
206	Porter,	6	5–2, 1787	unm.,	Tashua,	2–10, 1808	Tashua.
207	Capt. Abel,	6	1–27, 1789			11–27, 1877	"
	Naomia Gregory,		9–23, 1784		"	2–2, 1856	"
208	Olive,	6	5–18, 1791	12–25, 1813	"	12–1, 1853	"
	Capt. John Nichols,		7–21, 1775			5–13, 1862	"
209	Seth,	6	11–7, 1793	9–10, 1819		3–11, 1823	
	Rhoda (d. of Cyrus) Silliman,		11–18, 1797			10–27, 1841	Easton.
210	Capt. Jesse.	6	4–30, 1798	8–27, 1828	Tashua,	8–27, 1862	Tashua.
	Jennette Sherman,		7–10, 1805			12–10, 1839	"
	Mary Smith,		8–31, 1818	6–9, 1850		1–13, 1887	
	Children of 50 Ebenezer Mallett,[5]						
211	Josiah Burr Mallett,	6	2–11, 1798	unm.,	Tashua,	5–28, 1882	Tashua.
212	Fanny Maria,	6	1811			3–29, 1843	"
	587 Amariah Mallett,[7]		1805			3–29, 1863	
	Children of 51 Joseph Mallett,[5]						
213	Mary Mallett,	6					
	—— Franklin,						
	Children of 56 Philo Mallett,[5]						
214	Polly Mallette,	6	bap. 5–31, 1789	1804	Newtown, Ct.		
215	William,	6					
	Eunice Curtis,						
	Sarah D. Wakeley,						
216	Roswell,	6	6–7, 1794	12–7, 1819	Ames, N. Y.,	4–3, 1865	Ames, N. Y.
	Sally Parmelia Beach,		2–15, 1799			4–15, 1839	"
	Christianna Eckerson,		3–21, 1832	6–20, 1839		1–9, 1893	"

No.	Name of Wife (or Husband).	Date of Birth.	Date of Marriage.	Residence.	Date of Death.	Place of Burial.
217	Philo, ... 6	2-16, 1790	5-6, 1812	Hadley, N. Y.,	10-25, 1865	Canajoharie.
	Rhoda Ellen Taylor,			"	11-13, 1877	
218	Dilizon, ... 6	8-5, 1794			4-14, 1882	
	Ann Maria Davis,	1796			4-9, 1867	
219	Grandison, ... 6			Toledo, O.		
	Keziah Elliott,					
220	Benjamin, ... 6			Toledo, O.		
221	Esther, —— *Bradshaw,* . . . 6					
222	Lois, ... 6					
	Marlyn Hoyt Stevens,					
223	Elizabeth, ... 6			Canajoharie.		
	Peter Welch.					
	Children of 58 HANNAH MALLETT EDWARDS.[5]					
224	David Mallett Edwards, ... 6	bap. 10-19, 1790		Waterville, N. Y.		
	Children of 59 ZACHARIAH MALLETT.[5]					
225	Wheeler Mallett, ... 6	bap. 10-19, 1770			dec.	
226	Wheelor, ... 6	" 3-30, 1791				
	Children of 60 AARON MALLETT.[5]					
227	Mary Eliza Mallett, ... 6	7-3, 1806		Tashua,	6-3, 1817	Tashua.
228	George Albert, ... 6	1-24, 1808	12-24, 1833	"	3-19, 1893	"
	571 Charity Nichols.[7]					
229	David Beach, ... 6	8-6, 1814	unm.,	"	12-15, 1891	"
		6-14, 1810				
230	Stephen Summers, ... 6	5-1, 1812	5-17, 1843	Oxford, Ct.	9-13, 1846	"
	Flora M. (d. of Nath'l) Sherman,	11-13, 1817				
231	Rhoda Clarissa, ... 6	8-16, 1814	12-24, 1849	Tashua.		
	Ebenezer T. Sanford,	4-, 1794		Easton, Ct.,	11-22, 1873	Easton.
232	Aaron Benjamin, ... 6	12-11, 1816	11-1, 1843	Tashua.		
	Jane Elizabeth Howley,	5-1, 1822			5-25, 1851	Tashua.
	Lydia A. Sherman,	12-13, 1811	12-22, 1851		4-24, 1884	"

No.	Name		Born	Married	Place	Died	Place
233	Mary Melissa,	6	3-8, 1819	4-19, 1846	Tashua,	2-27, 1852	Tashua.
	William Nichols,		11-30, 1811		"	1-10, 1887	"
234	William Alanson,	6	5-25, 1821	9-28, 1851			"
	Sarah Augusta Wakeley,		10-5, 1830			1-23, 1861	
	Hannah Elizabeth Walker,		12-17, 1830	6-18, 1862			
235	Parthenia Eliza,	6	4-27, 1824	5-11, 1864	Tashua. Easton,	3-18, 1878	Easton.
	William W. Wheeler,		1- , 1813				
	Children of 62 BETHIAH MALLETT NICHOLS,[5]						
236	Maria Nichols,	6	8- , 1801			1-3, 1806	Tashua.
	Children of 65 CHARITY MALLETT BEACH,[5]						
237	David Youngs Beach,	6	5-30, 1813	4-19, 1838	Trumbull,	7-21, 1881	L. H. Trum.
	Sally Eliza French,		4-17, 1816			1-22, 1877	
238	Mary Eliza,	6	1-26, 1819	9-27, 1837		10-16, 1892	Sumter, S. C.
	Charles Curtis,		1807			8-22, 1890	"
	Children of 66 ELIZABETH MALLETT MIDDLEBROOK,[5]						
239	Elizabeth Middlebrook,	6		3-8, 1855	Monroe,	11-5, 1885	Monroe.
	Hiram Beardsley,				"	1-2, 1879	"
240	Jerusha,	6	5-31, 1790			2-7, 1826	Trumbull.
	Eli Burnam Beach,		3-24, 1790		Trumbull,	3-24, 1857	
241	Huldah,	6	5-14, 1792	10-19, 1815	Easton,	12-29, 1862	Easton.
	Eli Adams,		1-10, 1784			2-19, 1861	"
242	Mary,	6	6-8, 1803	10-22, 1823		4-27, 1878	L. H. Tr.
	Lucius Jackson,		3-5, 1801		West,	3-22, 1879	"
243	Ephraim,	6	9-20, 1799	1-7, 1824	Trumbull,	12-13, 1863	
	Mary Cynthia (d. of Silas) Nichols,		9-11, 1802			4-11, 1859	
244	David,	6	7-31, 1805	1-2, 1828		4-8, 1868	
	Hepsabah Beardsley,		1-21, 1804			8-2, 1868	
	Children of 68 ELIJAH MALLETT,[5]						
245	Ephraim "Sanford" Mallett,	6	1-6, 1796	4-2, 1828	Tashua,	3-15, 1881	Tashua.
	Cynthia Sherman,		4-1, 1792			8-10, 1881	"
246	Josiah,	6	4-23, 1798	11-20, 1833	Easton,	6-11, 1886	Stepney, Ct.
	Huldah Winton,		2-12, 1807		"	1-23, 1890	"

No.	Name of Wife (or Husband).		Date of Birth.	Date of Marriage.	Residence.	Date of Death.	Place of Burial.
247	Esther,	.6	1-17, 1802	} 10-10, 1842	Tashua,	7-6, 1876	Laceyville.
	Benjamin Edwards,		9-1, 1793		Laceyville, Pa.,	2-24, 1876	"
	Children of 69 ROBERT MALLETT,[5]						
248	John "Clark" Mallett,	.6	10-5, 1805	} 6-7, 1832	Tashua.	11-13, 1869	Tashua.
	Sally P. Nichols,		5-27, 1811		.	2-5, 1884	"
249	Caroline,	.6	5-26, 1807	} 2-23, 1825	Tashua,	9-4, 1838	Unity, Tr.
	Chas. Elliot (s. of Isaac) Booth,		11-5, 1801		Trumbull,	9-12, 1876	"
250	Emeline,	.6	6-29, 1809	} 3-8, 1826	Tashua,	12-21, 1890	Trumbull.
	Birdseye Booth Plumb,		8-8, 1804		Trumbull,	2-12, 1891	"
251	Catharine,	.6	7-8, 1812	} 5-16, 1832	Tashua,	12-1, 1849	"
	Daniel Stiles Brinsmade,		2-2, 1808		Trumbull,	5-28, 1872	"
252	Sally Ann,	.6	10-15, 1814	} 6-15, 1837	Tashua,	4-5, 1864	Unity, Tr.
	David Hinman,		1813		Trumbull,	1892	"
253	Cordelia,	.6	8-18, 1820	} 2-20, 1840	Bridgeport,	9-18, 1887	L. H. Tr.
266	*Ebenezer Wheeler,*[6]		11-18, 1812		L. H. Trum.		
	Children of 70 ESTHER MALLETT SEELEY,[5]						
254	Mallett Seeley,	.6	11-9, 1801	} 12-12, 1822,	Easton.	4-28, 1881	Easton.
	Caroline Bennett,		1-22, 1801			9-28, 1885	"
255	Roswell,	.6	6-24, 1804	unm.,	Easton,	11-27, 1832	"
256	Anna,	.6	11-4, 1807	unm.,	"	9-22, 1826	"
257	Arron Sherwood,	.6	1-2, 1810		"	1-18, 1810	"
258	Eunice,	.6	9-22, 1811	unm.,	"	11-27, 1848	"
259	Ezra Sherwood,	.6	6-22, 1818	} 6-1, 1854			
	Mary Ann Jackson,		8-, 1829				
260	Son,	.6	7-10, 1824		Easton,	7-11, 1824	Easton.
	Children of 72 DAVID WHEELER,[5]						
261	Eunice Wheeler,	.6					
	Hallett Smith,				Red Bank, Pa.		
262	Esther,	.6	2-3, 1796	} 12-26, 1821	Nichols,	1-2, 1893	Nichols, Ct.
	David Beach Plumb,		3-31, 1796			11-26, 1878	"
263	Abigail,	.6		unm.,			Brookfield, Mo.

No.	Name		Birth	Marriage	Married at	Death	Residence
	Children of 78 JOHN MALLETT,⁵						
264	Melissa Wheeler,	6	1797	6-3, 1824	Monroe,	4-13, 1867	Monroe.
	Jared Perry Beardsley,		1779			1-26, 1841	"
265	Walker,	6	1-21, 1803	3-15, 1826	L. H. T.,	4-28, 1885	L. H. T.
	Rebecca Sherwood,		4-23, 1805			8-27, 1881	"
266	Ebenezer,	6	11-18, 1812	2-20, 1840	Bridgeport.	9-18, 1887	"
	253 Cordelia Mallett,⁶		8-18, 1820				
	Children of 77 SALMON MALLETT,⁵						
267	Sidney Mallett,	6					
	Betsey Green,	6					
268	Munson,	6					
	Wealthy Wayland,	6					
269	Cyrenus,	6			Fairport, N. Y.,	1844	Fairport.
	Hannah (d. of Joseph B.) Tomlinson,					1830?	"
270	Phebe,	6	1790			1871	
	David Hubby,	6					
271	Laura,	6				5-7, 1887	Fairport.
	Gardner Hall,						
	Children of 78 MATTHEW MALLETT,⁵						
272	Asher Mallett,	6	8-4, 1796	12-18, 1822	New Milford, Ct.,	3-4, 1881	Northville.
	Harriet Ford,		1805			3-8, 1885	"
273	Ithemer,	6	1801	5-28, 1827	New Milford,	3-25, 1831	"
	Loiza Ford,		1800			6-11, 1881	
	Children of 86 ELI BEARDSLEY,⁵						
274	Lidia Beardsley,	6	1-2¹, 1787		Catharine?	7-15, 1844	Catharine.
	Lemuel Sherman,		11 1, 1790		Weston, Ct.,	12-20, 18.6	Stepney, Ct.
275	Hannah,	6	5-13, 1789		Catharine,	9-1, 1819	Catharine.
	Mason Jones,		10-24, 1786			8-19, 1853	"
276	Ammon,	6	4-8, 1791				
	Rachel Summers,		11-27, 1794			4-17, 1814	
	Sabria Goodwin,						
277	Abigail,	6	4-5, 1793	9-3, 1812	Weston,	9-3, 1835	Montour, N. Y.
	William Judd,		4-14, 1788			5, 1879	Dawagine, Mich.
278	Elam,	6	5-7, 1795			9-28, 1884	Havana, N. Y.
	Polly Clark,						

No.	Name of Wife (or Husband).	Date of Birth.	Date of Marriage.	Residence.	Date of Death.	Place of Burial.
279	Hiram. . . . . [6]	5-15, 1797				
280	*Lyda Knapp.*					
	Irad, ... [6]	9-2, 1799	10-23, 1842	Catharine, . . .	6-17, 1863	Catharine.
	Fannie Cordelia Stuart (Ogden), [6]	4-23, 1805			12-16, 1887	"
281	Mehitable. . . . . . [6]	11-22, 1801		. . . .	11-25, 1843	"
	Philo Beardsley, . . . [6]	2-13, 1797	6-1, 1817	Catharine,	2-3, 1849	H. Montour,
282	Cyrus, ... [6]	8-24, 1804		"	7-31, 1890	"
	Mary Wakeman, . . . [6]	1-25, 1807	3- , 1825		10-8, 1887	"
283	Stiles, ... [6]	4-7, 1807		Catharine,	1-25, 1892	"
	Frances L. Howard, . . [6]	11-12, 1810			1-20, 1851	
	Sally Wayland (Lewis), . [6]		9-12, 1855			
284	Othniel, ... [6]	10-16, 1809	. . . . .	. . . .	3-13, 1827	H. Montour.
	Children of 87 HANNAH BEARDSLEY, WALKER,[5]					
285	Mercy Walker, ... [6]					
286	Mehetable, ... [6]					
287	Betsey, ... [6]					
288	Charles, ... [6]					
	Children of 88 ESTHER BEARDSLEY FRENCH,[5]					
289	Phebe French, ... [6]					
290	Eli, ... [6]					
291	Sally, ... [6]					
292	Lemuel, ... [6]					
293	Eliza, ... [6]					
294	Caty, ... [6]					
	Children of 89 ISAAC BEARDSLEY,[5]					
295	Fanny Beardsley, . . . [6]					
296	Charles, ... [6]					
297	Silas, ... [6]					
298	Eliza, ... [6]					
299	Jared, ... [6]					

No.	Name	Gen	Birth	Marriage	Married at	Death	Residence
300	Jacob L.,	6					
301	Mary,	6					
302	Nelson,	6					
	Children of 91 POLLY BENNETT MALLETT,[5] (See 45.)						
	Children of 94 JOHN LEWIS MALLETT,[5]						
303	Sarah Mallett,	6	7-14, 1795		Tashua,	7-14, 1837	Tashua.
	197 Daniel Mallett,[5]		11-22, 1794		"	8-20, 1832	"
304	Fanny,	6	1-15, 1801	9-24, 1823	"	1-15, 1828	M. G. C. B. C.
	Munson Seeley,		1-15, 1800		Bridgeport,	6-11, 1876	"
	Children of 96 LUKE BEARDSLEY,[5]						
305	Peter Beardsley,	6	4-26, 1791	10-, 1825	Huntington,	6-27, 1870	Huntington.
	Delia Bennett,						
306	Eli,	6	1-7, 1793				
307	Abner,	6	1-7, 1793				
308	Sally,	6	11-4, 1795				
309	Anthony,	6	11-, 1797	12-4, 1825	Hartland, N. Y.,	9-, 1824	New Orleans.
	Almira Baker,		1-20, 1793		Parma, N. Y.,	3-11, 1875	Hartland.
310	Cyrus,	6	4-24, 1799			5-26, 1881	"
311	Eunice,	6	9-22, 1803				Albion, Mich.
	Children of 97 DAVID BEARDSLEY,[5]						
312	Lewis Beardsley,	6	3-4, 1796	3-11, 1821	Catharine,	3-2, 1885	Catharine.
313	Michael,	6	2-5, 1802	1823	Chandlersville,	1872	Cass Co., Ill.
314	Lucy,	6	8-2, 1806	1824	Virginine, Ill.,		Catharine.
315	Lucius,	6	9-1, 1812	2-11, 1836	Catharine,	5-3, 1887	Catharine.
	Mariette Aiken,						
	Children of 98 JAMES BEARDSLEY,[5]						
316	Lewis Beardsley,	6	7-8, 1796	3-3, 1818	Catharine,	2-13, 1882	Montour.
	Harriet Agard,		8-24, 1796			7-11, 1870	"

No.	Name of Wife (or Husband).		Date of Birth.	Date of Marriage.	Residence.	Date of Death.	Place of Burial.
317	Stephen,	.6	11-22, 1797 / 1799	9-1, 1819	Catharine,	8-19, 1871 / 7-15, 1880	Catharine.
	Sally Bennett,						
	Maria Lockerby,		10-1, 1802	3-2, 1831		2- , 1873	"
318	Elias,	.6	8-19, 1799	1833	Veteran,	9-22, 1873	Michigan.
	Polly Maria Cornell,						
	Maria (Cassady),			1845		12- , 1844 / dec.	
319	Levi,	.6	6-24, 1801	11-24, 1823	Catharine.	1-28, 1883	Catharine.
	Loraine Agard,		11-12, 1803			2-25, 1866	
320	Susannah,	.6	5-16, 1803	10-15, 1822	Veteran,	7-14, 1884	Montour.
	Jonathan Howard,		10-14, 1793			10-10, 1875	"
321	Sarah,	.6	2-18, 1805	1-14, 1834	Sullivan,	3-11, 1887	Sylvania.
	Orin Ruggles,		12-10, 1799			8-21, 1880	Sylvania, Pa.
322	Nehemiah Beach,	.6	1-2, 1807			3-5, 1833	Genessee Co.
323	Eunice,	.6	8-28, 1809			1-26, 1812	Catharine.
324	James,	.	8-10, 1811	2-18, 1836	Catharine,	12-20, 1871	Montour.
	Nancy Fritz Gerald,		3-9, 1818			5-1, 1845	"
	Margaret Lockerby,		9-11, 1809	2-11, 1846		6-2, 1888	"
325	Abel Northrop,	.6	1-12, 1814	12-31, 1836	Catharine,	10-4, 1852	"
	Martha Ann Lambert,		3-24, 1820			1-16, 1876	"
326	Hannah,	.6	3-12, 1816	12-31, 1834	Catharine,	7-27, 1866	"
	Shuman W. Evans,		7-25, 1810		"	3-16, 1891	

Children of 99 REV. ELIAS BEARDS-LEY.[5]

No.	Name of Wife (or Husband).		Date of Birth.	Date of Marriage.	Residence.	Date of Death.	Place of Burial.
327	Phebe Beardsley,	.6	1808	1830	Austin, Minn.,	4-2, 1884	Sullivan.
	Isaac Baker,				Sullivan, Pa.,		"
328	Eden,	.6	8-5, 1811	1840	Vermont,	5-29, 1879	St. Oloff.
	Miranda Tinkham,		8-31, 1818				
329	Samuel A.,	.6	11-11, 1812	1832	Ashby, Minn.,	1-9, 1886	
	Margaret M. Loce,		1-23, 1814				
330	Roswell,	.6	1818	unm.,	Catharine,	1810	Catharine.
331	Harry,	.6	1821	1845	Elmira, N. Y.,		
	Margaret Dewyee,		1824				
332	Zilpha,	.6	1825	1843	Hornby, N. Y.,	1890	Hornby.
	Joseph R. Van Notrick,		1820				

Children of 100 POLLINA BEARDSLEY BONNEY,[5]

No.	Name		Born	Married	Residence	Died	Place
333	Maria Bonney,	6					
	Walter Daily.						
334	Eunice,	6					
	—— Brown.						
335	Aaron,	6					
336	Amos,	6					
337	Polly (Martha),	6					
338	Mary,	6					
339	Lydia,	6					

Children of 108 *Lewis Mallett*,[5]

No.	Name		Born	Married	Residence	Died	Place
340	Anna Mallett,	6	5-14, 1779	about 1828	Bridgeport,	6-4, 1859	Damascus.
	David Hubbell,		1778		Damascus, Pa.,	1-23, 1832	M. G. C. B. C.
341	Abigail,	6	5-31, 1781		Bridgeport,	1857	"
	Joseph Knapp,						
342	Lewis,	6	6-28, 1788	2-, 1818	Bridgeport,	5-29, 1856	M. G. C. B. C.
	Sibbe (d. of Dr. Richard) Treat,		4-12, 1785		Milford,	12-26, 1838	"
343	Eunice,	6	3-28, 1786	1-2, 1812	Bridgeport,	10-1, 1867	Milford.
	Thomas B Clark,		7-8, 1786		Milford,	12-15, 1854	"
344	Mary,	6	5-20, 1788	6-9, 1808	Bridgeport,	11-16, 1856	M. G. C. B. C.
	Ezra Wheeler,		9-7, 1785		"	10-8, 1873	"
345	Harriet,	6	7-15, 1790	8-2, 1831	Huntington,	3-15, 1867	Huntington.
	Samuel Buckingham,		4-2, 1780		Bridgeport,	11-30, 1879	"
346	Laura,	6	2-26, 1793	unm.,	"	4-3, 1795	Stratfield.
347	Lauretta,	6	10-21, 1795	"	"	3-14, 1869	M. G. C. B. C.
348	Avis,	6	3-20, 1798	"	"	8-23, 1819	"
349	Lucy,	6	7-12, 1802			6-23, 1889	

Children of 109 JOHN MALLETT,[5]

No.	Name		Born	Married	Residence	Died	Place
350	John Mallett,	6	1783	1-7, 1810	New Milford,	6-27, 1852	N. Milford.
	Polly (d. Dan'l) Fenn,		1783		Milford,	9-24, 1850	"
351	William,	6		10-1, 1808	Milford,	dec. ae. 82	Milford.
	Sally Bowers,						
352	Mark,	6				1820	
353	Mehetable,	6		1-12, 1809		1823	
	Michael (s. of M.) Peck,						
354	Lucy Ann,	6	4-14, 1795	6-9, 1814		7-23, 1857	
	Sam'l Galpin (s. of Sam'l) Higby,		3-14, 1791			9-7, 1869	

No.	Name of Wife (or Husband).	Date of Birth.	Date of Marriage.	Residence.	Date of Death.	Place of Burial.
	Children of 111 Miles Mallett,[5]					
355	Sally Mallett, . . . [6]	8-13, 1788	3-5, 1812			
356	Charles Bowers, Daniel, . . [6]	3-11, 1790				
357	Maria, ——, *Steele,* . [6]	12-20, 1791			2-24, 18·0	
358	Mary, —— *Steele,* . [6]	10-18, 1793		Woodbridge, Ct.		
359	*Darius Ford,* Lewis, *Drownell,* . [6]	5-27, 1796	1816			
360	Miles, . . . [6]	7-7, 1798			4-7, 1817	
361	Betsey, *Burr (s. of Dea. Bradford) Steele,* . [6]	2-9, 1801 6-7, 1800	11-7, 1822		4-7, 1824 8-11, 1823	
362	Phebe, . . . [6]	4-3, 1803				
363	Luke, *Julina (d. of Isaac) Bristol,* . [6]	6-13, 1800 4-3, 1803	12-21, 1828		8-14, 1857 6-13, 1882	
364	Lucy, . . [6]	3-16, 1806	unm., . .		1881	
365	*Falle,* —— *Steele,* . [6]			New Haven.		
366	*Fowler,* Charlotte G. *(d. of Miles) Smith,* . [6]	9-5, 1808 4-12, 1807			7-16, 1862 9-8, 1886	
	Children of 113 Ann Mallett Wordin,[5]					
367	Lucy Wordin, *Seeley Peet,* . [6]	9-18, 1798		Fairfield Co.,	6-26, 1860	Bridgeport.
368	Clary, . . . [6]	1-1, 1795	unm.,		11-1, 1827	
369	Mary A., . . [6]	8-18, 1796	"		10-23, 1820	
370	Samuel W., . . [6]	9-2, 1798	"		11-22, 1837	
371	Laura, *Alfred Hubbell,* . [6]	10-24, 1800			2-7, 1883	
372	Eunice A., *David Wheeler,* . [6]	10-25, 1804			1-15, 1890	

No.	Name		Born	Place	Married / Died	Residence
	Children of 115 PETER MALLETT,[5]					
373	David Mallett,	6	1795	Milford,	} 4-24, 1816	1854	Milford.
	Eliza (d. of Joseph) Clark,					dec.	"
374	Susan,	6	1797	Milford,	...	1856	
	Abraham (s. of David) Burns,		1800		...		
375	Alfred,	6	7-16, 1799	Milford,	11-25, 1822	11-21, 1885	Milford.
	Dianna (d. of Benedict) Tibbals,		4-3, 1801				
376	Stephen,	6	11-1, 1804				
377	Eliza,	6	12-, 1809	Milford.	11-11, 1833	11-1, 1882	
	Julia (d. of Jedidah) Stow,		7-30, 1813				
378	Horace,	6	1810				
379	Mary,	6					
	Nathan (s. of Nathan) Fenn,						
380	Peter,	6		Derby, Ct.,	...	dec.	
	Nancy Hotchkiss,			New York.	...		
	Children of 117 ISAAC MALLETT,[5]						
381	*Isaac Mallett,	6	1799		} 4-18, 1822	11-21, 1866	Danbury, Ct.
	Eliza Keeler (d. of Dan'l and Anna),		7-, 1803			2-26, 1827	O. C. Bridgewater.
	Harriet E.,		1810			4-3, 1872	Danbury.
382	William,	6					
	Children of 121 NATHAN BALDWIN,[b]						
383	David Lewis Baldwin,	6	8-7, 1785	Milford.	6-10, 1814	9-2, 1868	Milford.
	Martha (d. of Abraham V. H. De Witt,)		9-15, 1790				
384	Eunice,	6	8-16, 1787	"			"
385	Samuel Miles,	6	6-6, 1790	New Milford,		1870	"
	Jerusha Parsons,						
386	Martha,	6	7-13, 1792	Bridgeport.	unm.,	3-13, 1842	
387	Adolphus,	6	10-28, 1794	Milford,	4-13, 1823	5-17, 1875	
	Lucy Higgins,			"		12-21, 1869	
388	Samuel D.,	6	5-26, 1797	"	11-27, 1827	7-15, 1873	
	Susan Peck,			"			
389	Charlotte,	6	3-14, 1799	Bridgeport.	1824		M. G. C. B. C.
	Harvey Higby,						

*The continuation of this man's record is a probability only.

No.	Name of Wife (or Husband).	Date of Birth.	Date of Marriage.	Residence.	Date of Death.	Place of Burial.
390	Nathan, [6] *Esther Stone,*	1-5, 1801 2-27, 1803	8-9, 1824	Milford. "	9-7, 1875	
	Children of *129* ABIAH SUMMERS BEACH,[5]					
391	Alfred Beach, [6] *Sibyl ——,*	12-11, 1776 1775	11-16, 1800	Trumbull,	12-9, 1849 4-23, 1829	Trumbull. "
392	Elihu, [6] *Polly Walker,*	1783 1-11, 1787			6-13, 1865 4-22, 1870	"
393	Nancy, [6] *Isaac Jennings, M. D.,*	11-7, 1788	9-15, 1813		3-13, 1874	Oberlin, O.
	Children of *134* MARTHA SUMMERS EDWARDS,[5]					
394	Hosea Edwards, [6]	6-22, 1794	unm.,	Trumbull,	3-18, 1874	New Orleans.
395	David Shelton, M. D., [6] *Harriet Eliza Henry,*				1-8, 1890	L. H. Trum. "
	Children of *135* RUTH SUMMERS BEARDSLEY,[5]					
396	Hepzibah Beardsley,[6] *Abijah Wheeler,*	11-27, 1797 10-15, 1793	6-18, 1826	Huntington,	6-5, 1884 2-19, 1869	Huntington.
397	Edwin, [6]	1800	unm.,	Trumbull,	3-4, 1846	Trumbull.
398	Mary Esther, [6]	1806	"	"	5-14, 1843	"
399	James Madison, [6]	11-24, 1807			7-3, 1877	
400	David Summers, M. D., [6] *Laura Farnham Carr,*	4-8, 1810	11-24, 1841			
	Children of *138* PHEBE SUMMERS BEACH,[5]					
401	Elijah Beach, [6]	1799		Trumbull,	3-7, 1800	Trumbull
402	Mary Ann, [6]	1803	unm.,	"	9-18, 1823	"
403	Elijah Summers, [6] *Lydie E. Pardee,*	12-24, 1808 1813	1834	"	5-11, 1869 9-20, 1870	"

Children of 143 NAOMIA SUMMERS BURTON,⁵

		Born	Married	Residence	Died	Buried
404	Alden Burton, . . . 6	10-31, 1800	} 3-12, 1826	Bridgeport, .	2-26, 1879	M. G. C. B. C.
	Clarissa (d. of David) Nichols,	4-13, 1801	} 5-3, 1840	Trumbull, . .	4-13, 1839	Trumbull.
	Abigail Avis (d. of Sam'l F.) Shelton,	11-19, 1811			8-31, 1852	M. G. C. B. C.
	Charity Seeley,				2-2, 1889	"
405	Polly, . . . 6	2-19, 1803	6-7, 1832	Trumbull.	10-18, 1873	Huntington.
	George L. Nichols,	1-17, 1808		Huntington,	5-14, 1894	"
406	Eloise, . . . 6	10-15, 1805	5-21, 1826	Trumbull,	5-7, 1852	M. G. C. B. C.
	Legrand (s. of Nath'l) Sterling,	6-12, 1802		Bridgeport,	8-21, 1877	"
407	Stiles, . . . 6	4-6, 1808	1-9, 1844	Chicago,	1-12, 1885	Chicago.
	Ann Wealthy Germain,	11-20, 1820		"		
408	Benjamin, . . . 6	10-17, 1811	11-10, 1835	Trumbull,	8-10, 1894	
	Harriet Alice (d. of Eli) Plumb, .	1816			5-27, 1854	

Children of 144 IRA SUMMERS,⁵

		Born	Married	Residence	Died	Buried
409	Laura Ann Summers, . . . 6	7-28, 1802	11-13, 1822	. L. H. Trum.,	9-4, 1874	L. H. Tr.
	James Jones,	12-4, 1799			7-12, 1879	"
410	Lucinda, . . . 6	10-2, 1805	2-24, 1833		12-2, 1881	M. G. C. B. C.
	Manson Seeley,	1800		Bridgeport,	6-11, 1876	"
411	Miranda Emeline, . . . 6	8-12, 1810	4-24, 1837	Port Deposit, Md.,	8-13, 1883	Nottingham, Md.
	982 Sheldon Beach,⁷	1-1, 1808		Birmingham.	10-13, 1887	"
412	Stephen N., . . . 6					
	Mary Phillips,		12-24, 1867			
	Henrietta Sherman,					

Children of 157 EBEN BOOTH,⁵

413	
414	
415	
416	
417	
418	

No.	Name of Wife (or Husband).	Date of Birth.	Date of Marriage.	Residence.	Date of Death.	Place of Burial.
	*Children of 159 ELIJAH BOOTH,*⁵					
419	Ransom E. Booth, ... 6				dec.	
420	Solomon Smith, . . . 6	3-11, 1798	2-6, 1826	Catharine,	10-16, 1864	Catharine.
	—, *Fanny Goodspeed Evans,* 6	4-29, 1798		Nichols, N. Y.,	9-30, 1841	"
421	Winthrop, Elijah, M. D., . 6	1-1, 1802	1-1, 1842	Watkins,	11-7, 1875	Watkins.
	Harriett M. Thayer, . 6	7-13, 1818		Ithaca,	9-26, 1865	"
422	John Isaac, . . . 6				dec.	
	Hannah Thompson, . .	10-13, 1814			6-20, 1842	
	Mary Hawley, . . .					
	*Children of 163 NANCY BOOTH CAR-PENTER,*⁵					
422-1	Phebe Adeline Carpenter, . 6	6-10, 1817				
422-2	Joseph B., . . . 6	7-2, 1819				
422-3	Daniel D., . . . 6	9-2, 1821				
422-4	Susan Maranda, . . 6	10-16, 1827			3-28, 1842	
	James B. Farrington, .		10-30, 1849	Elmira.		
422-5	Winthrop. . . 6	6-12, 1832			dec.	
	*Children of 165 MARY ELIZABETH MALLETT JONES,*⁵					
423	Peter Stephen Jones, . . 6	4-25, 1791			4-30, 1791	
424	Peter Du Ponceau, . . 6	2-6, 1793			8—, 1793	
425	John Haywood, . . . 6	9-8, 1795			3-4, 1796	
426	Frances Pollock, . . 6	1798	1814	Fayetteville,	3-10, 1863	Fayetteville.
	William Hooper, D. D., LL. D., 6	1792			8-19, 1876	Chapel Hill, N. C.
427	Elizabeth Pearson, . . 6	5—, 1800	1820	Fayetteville,	1856	Fayetteville.
	John D. Eccles,	3—, 1792		"	1856	"
428	Charlotte, . . . 6	5-5, 1802	1-3, 1888	Fayetteville,	12-17, 1881	O. C.,Raleigh,N. C.
	William Hardin, .	3-1, 1797			8-5, 1885	"
429	Eunice Sarah, . . 6	4-30, 1804			12-27, 1805	
430	Louisa Maria, . . 6	1807			1883	Pittsboro, N. C.
	Gov. Abraham Renehor,			N. Mexico,		

No.	Name		Born	Married	Place of Marriage	Died	Place
431	Du Ponceau Devereux,	6	10-6, 1809	unm.,		11-14, 1832	Pittsboro, N. C.
432	Murphy Valentine,	6	1811			1858	Texas.
	450 Henrietta Mallett Campbell,[6]						
433	Johnston Blakeley, M. D.,	6	10-10, 1818			3-1, 1889	Charlotte, N. C.
	Mary Penelope Stuart,		1814				
	Children of 166 SARAH JANE MAL- LETT SMITH,[5]						
434	William Isaac Smith,	6	3-7, 1801			8- , 1801	1 Fayetteville.
	Children of 170 CAROLINE M. MAL- LETT WALKER,[5]						
435	Carlton Scott Walker,	6	3-14, 1808			12-14, 1809	Hillsboro.
436	Sarah Jane,	6	11-1, 1809			dec.	N. York.
	Edward Jones Hale,				Fayetteville,		"
437	Eliza Henrietta,	6	1-24, 1812		Fayetteville.	1844	Fayetteville.
	Robert Belden,						
438	James,	6	1-5, 1814			10- , 1818	Hillsboro.
439	Mary Pearson,	6	12-13, 1815			3-26, 1888	Montgomery, Ala.
	Thos. H. Byrne,						
440	Peter Mallett,	6	4-13, 1814			2-16, 1880	Opelika, Ala.
	Wm. Jackson Adams,		10-13, 1817	4-24, 1845	Wilmington, N. Hanover co.,N.C.	1-7, 1862	Wilmington.
	Margaret Hill Lane,		12-24, 1821			dec.	"
441	Caroline de Berniere,[6]	6	3-11, 1820	1841	Chapel Hill, N. C.	1889	Wilmington.
	457 Wm Peter Mallett,[6]		1-19, 1819				
442	Margaret Isabella,	6	12-27, 1824	7-18, 1852	Nashville, Tenn.		Nashville, Tenn.
	Heinrich Weber,						
443	John Moseley,	6	12-27, 1824		Blowing Rock, N.C.	6-30, 1894	Blowing Rock.
	Eliza James Gibbs,						
444	Catharine Burke,	6	1-7, 1827		Hillsboro, N. C.,	1879	Pittsboro.
	John A. Hanks, M. D.,		4-19, 1812	7-4, 1851	Pittsboro, N. C.,	1890	"
445	Sophia Woodhouse,	6	11-20, 1830		Hillsboro, N. C.,	dec. infancy	Hillsboro.
	Children of 171 HENRIETTA A. MAL- LETT CAMPBELL,[5]						
446	Carlton John Campbell,	6	1-14, 1810		Fayetteville,	8-15, 1814	1 Fayetteville.
447	Hugh J.,	6	6-1, 1812		"	8-14, 1825	P. P. "
448	Elizabeth Caroline,	6	5-1, 1814		Mobile, Ala.,	12- , 1890	Mobile, Ala.
	Joseph Seawell,						
449	John,	6	9-1, 1816	6-24, 1837	Fayetteville,	12-27, 1816	Fayetteville.

No.	Name of Wife (or Husband).		Date of Birth.	Date of Marriage.	Residence.	Date of Death.	Place of Burial.
450	Henrietta Mallett,⁶	6	10-10, 1818	3-14, 1839		4-, 1873	Greenville, Ala.
	452 Murphy V. Jones,⁶		1811			1858	Texas.
451	Carlton John,	6	1-15, 1820	6-25, 1845		9-5, 1849	Fayetteville.
	Christian Fleming Gibbs,		1820			3-28, 1892	Wilmington.
452	Donald W..,	6	1-5, 1824			8-9, 1828	P. P. Fayetteville.
453	Margaret Sarah,	6	2-9, 1826			1828	P. P. "
454	Sarah M..	6	2-17, 1828			2-17, 1828	P. P. "

Children of 172 CHARLES PETER MALLETT,⁵

No.	Name of Wife (or Husband).		Date of Birth.	Date of Marriage.	Residence.	Date of Death.	Place of Burial.
455	Caroline Eliza Mallett,	6	5-7, 1814	1886	Fayetteville,	1873	Montgomery, Ala.
	Judge Geo. de B. Hooper,		7-9, 1809		Opelika, Ala.,	3-19, 1892	"
456	Charles Beattie,	6	6-18, 1816	1841	Fayetteville,	7-7, 1872	Fayetteville.
	Margaret Wright,		2-18, 1831		"	8-4, 1859	"
	Marion Winslow,			1862		11-19, 1886	
457	William Peter,	6	1-19, 1819	1841	Chapel Hill,	1889	Chapel Hill.
	441 Caroline de B. Walker,⁶		3-11, 1820				
458	Alexander Fridge,	6	1820		Fayetteville,	1889	Morehead, N. C.
	Susan Hardin,					dec.	Niles, Mich.
459	Peter,	6	1822		Brooklyn.	1865	Chapel Hill.
	Anna Bella Gibbs,		5-18, 1824	11-13, 1848	Wilmington.	1869	"
460	Edward,	6	1824		Chapel Hill,	1829	
	Mary Hunter,					8-25, 1863	1. Fayetteville.
461	Sophia Sarah,	6	1829		Fayetteville,		l.
462	Richardson,	6	1840		"		
463	Cecil,	6	3-1, 1843	6- , 1874	Bastrop, La.		
	Louisa ——,					5-14, 1879	n. Monroe, La.
464	Margaret (Meta) Wright,	6	6-25, 1845	unm.,	Bastrop,	9-18, 1878	Bastrop.
465	Herbert,	6	1-11, 1848	11-26, 1874	"	11-, 1878	"
	Lee Warren Taylor,		1855				

Children of 173 PETER JAMES MALLETT,⁵

No.	Name of Wife (or Husband).		Date of Birth.	Date of Marriage.	Residence.	Date of Death.	Place of Burial.
466	Charles Gibbs Mallett,	6	6-3, 1817	unm.,	Memphis,	10- , 1866	Memphis, Tenn.

No.	Name		Born	Married	Place	Died	Residence
467	Sarah Louisa,	6	8-7, 1819	5-30, 1842	Fayetteville,		Hamden.
	Rev. C. W. Everest,	6			Hamden, Ct.	6-29, 1843	
468	Margaret Isabella,	6	4-13, 1821	4-4, 1848	Brooklyn.	4-13, 1872	Brooklyn.
	Lothrop Lewis Smith,		8-24, 1817			11-18, 1851	1. Fayetteville.
469	Johnson de Berniere,	6	2-9, 1827	unm., . .	Fayetteville,		

Children of 174 EDWARD JONES MALLETT,[5]

No.	Name		Born	Married	Place	Died	Residence
470	Sarah Fenner Mallett,	6	8-14, 1821	4-30, 1840	Baltimore.	8-22, 1892	Baltimore.
	Stephen States Lee,	6	10-8, 1812		Baltimore, Md.,		
471	James Fenner,	6	2-25, 1823	10-22, 1849	Illinois.		
	Maria Louisa Steinhauer,	6					
472	Charles Peter.	6	12-20, 1824	1-26, 1847		7-4, 1886	
			2-1, 1829			dec.	
473	Edward Jones,	6	6-27, 1826		Providence.		
474	Ellen Madelene de Berniere,	6	8-26, 1828	6-28, 1849	"		
	Hon. J. Hilyard Cameron,	6			Toronto, Can.,	11-14, 1877	Toronto.
475	George Russell,	6	11-27, 1832			dec.	
476	Arthur Fenner,	6				dec.	
477	Alice,	6					
478	Amy Fenner,	6	8-27, 1835	4-12, 1859	Providence.		
	Wm. D. Murray,	6			"		
479	Edward Jones,	6	11-6, 1846	1-25, 1868	N. York,	8- , 1888	N. York.
	Mary Ada McNally,	6			"		

Children of 176 LALLERSTEDT D. MALLETT,[5]

No.	Name		Born	Married	Place	Died	Residence
480	William Smith Mallett,	6			Brennan, Tex.		
	Harriet Hardin,	6			Fayetteville.		
481	Ellen "Sophia,"	6		unm..	"		
482	Elizabeth,	6		"			

Children of 178 GILES MUMFORD MALLETT,[5]

No.	Name		Born	Married	Place	Died	Residence
483	Giles Mallett,	6					dec.
484	David,	6					"
485	Mordecai,	6		unm.			"
486	Caroline,	6					
487	Joseph,	6					

No.	Name of Wife (or Husband).	Date of Birth.	Date of Marriage.	Residence.	Date of Death.	Place of Burial.
	Children of 180 CATHARINE MALLETT AGARD,[5]					
488	Daniel Mallett Agard, M. D., . .6	12-8, 1819		Catharine, ...	(4-13)? 1870	Catharine.
	Leonora Hurd,				1874	"
489	Eaton J., ...6	11-30, 1822	1867	Havana, N. York.	2-24, 1884	
490	*Jane Coryell,* 6	3- , 1827		Catharine.		
	Arabella,	1825				
	Dexter Horton,		9- , 1882	Seattle, Wash.		
	Children of 181 SAMUEL MALLETT,[5]					
491	Adeline Cannon Mallett, . .6	2-7, 1822	7-31, 1851	. . . .	4-3, 1891	Denver, Col.
	Israel Ludlow Wyckoff,	10-13, 1818			4-18, 1882	"
	Children of 183 DIMON MALLETT,[5]					
492	Eliza Mallett, ...6	8-24, 1801	7-10, 1828	Conn., . . .	10-21, 1881	Millport.
	Curtis P. Stuart,	12-16, 1802		Millport, N. Y.,	8-27, 1881	"
493	"Era" Couchlin, ...6	6-9, 1803	7-10, 1828	Havana, . .	9-1, 1873	"
	Sally E. Sherwood,	8-27, 1801			11-28, 1891	Catharine.
494	"Lucy", Parmelia, . . .6	8-5, 1805		Catharine, .	8-13, 1877	"
	Thomas (s. of Thom. & Mary S.) Couch,	1807		Odessa, N. Y.,	5-11, 1890	
495	Abel "Alanson," . . .6	1810	1833	Catharine, .	12-13, 1855	Millport.
	Polly (d. of Lemuel) Nichols,	6-26, 1809	2-18, 1849	Spencer, N. Y.,	6-5, 1848	"
	Ann (widow of Isaac) Mallett,	5-15, 1809		Pennington, N. J.	3-10, 1884	"
496	Daniel, ...6	4-4, 1805	7-25, 1833	Millport, .	12-11, 1871	"
	Elizabeth Lambert,	6-21, 1808		Hopewell, N. J.,	8-25, 1835	"
	Elsie McKinney,		1-1, 1887		11-10, 1891	Michigan
497	Jonathan "Nash," . . .6	11-23, 1811	10-16, 1833	Copper Creek,	5-15, 1857	Copper Creek, Ia.
	Julian Walker,	1-16, 1810		Catharine, .	6-2, 1855	
	Jane B. Gardner,		1855 or 6			
498	"Isaac" Dimon, . . .6	11-18, 1813	9-19, 1836	Millport, .	6-7, 1842	Millport.
	Ann (d. of John) Lambert,	6-26, 1809		Pennington, N. J.	3-10, 1884	"
499	"George" Booth, . . .6	2-15, 1815	10-27, 1836	Watkins, N. Y.		
	Hannah Smith,	7-19, 1811		Jacksonville, N. Y.	12-19, 1865	Millport.
	Mary Clark (Crippin),	2-2, 1819	6-27, 1867	Rutland, Vt.,	2-19, 1894	Troy, Pa.

No.	Name	Gen.	Born	Married	Place	Died	Residence
500	Eunice "Genet,"	6	6-8, 1817	1848	Catharine,	11-3, 1875	Millport.
	Hermon Denson,		1827		Millport,	5-10, 1890	California.
	Children of 184 DANIEL MALLETT,[5]						
501	Arron Mallett,	6	3-20, 1809	10-4, 1837	Danbury, Conn.,	12-30, 1889	Danbury.
	Abbie Hill,		10-25, 1820				
502	Mary,	6	3-6, 1814	unm.,	Danbury,	10-9, 1832	Danbury.
503	Samuel, D. D. S.,	6	9-7, 1816	11-1, 1841	New Haven,	4-21, 1876	New Haven.
	Elizabeth Ann Turney,				Bridgeport.		
	Children of 186 NAOMI MALLETT AVERILL,[5]						
504	Almira,	6		unm.,	Chemung,	dec.	
505	Miami,	6		"	"	dec.	
506	Thomas Averill,	6				3-10, 1855	Chemung.
507	Edward.	6			Waverly,	1864	Wheatland.
508	Sarah,	6	1810	10- , 1848	Wheatland, Wis.,	11- , 1890	Lebaron, Mo.
	Rev. Daniel D. Bacon,						
509	Amanda,	6		1850		dec.	
	David Smith,						
510	William,	6	1828 ?	unm.,		"	
511	Levi,	6			Horseheads, N. Y.,	10-5, 1888	Horseheads.
	Sarah Tubor,				Elmira.		
	Children of 187 LEVI MALLETT,[6]						
512	"Isaac" Betts Mallett,	6	4-4, 1810	9-28, 1830	Clifton Spr., N. Y.,	1-29, 1885	Clifton Spr.
	Elizabeth McKinney,		2-7, 1810		Veteran, N. Y.,	5-5, 1892	"
513	Sally,	6	6-19, 1814	5-16, 1839	Catharine,	2-12, 1847	Wheatland.
	Daniel D. Bacon,		1810		Wheatland,	11- , 1890	Lebaron, Mo.
514	John,	6	3- , 1820		Catharine,	2- , 1824	Catharine.
515	"Levi" Stocker,	6	6-26, 1821	6-6, 1841	Bath, N. Y.	4-26, 1847	Millport.
	Maria Perry,		1822	3-11, 1848	Millport,		
	Mary Bush,						
516	Jesse,	6	7-3, 1816	6-26, 1851	Leroy, N. Y.		
	Mary (d. of Rev. Asa) Story,		3-10, 1824				
517	Mary,	6	4-9, 1829	11-13, 1864	Catharine.	8-21, 1876	Alpine.
	Henry U. Bonnet,		10-2, 1826		Millport.		
			1819				
518	Lucy A.;	6	4-27, 1830	9-4, 1856	Catharine.	3-4, 1879	N. Elmira.
	Edward Hall,		1820		Millport.		

No.	Name of Wife (or Husband).	Date of Birth.	Date of Marriage.	Residence.	Date of Death.	Place of Burial.
	*Children of 188 PHILIP MALLETT,*5					
519	Sarah Mallett, ...6	10-4, 1831			before 3, 1841	
	*Children of 190 MARY MALLETT HUBBELL,*5					
520	Minerva Hubbell, ...6					
	David Blackman, . . .			Ridgefield, Ct.		
	*Children of 191 EUNICE MALLETT BENNETT,*5					
521	Sarah "Paulina" Bennett, . .6	10-29, 1798	unm., . .		4-24, 1833	Easton.
522	Hannah "Melinda," . . .6	12-30, 1804	} 4-22, 1829		4-3, 1865	L. H. Tr.
	Zalmon Hall, . . .	6-13, 1795			2-18, 1884	"
	*Children of 192 JOSEPH EDWARDS MALLETT,*5					
523	Emily Mallett, ...6	4-29, 1807	} 1-31, 1827	Tashua, . .	10-3, 1874	Tashua.
	John Legrand Nichols, . . .6	7-16, 1798		"	3-3, 1880	"
524	Charles, ...6	12-22, 1808	} 11-25, 1841	Bridgeport, Ct.,	10-9, 1883	M. G. C. B. C.
	Mary (d. of Thom. "Parker") Smith,	3-25, 1813		Brookfield, Ct.,	12-23, 1870	"
525	Sally, ...6	6-16, 1810	} 4-27, 1828	Tashua, . .	9-4, 1883	"
	John Consider Shelton, . .	9-19, 1804		Bridgeport, .	6-11, 1871	"
526	Huldah, ...6	1-22, 1814	} 3-14, 1835	Tashua, . .	9-6, 1891	Tashua.
	Marcellus Jackson, . . .	2-5, 1808		"	4-22, 1847	"
527	Louisa, ...6	4-28, 1816	} 4-7, 1841	Huntington, .	11-25, 1883	Huntington.
	Joel (son of Samuel) Shelton,	4-16, 1816			6-26, 1857	"
528	Charity, ...6	8-14, 1823	} 9-17, 1848	Tashua, . .	5-7, 1850	Tashua.
	Austin Sherman, . . .	9-16, 1822		Stepney, . .	5-17, 1889	"
	*Children of 193 SAMUEL MALLETT,*5					
529	Amy Maria Mallett, . . .6	7-22, 18 1	} . . .	Monroe, . .	10-21, 1827	Tashua.
530	"George" William, ...6	12-14, 1813	} 1-23, 1836	Lyme, O., . .	8-22, 1876	Sherman, O.
	Amanda Fanton, . . .	6-24, 1813		"	10-15, 1890	"
531	Harriet, ...6	12-26, 1815	unm., . .	Tashua, . .	1-28, 1853	Tashua.

No.	Name	Born	Married	Marriage place	Died	Death place
582	"Charles" Edward, ... 6	10-7, 1817	4-2, 1839	Lyme, O., . . .	12-16, 1888	Lyme, O.
	Dorothy Stanyer,				2-16, 1891	"
533	"Samuel" Edwards, . . . 6	8-30, 1819	6-6, 1847	Easton, Ct.,	6-5, 1892	M. G. C. B. C.
	538 Sylvia "Eliza" Edwards, 6	5-6, 1816		Bridgeport.		
534	Roger "Sherman," 6	6-14, 1821	3-11, 1860	Tashua, . . .	4 16, 1887	Tashua.
	Jane M. Hubbell,	3-2, 1826	5-30, 1882		8-24, 1879	"
	Sylvia Lamphear Sears,	5-1, 1827				
535	"Elizabeth" Ann, ... 6	7-14, 1825	10-1, 1845	Monroe.	11-22, 1886	Nichols.
	George E. Peet,	3-19, 1816		Nichols, Ct.,		
536	"Morse" Dwight, ... 6	5-2, 1827	10-26, 1853	Tashua.	8-23, 1891	Monroe.
	Harriet Esther Dimon,	1-8, 1832				
537	Martin "Jerome," 6	9-7, 1831	9-16, 1855	Monroe,		
	1295 Huldah "Catharine" Jackson, 7	1-8, 1836		Tashua.		

Children of 194 CHARITY MALLETT EDWARDS. 5

No.	Name	Born	Married	Marriage place	Died	Death place
538	Sylvia "Eliza" Edwards, . . . 6	5-6, 1816	6-6, 1847	Bridgeport.	6-5, 1892	M. G. C. B. C.
	533 Samuel E. Mallett, 6	8-30, 1819		Easton.		

Children of 195 PHEBE MALLETT LEAVITT. 5

No.	Name	Born	Married	Marriage place	Died	Death place
539	David Leavitt, ... 6	10-11, 1815	5-24, 1841	Gr. Rapids, Mich.,	dec.	
540	David "Sheldon," 6	5-24, 1824	3-31, 1870	Bristol, N. H.	3-19, 1887	L. H. Tr.
	Martha Ann Terrill,			L. H Tr.		
	Elizabeth Clark Dayton,					
541	Phebe Ann, ... 6			Grand Rapids.	9-10, 1853	Gr. Rapids, Mich.
	Joel Consider Guild,	3-25, 1816	8-23, 1851	Paris, Mich.	3-29, 1861	Paris, Mich.
542	"John" Burr, ... 6	5-26, 1825		Cayuga Co., N. Y.,		"
	Emeline V. Meach (Lyon),				before 1854	
543	Polly Ann, ... 6					
	Hiram Darling.					
544	Sarah Ann, ... 6	10-25, 1820	10-25, 1841	Paris, Mich.	3-15, 1845	
	Fletcher Terrill,	7-24, 1817				
545	George Munson, ... 6					
	Sophia Auble.					

Children of 197 DANIEL MALLETT, 5 *and of 303.*

No.	Name	Born	Married	Marriage place	Died	Death place
546	John Mallett, ... 6	10-9, 1814	5-3, 1837	Tashua,	12-21, 1864	Tashua.
	Harriet Dunning,	3-19, 1818				

No.	Name of Wife (or Husband).	Date of Birth.	Date of Marriage.	Residence.	Date of Death.	Place of Burial.
547	"Fanny" Eliza, Wakely, .6	11-29, 1823	7-1, 1840	Tashua.	6-14, 1846	L. H. Tr.
	Miles Burton Wakely,	12-14, 1817		Trumbull,		
	Nathaniel Hall, " .6	3-20, 1816	2-17, 1853			
548	Hannah " Melinda,"	11-25, 1825	5-6, 1846	Tashua.		Tashua.
	David Abijah Wakely, .6	8-, 1824		"		L. H. Tr. "
549	Lucy Maria, .6	, 1827			6-26, 1832	
550	Munson " Augusta " Edwards, .6	5-3, 1829	5-21, 1848	L. H. Tr.,	4-4, 1894	
		12-25, 1828			11-19, 1893	
	Children of 198 EPHRAIM MALLETT, 6					
551	David Mallett, .7					
552	Phebe, .7					
	Children of 199 DANIEL MALLETT, 6					
553	"Hannah" Mervina Mallett, .7	11-13, 1806	1-21, 1826		4-17, 1885	Stepney.
	Benjamin Hall,					Bridgewater.
554	Marcus " Beach,"	8-5, 1809	3-8, 1831	Stepney,	6-19, 1889	"
	Sarah (d. of Stephen B.) Keeler, .7	2-23, 1810		Bridgewater,	12-26, 1888	
555	Daniel Alonzo, .7	12-5, 1810	5-31, 1826	Stratford.	11-5, 1894	Stratford.
	Delia M. Judson,	3-6, 1815		"	3-7, 1886	Nichols.
556	Huldah Adaline,	5-19, 1813	9-20, 1835	Huntington,		"
	Ebenezer Burch, .7	4-18, 1813			3-4, 1889	
		3-15, 1815				
557	Polly Ann,		12-25, 1834	Woodbury, Ct.,	2-22, 1894	
	J. Stoddard Isbell, .7					
558	David " Harvey,"	1-25, 1817	4-21, 1839	Bridgewater,	12-13, 1860	N. C. Bridgewater.
	Anna Maryetta Skidmore, .7	5-18, 1818		Roxbury,	5-10, 1875	"
559	Eliza Jennett,	2-20, 1819	5-10, 1840		3-18, 1879	
	Amos Richmond, .7				12-8, 1856 dec.	Waterbury.
560	Susan,	3-2, 1821	4-22, 1839	Waterbury, Ct.,		
	Martin Isbell, .7					
561	Eunice,	12-8, 1822	2-11, 1844	Newtown, Ct.,	12-27, 1891	Newtown.
	William Minor, .7					
562	Sarahett,	3-14, 1826	7-18, 1845	Danbury,	1-21, 1894	
	Levi McKinney, .7					

No.	Name		Born	Married	Where married	Died	Where died
563	Emeline,	7	7-27, 1828	} 3-14, 1849	Meriden.	10-15, 1855	Trumansburg.
	Edwin Dayton,						
564	Charles,	7	6-2, 1831		Woodbury.		
	Eliza J. Morgan,		10-24, 1830	10-16, 1853			
	Children of 200 HULDAH HANNAH MALLETT LYON, [6]						
565	Laura Lyon	7	12-10, 1801		Tashua, Trumansburg, N.Y.		
566	Catharine,	7	8-5, 1803		Tashua.		
	Reuben Bradley Gilbert,		9-27, 1801	1-12, 1824	Trumbull,	4-11, 1846	Easton, Ct.
	Children of 202 GIDEON MALLETT, [6]						
567	Mahala Mallett,	7	12-22, 1814	10-19, 1841	Tashua.	9-25, 1880	Monroe.
	Ephraim "Lee" Woodin,		12-21, 1818		Stratford,		
568	Esther Jane,	7	4-12, 1820	1-31, 1838	Tashua.	4-30, 1873	Monroe.
	Burton Wayland,		1-4, 1813				
569	Mary Frances,	7	9-26, 1831	12-25, 1850	Monroe.	6-1, 1864	L. H. Tr.
	Homer F. Wiford,		3-14, 1828		Trumbull,		
	Children of 205 REBECCA MALLETT TURNEY, [6]						
570	—— Turney,	7					
	Children of 208 OLIVE MALLETT NICHOLS, [6]						
571	Charity Nichols,	7	8-6, 1814	12-24, 1883	Tashua,	12-15, 1891	Tashua.
	223 George Albert Mallett, [6]	7	1-24, 1808		"	3-19, 1893	"
572	Charles Mallett,	7	8-, 1827	unm.,	"	6-25, 1832	"
	Children of 209 SETH MALLETT, [6]						
573	Amelia Malvina Mallett,	7	6-7, 1820			5-12, 1881	Easton, Ct.
	Morris Banks,		10-10, 1815	11-17, 1842			
574	John Silliman,	7	2-15, 1823	11-13, 1851	Trenton.	11-2, 1870	Trenton, N. J.
	Charlotte Bolmer Adams,		3-13, 1827				
	Children of 210 (Capt.) JESSE MALLETT, [6]						
575	Ann Rebecca Mallette,	7	11-19, 1829	9-22, 1851	Tashua,	3-8, 1861	Tashua.
	Ephraim "Lacy" Stanford,		7-11, 1824				

No.	Name of Wife (or Husband).	Date of Birth.	Date of Marriage.	Residence.	Date of Death.	Place of Burial.
576	Mary Jane, ... Burr (s. of Capt. Truman) *Davis*, [7]	5-4, 1831 1-7, 1828	3-24, 1850	Tashua. Mt. Vernon, N. Y.	2-27, 1860 4-22, 1891	Tashua. E. Bridgeport.
577	Hepsa Almira, [7]	10-29, 1832	unm., ...	Tashua, ...		
578	George Abel, [7] *Fanny Elizabeth Sanford*, [7]	8-20, 1834 3-7, 1836	1-2, 1860	Bridgeport, ...		
579	Edward Bronson, [7] *Cornelia A. Hill*, [7]	8-31, 1835 3-29, 1846	11-1, 1854	Thomaston, Ct.		
580	Frances Jannette, [7] *Wm. Hart (s. of John) Davis*, [7]	6-18, 1837 3-10, 1829	3-18, 1855	Tashua. Oxford, Ct.		
581	Sarah Elizabeth, [7] *Richard H. W. Griffin*, [7]	7-22, 1838 10-8, 1834	1-5, 1859	Tashua. Bridgeport.		
582	Porter Govrales, [7]	2-3, 1854	unm.			
583	Jessee Alphonso, [7] *Catharine E. Mulvaney Read*, [7]	1-30, 1856 9-20, 1858	11-18, 1891	Bridgeport.		

Children of 212 FANNY MARIA MALLETT,[6] see 587.

Children of 213 MARY MALLETT FRANKLIN,[6]

No.	Name of Wife (or Husband).	Date of Birth.	Date of Marriage.	Residence.	Date of Death.	Place of Burial.
584	Mary Franklin, [7]					
585	——, [7]					
586	——, [7]					

Children of 215 WILLIAM MALLETT.[6]

No.	Name of Wife (or Husband).	Date of Birth.	Date of Marriage.	Residence.	Date of Death.	Place of Burial.
587	Amariah Mallett, [7] *212 Fan-y Maria (d. of Ebenezer[4]) Mallett,[6]* *Polly Ann (d. of Eben Sherman,[6]* *Mary Curtis,*	1805 1811	}	Easton, Tashua,	3-29, 1863 4-29, 1843 5-26, 1850 1-16, 1882	Tashua. " "
588	Ann Merilla, [7] *Aaron Bennett,* [7]	4-18, 1808 4-16, 1805	7-4, 1826	Newtown. Bridgeport.		
589	Eunis. [7]	1812	unm., . . .		1831	Stepney.
590	Isaac Bronson, [7] *June Ann Clow,* [7]	2-14, 1815 2-13, 1816	11-19, 1840	New York,	3-16, 1874 2-, 1894	Sharon Springs.
591	Stephen Wheeler, [7]	4-17, 1817	unm., . . .		5-17, 1849	Stepney.

No.	Name	Gen.	Born	Married	Place	Died	Residence
592	Glover Z.,	7	4-4, 1819	3-12, 1849	Camptown, Pa.,	8-7, 1894	Camptown, Pa.
593	Julia A. Thorpe,	7	12-29, 1825	5-22, 1850	Weston, Ct.,	8-26, 1866	Tashua.
	Abel Wakeley,		6-6, 1822		Ansonia, Ct.,		
	Susan Marie Oakley,		1 1, 1827				
	*Children of 216 ROSWELL MALLETT,*6						
594	Maria Dorothy Mallett,	7	9-6, 1820		Ames, N. Y.,	6-22, 1841	Ames.
	John P. Snell,	7					
595	Charles,	7	12-21, 1823	unm.	Ames, N. Y.,	3-10, 1841	Ames.
596	Mary Eliza,	7	2-27, 1829		"	1-7, 1830	"
597	Charles,	7	11-10, 1842	1-9, 1867			
	Hattie L. Burlow,						
	*Children of 217 PHILO MALLETT,*6						
598	Eliza Jane Mallett,	7	12-25, 1812			11-14, 1814	
599	Rhoda Eunice,	7	10-26, 1814	3-6, 1833		9-20, 1890	
	John R. Loucks,	7	5-6, 1811		Erie, Pa.,	5-6, 1887	
600	Sarah Jane,	7	5-26, 1816	3-6, 1833		6-16, 1885	
	Henry Esmey,	7	10-21, 1811			5-25, 1867	
601	Jay Cady,	7	7-30, 1819	2-28, 1846	Eprutah, N. Y.		
	Catharine Howard,						
	Margaret Empire,		3-19, 1821	8-7, 1854			
602	Lucretia Ann,	7	4-14, 1821	1-12, 1853	Sprout Br'k, N. Y.,	11-3, 1882	Albion, Pa.
	Rev. David Wilcox,		12-28, 1800				
603	Daniel Parris,	7	3-9, 1823	9-23, 1868	Cherry Val., N. Y.	12-13, 1883	
	Salome Cath. Hemstreet (Walrath),	7	6-1, 1829				
604	Charles Eaton,	7	11-4, 1825	2-25, 1851	Richfield Spr.		
	Sarah Jane Jones,	7	7-20, 1829				
	Henry Seymour Smith,		7-16, 1827				
605	Henrietta Louisa,	7	6-23, 1827		Colliers, N. Y.	5-30, 1867	Sharon Spr.
606	William Wallas,	7	5-29, 1829	1-1, 1850	England.	dec.	
	Isabel Heith,		6-1, 1829				
607	George Philo, M. D.,	7	9-4, 1831	3-9, 1854	Sprout Brook.		
	Sarah Ann Fuller,	7	10-29, 1836				
608	Charlotta Maria,	7	6-4, 1884	9-23, 1868	Canajoharie.	5-24, 1888	Fonda, N. Y.
	Benjamin E. Jansen,		6-9, 1838				
609	James Henry, W. G. A.,	7	6-26, 1844	11-29, 1871	Unadilla, N. Y.	5-7, 1893	
	Ellen Louise Youmans,						

No.	Name of Wife (or Husband).	Date of Birth.	Date of Marriage.	Residence.	Date of Death.	Place of Burial.
	Children of 218 DELASON MALLETT,[6]					
610	Giles Mallett, [7]	4-4, 1822			11-18, 1823	Sprakers, N. Y.
611	Jane Ann, [7]	7-26, 1825			7-16, 1835	"
612	Aurelian, [7]	6-21, 1832				
	Sarah M. Day, [7]	2-10, 1834	3-18, 1852	Rual Grove, N. Y.	2-10, 1881	Charleston, N. Y.
613	Henry Delason, [7]	5-20, 1835				
	Ruth Esther Van Deveer, [7]	7-14, 1836	5-22, 1859	Gloversville, N. Y.		
614	Erasmus Darwin,	1-17, 1838				
615	Isabella, ——, [7]	10-6, 1843	12-2, 1863		2-28, 1867	Argusville, N. Y.
	Andrew Secoy,	9-9, 1841				
	Children of 219 CHAS. GRANDISON MALLETT.[6]					
615a	Stephen Wheeler Mallett, [7]	11-14, 1823	unm.,		12-15, 1843	
615b	Giles Fonda, [7]	10-9, 1825				
	Adaline Haughton.					
615c	Charles Grandison, [7]	10-16, 1829	6-24, 1851	Englewood, Ill.		
	Cassandra Maria Van Auken, [7]					
615d	George Washington, [7]	12-25, 1831				
615e	Mary Minerva, [7]				12-23, 1892	Toledo, O.
	O. S. Dewolf,				dec.	
615f	James Elliott, [7]				dec.	
615g	Valorous, [7]					
	—— Lake,					
615h	Sarah Jane, [7]	10-15, 1828			7-20, 1846	
	Hezekiah C. Carpenter.					
	Children of 220 BENJAMIN MALLETT,[6]					
615i	Sally Anne Mallett, [7]	1809			1892	
	William Lewis, [7]					
515j	Henry, [7]				dec. young	
615k	Benjamin, [7]	4-8, 1816	3-2, 1843		10-16, 1893	W. Toledo, O.
	Julia Anne,	3-2, 1823				

No.	Name	Gen.			Residence		Burial
615 l	Montiere,	7	2–13, 1893 }		W. Toledo,	9–7, 1887	W. Toledo.
	Jane Haynes,		9–20, 1834 }			dec.	
615m	Voltaire,	7					
615n	James,	7					
615o	Clementine,	7	4–2, 1842				

Children of *221* ESTHER MALLETT,[6] BRADSHAW,[6]

No.	Name	Gen.					
615p	Emma Bradshaw,	7					

Children of *222* LOIS MALLETT STEVENS,[6]

No.	Name	Gen.					
616	Sarah Stevens,	7					

Children of *223* ELIZABETH MALLETT WELCH,[6]

No.	Name	Gen.			Residence		
617	Anna Maria Welch,	7			Charlotteville, N. Y.		
	Allison Hartwell,						
618	Caroline,	7					
	John Perigo,	7			Ames, N. Y.		
619	Lyman,	7			Newark, N. Y.		
	Judith Stansell.						
620	Abram,	7			Oakland, Cal.		
	Eliza Kinskern.						
621	Jay,	7					
622	Benjamin,	7				dec.	
623	Adaline,	7					
	Jacob C. Anthony.						
624	Roswell Carlton,	7			Charlotteville.		
	Harriet Effie Bartlett.						

Children of *228* GEORGE A. MAL-LETT,[6] and of *571*,

No.	Name	Gen.			Residence		Burial
625	Charles Tomlinson Mallett,	7	9–16, 1835	unm.,	Tashua,	4–11, 1863	Tashua.
626	Mary Eliza,	7	10–10, 1842		"	8–9, 1891	Tashua.
	Albert Judson Clark,		11–1, 1889 }	10–26, 1864			

No.	Name of Wife (or Husband).	Date of Birth.	Date of Marriage.	Residence.	Date of Death.	Place of Burial.
627	*Children of 231* CLARISSA MALLETT SANFORD,[6]					
	Stephen "Mallett" Sanford, . . 7	12-3, 1850	} 11-13, 1872		4-4, 1881	Easton, Ct.
	Sylvia Alosia Clark,	1-4, 1853	{ 11-15, 1893			
	Ida Jane (d. of Eugene) Botsford,	12-4, 1855				
628	*Children of 232* AARON B. MALLETT,[6]					
	Orville Sherman Mallett, . . 7	7-20, 1844	9-20, 1866	Tashua.		
	Cornelia A. Clark, . . 7	8-25, 1842				
629	*Flora Jane,* . . 7	8-12, 1847	11-1, 1865	Redding, Ct.		
	Charles Edson Bradley, . . 7	7-12, 1840				
630	*Lydia Beach,* . . 7	2-19, 1853	unm., . .	Tashua.		
631	*Children of 233* MARY M. MALLETT NICHOLS,[6]					
	Mary Frances Nichols, . . 7	11-5, 1847		Tashua.		
632	*Seth Hill, M.D.,* —— 7	6-16, 1837	} 6-19, 1872	"	2-27, 1852	
		2-27, 1852				
633	*Children of 234* WM. A. MALLETT,[6]					
	Emma Louisa Mallett, . . 7	3-31, 1852	} 9-9, 1874	Tashua.	3-10, 1891	L. H. Tr.
	Charles Henry Walker, . . 7	11-5, 1844		L. H. Tr.,		
634	Franklin Beach, . . 7	6-29, 1856	} 5-30, 1882	Tashua.		
	Nellie Staples, . .	11-29, 1863				
635	William Blackman, . . 7	10-12, 1859	} 9-26, 1881	Tashua.	3-16, 1882	Tashua.
	Sadie J. Wilson, . .	1-1, 1862				
636	*Minnie F. Staples,* . . 7	11-11, 1866	} 9-26, 1883		1-23, 1861	Tashua.
	Son, . .	1-23, 1861				
637	*Children of 237* DAVID Y. BEACH,[6]					
	Mary Frances Beach, . . 7	9-4, 1840	} 1-13, 1863	Trumbull.		
	Horace Abbey Smith, . . 7	3-26, 1832		East Haven, Ct.		
638	David Clinton, . . 7	7-21, 1844	} 5-18, 1865	Trumbull.	7-10, 1876	L. H. Tr.
	Fannie Augusta Hawley, . .	3-9, 1842				
	Martha Murr, . .					

No.	Name		Birth	Marriage	Residence	Death	Place
	Children of 238 MARY E. BEACH CURTIS,[6]						
639	George Henry Curtis,	7	5-26, 1838	4-4, 1875	Sumter, S C.		
	S. Ella King,		8-26, 1856				
640	Horace Beach,	7	4-, 1851	2-20, 1888			
	Maggie E. Boyden,		10-29, 1858				
641	Charles Stephen,	7	11-, 1854	(1-, 1895)?			
	Children of 240 JERUSHA MIDDLE-BROOK BEACH,[6]						
642	David Middlebrook Beach,	7	9-28, 1820	1-12, 1846		1-28, 1890	
	Emily Buckingham,			10-9, 1853		9-17, 1852	
	Marietta Seeley,			11-4, 1885		4-16, 1888	
	Elizabeth Burr,						
643	John Calvin,	7	1-, 1826	1-8, 1852			
	1403 Jane Gilbert,[8]						
644	Wheeler,	7	3-28, 1824			3-26, 1825	
	Children of 241 HULDAH MIDDLE-BROOK BROOKS ADAMS,[6]						
645	John Sherwood Adams,	7	9-18, 1816	11-27, 1888	Easton,	3-7, 1875	Easton.
	Marietta Sherwood,		11-5, 1821				
646	George W.,	7	5-11, 1822	unm., ...	Easton,		
647	Mary Elizabeth,	7	8-6, 1827	11-2, 1848	"		
	Ebenezer S. Gillette,		7-27, 1821			10-17, 1851	Easton.
	Children of 242 MARY MIDDLE-BROOK JACKSON,[6]						
648	Charles Burton Jackson,	7	9-15, 1824	12-2, 1846		6-6, 1864	
	Rebecca Jane Clark,		10-22, 1828			1878	
649	Anna Elizabeth,	7	7-8, 1826	9-5, 1847		2-27, 1853	
	Nathan Harris,						
650	Emily Jerusha,	7	11-2, 1828	11-3, 1852	Sparta, O.	9-29, 1894	
	A. Jackson Scarborough,		1-29, 1829				
651	John Wesley,	7	10-16, 1830	10-5, 1853	Monroe, Ia.		
	Mary Jane Lineweaver,		6-19, 1830		Mt. Liberty, O.		
652	Margaret Esther,	7	10-5, 1832	5-3, 1854		11-25, 1889	
	Morgan Bliss Gloyd,		8-26, 1826				

No.	Name of Wife (or Husband).		Date of Birth.	Date of Marriage.	Residence.	Date of Death.	Place of Burial.
653	James Fletcher,	7	3-22, 1834	10-14, 1851	Monroe, Iowa,	9-14, 1893	
	Lucy Jane Gardner,		2-10, 1831				
654	Julia Samantha,	7	4-9, 1836			1-4, 1887	
	Ezekiel Roberts,		6-22, 1835	6-13, 1858		3-2, 1885	Bloomfield, O.
655	Victorine Phadrina,	7	9-21, 1838	2-11, 1857		1-27, 1867	Monroe, Ia.
	Joseph Pearsal Wright,		2-26, 1835			6-18, 1891	
656	William McKendre,	7	5-20, 1843	1-9, 1867	Columbus, O.,	11-25, 1892	
	Olive Malinda Osborn,						
	Children of 244 DAVID MIDDLEBROOK.[6]						
657	Arthur McLane Middlebrook,	7	5-30, 1827				
658	Lucy Ann,	7	1-5, 1829		Norofon.	10-5, 1829	Trumbull.
659	Samuel Hoyt,	7	8-1, 1830				
660	Mary Ophelia,	7	1-1, 1832	2-19, 1892	Erie, Pa.		
	Arthur McLane,						
661	Jerusha Beach,	7	1-28, 1834	5-3, 1858	Bridgeport, Ct.,		
	George Royal Stowell.		8-19, 1827				
662	Lorintha Augusta,	7	10-6, 1835	10-6, 1853	Bridgeport.		
	Charles Alonzo Booth,		1-22, 1826		Stratford.		
663	Nathan Barnum,	7	11-26, 1838	8-31, 1863			
	Susan Mary Batterson,		6-4, 1837				
664	Sarah Louisa,	7	2-5, 1841	12-23, 1863	Brooklyn, N. Y.		
	Charles Alfred Bogue,		1-30, 1841		Bridgeport.		
665	Henry Bronson,	7	9-11, 1843	1875		1876	Alliance, O.
	Alice Spencer,			8-2, 1877			
	Elva Evans,		9-28, 1856				
	Children of 245 SANFORD MALLETT.[6]						
666	Sarah Ann Mallett,	7	2-22, 1830		Tashua.	8-21, 1834	Tashua.
667	Emmeline,	7	9-29, 1831	4-27, 1851	"		
	James Sturges Cole,		9-19, 1825		Bridgeport.		

No.	Name		Born	Married	Residence	Died	Church
668	Mary Esther,	7	12-16, 1835	10-11, 1854	Shelton.	4-21, 1877	M. G. C. B. C.
	Chas. Middlebrook Jennings,	7	10-13, 1828				
669	Josiah "Hobart,"		2-16, 1838	12-14, 1870	Tashua.		
	Juliette Sherwood,		4-5, 1847				
	Children of 247 ESTHER MALLETT EDWARDS,⁶						
670	Bradley W. Edwards,	7	8-19, 1843	4-19, 1868	Laceyville, Pa.		
	Electa J. Stevens,		5-20, 1848				
	Children of 248 CLARK MALLETT,⁶						
671	Caroline Augusta Mallett,	7	9-15, 1833	unm., . .	Lockport, N. Y.		
672	"Theodore" Augusta,	7	5-13, 1835	10-6, 1856	Trumbull.		
	Lucy Cornelia (d. of John) Foster,		4-13, 1836				
673	"Lorenzo" Nichols,	7	11-13, 1839	3-16, 1864	Tashua.	4-13, 1861	L. H. Tr.
	Sarah E. (d. of Philo) Wooster,						
	Jennie Wills,		7-2, 1849	1-27, 1887			
674	Sarah Ann,	7	3-23, 1844	2-13, 1872	Shelton.		
	Horace Wheeler,						
675	Emeline Amalia,	7	4-26, 1851	6-2, 1882	L. H. Tr.		
	Austin A. Hall,		4-11, 1844				
	Children of 249 CAROLINE MALLETT BOOTH,⁶						
676	—— Booth,	7				dec. inf.	
677	—— Booth,	7				dec. inf.	
	Children of 250 EMELINE MALLETT PLUMB,⁶						
678	Betsey Anne Plumb,	7	12-15, 1827	11-21, 1854	Trumbull,	1-17, 1864	M. G. C. B. C.
	Thomas Cook Worden,		10-31, 1826		Bridgeport,	10-31, 1878	"
679	Charles Elliott,	7	1-12, 1832	5-5, 1856	Trumbull,	6-24, 1873	Trumbull.
	Susan Ann Hall,		1-23,				
	Children of 251 CATHARINE MALLETT BRINSMADE,⁶						
680	Frances Adelia Brinsmade,	7	7-16, 1834	11-21, 1854	Trumbull.		
	James Robert Middlebrook,		10-27, 1832		Hartford, Ct.		
681	James R.,	7	8-25, 1839	2-16, 1876	Trumbull.		
	Martha A. (d. of Orville Hall) Beardsley,						

No.	Name of Wife (or Husband).	Date of Birth.	Date of Marriage.	Residence.	Date of Death.	Place of Burial.
682	Daniel "Seymour," . . . . . .⁷ *Janetta Salina (d. of John) Pardee,*	2-17, 1845 12-28, 1845	12-28, 1870			
683	*Children of 252* SALLY ANN MALLETT HINMAN,⁶ Edward Wellington Hinman, . . .⁷	3- , 1889	unm., . . .	Trumbull, ...	1-31, 1860	Unity, Tr.
684	*Children of 253* CORDELIA MALLETT WHEELER,⁶ *and of 261,* Hobart Rutledge Wheeler, ...⁷ *Antoinette S. (d. of Dan'l) Fairchild,*	11-20, 1840 3-15, 1843	6-15, 1864	Bridgeport. Trumbull. L. H. Tr.		
685	Wilmot Clark, ...⁷ *Sarah (d. of Peter) Curtis,* . . .	3-11, 1848	6-4, 1873	Stratford.		
686	*Children of 254* MALLETT SEELEY,⁶. Bennett Seeley, ...⁷ *Virginia Gregory,* . . . . . . .⁷	6-16, 1824	3-16, 1853	Easton.		
687	Mary Esther, ...⁷	8-27, 1828		Easton,		
688	Anna Frances, ...⁷	1-5, 1842		"	5-3, 1894	Easton.
689	*Children of 259* EZRA S. SEELEY,⁶ Samuel Jackson Seeley, ...⁷	8-21, 1856		Easton.		
690	Frank Sherwood, ...⁷	5-16, 1858		"		
691	Charles S., ...⁷	10-31, 1861		"		
692	Mary Eunice, ...⁷	9-19, 1864		"		
693	*Children of 261* EUNICE WHEELER SMITH.⁶ John Smith, ...⁷			Red Bank, Pa.		
694	Henry, ...⁷			"		
695	*Children of 262* ESTHER WHEELER PLUMB,⁶ Abigail Melissa Plumb, ...⁷ *Elliott Plumb Nichols,*	12-7, 1822 8-18, 1824	5-29, 1848	Nichols, Ct.		

No.	Name	Gen.	Born	Married	Residence	Died	Place
696	Ezra Wheeler,	7	2-25, 1825	3-21, 1853	Nichols, Ct.		
	Julia Ann Drew,	7	9-12, 1825		Nichols, Ct.		
697	Orange Beach,	7	10-11, 1827	5-18, 1862	Trumbull.	11-18, 1863	Nichols.
	1015 C. Betsey (d. of Benj.) Burton,	7	1-19, 1837				
698	Mary Esther,	7	3-2, 1830	2-26, 1863	Weston.		
	William Lockwood,	7	3-11, 1821				
699	Catharine Eunice,	7	2-4, 1833	8-17, 1864	Nichols.	8-29, 1879	Nichols.
	John Beach Nichols,	7	8-16, 1817		Nichols. "		
700	David Elliott,	7	11-28, 1835	4-26, 1893	Nichols.		
	Ermina Nichols,	7	9-5, 1853				
701	Frances Ann,	7	9-8, 1841	unm., . . .	Nichols.	11-16, 1894	Nichols.

Children of 264 MELISSA WHEELER BEARDSLEY,[6]

No.	Name	Gen.	Born	Married	Residence	Died	Place
702	Lyman Beardsley,	7	8-16, 1827				
	Almira (d. of Birdseye) Curtis,	7					
703	Melissa Ann,	7	7-4, 1825		Monroe,	12-16, 1879	Monroe.
	Edwin C. Hurd,	7	8-2, 1832				
704	Walter,	7		2-6, 1859	Stepney.	11-23, 1893	Stepney.
	Sarah Louisa (d. of David) Shelton,	7					

Children of 265 WALKER WHEELER,[6]

No.	Name	Gen.	Born	Married	Residence	Died	Place
705	Walker Sherwood Wheeler,	7	5-21, 1828	unm., . . .	Trumbull, . . .	10-1, 1848	L. H. T.
706	Melissa,	7	5-11, 1832	10-11, 1855	Bridgeport.		
	William Augustus Tomlinson,	7	10-30, 1825				
707	Margaret,	7	1-23, 1827	3-25, 1846	Trumbull.		
	Abel Stiles Beach,	7	4-5, 1824				
708	John Mallett,	7	6-13, 1835	1-16, 1867	Bridgeport.		
	Mary Isabell Bartram,	7	2-22, 1848				
709	Marcus Ormel,	7	5-25, 1838	10-24, 1861	Trumbull.		
	Susan Eloise Beardsley,	7	5-30, 1841				

Children of 266 EBENEZER WHEELER.[6]
See 253.

Children of 267 SIDNEY MALLETT,[6]

No.	Name	Gen.	Born	Married	Residence	Died	Place
710	Maria Mallett,	7	10-12, 1816		Fairport, N. Y.		
711	Sidney,	7			Cory, Pa.		
	Mary A. Ray,	7					

No.	Name of Wife (or Husband).	Date of Birth.	Date of Marriage.	Residence.	Date of Death.	Place of Burial.
712	Salmon,					
713	S. Dewitt,		unm.,		dec.	
	Julia Gates,					
714	Sylvanus,		18—			
715	Elizabeth,	1833				
	Daniel Eldridge,					
	Children of 268 MUNSON MALLETT.[6]					
716	Helen Mallett,			Rochester.		
	E. G. Billings,					
717	Charles,				dec. infant	
	Children of 269 CYRENUS MALLETT.[6]					
718	Cordelia Mallett,				dec. infant	Fairport.
	Children of 270 PHEBE M. HUBBY.[6]					
719	Leander M. Hubby,	1814		Cleveland, O.		
	Children of 271 LAURA MALLETT HALL.[6]					
720	Matthew Hall,					
721	Lyman,					
722	William,					
723	Cyrenus,					
724	Norman,	1816		Rochester, N. Y.		
725	Malissa,					
	Shaw,					
	Children of 272 ASHER MALLETT.[6]					
726	Nathaniel Lee Mallett,			Harlem, N. Y.	dec.	Ohio.
727	Car Matthew,					

No.	Name					
	Children of 273 ITHEMAR MALLETT,⁶ . .7					
728	Henry William Mallett, . . .7	10-11, 1821	New Milford.	} 10-11, 1846 / 3-26, 1868	6-11, 1866	New Milford.
	Jane O. Benedict,	1823				
	Harriett L. Sherwood, . .7					
729	Madison J.; 7	1828	New Milford, . .	unm., . . .	6-8, 1855	Northville.
	Children of 274 LIDIA BEARDSLEY SHERMAN,⁶					
730	Betsey Sherman, ...7	12-11, 1809	Stepney, . .	1-9, 1881	6-7, 1880	Catharine.
	Thomas L. Fanton, . .7	6-25, 1805	Catharine, . .		8-22, 1885	"
731	Janet, ...7	1812 ?	"		1-4, 1877	"
	Isaac Lyon, ...7					
732	Ann, ...7	4-26, 1815	unm., . .	12-3, 1887	1813	Catharine.
	Archibald Updike, . .7					
733	Polly, —— *Culver.* .7					
734	Eli B., ...7		Catharine, Brooklyn, Mich.	unm., . .		Elmira.
735	Jane A. 7					
736	Mary, —— *Fitzgerald,* . .7		Manchester, Mich.,		1880	Brooklyn, Mich.
737	Walker B., . . .7		Booklyn, . .	unm., . .	1-26, 1892	
	Children of 275 HANNAH BEARDSLEY JONES,⁶					
738	Rhoda Delilah Jones,⁷	11-26, 1814	Bridgeport, . .	} 4-5, 1839	10-22, 1878	Trumbull.
	*747 Reuben (s. of Wm.) Judd,*⁷ .	5-31, 1813			4-28, 1885	"
	Children of 276 AMMON BEARDSLEY,⁶					
739	Edwin Beardsley, . . .6		New York			
740	Irad, ...7					
741	Edward, ...7					
742	Eli, ...7					
743	Edgar, ...7					
744	Emerus, ...7					
745	Edmond, ...7					
746	Mirah, ...7					

No.	Name of Wife (or Husband).	Date of Birth.	Date of Marriage.	Residence.	Date of Death.	Place of Burial.
	Children of 277 ABIGAIL BEARDSLEY JUDD,[6]					
747	Reuben Judd,[7]	5–31, 1818	4–5, 1839	Bridgeport,	4–28, 1885	Trumbull.
	738 *Rhoda Delilah Jones,*[7]	11–26, 1814			10–22, 1878	"
748	Rhoda Ann,[7]	6–9, 1815	unm.			Kalamazoo, Mich.
749	Stephen Hubble,[7]	7–29, 1817				
750	Sylvia Marietta,[7]	2–29, 1820		Oregon.		
751	Harvey,[7]	10–26, 1822				Sou. Calif.
752	Eunice,[7]	12–9, 1825				
753	Pauline,[7]	7–3, 1828				California.
754	Mark,[7]	6–18, 1832				
	Children of 278 ELAM BEARDSLEY,[6]					
755	Polly Beardsley,[7]				7– , 1889	Havana.
	— Whappy, *M. D.,*					
	— *Arnold,*					
756	Othniel,[7]				1888	Missouri.
	Children of 279 HIRAM BEARDSLEY,[6]					
757	Rebecca Beardsley,[7]					
758	Clara,[7]					
759	Lucy, *Judson Crawford.*			Catharine.		

No.	Name	Gen.	Born	Married	Residence	Died	Where
	Children of 280 IRAD BEARDSLEY,6						
760	Eli John Beardsley,	7	9-6, 1843	unm.,	Catharine,	11-19, 1863	Catharine.
761	Mary Elizabeth,	7	10-7, 1845	1-14, 1873	"		
	George S. Hitchcock,	7	8-5, 1833		"		
762	Ann Eliza,	7	11-8, 1849	unm.,	"	4-11, 1887	Catharine.
	Children of 281 MEHITABLE BEARDSLEY.6						
763	Roswell F. Beardsley,	7	7-26, 1818		Wisconsin.		
764	Agur, ——,	7	12-20, 1820		Catharine,	3-10, 1823	Catharine.
765	Eli,	7	8-11, 1823		"	8-29, 1843	"
766	Rhoda,	7	11-15, 1825	2-5, 1845	"		
	Courtland C. Smith,	7			Jacksonville, N.Y.		
767	Henry,	7	6-21, 1828		Minnesota.		
768	Oscar, ——,	7	2-9, 1832		Catharine,	3-10, 1832	Catharine.
769	Elizabeth,	7	5-31, 1834	4-24, 1850	"		
	Darius Bulkley,	7			"		
770	Daniels,	7	10-21, 1838			11-14, 1852	Catharine.
	Children of 282 CYRUS BEARDSLEY,6						
771	Alonzo Sherman Beardsley,	7	1-23, 1826	12-30, 1862	Catharine.	9-10, 1886	Southport, Ct.
	Sarah Augusta Lewis,		10-24, 1837		"		"
772	Marie Antoinette,	7	3-27, 1831	10-7, 1856	Southport,	4-11, 1892	
	David Hull Sherwood,		6-29, 1829				
	Children of 283 STILES BEARDSLEY,6						
773	Mary Marilla Beardsley,	7	3-26, 1830		Catharine,	1-1, 1851	Montour, N. Y.
774	George Robert,	7	4-9, 1832	1-8, 1855	St. Helena, Cal.	5-16, 1871	Chicago, Ill.
	Elizabeth McGregor,		1-7, 1886		Bridgeport, "		
	Adella A. Chapin,		7-3, 1846	11-12, 1872	Independence,N.Y.		
775	Annie Irving,	7	4-12, 1834		Catharine,		Montour.
776	Marinda,	7	10-22, 1838		"	12-19, 1888	"
777	Frances,	7	7-26, 1841			5-19, 1853	
	Truxton Slocum,						
778	William "Irving,"	7	11-1, 1844		San Francisco.		
779	Edwin Stiles, ——,	7	3-23, 1847			11-21, 1872	Wadsworth.

No.	Name of Wife (or Husband).	Date of Birth.	Date of Marriage.	Residence.	Date of Death.	Place of Burial.
	Children of 303 SARAH MALLETT,[6] *see 197.*					
	Children of 304 FANNY MALLETT SEELEY,[6]					
780	Lewis "Mallett" Seeley, . . . 7	5-22, 1824		Bridgeport, . .	9-20, 1888	M. G. C. B. C.
	Mary Julia Beach, . . .	5-18, 1825				
781	Clark, ... 7	9-12, 1823	6-30, 1844	Bridgeport, . .	7-16, 1871	Milford.
	Caroline "Cornelia" Peck, . .	10 10, 1823	9-3, 1848	Milford.		
	Children of 305 PETER BEARDSLEY,[6]					
782	John Bennett Beardsley, . . . 7	7-6, 1827		Huntington, . .	12-26, 1828	Huntington.
783	John Lovejoy, ... 7	4-28, 1831	5-20, 1855	"	9-11, 1868	Huntington.
	Mary Ann Squire,	1-25, 1833				
	Mary Jane Hubbell (Sherman), . .	5-30, 1833	3-24, 1870	"	12-14, 1891	
	Children of 309 ANTHONY BEARDS-LEY,[6]					
784	John L. Beardsley, ... 7	9-12, 1829	10-3, 1867	Hartland.		
785	*Georgianna T. (d. Aaron T.) Beardsley,* 7	10-3, 1841		Bridgeport.	1-8, 1893	La Grange, Ill.
	Mary Jane, ... 7	5-30, 1832	11- , 1857	Hartland. . .		
	Wm. S. Banker,			Western Sp'gs, Ill.		
	Children of 315 LUCIUS BEARDSLEY,[6]					
786	Dell Beardsley, ... 7			Catharine.		
	Eli Stanley, ... 7					
787	Frelich, ... 7					
	Lucretia Kendle.					
	Children of 316 LEWIS BEARDSLEY,[6]					
788	Samuel Agard Beardsley, . . . 7	6-15, 1819	6-17, 1843	Catharine.		
	Phebe Kendall.	1823				
789	Cicero, ... 7	5-17, 1821		Sandwich, Ill.		
	Helen Kilburn.					
790	Seneca L., ... 7	5-22, 1824				

No.	Name		Birth	Marriage	Residence	Death	Place
791	Scipio C.,	7	10-8, 1826	{12 22, 1852 / 1-31, 1878}	Watkins.	2-10, 1877	
	Caroline M. Coates,		9-24, 1826				
	Mary Jane (Cooke),		4-27, 1825		Havana.		
792	James E.,	7	12-12, 1829	1857			
	Letitia B. Coe,		1830				
793	John W.,	7	6-24, 1832		Anderson, Cal.		
	Children of 317 Stephen Beardsley,[6]						
794	Ruana Beardsley,	7	4-17, 1821		Chicago,	1-14, 1892 dec.	Chicago.
	Levi Lyon,						Odessa.
	Floyd Higgin.						
795	Alice Genett,	7	6-24, 1822		Ft. Leavenw'h, Ks.		
	Aaron E. Mallory.						
796	James Bennett,	7	5-23, 1824	1845	Catherine.	10-20, 1893	Montour.
	Almira Hagar,		10-14, 1822				
797	Aaron Bennett,	7	10-17, 1825		Southport, N. Y.		
798	Ruth Ann,	7	6-3, 1827		Flint, Mich.		
799	Eunice,	7	9-15, 1828			3-, 1878	
800	Beach,	7	5 8, 1836			5-17, 1886	
	Children of 318 Elias Beardsley,[6]						
801	Elizabeth Beardsley,	7	1837			1837	
802	Melissa Jane,	7	7-19, 1888				
803	Hannah Ursula,	7	12-4, 1840		Petersburg, N. D.	3-24, 1880	
804	Orren,	7	1844		Iowa,	1844	
805	Julia A.,	7	11-27, 1846		Corning, N. Y.		
	William Burrel.						
	Children of 319 Levi Beardsley,[6]						
806	Lucina M. Beardsley,	7	10-29, 1824	11-24, 1840	Catharine,	3-18, 1888	Catherine.
	Israel C. Gibbs,		9-6, 1818		Odessa.		
807	Clarissa,	7	4-7, 1827		Catharine.	5-14, 1834	
808	Harriet A.,	7	10-27, 1829	5-3, 1848	S. Danby, N. Y.		S. Danby.
	Wm. M. Rittenhouse,		9-10, 1821		?		
809	Nancy I.,	7	12-11, 1832	unm.,	Catharine,	4-7, 1876	
810	Anna C.,	7	7-19, 1834	unm.,	Catharine.	5-18, 1889	
811	Horace A.,	7	1-16, 1840	12-23, 1865	Catharine.		
	Emily G. Coe,		2-1, 1842				

No.	Name of Wife (or Husband).	Date of Birth.	Date of Marriage.	Residence.	Date of Death.	Place of Burial.
812	Elizabeth Hannah, ...7	12–28, 1842	. . . .	Gates Co., N. Y.		
	Children of 320 SUSANNAH BEARDS-LEY HOWARD,[6]					
813	Mary Howard, ...7 *John Kingsbury,* *James Campbell,*	7–10, 1823 1824 1821	} 1843 1847	Elmira. Elmira.	1845	Auburn.
814	Sarah, . *Stuart Hamilton,* . .7	10–30, 1824	1850	Sullivanville. "	1884	Catharine.
815	Hannah, *James Palmer,* . . .7	10–29, 1826 1821	1849	Cator.	1888	Cator.
816	Harriet, *Clark Brotherton,* . .7	6–25, 1828	1847	Allendale, Mich. .		
817	Alvira, ...7	10–21, 1830		. . . .	9–3, 1832	Veteran.
818	Almira, *John Kingsley,* . . .7	10–21, 1830	1852	Pine Valley.		
819	Josephine, *Joseph Lattin,* . .7	7–5, 1837	1857	Alpine.		
820	John W. —— *Boas,* 7	4–24, 1839		Bay View, Mich.		
821	Maria, ...7 *John Grimes,*	5–15, 1844	9–2, 1864	Millport.		
	Children of 321 SARAH BEARDSLEY RUGGLES,[6]					
822	Hannah Ruggles, ...7 *James Lay,*	6–19, 1837	}	Sullivan, Pa.		
823	Mary Louise, ...7 *Daniel (s. of Garret) Compton,*	1–5, 1839 8–8, 1835	5–31, 1858	Troy, Pa.	2–18, 1841	
824	Mahaia, ...7	11–8, 1840	. . . .			
	Children of 324 James Beardsley,[6]					
825	Matilda Beardsley, ...7 *Henry Lattin,*	4–9, 1837 10–3, 1830	} 6–4, 1854	Catharine.		

No.	Name	Gen.	Born		Place		Place
826	Sarah,	7	8-5, 1838	1855	Norwalk, O.	8-11, 1863	Alexandria, Va.
	Chas. Wm. Hawes,		8-15, 1834				
827	Nehemiah Beach,	7	12-20, 1839		San Francisco.	1890	Bridgeport.
828	James Watson,	7	12-21, 1841	1871	Bridgeport,		
	Helen Coryell,						
829	Nancy "Charlotte,"	7	2-2, 1845	9-10, 1865			
	Wesley Stanley,		7-11, 1840				
830	Mary Jane,	7	9-16, 1848	4-24, 1870	Odessa.		
	James Keyser,						
	Charles Lockhart,			4-15, 1890	Odessa.		

Children of 325 ABEL N. BEARDSLEY,[6]

No.	Name	Gen.	Born		Place		Place
831	Melissa Beardsley,	7	6-16, 1838		Catharine.		
	James Corby,						
832	Albert,	7	2-24, 1841			4-28, 1884	Montour.
	Irene Gernard,						
833	Jeremiah.	7	1843			1843	
834	John Lambert,	7	6-18, 1845		Catharine.		Montour.
	Sarah Cooper,						
835	Levi,	7	3-1, 1848		Catharine.	1850	

Children of 326 HANNAH BEARDSLEY EVANS,[6]

No.	Name	Gen.	Born		Place		Place
836	Maria L. Evans,	7	9-28, 1838	1-29, 1865			Catharine.
	Timothy Sanford Couch,		1-20, 1832				
837	Estus D.,	7	10-5, 1845			1-12, 1846	

Children of 327 PHEBE BEARDSLEY BAKER,[6]

No.	Name	Gen.	Born		Place		Place
838	Margaret,	7			Austin, Minn.		
	—— Raiser,						

Children of 328 EDEN BEARDSLEY,[6]

No.	Name	Gen.	Born		Place		Place
839	Sarah Beardsley,	7	1-19, 1843	3 31, 1867	Richmond, Pa.	4-27, 1882	Sullivan.
	Aden Cleveland,		7-6, 1888		Sullivan,		
840	Susan,	7	12-31, 1845	12-31, 1870	Rutland, Pa.		
	Henry Makley,		9-23, 1834				
841	George G.,	7	1-11, 1849	1-11, 1882	Troy, Pa.		
	Alice E. Tears,		2-28, 1858				

No.	Name of Wife (or Husband).	Date of Birth.	Date of Marriage.	Residence.	Date of Death.	Place of Burial.
842	Hattie,[7]	6-21, 1856	} 6-8, 1878	Lamb's Creek, Pa.	8-, 1836	
	Asa R. Harvey,				3-23, 1862	
	Children of 329 SAMUEL BEARDS- LEY.[6]					
843	Mary Beardsley,[7]	1833				
843a	Stephen L.,[7]	1-10, 1834				
	Sarah Croy,					
843b	Henrietta M.,[7]	7-19, 1836	} 9-24, 1852			
	Clinton Williams,					
843c	Adelia F.,[7]	5-26, 1838	1855			
	—— Hull,		} 1864			
	—— Triggs,		}			
	Chester F. Francis,		10-11, 1870			
843d	Roswell,[7]	6-16, 1846	} 10-3, 1869	Ashby, Minn.		
	Kizzie Timberlake,	2-6, 1840				
843e	William H.,[7]	1-17, 1849				
	Jane Corliss.	7-13, 1841				
843f	Mary M.,[7]	5-16, 1842				
	Ira Ingraham.					
843g	Angeline.[7]	9-30, 1845	}			
	Jefferson Holman,		}			
	Michael Q. Caldwell,					
	George Albright,					
843h	George A.,[7]	8-22, 1851			1852	
843i	Malisa E.,[7]	6-20, 1854			1867	
843j	Sarah M.,[7]	9-22, 1859			1867	
	Children of 331 HARRY BEARDSLEY.[6]					
844	William H. Beardsley,[7]	1849				
845	Frederick,[7]	1852	}			
	Ella Grant,	1856	}			
846	Norton L.,[7]	1854	}			
	Catharine Westlake,	1858	}			

No.	Name	Gen.	Birth	Marriage	Marriage / Residence	Death	Death place
847	Albert H.,	7	1857				
	Sarah Tagart,	7	1862				
848	Roswell E.,	7	1861				
	Margaret Light,		1867				

Children of 332 ZILPHA BEARDSLEY VAN NOTRICK,[6]

No.	Name	Gen.	Birth	Marriage	Marriage / Residence	Death	Death place
849	George W. Van Notrick,	7	1844	1882			
	Melissa A. Kendrick,	7	1847				
850	Susan E.,	7	1851				
851	Sarah E.,	7	1857	1874			

Children of 340 ANNA MALLETT HUBBELL,[6]

No.	Name	Gen.	Birth	Marriage	Marriage / Residence	Death	Death place
852	Susan Hubbell,	7	1804?	unm.,		9- , 1856	Damascus, Pa.
853	Ira,	7	1806?				At sea.
854	William,	7	1808?	unm.,		1828?	Bridgeport.
855	Laura,	7	9-26, 1810	9- , 1841	Honesdale, Pa.,	6-23, 1881	Damascus, Pa
	William Rolston,	7	11- , 1813		New Haven, Ct.,	10-9, 1885	
856	Levi B.,	7	4-15, 1812	1836?	Milford.	8-23, 1885	N. Haven.
	893 b Catharine Mallett,						
857	Charles,	7	11- , 1816	1842?	Easton, Ct.		
	Martha Gunn,						

Children of 341 ABIGAIL MALLETT KNAPP,[6]

No.	Name	Gen.	Birth	Marriage	Marriage / Residence	Death	Death place
858	George Knapp.	7	3-1, 1804	unm.,	Bridgeport,	12-12, 1822	Bridgeport.
859	William P.,	7	11-24, 1808	1827	New York,	8-20, 1857	"
860	Isaac M.,	7	7-3, 1812	1843	Columbus, Miss.,	10-6, 1870	Columbus.
	Happy Wakeman,						
	Mary Jane Glover,						
861	Levi,	7	11-4, 1814	unm.,	Bridgeport,	6-21, 1813	Bridgeport.
862	Elizabeth,	7	10-18, 1818	9-20, 1837	New Milford, Ct.,	2-20, 1892	New Milford.
	Frederick L. Curtis,						
	Charles C. Noble,		5-26, 1864				
863	Lucy A.,	7	12-21, 1821	3-4, 1850	East Northport, L.I.		
	James Rudyard,				"		

No.	Name of Wife (or Husband).	Date of Birth.	Date of Marriage.	Residence.	Date of Death.	Place of Burial.
	Children of 342 LEWIS MALLETT,⁶ ⁷					
864	Julia Ann Mallett,	3-21, 1823	12-1, 1844	Bridgeport,	4-26, 1891	M. G. C. B. C.
	Stephen Hawley,	5-21, 1817		"	1-7, 1892	"
865	Amelia,	2-5, 1825	unm.,	"	7-22, 1826	"
866	Jennette,	3-6, 1827		"	4-28, 1891	"
867	Mary A., "Treat,"	12-1, 1818	"	"	1-4, 1882	"
868	Richard "Treat,"	1-10, 1820	"	"	10-8, 1853	"
	Children of 343 EUNICE MALLETT CLARK,⁶					
869	Lewis Elisha Clark,⁷	4-4, 1813	11-4, 1833	Milford,	6-29, 1846	
	Nancy Eliza Benjamine,	3-12, 1812		"		
870	Alanson Beach,⁷	6-19, 1815	4-9, 1846	"	3-5, 1866	Milford.
	Nancy Lyra Palmer,	10-25, 1820			3-27, 1871	"
871	Sarah Ann,⁷	12-20, 1817	4-9, 1843	West Haven.	9-4, 1880	W. Haven.
	John Peck Hubbard,	7-23, 1811		"	10-13, 1883	Milford.
872	Avis Mallett,⁷	2-13, 1820	4-13, 1851	Milford,		
	Jonas Buckingham,	2-16, 1819		"		
873	Nehemiah Thomas,⁷	5-5, 1823	12-23, 1858	"		
	964 Abigail Peck Baldwin,⁷	3-27, 1829		"		
874	Harriet Abigail,⁷	7-3, 1825	4-24, 1851	"	3-12, 1891	
	Wyllis Andrew Law,	9-2, 1820		New Haven.		
875	Mary Elizabeth,⁷	7-11, 1829		Milford.	10-15, 1830	Milford.
	Children of 344 MARY MALLETT WHEELER,⁶					
876	Henry Timothy Wheeler,⁷	1-1, 1809		New York,	3-9, 1887	M. G. C. B. C.
	Jane Amanda Griffing,		12-5, 18—		3-28, 1859	"
	Mary Elizabeth (Durand),					
877	Francis Mallette,⁷	5-5, 1810		Bridgeport,	9-15, 1810	M. G. C. B. C.
878	Laura Ann,⁷	8-6, 1812	9-22, 1835	"		
	Orlando Beach Hall,	10-29, 1814				
879	Francis Ezra,	7-9, 1817		Bridgeport,	11-5, 1823	M. G. C. B. C.
880	Alfred Merwin,	6-27, 1820		"	12-2, 1821	"
881	Miles Mallett,					

No.	Name	Gen.	Born	Married	Residence	Died	Place
882	Maria Avis,	7	2–24, 1824	4–20, 1852	Bridgeport.	6–14, 1876	Milford.
	Caleb Tomlinson Mervin,	7	6–1, 1828		Milford.	dec.	"
883	George Benjamin,	7					
	Antionette Burns,						
884	Austin Atwater,	7	11–25, 1830	11–9, 1853	Louisville, Ky.	9–14, 1893	M. G. C. B. C.
	Atlanta Maria Gage,						
	Children of 345 HARRIET MALLETT[6] BUCKINGHAM,[6]						
885	Harriet Ann Buckingham,	7	8–8, 1832	4–21, 1858		4–21, 1858	
	John R. Lattin,		9–18, 1836				
	Children of 350 JOHN MALLETT,[6]						
886	Fenn Mallett,	7	1–20, 1811	9–24, 1887	Southbury,	4–26, 1851	
	Susan C. Downs,						
887	Sally,	7	10–24, 1812	10–4, 1883			
	Eli S. Peet,						
888	John,	7	2–9, 1814		New Milford,		
889	Thomas Hall,	7	9–17, 1815	1–15, 1845	Woodbury.	3–16, 1892	N. Milford.
	Lamira E. Hurd,						
890	Dan,	7	4–10, 1818	unm.,	Savannah, Ga.,	3–17, 1869	Savannah.
891	Betsey,	7	2–18, 1820	"		1–21, 1844	
892	Benjamin S.,	7	4–9, 1822			1–25, 1875	
893	Charlotte,	7	2–13, 1826	7–28, 1853	Savannah.	1–8, 1880	
	John Rutherford,						
	Children of 351 WILLIAM MALLETT,[6]						
893a	Susan Mallett,	7	1816				
893b	Catharine,	7	1818				
856	*Levi B. Hubbell,*		4–15, 1812				
893c	Lucy,	7	1820			8–23, 1885	New Haven.
	Children of 352 MARK MALLETT,[6]						
894	Maria Mallett,	7					
	Children of 353 MEHETABLE MALLETT PECK,[6]						
894a	Fenn Peck,	7					
894b	Mark,	7					

No.	Name of Wife (or Husband).	Date of Birth.	Date of Marriage.	Residence.	Date of Death.	Place of Burial.
	Children of 364 LUCY ANN MALLETT HIGBY,[6]					
895	Samuel Higby,[7]	3-17, 1815				
	Harriett Thomas,					
895a	Lucy Ann,[7]	1-13, 1817	9-21, 1843	Milford.	1-6, 1881	
	952 Samuel B. Baldwin,[7]					
895b	Elizabeth,[7]	3-12, 1819	10-27, 1844		4-27, 1887	
	Amos S. Bristol,					
895c	Riley,[7]	3-5, 1821			2-19, 1888	
	Mary Disbrow,					
895d	Ruth,[7]	1-29, 1823	5-31, 1847	Milford.		
	953 A. Brooks Baldwin,[7]	10-31, 1823				
895e	Mehetable,[7]	4-26, 1825				
	James P. Disbrow,					
895f	Marcus,[7]	1-13, 1828			1888	
895g	Mary Jane,[7]	2-6, 1830				
	Euselius H. Bristol,[7]					
895h	Charlotte Augusta,	6-13, 1833	6-6, 1867		6-5, 1886	
	Charles Brian,	12-29, 1819				
	Children of 361 BETSEY MALLETT STEELE,[6]					
896	Burr Steele,	3-19, 1824			9-4, 1844	
897	Betsey,[7]	3-19, 1824			4-7, 1824	
	Children of 363 LUKE MALLETT,[6]					
898	Lewis Bryant Mallett,[7]	6- , 1832				
	Mary (d. of Sam'l) Oviatt,					
899	Caroline Matilda,[7]					
900	Luke,[7]					

No.	Name					
	Children of **367** LUCY WORDIN PEET.[6]					
901	Mary A. Peet, [7]		unm.,	Bridgeport,	10-27, 1852	Bridgeport.
902	Charles W., [7]		—,			
	Children of **371** LAURA WORDIN HUBBELL.[6]					
903	Isaac Hubbell, [7]				dec. inf.	
904	George A., [7]	7-16, 1826		Easton, Ct.		
	Huldah A. Mills,					
905	Clarissa W., [7]	12-23, 1828	12-23, 1850	Bridgeport.		
	Alfred B. Corbusier,					
	Children of **372** EUNICE WORDIN WHEELER.[6]					
906	William W. Wheeler, [7]				8-29, 1868	
907	Elizabeth, —; [7]		unm.			
	— *Hubbell,*					
908	Elmer, [7]		unm.			
	Children of **373** DAVID MALLETT.[6]					
909	Abbie C. Mallett, [7]	11-23, 1816		Milford,	1888	Cypress Hill, Bkln.
	Henry Hubbell,			Bridgeport,	dec.	" "
910	Harvey Swain, [7]			Nantucket,		Quaker Cem., "
	Eliza Ann, [7]	2-14, 1819		Bridgeport.	1893	Bridgeport.
	Richard Davis,					
911	Alfred, [7]	4-7, 1821	unm.,			
912	Josephine, [7]	9-7, 1823		Newark, N. J.	9-29, 1853	M. G. C. B. C.
913	Sarah Frances, [7]	9-7, 1823		Milford,	1876	" "
	Curtis Rich,			Bridgeport,	dec.	
914	David, [7]	3-81, 1826				
915	*Sarah Burns,*					
	Mary, [7]	3-7, 1828		Milford,	1884	Milford.
	Lewis Clark,			W. Stratford.		
916	Joseph, [7]	10-30, 1830				
917	Stephen, [7]	2-24, 1833				
918	Crawford, [7]	7-11, 1835			1847	

No.	Name of Wife (or Husband).	Date of Birth.	Date of Marriage.	Residence.	Date of Death.	Place of Burial.
919	Charles B., ... 7	9-29, 1839		Jersey City.		
919a	*Maria,*			"		
	Sarah E., ... 7	6-14, 1842		New York.	1882	Milford.
	Newton Beach, . .			"	1880	Newark.
919b	Zachary Taylor, . . 7	2-16, 1847		Newark, . .	7- , 1880	
	Julia Isbell, . .			"		
	Children of 374 Susan Mallett Burns,[6]					
919c	Stephen Burns, . . 7	10-16, 1819				
919d	David, ... 7	4-10, 1822				
919e	Henry Storer, . . 7	7-29, 1824				
919f	Sarah Elizabeth, . . 7	12-17, 1829				
919g	Wayne, ... 7	3-21, 1832				
919h	Susan Storer, . . 7	11-8, 1834				
919i	Abraham D., . . . 7	1-23, 1840			10-24. 1878	
	Children of 375 Capt. Alfred Mallett,[6]					
920	Mark Mallett, . . . 7	6-19, 1825		Milford, Ct., .	9-19, 1828	
921	Caroline, ... 7	10-1, 1826		"		
	Capt. Sylvester Blakeman, 7	7-25, 1825	4-4, 1847	Stratford, Ct.,		Stratford.
922	Mark S., ... 7	11-12, 1828	8-14, 1852	. . . .		
	Susan C. (d. of Hezekiah) Baldwin, 7	12-10, 1825				
923	Henry Curtis, . . 7	4-17, 1834	4-14, 1855	Milford, . .	4-5, 1882	
	Mary A. Somers, . .	8-24, 1834		New York, . .	6-1, 1867	
	Mary Tibbals (d. of Chas.) Curtis, 7	12-25, 1834	1-29, 1873	Stratford.	10-20, 1870	
924	Alfred B., ... 7	8-16, 1837	3-22, 1844		9-8, 1876	
	Cornelia Stannard, . .		unm, ...	Milford.	8-5, 1870	
925	Mary Diana, . . . 7	11-11, 1840				
926	Charlotte, ... 7	10-12, 1842	12-22, 1875			
	James N. Hyde, . .	4 18, 1827				
927	Maria Louisa, . . 7	9-18, 1845	2-25, 1886			
	Hezekiah (s. of Hez.) Clark,					

No.	Name	Gen.	Born	Married	Place	Died	Place
	Children of 378 HORACE MALLETT,	6					
928	George Mallett,	7	2-20, 1855				Milford.
	Harriet Parsons,						
929	Elizabeth ——,	7	10-19, 1839		Milford,	1-24, 1841	Milford.
930	Elizabeth ——,	7	5-22, 1841				
	Albert Plumb,						
931	William,	7	6-8, 1839	9-26, 1866			
931a	Horace Edgar,	7	4-4, 1845			6-16, 1849	
	Children of 380 PETER MALLETT,	6					
931b	Margaret Mallett,	7					
	William Miles.						
	Children of 381 ISAAC MALLETT,	6					
932	Martha Eliza Mallett,	7	1835			12-27, 1864	Danbury.
933	Charles Lewis,	7	2- , 1836			10-30, 1844	"
934	Harriet Isabel,	7	12- , 1845			1-31, 1846	
	Children of 383 DAVID LEWIS BALDWIN,	6					
935	Richard L. Baldwin,	7	5-17, 1815	4 2, 1846	New York.		
	Julia Philips,				"		
936	Martha P.,	7	2-7, 1817	9-27, 1843	Milford.		
	David (s. of David) Miles,				"		
937	Mary Dewitt,	7	4-4, 1819		"	12-24, 1842	
938	Henry A.,	7	4-22, 1821	4-8, 1852	Orange, Ct.		
	Emily (d. of David) Nettleton,						
939	Charlotte C.,	7	12-18, 1823			4- , 1824	
940	Adam P.,	7	6-19, 1825	9-29, 1852	New York.		
	Anna P. Doremus,				"		
941	Abraham Dewitt,	7	10-15, 1828	10-24, 1877	"	8-26, 1880	
	Mamie E. Christie,						
942	Charles S.,	7	3-12, 1831				Milford.
	Elizabeth Hickson,						
943	Charlotte,	7	5-2, 1834				
	Lewis J. Nettleton,						

No.	Name of Wife (or Husband).	Date of Birth.	Date of Marriage.	Residence.	Date of Death.	Place of Burial.
	Children of 384 EUNICE BALDWIN MILES,⁶					
944	Nathan Miles,⁷		unm.,	Milford,	dec.	
945	Mary,⁷			"		
	Edwin Sperry,			Waterbury.		
946	Charlotte,⁷			Milford.		
947	Sarah, ____,⁷					
948	Samuel A..,⁷			Mass.	dec.	
949	Samuel A..,⁷			Milford,		
	*Ellen G. (d. of Selah) Strong,*⁷			"		
950	Catharine,⁷			"	dec.	
951	Infant,⁷					
	Children of 385 MARCUS BALDWIN,⁶,⁷					
952	Samuel Burton Baldwin,⁷	1–13, 1817	(5–30, 1847)?	Milford.	1–6, 1881	
	*895a Lucy A. Higby,*⁷	10–31, 1823				
953	Aaron Brooks,⁷	1–29, 1823	5–30, 1847	"		
	*895d Ruth Higby,*⁷					
954	James Ball,⁷	3–7, 1826	11 28, 1849	"	7–12, 1854	
	Esther (d. Amos; g.d. Amos) Baldwin,					
	Diana, "					
955	Elizabeth, .⁷	2–7, 1829	9–25, 1855	"	9–13, 1881	
	*Theodore Stow,*⁷		8–18, 1853	"		
956	Albert A..,⁷	11–7, 1831	9–26, 1855	"	8–14, 1872	
	*Sarah A. (d. of Enoch B.) Peck,*⁷					
	Susan J. "		9–3, 1873	"		
	Children of 387 ADOLPHUS BALDWIN,⁶					
957	Nathan Adolphus Baldwin, .⁷			New York.		
	Maria L. Fitch (Whitney).					
958	Laura Augusta, .⁷	1–11, 1826	9–26, 1846	Milford.		
	*George Cornwall,*⁷	3–21, 1821		Gunnison, Col.		

No.	Name	Gen.	Born	Married	Residence	Died	M. G. C. B. C.
959	Timothy Higgin,	7	1–13, 1828	. . .	Milford.		
	Sarah W. Smith,				"		
960	Henry Clay,	7	1–17, 1830	. . .	"	1–1, 1831	
961	Emily,	7	4–11, 1832	11–19, 1856	Cincinnati.	4–13, 1864	
	Frank T. Lockwood,				Milford.		
962	Lucy,	7	2–22, 1834	1–27, 1859	New York.		
	John B. Stevens.				Brooklyn, N. Y.,	6–19, 1877	
963	Henry Clay,	7	3–25, 1836	. . .	New York.		
	Emma Blauvelt,						

Children of 388 SAMUEL D. BALDWIN.[6]

No.	Name	Gen.	Born	Married	Residence	Died	M. G. C. B. C.
964	Abigail Peck Baldwin.	7	3–27, 1829	12–23, 1858	Milford,	3–12, 1891	
	873 Nehemiah Clark,[7]		5–5, 1823		"		
965	Calvin Durand,	7	4–1, 1832	12–23, 1858	"		
	Mary (d. of Hezekiah) Baldwin,				"		
966	Edwin,	7	2–14, 1835		"	6–7, 1879	
	Emelia (d. of Harvey) Minor,				N. Y. & Milford,		
967	Catharine Miles,	7	5–28, 1888	unm., . .	Milford.		

Children of 389 CHARLOTTE BALD-WIN HIGBY.[6]

No.	Name	Gen.	Born	Married	Residence	Died	M. G. C. B. C.
968	William Riley Higby,[6]	7	8–6, 1825	9–22, 1846	Bridgeport.		
	Mary Ann Johnson,		4–15, 1825				
969	Edwin Burr,	7			Bridgeport,	8–29, 1829	M.
970	Charlotte Augusta,	7			"	10–1, 1831	G. "
971	Susan Augusta,	7			"	9–15, 1832	C. "
972	Mason Durand,	7			"	9–7, 1836	B. "
973	Martha Louisa,	7			"	6–10, 1842	C. "

Children of 390 NATHAN BALDWIN.[6]

No.	Name	Gen.	Born	Married	Residence	Died	M. G. C. B. C.
974	Louisa Baldwin,	7	9–10, 1825	. . .	Milford.	3–7, 1826	
975	Sarah B.,	7	12–8, 1827	8–21, 1851	"		
	John Crockett,				New Haven, Ct.,	dec.	
976	Eliza J.,	7	5–9, 1830	4–21, 1852	Milford.		
	Noah B. Welton, M. D.,				Cheshire, Ct.		
977	William Pond,	7	1–10, 1834	7–, 1856	New York.		
	Hattie Oliver,				Milford.		
978	Caroline S.,	7	7–26, 1836	. . .	Memphis, Tenn.	4–13, 1837	
979	Anthony S.,	7	10–6, 1842	. . .			

No.	Name of Wife (or Husband).	Date of Birth.	Date of Marriage.	Residence.	Date of Death.	Place of Burial.
	Children of 391 ALFRED BEACH,[6]					
980	Samuel Beach, M. D., [7]	7-27, 1802		Bridgeport,	5-6, 1853	M. G. C. B. C.
	Mary Swift,	5-25, 1808			3-1, 1874	"
981	Cornelia, [7]	9-17, 1804	3-4, 1829	Bridgeport,	6-21, 1835	"
	Daniel Curtis,	1-26, 1801		"	10-27, 1868	
982	Sheldon, [7]	1-1, 1807			10-15, 1887	
	411 Miranda E. Summers,[6]	8-12, 1810			8-13, 1883	
983	Julia, [7]	3-7, 1814	6-7, 1843	Bridgeport,	10-27, 1868	M. G. C. B. C.
	Daniel Curtis,	1-26, 1801			2-12, 1893	Trumbull.
984	Elijah, [7]	10-31, 1817	1-19, 1842			
	Emily Hawley,	9-19, 1820				
985	Louisa, [7]	5-23, 1821	9-27, 1841	Nichols, Ct.,	8-12, 1845	Nichols.
	Charles Nichols Fairchild,	10-27, 1818			9-6, 1891	"
	Children of 392 ELIHU BEACH,[6]					
986	Elizabeth Ann Beach, [7]		5-23, 1827		3-18, 1870	
	Daniel Ufford, M. D.,					
987	William, [7]	3-29, 1810	9-24, 1835	Elmira.	1-5, 1891	Elmira.
	Juliana Lewis,	4-12, 1813				
988	Mary E., [7]	3-20, 1816	11-17, 1836	Bridgeport,	10-10, 1892	M. G. C. B. C.
	Horace Lyon,	7-8, 1813		"	10-19, 1887	"
989	James Walker, [7]	7-2, 1821	9-1, 1844		7-4, 1847	"
	Harriet E. Lewis,	5-27, 1822				
	Laura Silliman,	11-7, 1829	12-31, 1849			
	Children of 393 NANCY BEACH JEN- *NINGS,*[6]					
990	Rebecca Jennings, [7]	7-24, 1816			11-21, 1828	Derby, Ct.
991	Rev. Isaac, [7]	7-24, 1816			8-25, 1887	Bennington, Vt.
	Sophia (d. of Matthias) Day,					
992	Abigail, [7]	7-20, 1819			3-1, 1824	Derby, Ct.
993	Elizabeth Ann, [7]	12-16, 1820	1841		2-3, 1847	Oberlin, O.
	Elihu Hosford,					
994	Catharine, [7]	8-30, 1823	12-11, 1849		9-, 1890	Washington, D. C.
	Justin R. Parsons, D. D.,					

No.	Name	Born	Married / Died	Residence	Died	Place
996	John Giles, · · · · · · · ·7			· · ·		
996	*Caroline R.* (d. of Dan'l) *Conkling,*7	11-5, 1825 }	5-9, 1855 }		11-1, 1849	Oberlin, O.
996	Frederick Beach, · · · · ·7	1-7, 1828	· · ·	· · ·		
	Children of 395 DAVID S. EDWARDS.6					
997	William Stout Edwards, · · ·7	9-19, 1831	4-29, 1865	Bridgeport, · · ·	2-2, 1882	
	Lucy Woodworth Beebe,6			San Francisco.		
998	Harriet Summers, · · · ·7	9-13, 1823	9-29, 1859	Bridgeport, · · ·	12-8, 1881	
	William Gustavus Wuller,	6-7, 1813			6-13, 1891	
	Children of 396 HEPZIBAH BEARDS-LEY WHEELER.6					
999	James Beardsley Wheeler, · ·7	4-7, 1827	unm., · · · ·	Huntington, Ct.		
1000	William Summers, · · · ·7	7-9, 1834	3-30, 1864	Trumbull.		
	Rebecca Frances,	10-21, 1839				
1001	Albert, · · · · · · ·7	6-22, 1836	unm.,	· · ·	12-24, 1875	Trumbull.
	Children of 403 ELIJAH S. BEACH.6					
1002	Theodore Wells Beach, · · ·7	10-22, 1836	10-2, 1872	Bridgeport, · · ·	5-23, 1889	M. G. C. B. C
	Adaline Louisa (d. of Legrand) *Beers,*7	9-25, 1846				
1003	Mary Ann, · · · · · ·7	9-10, 1888	unm., · · ·	Trumbull, · · ·	1-24, 1839	Trumbull.
1004	Amanda, · · · · · · ·7	9-10, 1888	" · · ·	" · · ·		
1005	Anna Maria, · · · · · ·7	10-, 1841	"	" · · ·	8-9, 1867	Trumbull.
	Children of 404 ALDEN BURTON.6					
1006	James Burton, · · · · ·7		· · ·	· · ·	10-22, 1844	
1007	John, _____ · · · · ·7					
	Children of 405 POLLY BURTON NICHOLS.6					
1008	Stiles Burton Nichols, · · ·7	12-1, 1835 }	2-26, 1857 }	Huntington, Ct.		
	Ann Elizabeth Drew,	3-10, 1886				
	Children of 406 ELOISE BURTON STERLING.6					
1009	John Burton Sterling, · · ·7	1828 }	unm., · · ·	Bridgeport, · · ·	8-9, 1855	M. G. C. B. C.
1010	Emily Eloise, · · · · · ·7	4 6, 1838 }	1-20, 1860	Chicago.	4-1, 1860	"
	Frank W. Smith,					

No.	Name of Wife (or Husband).	Date of Birth.	Date of Marriage.	Residence.	Date of Death.	Place of Burial.
	Children of 407 STILES BURTON, [6]					
1011	Virginia Burton, [7]	10-11, 1844	6-19, 1866	Chicago.		
	Ira Holmes, [7]	11-19, 1889		"		
1012	Legrand Sterling, [7]	9-27, 1846	4-7, 1875	"		
	Mary Roberts, [7]	4-7, 1859		"		
1013	Stiles, [7]	3-13, 1856	. . . .	"	8-12, 1856	Rose Hill, Chic.
1014	Stephen Lester, [7]	10-10, 1864	5-14, 1875	"		
	Ada Perkins, [7]	11-16, 1856				
	Children of 408 BENJAMIN BURTON, [6]					
1015	Caroline Betsey Burton, [7]	1-19, 1887	5-18, 1862	Trumbull,	11-18, 1863	Nichols.
	697 *Orange Beach Plumb*, [7]	10-11, 1827		"		
1016	Eli Plumb, [7]	1-16, 1889	11 23, 1870	"		
	Mary Lavina Brewer,	7-8, 1847				
1017	Rollin Stiles, [7]	4-12, 1841	unm.,	Trumbull,	6-30, 1863	New Orleans.
1018	Lorena Naomi, [7]	9-27, 1843	10-31, 1865	Riverhead, N. Y.		
	Abaz Bradley, [7]	7-10, 1821				
1019	Orville Benjamin, [7]	10-22, 1852	11 25, 1879	Trumbull.		
	Carrie Rosa "bell" (d. of Harvey Hurd),	12-23, 1852				
	Children of 409 LAURA A. SUMMERS JONES, [6]					
1020	Mary Ann Jones, [7]	10-17, 1823	11-1, 1869	Trumbull.		
	George Beckwith, [7]	5-23, 1833		Bridgeport.		
1021	Harriet Edwards, [7]	6-2, 1832	. . . .	Plattsville, Ct.		
1022	Emily Laura, [7]	11-1, 1835	5-10, 1857	Trumbull,	10-30, 1889	L. H. Tr.
	Sherwood S. Reynolds,	1-10, 1835				
	Children of 410 LUCINDA SUMMERS SEELEY, [6]					
1023	Fannie Maria Seeley, [7]	12-10, 1836	3-5, 1856	Bridgeport,	5-3, 1867	M. G. C. B. C.
	George Beckwith, [7]	5-23, 1833		"		

Children of *411* MIRANDA SUMMERS BEACH[6], *and 982.*

No.	Name	Born	Married/Died	Residence	Died
1024	Sheldena Amanda Beach, [7]	5-12, 1840	3-14, 1861	Virginia.	
	John Humpden Macrae, [7]	12-25, 1824			
1025	Martha Edwards, [7]				
1026	Elliott Edgar, [7]	8-12, 1845	8-13, 1870	Philadelphia.	
	Mary Harned, [7]	7-24, 1847		"	

Children of *412* STEPHEN SUMMERS,[6]

No.	Name	Born	Married/Died	Residence	Died
1027	George E. Summers, [7]		11-9, 1858	Birmingham, Ct.	
	Sarah Jane Noble, [7]			Southbury.	
1028	Jane M., [7]			Waterbury.	

Children of *420* SOLOMON SMITH BOOTH,[6]

No.	Name	Born	Married/Died	Residence	Died
1029	Henry Delos Booth, [7]	8-28, 1827		Catharine,	8-14, 1828
1030	Myron Delos, [7]	3-20, 1829		"	1-29, 1847
1031	Ann Elizabeth, [7]	7-24, 1831		Owego.	
1032	Emeline Archabel, [7]	4-30, 1833	3-1, 1854	Catharine.	
	Harman L. Estabrook, [7]			Ithaca.	
1033	Harriet Goodspeed, [7]	1-25, 1835	5-16, 1858	Catharine.	10-14, 1860
	William W. Whitney, M. D., [7]			Hartford, Wis.	
1034	Frances Terissa, [7]	11-20, 1838			9-22, 1841
1035	Ivah Adelia, [7]	12-20, 1840	12-18, 1868	Tioga.	
	Abram Horton, [7]				

Children of *421* Dr. WINTHROP E. BOOTH,[6]

No.	Name	Born	Married/Died	Residence	Died
1036	—— Booth, [7]			Watkins, N. Y.,	dec. inf.
1037	——, [7]			"	"
1038	——, [7]			"	"
1039	Henrietta M., [7]	7-13, 1845	6-6, 1867	Watkins.	
	E. Baxter Stull, [7]				
1040	John M., [7]	12-11, 1849		Valley City, N. D.	
	Mary Freer, [7]				
1041	Ebenezer S., ——, [7]	8-22, 1856		Watkins.	

No.	Name of Wife (or Husband).	Date of Birth.	Date of Marriage.	Residence.	Date of Death.	Place of Burial.
	Children of 422-4 SUSAN M. CARPENTER FARRINGTON,[6]					
1042	Elizabeth Farrington, [7]	10-8, 1850	3-12, 1878			
	Horace B. Stafford,					
1043	Ebenezer Ward, [7]	12-24, 1855	10-8, 1879			
	Estella F. Gerity,					
1044	Mary Ellen, [7]	6-13, 1868	10-22, 1879			
	John Cushing,					
	Children of 422-5 WINTHROP CARPENTER,[6]					
1045	Clarace Carpenter, [7]					
1046	Estella, [7]					
	Children of 426 FRANCES JONES HOOPER,[6]					
1047	William Wilberforce Hooper, [7]	1-2, 1816	12-23, 1852	Birmingham, Ala.,	186-	Alabama.
	Mary Jane Kearney,	8-10, 1830				
1048	Edward Jones, [7]	3-24, 1818	11-27, 1845	N. Car.,	10-21, 1850	N. Car.
	Amelia Jones (Massey),	11-27, 1821			10-17, 1851	"
1049	Mary Elizabeth, [7]	9-26, 1819	12-20, 1837	N. Car.,	6-23, 1894	O. C. Raleigh.
	Prof. J. De Berniere Hooper,	9-6, 1811			1-23, 1886	"
1050	Joseph Caldwell, [7]	10-27, 1823	1859	Jacksonville, Fla.,	5-29, 1892	Fayetteville.
	1055 Mary Eccles,[7]	1824		Fayetteville,	186-	
1051	Elizabeth Walters, [7]					
1052	Thomas Clark, [7]	11-15, 1827	11-26, 1849	Blackville, S. C.,	10-27, 1884	Blackville.
	Mary Elizabeth Stevenson,	10-10, 1828		Wilmington, N. C.,	3-20, 1894	Wilmington.
1053	Du Ponceau Jones, M. D., [7]	1831	unm.,	Fayetteville,	1863	Fayetteville.
	Children of 427 ELIZABETH JONES ECCLES,[6]					
1054	John Eccles, [7]	1821	unm.,	Fayetteville,	1862	Lake City, Fla.
1055	Mary Jones, [7]	10-27, 1823	3-23, 1859	Jacksonville, Fla.	5-29, 1892	Fayetteville.
	1050 Joseph Hooper,[7]	1821				

No.	Name						
1056	Frances, ... 7	}	3-22, 1825		1857	Jacksonville, Fla.	7-12, 1860	Oakland, Col. c. Miss
	Rev. Bazile Edward Lanneau, .		1830			Charleston, S. C., . .		Fayetteville
1057	Edward Jones, ... 7	}	1827			Fayetteville, . .	1843	
1058	Elizabeth, ... 7	}	1829		1853	Jacksonville.	11-16, 1883	Lake City, Fla.
	Duncan McLaurin, .		5-15, 1818			Jacksonville, Fla.,		
	Children of 428 CHARLOTTE JONES HARDIN,6							
1059	Edward Jones Hardin, . . . 7					Tyler, Tex.		
	Sophia Manly.							
1060	Cynthia Ellen, ... 7					Tyler, Tex.		
	Children of 430 LOUISA JONES RENCHOR,6							
1061	Mary Renchor, ... 7							
1062	John Renchor, ... 7							
1063	William, ... 7							
1064	Sarah, ... 7							
	Col. Latham (s. of Gov. A.) Anderson.							
1065	Eva, ... 7					Franklinton, N. C.	dec. inf.	
	Robert Winston, ...							
	Children of 432 MURPHY V. JONES,6 and 450,							
1066	Fanny Hooper Jones, . . . 7				1870	Greenville, Ala.,	dec.	
	J. R. Thames,							
1067	Elizabeth, ... 7				1878	Alabama.	dec.	
	Wright S. Massey, .							
1068	Murphy Renchor, . . . 7					Alabama.		
	___.							
	Children of 433 JOHNSTON JONES, M. D.,6							
1069	Mary de Berniere Jones, . . 7					Chapel Hill, N. C.,	dec.	Pittsboro, N. C.
	Thomas S. Armstead, .							
1070	Edward, ... 7						dec.	
1071	Johnson, ... 7					Charlotte.		
1072	Simmons Baker, M. D., . . 7					Charlotte.		
	Margaret Morehead.							

No.	Name of Wife (or Husband).	Date of Birth.	Date of Marriage.	Residence.	Date of Death.	Place of Burial.
1073	Annie Stuart, ...7			Charlotte.		
	1088 Lucian Walker.7					
1074	Caroline Daly, ...7			Charlotte.		
	Children of 436 SARAH JANE WALKER HALE.6					
1075	Peter Mallett Hale,6 . . .7			Fayetteville, . . .	dec.	Fayetteville.
	Mary Badger, ...					Raleigh.
1076	Sarah Caroline,7 . . .			Fayetteville, . . .	"	Fayetteville.
	George H. Haigh,7					
1077	Edward Joseph,7 . . .	12-25, 1889		Fayetteville.		
	Maria Rhett Hill,					
	Children of 439 MARY P. WALKER ADAMS.6					
1078	William Gilmer Adams,7 . .	6-4, 1848	12-27, 1871	Birmingham, Ala.		
	Ida Youngblood,7			Union Spr., Ala.		
1079	Caroline Mallett,7 . . .	12-14, 1849		Birmingham, . .	2-27, 1860	LaFayette, Ala.
1080	John Carlton,7	4-3, 1853		"	2-27, 1882	Opelika, Ala.
1081	Margaret Martha,7 . . .	2-24, 1856				
1082	De Berniere Owens,7 . .	10-1, 1857				
	Children of 440 PETER MALLETT WALKER.6					
1083	John Moseley Walker, . . .7	6-27, 1846	4-18, 1882	Fayetteville.		
	Mary Lippitt,7					
1084	Margaret Moore, ...7	4-7, 1852		Hickory, N. C.		
1085	Caroline Carlton, ...7	8-26, 1858		Richmond.		
	Children of 441 C. DE BERNIERE WALKER MALLETT,6 see 457.					

No.	Name	Gen.			Place	Note
	Children of 442 MARGARET WALKER WEBER,[6]					
1086	John Walker Weber,	7	5-2, 1853		Nashville.	
	Maude Groves,			3-18, 1879	"	
1087	Henri "Carleton,"	7	11-7, 1860		"	
	Beulah Beaumont,			6-13, 1882	Clarksville, Tenn.	
	Children of 443 JOHN MOSELEY WALKER,[6]					
1088	Lucian Holmes Walker,	7			Charlotte, N. C.	
	1073 Annie S. Jones,[7]					
1089	John Moseley,	7			Charlotte, N. C.	
1090	Caroline Mallett,	7			Greensboro.	dec. infancy
1091	Mary Fleming,	7			Hickory.	dec. infancy
1092	Eliza James,	7				
1093	Margaret Isabella,	7				
	Children of 444 CATHARINE B. WALKER HANKS,[6]					
1094	Carleton Walker Hanks,	7	12-, 1855		Charlotte.	
1095	Sarah Caroline,	7	1857		Pittsboro.	dec. infancy
1096	Thomas Ashe,	7	8-, 1860			
	Children of 448 ELIZA C. CAMPBELL SEWELL,[6]					
1097	Joseph Sewell,	7		1881	Mobile, Ala.	
	Florence Hamilton,					
	Children of 450 HENRIETTA M. CAMPBELL JONES,[6] *see 432.*					
	Children of 451 CARLTON JOHN CAMPBELL,[6]					
1098	Hugh Campbell,	7	1846		Fayetteville, N. C.,	dec.
1099	James Donald Angus,	7	1847		"	"
1100	Sophia Gibbs,	7	1850		Wilmington.	
	Children of 455 CAROLINE E. MALLETT HOOPER,[6]					
1101	Sophia Beatty Hooper,	7			Opelika, Ala.,	dec. child.

No.	Name of Wife (or Husband).	Date of Birth.	Date of Marriage.	Residence.	Date of Death.	Place of Burial.
1102	George William, 7			Opelika, Ala.,	9– , 1883	Opelika, Ala.
	Charlotte J. Waddell,					
1103	Charles Mallett, 7			Ocala, Fla.		
	Lucy Yonge,					
1104	Charlotte Mary, 7				dec.	
1105	William, 7				"	
1106	Archibald Maclaine, 7				"	
1107	Caroline Mallett, 7					
1108	John de Berniere, 7	3–23, 1853		Birmingham, Ala.		
1109	Caroline Alice, 7	4–1, 1857		Newark, N. J.		
	Children of 456 CHARLES BEATTIE MALLETT,[6]					
1110	John Wright Mallett, 7	10–15, 1842	11–20, 1873	Leighton, Ga.		
	Nannie Strange, 7	11–18, 1848				
1111	Charles Peter, 7	9–12, 1841	1867	Leighton, Ga.		
	Pattie Aiken, 7	12–12, 1846				
1112	William Anderson, 7	6–9, 1846		Fayetteville,	2–15, 1876	Fayetteville.
1113	Caroline Green, 7	4–29, 1848		"	3–16, 1847	"
1114	Margaret Anderson, 7	6–6, 1850				
1115	Charles Beattie, 7	11–27, 1851		Leighton.		
1116	Mercer, 7	5–1, 1854		Fayetteville,	1–24, 1875	Fayetteville.
1117	Alice Hazleton, 7	4–9, 1857		"		
	Children of 457 WILLIAM PETER MALLETT,[6] *and 441,*					
1118	Caroline Eliza Mallett, 7	6–21, 1812				
1119	Sophia Beatty, 7	3–7, 1847	1881	Chapel Hill.		
	Virginius St. Clair McNider, 7					
1120	John Walker, 7	3–14, 1852	1884	Chapel Hill.		
	Josephine Steele, 7					
1121	Mary Godena, 7	1856				

No.	Name		Born		Residence	Died	Death Place
	Children of 458 FRIDGE MALLETT,[6]						
1122	Virginia Mallett,	7	. .	. .	Niles, Mich.	1893	Niles.
	Landon.						
1123	Caroline,	7	. .	. .	Niles, Mich.		
	Jacks.						
1124	H. Seymour,	7	. .	. .	. .		
	Children of 459 PETER MALLETT,[6]						
1125	Susan Gibbs Mallett,	7	10– , 1849		Wilmington, N. C.	1–5, 1881	
	Gabriel Holmes.						
1126	Charles Edward,	7	1851	1890	Brooklyn.		
	Ida Beach.						
1127	Robert Gibbs,	7	3–27, 1853		Birmingham, Ala.		
1128	James Fleming,	7	1856		Brooklyn.		
1129	Colden Murray,	7	1858			1859	Wilmington.
1130	Eugene Pierre, M. D.,	7	4–1, 1861		Atchison, Kan.		
1131	George Hooper, M. D.,	7	5–5, 1863		New York.		
1132	Richard,	7	1866			1866	Wilmington.
	Children of 460 EDWARD MALLETT,[6]						
1133	Sally Smith Mallett,	7	1850	unm.,			
1134	Simmons Baker, M. D.,	7	1852		Texas.		
1135	Joseph Hunter,	7	1854		Ocala, Fla.	1870	Opelika, Ala.
1136	Pattie,	7	1857		Hickory, N. C.		
	Oliver Royster.						
1137	Johnson de Berniere,	7	. .	. .	. .	dec.	
	Children of 463 CECIL MALLETT,[6]						
1138	May Mallett,	7	5–28, 1875		Bastrop, La.		
1139	Lilie,	7	4–2, 1877		"		
1140	Cecil,	7	2–17, 1879		"		
1141	Ernest Green,	7	3–10, 1880		"		
1142	Carrie,	7	12–7, 1882		"		
1143	Charles Pierre,	7	11–30, 1885		"		
1144	Earl,	7	4–27, 1889		"	9–28, 1890	Bastrop.
1145	Virginia,	7	10–22, 1892		"		

No.	Name of Wife (or Husband).	Date of Birth.	Date of Marriage.	Residence.	Date of Death.	Place of Burial.
	Children of 465 HERBERT MALLETT,[6]					
1146	Herbert Mallett,[7]	10-9, 1875		Bastrop.		
	Children of 467 SARAH L. MALLETT EVEREST,[6]					
1147	Sarah Louisa Everest,[7]				dec.	
	Children of 468 MARGARET I. MALLETT SMITH,[6]					
1148	Lothrop Lewis Smith, Jr.,[7]	1849	unm.,			
1149	Johnson Mallett "de Berniere,"[7]	3-19, 1853	9 17, 1878	London, Eng.	1885	Stockton, Cal.
	Margaret Zoe Ford,					
1150	Percy Hamilton Mallett,[7]	1-18, 1856	10-25, 1887	Brooklyn, N. Y.		
	Emily E. Parsons,	8-4, 1864				
1151	Logan McKnight,[7]	1-31, 1859	unm.,		3- , 1891	Palestine, Tex.
	Children of 470 SARAH F. MALLETT LEE,[6]					
1152	Edward Jones Lee,[7]	7-9, 1843				
1153	James Fenner,[7]	12-25, 1839	6-28, 1866	Baltimore, Maryland.		
	Mary Cornelia Read (Carroll),	11-2, 1845		"		
1154	Julian Henry,[7]	4-5, 1853	6-1, 1873	"		
	Elizabeth Dawson Tyson,	12-18, 1855		Baltimore.		
1155	Hilyard Cameron,	6-14, 1858		"		
1156	Amabel,	3-25, 1858	12-18, 1879	"		
	John Cowman George,				dec.	
	Children of 471 JAMES FENNER MALLETT,[6]					
1157	James Fenner Mallett, Jr.,[7]	5-11, 1851				
1158	George Steinhauer,[7]	12-3, 1852				
1159	Robert Sterry,[7]	6-29, 1856				
1160	William Paul Russell,[7]	7-17, 1859				

Children of *472* CHARLES PETER MALLETT,[6]

No.	Name	Gen.	Birth	Death
1161	Edward Jones Mallett,	7	11–16, 1847	7–22, 1848
1162	Ellen Madeline de Berniere,	7	5–20, 1850	
	Elliott.			
1163	Arthur Fenner,	7		
1164	Charles Pierre,	7	4–26, 1857	dec.

Children of *474* ELLEN MALLETT CAMERON,[6]

No.	Name	Gen.	Birth	Death
1165	Allan Cameron,	7		
	Florence Grissell.			
1166	Ellen Elizabeth,	7		
	Arthur Spragge.			
1167	Madeline de Berniere,	7		
	Foster.			
1168	Frank Robert,	7		dec.
1169	Kenneth,	7		

Children of *478* AMY MALLETT MURRAY,[6]

No.	Name	Gen.	Birth	Death
1170	Mary Amy Murray,	7	10–15, 1860	
1171	Edith Bruce,	7	11–7, 1861	
1172	Davidson Munroe,	7	9–12, 1863	
1173	Sarah Fenner,	7	3–8, 1865	
1174	Julian Harry,	7	10–16, 1867	dec.
1175	Amy Fenner,	7	6–15, 1870	

Children of *479* EDWARD JONES MALLETT, JR.,[6]

No.	Name	Gen.	Birth	Death
1176	Therese Mallett,	7		dec.
1177	Therese Mallett,	7		"

Children of *480* WILLIAM SMITH MALLETT,[6]

No.	Name	Gen.	Birth	Death
1178	Louisa Mallett,	7		
1179	Thomas,	7		
1180	Ellen Sophia,	7		
1181	Harriet,	7		

No.	Name of Wife (or Husband).	Date of Birth.	Date of Marriage.	Residence.	Date of Death.	Place of Burial.
	*Children of 485 MORDECAI MALLET,*⁶					
1182	—— Mallett, ⁷					
1183	——, ⁷					
	*Children of 491 ADALINE C. MALLETT WYCKOFF,*⁶					
1184	Adaline Mallett Wyckoff, ⁷	5-20, 1852	1-24, 1884		5-22, 1891	Denver, Col.
1185	*Joseph S. Foulke,*	9-11, 1862		Denver.		
1186	Dayton Ludlow, ⁷	8-17, 1854			8-9, 1861	Bushwick, L. I.
	Elizabeth, ⁷	4-19, 1856	12-15, 1880			
	Harry Foulke,	9-1, 1858				
1187	George Harry, ⁷	6-20, 1861			4-18, 1863	New York.
	*Children of 492 ELIZA MALLETT STUART,*⁶					
1188	Laura "Minerva" Stuart, ⁷	3-26, 1831	5-18, 1850	Millport.	4-10, 1874	Millport.
	Nathaniel Goodwin,	1-24, 1824				
1189	George, ⁷	7-4, 1835	7-4, 1858			
	Sarah A. Gary,	5-30, 1842				
1190	Mary "Elizabeth," ⁷	1-4, 1841	12-2, 1855	Millport.		
	Robert Goodwin,	2-19, 1829				
	*Children of 493 "ERA" COUCHLIN MALLETT,*⁶					
1191	Sherman Mallett, ⁷				dec.	
1192	Sarah, ⁷				dec. inf.	
1193	William, ⁷	1836?		Havana.		
1194	Mary, ⁷	1851?	11-22, 1893			
	Robert Ralph Erskine, ⁷			Battle Creek, Mich.		
1195	George, ⁷				dec.	
	*Children of 494 LUCY MALLETT COUCH,*⁶					
1196	Mary Couch, ⁷	1831	1863	Odessa.	1860	Odessa, N. Y.
	George James Chapman,	1828				

No.	Name	Gen	Born	Married	Residence	Died	Death Place
1197	Edward J.,	[7]	1832		Iowa.		
	Anna Maria Littler,		1-25, 1843			8-29, 1871	
1198	Esther,	[7]	1832			1861	Odessa.
	George Carpenter,		9-28, 1827	1856	Odessa.		
1199	Emily,	[7]	1834		Odessa.		
1200	Samuel T.,	[7]	2-8, 1838		Odessa.		
	Vian Woodward,		8-11, 1839	8-11, 1862			
1201	Myron,	[7]	1843	unm.,		5-5, 1865	
	Children of 495 A. ALANSON MALLETT.[6]						
1202	Amarilla Mallett,	[7]	1835?	5-18, 1850		1872? dec.	Millport.
	Matthew Christman,						
1203	Eunice,	[7]	5-4, 1837	8-, 1867			
	John Sterling,				Gilletts, Pa.		
	Charles Ostrander.		11-25, 1826	12-25, 1872	Odessa.	10-11, 1869	Millport.
1204	Ephraim,	[7]	8-11, 1841	11-, 1861	Odessa.		
	Jennie Lottie Hamilton,						
	Mary Woodward,			3-18, 1874			
	Children of 496 DANIEL MALLETT.[6]						
1205	Richard Mallett,	[7]	3-20, 1835		Millport.	1-3, 1888	Millport.
1206	Sylvester Fellows,	[7]	10-15, 1837	11-4, 1864	Fairmont, W. Va.	2-1, 1884	Rowellsburg, W. Va.
	Ella Courtney,						
1207	"Ellen" Jane,	[7]	3-17, 1840		W. Virginia.		
	James Woodward,						
1208	"Henry" Wisner,	[7]	8-10, 1841		Howard City, Mich.	8-9, 1891	Howard City.
	Dell Hastings,						
1209	"Francis" Asbury,	[7]	8-27, 1843		Millport.		
	Ellen Maria Sinclair,		3-22, 1851				
	Children of 497 J. NASH MALLETT.[6]						
1210	Mary A. Mallett,	[7]	8-24, 1834	4-28, 1856	Buffalo Prairie, Ill.	6-29, 1858	
	James Kinnaman,		1-17, 1828	11-10, 1859	Laurens, Ia.		
	Ransom Ferguson,						
1211	Abram W.,	[7]	6-10, 1836	4-, 1859	Huntington, Neb.	10-, 1860	
	Nancy Hayes,						
	Leah Tyrrell.						
1212	Isaac D.,	[7]	4-8, 1838	1866	Gilman, Ia.		
	Amarillas Wynn,		7-8, 1849				

No.	Name of Wife (or Husband).	Date of Birth.	Date of Marriage.	Residence.	Date of Death.	Place of Burial.
1213	Rhoda, ... 7	11-24, 1840	3- , 1867	Illinois Cy, Ill.		
	Peter Seedam, . . .			Audobon, Ia.		
	George Chamberlain, .					
1214	Adelia, ... 7	4-25, 1843	. . . , 1866			
	Wiley T. Jackson, . .		1-1, 1866	Wichita, Kas.		
1215	Jacob W. 7	7-2, 1845	2-9, 1881	Guthrie, Ia.		
	Alice Summers, . .					
	Emma Nagel, . . .					
1216	Jerome W., ... 7	9-30, 1847		Guthrie, Ia.		
	Catharine Krontz, . .					
1217	Albert R. 7	6-5, 1850	9-19, 1869	Marshalltown, Ia.		
	Hattie Fagan, . . .					
1218	Charlotte Ersulia, . . 7	11-2, 1854	9-9, 1873	Hartwick, Ia.		
	Decatur Parks, . .	12-4, 1850				
	Children of 498 Isaac D. Mallett.6					
1219	John "Wesley" Mallette, . 7	11-24, 1836	1871	Bennettsburg, N.Y.		
	Eleanor Smith, . . .					
1220	Rebecca, ... 7	2-24, 1840	10-4, 1865	Millport.		
	Julius Lattin, . . .	10-4, 1840		?		
1221	Jane, ... 7	5-10, 1842	unm., . .		6-27, 1859	Millport.
	Children of 499 George B. Mallett.6					
1222	William "Smith" Malette, . 7	10-21, 1837	5-23, 1861	Elmira.		
	Lestina Tanner, . . .	5-30, 1842		Millport.		
1223	"John" Fiddler, . . . 7	1-12, 1840	8-14, 1869	Rochester.		
	Adeline M. Benham, . .	7-7, 1847		Watkins.		
	Children of 500 Genet Mallett Denson.6					
1224	John Denson, . . . 7	1849		May's Point, N.J.		
	Julia Gowers.					
1225	Frank, ... 7		1-26, 1872	Bennettsburg, N.Y.		
	Eva King,			Catharine.		

No.	Name	Gen	Born	1888?	Place		
1226	Charles,	7		1888?			
	Children of 501 ARRON MALLETT,6						
1227	Mary Jane Mallett,	7	10-17, 1840		Danbury, Ct.		
1228	Arron Hill,	7	9-11, 1856	8-21, 1878	"		
	Effie Aruminta Barnum,		3-4, 1862				
	Children of 508 SAMUEL MALLETT,6						
1229	Elizabeth Turney Mallett,	7	1851	1874	New Haven.		
	Walter Judson, M. D.,	7			"		
1230	"Samuel" Sanford,	7	1852		Albany, N. Y.		
	Carrie Catchum,						
1231	Daniel "Trowbridge,"	7	1862	6-11, 1890	New York.		
	Aleine Rowland,						
	Children of 508 SARAH AVERILL BCAON,6						
1232	Marilla Bacon,	7	1849		Wheatland, Wis.		
1233	Ruth Naomi,	7					
	Children of 509 AMANDA AVERILL SMITH,6						
1234	Harriet Smith,	7		10-17, 1876	Rochester.		
	William Cramer,	7			"		
1235	Edward, ——,	7					
1236	Florence, ———,	7			Rochester.		
	Children of 511 LEVI AVERILL,6						
1237	Anna Averill,	7			Elmira.		
	J. A. Price, M. D.,	7					
1238	Louisa,	7		12-18, 1883	Horseheads, N. Y.		
	Louis Van Duzer,	7					
	Children of 512 ISAAC B. MALLETT,6						
1239	Son, ——,	7	7-12, 1832	1-3, 1856	Geneva, N. Y.		
1240	James B. Mallette,	7	10-, 1832	unm.,		9-20, 1885	Geneva.
	Rachel H. McKendric,	7	1834			3-2, 1859	Clifton Spr.
1241	John W.,	7					

No.	Name of Wife (or Husband).	Date of Birth.	Date of Marriage.	Residence.	Date of Death.	Place of Burial.
1242	Charlotte E., ... 7	2-17, 1837	11-12, 1857	Clifton Spr.	9-28, 1894	Clifton Spr.
	James Watson Griffith,	3-25, 1830		"	11-11, 1891	
1243	Sarah Jane, ... 7	9-22, 1839				
	John Garlock, . . .	8-12, 1839	3-4, 1860	Palmyra, N. Y.		
	Children of 513 SALLY MALLETT BACON,[6]					
1244	David G. Bacon, ... 7	5-15, 1840	unm., ...	Arizona.		
1245	Charles, ... 7	10-19, 1848			1861	Missouri.
1246	Elizabeth, ... 7	5-11, 1846		Wheatland, Wis., Catharine.		Catharine.
	Sevellon A. (s. of John) Stuart, .	4-2, 1844	12- , 1867		1-12, 1881	
	Children of 515 LEVI STOCKER MALLETT,[5]					
1247	Harriet Mallett, ... 7	6-30, 1842	3-17, 1869	N. Elmira.	1-12, 1865	Salisbury, N. C.
	Samuel Scott, ... 7	8-13, 1845	unm., ...		1- , 1847	
1248	Huson William, ... 7	9- , 1846				
1249	Maria, ... 7					
	Children of 516 JESSE MALLETT,[6]					
1250	Helen Mallett, ... 7	6-17, 1852	6-17, 1882	Omaha, Neb.		
	Nelson Swanson,					
1251	Emma, ... 7	12-19, 1854	5-8, 1878	LeRoy, N. Y.		
	Eugene Cochran, . . .					
1252	Jessie Caroline, ... 7	11-1, 1857	. . . . .	LeRoy, N. Y.	8-20, 1869	LeRoy, N. Y.
1253	Clotilda, ... 7	7-22, 1861	12-27, 1884	Port Gibson, N. Y.		
	Alva Sibbett, ...					
1254	Levi, ... 7	10-17, 1863	. . . . .	. . . . .	4-9, 1869	LeRoy, N. Y.
1255	Arthur, ... 7	8-31, 1868	unm., ...		7-6, 1889	LeRoy, N. Y.
1256	William Jesse, ... 7	9-24, 1870		LeRoy.		Catharine.

Children of 518 LUCY A. MALLETT HALL,⁶

No.	Name	Gen.	Birth		Place	
1257	Emeline Hall,	7	1-9, 1858	6-5, 1892	Millport.	
	William Davis,		1838		"	
1258	Walter,	7	5-16, 1863		Millport.	4-28, 1872
1259	Herbert,	7	11-24, 1870		"	8- , 1878

Children of 520 MINERVA HUBBELL BLACKMAN,⁶

No.	Name	Gen.				
1260	Daniel Blackman,	7				
1261	Mary,	7				
1262	Eliza,	7				
1263	Sally,	7				
1264	Paulina,	7				
1265	Phebe,	7				
1266	George,	7				
1267	Munson,	7				

Children of 522 MELINDA BENNETT HALL,⁶

No.	Name	Gen.	Birth		Place	
1268	Beach Hall,	7	6-28, 1830	2-11, 1852	Trumbull.	
	Amelia Buck,					
1269	Louisa,	7	3-5, 1832		Trumbull.	
1270	Bennett,	7	7-22, 1834	5-29, 1860	Carthage, Mo.	
	Isabel Smith,		10-4, 1838			
1271	Pauline,	7	11-12, 1837		Trumbull.	
1272	Horace,	7	4-3, 1842		"	
1273	Clarissa,	7	3-18, 1844		"	
1274	Ormel,	7	10-17, 1845			

Children of 523 EMILY MALLETT NICHOLS,⁶

No.	Name	Gen.	Birth		Place	
1275	"Sylvia" Marina Nichols,	7	1-5, 1828	11-9, 1851	Tashua.	
	Horace Northrop,		12-12, 1827		Newtown, Ct.	
1276	"Stephen" Gregory,	7	5-31, 1829	12-29, 1869	Stepney, Ct.	11-21, 1892 Perth Amboy, N. J.
	Elizabeth Maria Rawson,		12-29, 1844		Hornellsville, N.Y.	
1277	Hannah "Amanda,"	7	10-13, 1831		Tashua.	
1278	Huldah "Augusta,"	7	3-11, 1834		"	
	Henry E. Hurd,		7-13, 1828	12-30, 1863	Monroe.	
1279	Sarah Jane,	7	2-21, 1836		Tashua.	

No.	Name of Wife (or Husband).	Date of Birth.	Date of Marriage.	Residence.	Date of Death.	Place of Burial.
1280	John Edwards, [7]	4-19, 1840	unm, ...	Tashua, ...	10-15, 1873	Tashua.
	Children of 524 CHARLES MALLETT,[6]					
1281	Anna Smith Mallett, ...[7]	11-7, 1845	....	Washington, D. C.		
	Children of 526 HULDAH MALLETT JACKSON,[6]					
1282	Huldah "Catharine" Jackson, [7]	1-8, 1836	9-16, 1855	Monroe.	8-23, 1891	Monroe.
	557 *Martin "Jerome" Mallet,[6]*	9-7, 1831		"	8-14, 1839	Tashua.
1283	Daughter, [7]	8-7, 1839		Stepney,	11-11, 1844	"
1284	Isaac Edwards, [7]	8-16, 1842		?		
1285	John Marcellus, [7]	4-7, 1845		"		
1286	Charles Judson, [7]	11-11, 1847		Trumbull.		
	Julia (d. of Nath'l) Sterling,					
	Children of 527 LOUISA MALLETT SHELTON,[6]					
1287	Mary Louisa Shelton, [7]	2-18, 1812	9-30, 1863	Huntington, Ct.		
	2190 *Henry Charles Fairchild,[8]*	7-17, 1842		Bridgeport.		
1288	John Consider, [7]	7-8, 1853	3-1, 1881	"		
	Jennie E. Watson,	8-1, 1853				
	Children of 528 CHARITY MALLETT SHERMAN,[6]					
1289	Isaac Edwards Sherman, [7]	10- , 1849	10-18, 1871	Tampa, Fla.	1885	Norfolk, Va.
	Eliza Sherwood,			Bridgeport,		
	Alice G. (d. of Wm.) Woodruff,		11-10, 1887	Canandaigua, N. Y.		
	Children of 530 GEORGE W. MALLETT,[6]					
1290	Adelaide Augusta Mallett, [7]	3-21, 1840	10 21, 1857	Lexington, O.		
	William Lane Harrod,	8-8, 1835				
1291	Isabella Amanda, [7]	11-30, 1844	1-1, 1873	Hudson, Mich.		
	Munson L. Squire,	1845				
1292	Morse George, [7]	1-9, 1848			4-11, 1855	Sherman, O.

Children of *532* CHARLES E. MALLETT,⁶

No.	Name					
1293	Stephen Edward Mallett, 7	12-19, 1839	12-6, 1882	Concordia, Kan.		
	Mary Cole,	1-14, 1853				
1294	Dorothy Elizabeth,⁷	8-29, 1841			3-14, 1843	Lyme, O.
1295	Betsey Ann,⁷	1-14, 1844	4-14, 1873	Norwalk, O.		
	Henry Griswold,	7-6, 1826				
1296	*Dorothy,*	10-30, 1845			10-16, 1890	Lyme, O.
1297	Isaac,⁷	4-28, 1848	1-14, 1879	Garden Grove, Ia.	9-7, 1847	"
	Susie Young,	7-10, 1856				
1298	Charles D.,⁷	11-17, 1849	1-17, 1884	Garden Grove, Ia.		
	Emeline Manny,	3-15, 1855		Plymouth, Wis.		
1299	Harriet,⁷	1-3, 1851		Bridgman, Mich.	7-20, 1854	Lyme, O.
1300	Sylvanus,⁷	11-2, 1853		Keokuk, Iowa.		
	Araminta Stotts,	11-24, 1858	11-28, 1893	Bellevue.		
1301	Angeline,⁷	3-9, 1858				

Children of *533* SAMUEL E. MALLETT,⁶ and *538.*

No.	Name					
1302	Charity Edwards Mallett,⁷	5-15, 1849	6-30, 1874	Easton, Ct.,	1-15, 1876	M. G. C. B. C.
	*Everett L. Spencer,*⁷			Norwich, Ct.		
1303	Daniel "Sylvanus" Sterling,⁷	7-23, 1854		Easton.		

Children of *534* SHERMAN MALLETT,⁶

No.	Name					
1304	"Jennie" Verona Mallett,⁷	6-5, 1862		Tashua.	10-16, 1863	Tashua.
1305	Charlotte Amy,⁷	8-1, 1863		"		
1306	"Charles" Sherman,⁷	5-28, 1865	9-16, 1891	Easton.		
	*Florence (d. of Wakeman) Williams,*⁷					
1307	Mary "Elizabeth,"⁷	9-11, 1867	11-28, 1889	Tashua.		
	*Oliver Northrop,*⁷	10-30, 1861		Newtown.		

Children of *535* ELIZABETH MALLETT PEET,⁶

No.	Name			
1308	William Peet,⁷	6-15, 1849	Concord, Va.	
1309	Emma,⁷	6-9, 1852	Nichols, Ct.	
1310	Evanna,⁷	2-18, 1854	"	
1311	Gertrude,⁷	11-26, 1858	"	

No.	Name of Wife (or Husband).	Date of Birth.	Date of Marriage.	Residence.	Date of Death.	Place of Burial.
	Children of 586 MORSE D. MALLETT,[6]					
1312	George Dimon Mallett. . . . .[7]	8-20, 1854	10-25, 1882	Tashua.		
	Arabella Eliza (d. of Chas.) Sterling.	6-11, 1859				
	Children of 587 JEROME MALLETT,[6] *and 1282,*					
1313	Frank A. Mallett, ...[7]	10-27, 1856				
	Carrie J. Lake, ...[7]	5-28, 1861	2-21, 1884	Monroe.		
1314	"Ida" Marian, ...[7]	8-20, 1860	10-30, 1880	Monroe.		
	Frank Beardsley, ...	11-25, 1857		"		
	Children of 538 ELIZA EDWARDS MALLETT,[6] *see 533,*					
	Children of 540 SHELDON LEAVITT,[6]					
1315	Frances Isabel Leavitt, ...[7]	11-2, 1842	10-30, 1861	Gr. Rapids, M.		
	Levi Shultus, ...[7]			"		
1316	Sylvia E., ...[7]	8-2, 1844	6-7, 1865	Lyons, M.	1889	Gr. Rapids.
	Lyman Hizer, ...[7]	3-23, 1831				
1317	Amanda, ...[7]	4-9, 1848		Chicago.		
1318	Sheldon, M. D., ...[7]	7-, 1847	12-24, 1868	Portland, Mich.	dec.	
	Marcella E. Smith, ...[7]	10-22, 1850		Gr. Rapids.		
1319	Martha, ...[7]	2-13, 1850	12-27, 1870	"		
	Rev. Wilbur Israel Cogshall, . .	5-20, 1852				
1320	David, ...[7]	3-9, 1854			10-26, 1861	
1321	Adelman, ...[7]	11-10, 1861			5-, 1872	
1322	Frederick E., M. D., ...[7]	6-12, 1863	8-14, 1882	St. Paul, Minn.		
	L. Eva Avery, ...[7]			Centreville, Mich.		
1323	David Sherwood, ...[7]	12-23, 1870	12-31, 1890	Stepney, Ct.		
	Betsey Maranda Peet, ...	10-12, 1869				
	Children of 541 PHEBE ANN LEAVITT GUILD,[6]					
1324	(son) Guild, ...[7]					dec.
1325	Joel, ...[7]	1842			dec. 1861-5	

1826	Gilbert, ...	7	4– , 1853		Gd. Rapids.	
1327	*Children of 542* JOHN LEAVITT,[6] Mary V. Leavitt, ... *Earle A. Hoag*, ...	7	12-19, 1854 1-20, 1854	12-13, 1882	"	
1328	*Children of 544* SARAH LEAVITT TERRILL,[6] Olive Mallett Terrill, . . .	7	3-1, 1843			
1329	Elida, ...	7	12-7, 1844			
1330	*Children of 545* GEORGE LEAVITT,[6] Carrie Leavitt, ...	7				dec.
1331	Juliet, . *Towser, M. D.*, . .	7		unm.,	Caledonia, Mich.	
1332	——, ...	7				
1333	Son, ...	7				
1334	"	7				dec.
1335	*Children of 546* JOHN MALLETT,[6] Sarah Maria Mallett, ... *Joseph A. Treadwell*, . . .	7	4-5, 1838 8-12, 1834	10-7, 1857	Tashua. "	
1336	*Children of 547* FANNY MALLETT WAKELY HALL,[6] "Mary" Elizabeth Wakely, . . *George Thompson*, . . .	7	12-16, 1843 4-16, 1844	12-22, 1864	Trumbull. Stamford, Ct.	
1837	Miles Burton "Lewis," . . . *Julia M. Hoyt*, . . .	7	2-6, 1845 5-3, 1854	12-22, 1872	L. H. Trumbull. "	
1338	"Fannie" Augusta Hall, . . .	7	5-20, 1856		"	
1339	Sarah Mallett, ... *John Marcus Haugh*, . .	7	8-20, 1857 6-17, 1858	7-17, 1886	"	
1340	Cornelia, ... *Charles Prindle Jennings*, .	7	8-19, 1856 8-9, 1861	6-8, 1878	"	
1341	Charles Austin, ... *Mary Dayton*, . . .	7	6-10, 1866	10-24, 1886	Newtown.	
1842	Clara Louisa, ...	7	2-11, 1870		L. H. Tr.	

No.	Name of Wife (or Husband).	Date of Birth.	Date of Marriage.	Residence.	Date of Death.	Place of Burial.
	Children of 548 MELINDA MALLETT WAKELEY.[6]					
1343	"Melvin" Abijah Wakely, . . . [7]	8-30, 1848	⎱ 12-24, 1867	Trumbull.		
	Abigail E. Williams, . . . [7]	2-11, 1850	⎰			
1344	Harriet "Estella," . . . [7]	8-30, 1854		Trumbull.		
1345	"Annie" Loretta, . . . [7]	7-14, 1863	⎱ 10-25, 1882	"		
	2574 John W. Treadwell, . . .	5-18, 1859	⎰			
	Children of 550 MUNSON MALLETT,[6]					
1346	Frances Isabella Mallett, . . . [7]	1-31, 1850	⎱ 4-21, 1874	L. H. Trum.		
	John Kennedy, . . . [7]	4-21, 1851	⎰	"		
	Children of 553 HANNAH MALLETT Hall.[7]					
1347	Priscilla Amanda Hall, . . . [8]	2-26, 1827	⎱ 8-1, 1852	Stepney, Ct.		
	George M. Curtis, . . .	12-3, 1831	⎰	"		
1348	Daniel Mallett. . . . [8]	10-11, 1828	⎰ 5-30, 1852	"		
	Sarah A. Curtis, . . .		⎱ 9-26, 1880			
	Frances E. Clark, . . .					
1349	Mary, . . . [8]	10-17, 1830	unm,, ...	Stepney, Ct.	6-6, 1855	Stepney.
1350	David, . . . [8]	4-18, 1832	"	"	8-11, 1849	"
1351	Mary Esther, . . . [8]	3-9, 1837				
1352	Benjamin Turney (Rev.), . . [8]	11-7, 1838	⎱ 3-27, 1860	Pleasantville, N. Y.		
	Laura A. Ford, . . .		⎰ 5-24, 1866			
	Emily Kenfield, . . .					
	Children of 554 MARCUS BEACH MALLETT.[7]					
1353	Sarah Elizabeth Mallett, . . . [8]	2-29, 1832	⎱ 10-3, 1854			
	Arza C. Morris, . . .	8-10, 1828	⎰			
1354	"Burr," . . . [8]	2-25, 1834	⎰ 9-28, 1856		10-2, 1856	O. C. Bridgewater.
	Mary E. (d. of Grandison R.) Warner,	2-14, 1836	⎱ 6-1, 1861			
	Emelia C. (d. of Fred.) Boland, . . .	1-22, 1885				
1355	Alvira, . . . [8]	7-25, 1840	⎱ 11-4, 1861		5-30, 1868	Bridgewater.
	Levi W. Warner, . . .	6-10, 1888	⎰			

No.	Name		Birth	Marriage	Place	Death	Death Place
	Children of 555 DANIEL A. MALLETT,⁷						
1356	Margaret Ann Mallett,	.⁸	4-23, 1838	. . . .	Stratford, Ct.	11-11, 1840	Stratford.
1357	Margaret A.,	.⁸	9-2, 1841	. . . .	"		
1358	Isabella,	.⁸	1-20, 1844	. . . .	"	5-22, 1894	Stratford.
	John Beach,		1848	4-29, 1869	"		
	Children of 556 HULDAH MALLETT BURCH,⁷						
1359	Arresta Burch,	.⁸	. .	2-10, 1861			
	Wilbur Selleck,		. .				
1360	Elosia Ann,	.⁸	. .				
	Children of 557 POLLY ANN MALLETT ISBELL,⁷						
1361	Mary Isbell,	.⁸	. .	unm.			
1362	William,	.⁸	. .			dec.	
1363	George, ——,	.⁸	. .		Woodbury.		Woodbury, Ct.
	Children of 558 HARVEY MALLETT,⁷						
1364	Albert Beach Mallett,	.⁸	12-21, 1845	5-13, 1868	Bridgewater.	9-11, 1884	Bridgewater.
	Betsie Maria Frost,		6-14, 1849				
	Children of 559 ELIZA JENNETT MALLETT RICHMOND,⁷						
1365	Anna Richmond.	.⁸					
1366	Sherman,	.⁸					
	Children of 560 SUSAN MALLETT ISBELL,⁷						
1367	Charles Isbell,	.⁸					
1368	Isabella,	.⁸					
	Frank Knox.						
1369	Frank,	.⁸					
	Children of 561 EUNICE MALLETT MINOR,⁷						
1370	Sarah Emeline Minor,	.⁸	12-25, 1845	10-22, 1863	Bridgeport.		
	Franklin A. Warner,		9-9, 1842		New Milford.		

No.	Name of Wife (or Husband).	Date of Birth.	Date of Marriage.	Residence.	Date of Death.	Place of Burial.
1371	Charles E., ...8	4-29, 1848	2-17, 1869	Newtown.	5-11, 1860	Bridgewater.
	Naomi R. Beardsley,	2-17, 1850			4-20, 1855	Newtown.
1372	Garrey P., ...8	5-20, 1850				
1373	William Harvey, ...8	11-8, 1853				
1374	Eunice "Adelia," 8	11-11, 1855	8-1, 1878	Newtown.		
	James Partridge,	4-22, 1834				
1375	Daniel Edwin, ...8	12-13, 1857				
	Katie Wengel,	8-23, 1859	4-, 1879			
1376	Lizzie A., ...8	5-24, 1860	10-13, 1880	Hattertown, Ct.,		
	Edward Booth,	3-7, 1844				
1377	Alice Amanda, ...8	4-9, 1865		"	4-3, 1872	

Children of 562 SARAHETT MALLETT McKINNEY,[7]

No.	Name of Wife (or Husband).	Date of Birth.	Date of Marriage.	Residence.	Date of Death.	Place of Burial.
1378	Hattie McKinney, ...8			Danbury.		
	Charles Ball,					

Children of 563 EMELINE MALLETT DAYTON,[7]

No.	Name of Wife (or Husband).	Date of Birth.	Date of Marriage.	Residence.	Date of Death.	Place of Burial.
1379	Charles Dayton,[7] ...8					
1380	Adela, ...8					
1381	Carrie, ...8					

Children of 564 CHARLES MALLETT,[7]

No.	Name of Wife (or Husband).	Date of Birth.	Date of Marriage.	Residence.	Date of Death.	Place of Burial.
1382	Daniel E. Mallett, ..8	10-4, 1854	10-4, 1883	Woodbury, Ct.		
	Lilian G. Winton,					
1383	George H., ...8	10-14, 1857	10-9, 1878	Woodbury, Ct.		
	Cornelia Smith,					
1384	Carrie A., ...8	11-4, 1867		Woodbury, Ct.		

Children of 565 LAURA LYON FOOTE,[7]

No.	Name of Wife (or Husband).	Date of Birth.	Date of Marriage.	Residence.	Date of Death.	Place of Burial.
1385	Harriet Foote, ...8	1834				
	Harrison Van Orden,					

					Michigan.		
1386	Eli,	.	.	.	.		
	Children of *566* CATHARINE LEYON GILBERT,⁷						
1387	Sarah Gilbert,	8	5-27, 1825	unm,	Trumbull,	9-16, 1878	Easton, Ct.
1388	Marietta,	8	4-11, 1827	"	"		
1389	Frances Janet,	8	8-7, 1829	"			
1390	Hannah Jane,	8	12-10, 1832	1850		4-2, 1888	Easton, Ct.
	*643 John Calvin Beach,*⁷	.					
1391	Emeline,	8	12-11, 1835	12-10, 1852	Trumbull.		
	William B. Wakeman,	.					
1392	Amanda Louisa,	8	2-16, 1838	.	Trumbull,	1-6, 1843	Easton, Ct.
	Children of *567* MAHALA MALLETT WOODIN,⁷						
1393	Milton Austin Woodin,	8	7-5, 1844				
1394	Edward,	8	1845				
	Estelle,	.					
	Children of *568* ESTHER JANE MALLETT WAYLAND,⁷						
1395	Mary C. Wayland,	8	10-18, 1841				
1396	Helen Mahala,	8	4-19, 1843	6-24, 1874			
	Philo James Burr,	.	2-18, 1840				
	Children of *569* MARY FRANCES MALLETT TILFORD,⁷						
1397	Arthur Reed Tilford,	8	12-27, 1851	.	L. H. Tr.,	12-27, 1857	L. H. Tr.
1398	Homer Herrick,	8	7-24, 1864	.	L. H. "	8-6, 1864	L. H. "
	Children of *571* CHARITY NICHOLS MALLETT.⁷ *See 228.*						
	Children of *572* AMELIA M. MALLETT BANKS,⁷						
1399	Horace Marsena Banks,	8	12-11, 1843				
1400	Sarah Louisa,	8	8-21, 1845				
1401	"Harriet" Amelia,	8	8-6, 1847	2-11, 1868			
	Andrew Barnum Curtis,	.	7-25, 1844				

No.	Name of Wife (or Husband).	Date of Birth.	Date of Marriage.	Residence.	Date of Death.	Place of Burial.
1402	"Sylvina" Antoinette, ... 8	8-1, 1850				
	Children of 574 JOHN SILLIMAN MALLETTE,[7]					
1403	"Eliza" Amelia Mallette, . . . 8	10-1, 1852				
1404	George Whitefield, ... 8	2-28, 1855	7-1, 1885			
	Margaret P. Gleason, . . 8	4-4, 1861				
1405	Metta Florence, ... 8	7-27, 1857				
1406	Charles Fremont, ... 8	6-30, 1859			9-11, 1859	
1407	Margaret Adams, ... 8	7-10, 1860				
1408	Sarah Maria, ... 8	12-13, 1862			10-6, 1872	
1409	Charlotte Olive, ... 8	8-29, 1870				
	Children of 575 ANN REBECCA MAL- LETTE SANFORD,[7]					
1410	Sarah Sanford, ... 8	9-2, 1853	3-11, 1874	Easton.		
	James Tyler, ... 8	12-24, 1850				
1411	Yula, ... 8	12-30, 1855	7-23, 1885	Tashua,	3-16, 1894	Tashua.
	Charles F. Osborn, ...	3-13, 1859				
	Children of 576 MARY JANE MAL- LETTE DAVIS,[7]					
1412	Franklin Truman Davis, . . 8	2-5, 1852	10-22, 1873			
	Emma Margret Coles, . .	5-10, 1852				
1413	Arthur Burr, ... 8	6-30, 1854			9-23, 1873	Woodlawn, N. Y.
1414	George Mallette, ... 8	12-24, 1857			8-30, 1858	"
1415	Edward Moulton, ... 8	10-24, 1859	2-22, 1883			
	Martha Estella Close, . .	7-16, 1858				
1416	Nellie Bridgham, ... 8	6-17, 1864	9-3, 1883			
	Arthur Andrew Jarvis, . .	2-25, 1862	1-7, 1890		8-1, 1884	Woodlawn.
1417	*George Laurie Fisher,* . . .	4-14, 1854				
1418	William Berrian, M. D., . . 8	4-13, 1868				
	Frederick Allen, ... 8	1-25, 1874				

Children of 578 GEORGE ABEL MALLETTE,[7]

No.	Name	Gen.					
1419	Irving "Sanford" Mallette,	8	4-2, 1862	6-2, 1886	Bridgeport, Ct.		
	Odilege E. Fricke,						
1420	Georgia,	8	5-18, 1874		Bridgeport.		
1421	Fanny Elizabeth,	8	10-21, 1876			12-27, 1878	E. Bridgeport.

Children of 579 EDWARD B. MALLETTE[7]

No.	Name	Gen.					
1422	Stanley Andrew Mallette,	8	5-6, 1870	10-12, 1892	Thomaston, Ct.		
	Effie J. Norton,						
1423	Edward Rutledge,	8	7-3, 1879		Thomaston, Ct.		

Children of 580 FRANCES MALLETTE DAVIS,[7]

No.	Name	Gen.					
1424	Lucy Adams Davis,	8	7-5, 1856	5-10, 1875		6-13, 1875	Oxford.
	Frederick C. Candee,		8-15, 1854				
1425	William Otis,	8	10-22, 1857	3-26, 1879	Oxford, Ct.		
	Hattie Anna Benham,		5-30, 1855				
1426	George McClellan,	8	7-19, 1862	7-24, 1883	Hartford.		
	Funnie Lenox,		7-24, 1865				
1427	Isaac Beecher,	8	5-22, 1864			5-22, 1870	Oxford, Ct.

Children of 581 SARAH E. MALLETTE GRIFFIN,[7]

No.	Name	Gen.					
1428	Jennetie Griffin,	8	8-1, 1860				
1429	Stephen Joseph,	8	12-20, 1862	6-17, 1889			
	Delphine Morrell,						
1430	Laura,	8	3-4, 1864			8-21, 1864	
1431	Louisa,	8	3-10, 1867			12-8, 1885	
1432	Sarah Elizabeth,	8	4-13, 1871	6-26, 1889			
	Atwood Rainous,		1-15, 1868				

Children of 587 AMARIAH MALLETT,[7] and (1st six) of 212,

No.	Name	Gen.					
1433	Fanny Maria,	7 and 8	4-30, 1829	1844	Easton, Ct.	4-30, 1883	U. Stephney.
	William Brown,						
1434	Sylvia Jane,	7 and 8	7-29, 1830	4-20, 1847	Bethel.	1861	Bethel.
	Henry Jenkins,		2-11, 1823				
	Philip Jacob Wardner, M. D.,		9-12, 1832	2-20, 1863			

No.	Name of Wife (or Husband).		Date of Birth.	Date of Marriage.	Residence.	Date of Death.	Place of Burial.
1435	John Wesley, . . .	7 and 8	1-25, 1832	4-24, 1859		1-6, 1875	Springfield, Ill.
	Mary Jane (d. of Benj. W.) Mead,	7 and 8	1-18, 1839				
1436	Asaph Burr Mallett, . .	7 and 8	2-12, 1833	9-4, 1860	Chicago.		
	Maria Haynes, . . .		4-17, 1840		Easton,		
1437	Harriet Phebe, . . .	7 and 8	5- , 1834	. . . . .	Danbury.	5-30, 1881	Cecil, Kan. Danbury, Ct.
	Theodore Fowler,						
	John Lane Jones,			7-7, 1869	Bartlett, Kas.		
1438	Antha Jane, . . .	7 and 8	1-31, 1831	9-21, 1862	Trumbull, Ill.	11-19, 1891	L. H. Trum.
	Daniel Edwards, . .		2-5, 1841				
1439	Charles Sherman, . .	8	10-20, 1821	8-16, 1870	Decatur, Ill.		
	Sarah Elizabeth White.		3-6, 1847				
1440	Mary Esther, . . .	8	2-20, 1848	2-17, 1864	Trumbull, "	dec.	
	William H. Downs,						
1441	Hannah, . . .	8	. . . . .			dec. 12 yrs.	
1442	Sarah Adelia, . . .	8	6- , 1854	11-4, 1874	Bridgeport,	10-24, 1888	
	Ferris William Plumb,						
1443	Amariah, Jr., . .	8	1-18, 1857				
	Minnie Bell Wilson,		5-10, 1863				
1444	Ferdinand, . . .	8	11-15, 1859	10-30, 1879			

Children of 588 Ann Merilla Mal-
lett Bennett,[7]

No.	Name of Wife (or Husband).		Date of Birth.	Date of Marriage.	Residence.	Date of Death.	Place of Burial.
1445	Emily Delight Bennett,		9-17, 1827	5-9, 1849	Milford, Ct.		
	Samuel Henry De Forest,		9-2, 1827				
1446	Sarah S., . . .	8	4-20, 1829	. . . .	. . . . .	7-19, 1841	Tashua.
1447	John S., . . .	8	6-27, 1831	. . . .	. . . . .	7-15, 1832	"
1448	Mary Jane, . . .	8	5-1, 1833				
	Wilber Frisk Gleason,			unm.,			
1449	James Zolutus, . .	8	6-23, 1835	. . . .	New York.	1-16, 1861	Tashua.
1450	Alexander Jerome, . .	8	9-7, 1838	12-7, 1865	Hornellsville, N. Y.	11-10, 1873	Tallahassee.
	Sarah A. Childers,		10-24, 1844		Tallahassee, Fla.		
	Katharine Martin, .			5-9, 1874	Hornellsville.		
1451	Clarissa Maria, . .	8	3-27, 1841	12-31, 1862	Bridgeport.	6-23, 1888	M. G. C. B. C.
	Sturges Drew Beers, .		8-13, 1841				

No.	Name		Born	M.	Married/Died	Residence	Death	M. G. C. B. C.
1452	Martha Augusta,	8	5-4, 1843		7-5, 1866	Bridgeport.	3-7, 1892	
	Cornelius E. Fowler,		6-12, 1845					
1453	Frank C.,	8	1-5, 1846		10-15, 1874	"	8-18, 1885	
	Laura R. Smith,		12-6, 1849					

Children of 590 ISAAC BRONSON MALLETT,7

1454	Sarah M. Mallett,	8	1-12, 1842					
1455	Cassius M.,	8	9-16, 1843		9-9, 1872	Sharon Spr.		
	Annie E. Hoag,		9-4, 1855					
1456	Frances C.,	8	3-8, 1845					
1457	William M.,	8	4-5, 1847					
1458	Roswell I.,	8	1-5, 1849					
1459	Elida C.,	8	8-27, 1850					
1460	Isaac Bronson, Jr.,	8	10-27, 1852				10-21, 1867	
1461	Ada D.,	8	8-10, 1855					
1462	Ida A.,	8	8-10, 1855					
1463	Emma J.,	8	9-19, 1859		3-9, 1890	Sharon Spr.		
	Geo. B. Warner,		2-19, 1866					

Children of 592 GLOVER Z. MALLETTE,7

1464	Sarah E. Mallette,	8	5-10, 1850		2-1, 1882	W. Auburn, Pa.		
	James Wiles Angle,		1-25, 1859					
1465	Jennie C.,	8	9-6, 1852		2-3, 1879	Cobleskill.		
1466	Charles Gerdon,	8	11-22, 1854			Wyalusing, Pa.,	2-19, 1889	
	Mary D. Branyen,				7-20, 1892	Cobleskill.		
	Amanda A. Draper,							
1467	Julia A.,	8	6-10, 1861					

Children of 593 ABEL W. MALLETT,7

1468	Eugene Sherwood Mallett,	8	5-11, 1853			Ansonia, Ct.	10-9, 1855	
1469	Francis Arthur,	8	8-7, 1855					
1470	Jennie Lilly,	8	2-9, 1859		5-12, 1885			
	Franklin Robert Nichols,		1860					

Children of 599 RHODA E. MALLETT LOUCKS,7

| 1471 | Helen Lucretia Loucks, | 8 | 12-28, 1833 | | 3-6, 1851 | La Fox, Ill. | | |
| | *Albert P. Flower,* | | 9-5, 1828 | | | | | |

No.	Name of Wife (or Husband).	Date of Birth.	Date of Marriage.	Residence.	Date of Death.	Place of Burial.
1472	William Philo, ...8	12-2, 1836	5-6, 1866	Lakin, Kas.		
	Amy McCoy Sturtevant,	8-28, 1843				
1473	Jane, ...8	3-28, 1839	9-12, 1858			
	W. K. Gates, ...8	3-12, 1836				
1474	Miles, ...8	4-29, 1841	6-9, 1863	Dorest, O.	9-11, 1877	Crawford, Pa.
	Ella Amelia Marsh,	2-10, 1845		New Lyme, O., . . .		
1475	Charles, ...8	2-24, 1845				
1476	George Benjamin, . . .8	1-29, 1847	4-10, 1873		11-20, 1851	
	Maggie Madona Russell,	4-10, 1854				
1477	Mary Eunice, ...8	4-11, 1849	9-2, 1867		3-16, 1875	Springboro, Pa.
	H. N. Havens, . . .	7-18, 1846				
1478	Jay Albert, ...8	11-30, 1851	9-30, 1879	Beaver Centre, Pa. . . .	12-2, 1865	
	Jennie Lamb,	4-21, 1855				
	Minnie Ellen Cordley,	12-25, 1855	4-6, 1885			
1479	John Zee, ...8	12-15, 1853	4-10, 1881			
	Martha Delia Dalrymple,	10-2, 1861				
1480	Dayton Rozell, ...8	5-23, 1856	10-15, 1889	Ellinwood, Kan.		
	Katie May Shultz, . . .	7-15, 1868				
	Children of 600 SARAH J. MALLETT ESMEY,[7]					
1481	David E. Esmey,[7] . . .8	1-24, 1838	1-16, 1861	Worcester, N. Y. . . .	8-14, 1864	
	Elsina M. Abbott,	. . .	9-13, 1865			
	Lillie Maynard, . . .	12-7, 1848				
1482	Jerome M., ...8	11-22, 1844			8-2, 1862	
	Children of 601 JAY CADY MALLETT,[7]					
1483	Sarah Jane Mallett, . . .8	6-10, 1862			1-22, 1863	
1484	Elizabeth, ...8	5-30, 1864			9-15, 1867	
	Children of 602 LUCRETIA MALLETT WILCOX,[7]					
1485	Etta Wilcox, ...8	3-17, 1857			10-7, 1857	Albion, Pa.

No.	Gen	Name	Born	Died	Residence	
		Children of 603 DANIEL PARRIS MALLETT,⁷				
1486	8	Jennie Salome Mallett,	9-20, 1869	2-7, 1894	Cherry Valley, N.Y.	Ames, N. Y.
		Romaine McFee,	4-12, 1872			
		Children of 604 CHARLES EATON MALLETT,⁷				
1487	8	Dayton Rozelle Mallett,	4-3, 1852	10-12, 1878		2-24, 1891
		Sisters } *Elizabeth Ann McEwen,*	8-3, 1856	4-24, 1892		
		Ellen McEwen,	5-6, 1842	12-25, 1892		
1488	8	Byron Earl,	3-5, 1854			
		Jennette Jane Ramsay,	5-10, 1873			
1489	8	Elizabeth Louisa,	4-7, 1856	2-13, 1889		
		Peter McEwen,	12-7, 1845			
1490	8	Helen Augusta,	6-6, 1858	12-19, 1877		12-7, 1879
		Livingston Lewis Hess,	4-6, 1858	11-25, 1885		
		Franklin Wickoff,	1-2, 1859			
1491	8	Martin Jones,	5-9, 1863		Ames, N. Y.	
1492	8	Charles Jay,	4-30, 1867			
1493	8	Delos Lester,	8-15, 1872			
		Children of 605 HENRIETTA L. MALLETT SMITH,⁷				
1494	8	Franklin P. Smith,	3-4, 1853		Ames, N. Y.	
1495	8	Andrew,	6-4, 1863		Sharon Spr. N. Y.	
1496	8	Dillie Creka,	8-11, 1865	1-28, 1885	Ames, N. Y.	
		Charles Abram Ehle,	11-12, 1864			
		Children of 606 WILLIAM WALLAS MALLETTE,⁷				
1497	8	Emma Lavina Mallett,	2-23, 1851	1-21, 1869	Otego, N. Y.	
		Ansel Bennett,	6-6, 1821			
1498	8	Estella Minerva,	9-21, 1852	11-10, 1875		
		V. C. Shumway,	8-22, 18 2			
1499	8	Charles Ansel,	12-2, 1855	10-27, 1880	Casselton, N. Dak.	
		Amit E. Hadren,	2-13, 1862			
1500	8	William Jam°s,	12-25, 1859	7-12, 1887	Albuquerque. N. M	
		Clar A ——,	1-12, 1867			
1501	8	Jerome Rufus,	4-14, 1861	8-7, 1889	Gallup, N. Mex.	
		Grace May Goodrich,	8-26, 1868			

No.	Name of Wife (or Husband).		Date of Birth.	Date of Marriage.	Residence.	Date of Death.	Place of Burial.
1502	Ernest Bennett,	8	6-10, 1877	} 9-14, 1892	Colliersville, N.Y.		
	Alice Hattie Doris,		10-7, 1872				
	Children of 607 GEORGE PHILO MALLETT, M D.,[7]						
1503	Florence Alvaretta Mallett,	8	1-13, 1855	} 7-4, 1873	Gloversville, N.Y.		
	Edward K. Farquharson,		3-31, 1852				
1504	Ann Gennetta,	8	6-29, 1857	} 1-5, 1881	Richmondville, "		
	Jarvis Johnson,		6-20, 1862				
1505	Charlotte Louisa,	8	2-9, 1860				
1506	Ella Rhoda,	8	8-26, 1862	} 10-31, 1892	Sprout Brook, . .		
	Charles Michael Hibbard,		7-20, 1857				
	Children of 609 JAMES HENRY MALLETT.[7]						
1507	William Youmans Mallett,	8	4-18, 1873				
1508	Ellen Louise,	8	4-7, 1876				
1509	Czar Youmans,	8	7-1, 1880				
1510	Nellie Elizabeth,	8	5-13, 1883				
	Children of 612 AURELIAN MALLETT,[7]						
1511	James Dey Mallett,	8	2-1, 1854	} 9-3, 1876	Amsterdam, N.Y.		
	Sarah Rebecca Acker,		11-29, 1857				
1512	Alvaro,	8	1-21, 1856	} 1-8, 1882	Fultonville, N.Y.		
	Mary Putnam,		7-3, 1862				
1513	Arlva,	8	9-5, 1859	} 1-1, 1878	Amsterdam, N.Y.		
	Willard Lathers,		5-5, 1856				
1514	Armenia.	8	12-24, 1861	} 1-13, 1884			
	John Roberts,		7-17, 1861				
1515	Sanford,	8	10-8, 1864	} 10-30, 1890	Lykers, N.Y.		
	Carrie Kills,		2-16, 1871				
1516	Kate,	8	7-28, 1867	} 10-5, 1887	Burtonville, N.Y.		
	Ira D. Vrinck,		8-12, 1863				
1517	Mark,	8	8-19, 1869	. . . .	Rual Grove, N.Y.		

No.	Name		Born	Died	Place		
1518	Isabella, ...	8	4-7, 1872 4-8, 1873	9-18, 1894	Rual Grove.		
	Lewis Allen,						
1519	Jenny, ...	8	10-15, 1873 10-1, 1865	6-15, 1892	Randall, N. Y.		
	Melvin Green,				Rual Grove.		
1520	Estella, ...	8	5-25, 1876	. . . .			
	Children of 613 HENRY DAV.S MALLETT,[7]						
1521	John Lyker Mallett, . . .	8	5-12, 1865	. . . .	Albany, N. Y.		
1522	Henry Vandeveer, . . .	8	6-2, 1874	. . . .	Pittsfield, Mass.		
	Children of 615 ISABELLA MALLETT SECOY,[7]						
1523	Darwin Erasmus Secoy, . .	8	3-21, 1865	. . . .	Nebraska.		
	Dunis Kidd,						
	Children of 615 b GILES FONDA MALLETT,[7]						
1524	Albert Eugene Mallett, . .	8		11-20, 1873			
	Emma Mills,						
1525	Marvin, ...	8	1-6, 1857 1-22, 1860	2-23, 1881		9-23, 1869	
	Katie Secor,						
1526	Ora Maria, ...	8	10-12, 1866				
1527	Cora Kezia, ...	8	10-12, 1866	9-16, 1891			
	Charles Pelton,						
1528	Charles Grandison, . . .	8	9-25, 1878		Auburndale, O.		
	Children of 615 c CHARLES G. MALLETT,[7]						
1529	Florence Eudora Mallett, . .	8	2-7, 1852 5-26, 1848	12-25, 1873	Petersburg, Mich.		
	George I. Gove,						
1530	Viola Luella, ...	8	4-11, 1853	11-23, 1870	Erie, Mich.		
	Josiah Hull,						
1531	Clarence J., ...	8	12-4, 1840 9-22, 1855	. . . .	Englewood, Ill.		
	Children of 615 d GEORGE WASHINGTON MALLETT,[7]						
1532	Cora Ann Mallett, . . .	8	11-16, 1862 6-13, 1864	8-8, 1884	Washington, O.,	5-28, 1865	Washington.
	Earl Grandison,				"		
1533	*Louise Caroline Shultz,*	8	7-12, 1864		Toledo, O.		

No.	Name of Wife (or Husband).	Date of Birth.	Date of Marriage.	Residence.	Date of Death.	Place of Burial.
1534	James Spencer, ... 8	8-19, 1868	} 4-9, 1890	Wolsey, S. D.	7-25, 1879	Washington.
	Jennie Lind Hammond,	2-19, 1871		Little Rock, Neb.		
1535	George Washington, ... 8	11-4, 1876		Washington, O.,		
1536	Maud May, ... 8	6-8, 1879		"		
1537	Manard, ... 8	4-10, 1881				
1538	Marguerite, ... 8	2-13, 1893		Huron, S. D.		
	Children of 615 e MARY MALLETT DE WOLF,[7]					
1539	Charles Russell De Wolf, ... 8	5-16, 1863	} 5-31, 1893			
	Elizabeth Gertrude Paskert,	9-23, 1869				
	Children of 615 g VALOROUS MALLETT,[7] *and of 615 o.*					
1540	James Solomon Mallett, ... 8	12-4, 1861			9-27, 1862	W. Toledo.
1541	Nellie Iona, ... 8	10-6, 1863			9-18, 1864	"
	Children of 615 i SALLY MALLETT LEWIS,[7]					
1542	Jane Ann Lewis, ... 8				dec.	Bedford, Mich.
1543	Maria, ... 8					
	Jacob Harwood,				1890	Bedford.
1544	David, ... 8	9-18, 1834	} 12-2, 1858	Auburndale, O.		
	Mary A Majors,	2-21, 1843				
1545	Florence, ... 8				dec.	
1546	Mariette, ... 8				"	
1547	Elizabeth, ... 8	4-15, 1839	} 5-15, 1858		9-30, 1894	W. Toledo.
	Lewis Benton,	7-26, 1837			2- , 1864	
	Archie Van Houten,	1843	5-15, 1866			
1548	Martin, V. B., ... 8	3-22, 1848	} 9-22, 1867	Toledo, O.	9-5, 1861	
1649	Adelbert, ... 8	12-14, 1847				
	Emily Butler,					

Children of 615 k BENJAMIN MALLETT,⁷

No.	Name	Gen.	Born	Married	Residence	Died	Died Place
1550	Benjamin Franklin Mallett,	8	6-28, 1846	5-10, 1870	W. Toledo, O.	6-20, 1879	W. Toledo.
	Ellen Rattenberg,		9-22, 1848		Loughboro, Eng.		
1551	Anna Louisa,	8	5-18, 1853	5-6, 1869		2-12, 1871	W. Toledo.
	Milton Dorr,						
1552	Sherman,	8	10-5, 1864				

Children of 615 l MONTIERE MALLETT,⁷

1553	Wallace Mallett,	8	9-10, 1858		W. Toledo,	2-22, 1859	W. Toledo.
1554	Milford,	8	6-25, 1860		"	3-15, 1865	"
1555	Ralph,	8	3-13, 1865				
1556	Bertie,	8	10-5, 1872		W. Toledo,	8-12, 1880	W. Toledo.

Children of 615 m VOLTAIRE MALLETT,⁷

1557	Adda Mallett,	8			Michigan.		

Children of 615 n JAMES S. MALLETT,⁷

1558	Mary Samantha Mallett,	8	2-7, 1850	2-3, 1869	Scitico, Ct.		
	James Bissel Pease,		12-19, 1843		"		
1559	Elmer Eugene,	8	4-3, 1851	unm.,	Findlay, O.		
1560	Ellen Augusta,	8	2-19, 1853				
1561	Edward Everett,	8	7-30, 1859		Scitico.		
1562	Amanda Amelia,	8	3-6, 1862	3-14, 1885		10-2, 1894	Findlay.
	Wilbur Alfred Spencer,		8-3, 1863		W. Fitchb'rg, Mass.		

Children of 615 o CLEMENTINE MALLETT,⁷ *see 615 g,*

Children of 615 p DEO (NATHAN DEGO) MALLETT,⁷

1563	Frances Marian Mallett,	8	10-29, 1840	10-19, 1872	W. Toledo, O.		
	William Brock,		1-21, 1830		"		
1664	Esther Ellen,	8	1-3, 1844		Ames, N. Y.		
	Charles Eff,				Ohio.		

No.	Name of Wife (or Husband).	Date of Birth.	Date of Marriage.	Residence.	Date of Death.	Place of Burial.
	Children of 617 ANNA M. WELCH HARTWELL,[7]					
1565	Alvin Hartwell, ... 8	7-12, 1828	} 12-31, 1851	Gilbertsville, N. Y.	8-9. 1892	Nicholas, Pa.
	Julia Eliza Teneyck,	11-2, 1834		"	dec.	
1566	Caroline, ... 8					
1667	Samantha, ... 8			Norfolk, Ct.	6-16. 1894	
	George B. Munn,					
1568	—— *Benjamin,* 8			Cazenovia, N. Y.	dec.	
	Children of 618 CAROLINE WELCH PERIGO,[7]					
1569	—— Perigo, ... 8				dec.	
	Children of 619 LYMAN WELCH,[7]					
1570	Daniel Lyman Welch, ... 8	4-9, 1839	} 8-9, 1865	Morley, Mich.		
	Susannah M. Soule,	6-22, 1843		Binghamton, N.Y.		
	Children of 623 ADALINE WELCH ANTHONY.					
1571	Emma Catharine Anthony, ... 8	5-23, 18—	} 3-19, 1867	Buffalo.	3-7, 1881	Leesville, N. Y.
	Seth Eldridge Anthony,	9-28, 18—				
1572	Edward Lyman, ... 8	6-28, 18—	} 6-6, 1877			
	Electa Hume,	6-6, 18—				
	Children of 626 MARY ELIZA MALLETT CLARK,[7]					
1573	Bertha Emily Clark, ... 8	7-18, 1867	} 1-8, 1890	Tashua.		
	George Baldwin Ferris,	6-16, 1864		Newtown.		
1574	George Albert, ... 8	12-20, 1868		Tashua.		
1575	Arthur Judson, ... 8	6-15, 1870	} 8-22, 1891			
	Addie May Godfrey,					
	Children of 628 ORVILLE S. MALLETT,[7]					
1576	Berton Clark Mallett, ... 8	8-23, 1867		Tashua,	9-23, 1873	Tashua.

No.	Name	Gen.	Birth	Place	Date	Place
1577	——,					
1578	——,					
	Children of 629 FLORA MALLETT BRADLEY,[7]					
1579	Benjamin Bradley,	[8]	7-6, 1866			
1580	Bertha Elizabeth,	[8]	4-11, 186?			
	Arthur S. Jones,		11-10, 1889			
1581	Edward Mallett,	[8]	5-27, 1868	2-1, 1871		
1582	Robert,	[8]	10-27, 1877		9-16, 1881	
	Children of 631 MARY F. NICHOLS HILL,[7]					
1583	—— Hill,	[8]				
	Children of 634 FRANK B. MALLETT,[7]					
1584	Mary Augusta Mallett,	[8]	4-26, 1885			
	Children of 635 WILLIAM BLACKMAN MALLETT,[7]					
1585	Howard William Mallett,	[8]	2 25, 1882		3-5, 1890	Tashua.
1586	Ethel Louise,	[8]	4-13, 1893		5-8, 1893	"
	Children of 637 MARY F. BEACH SMITH,[7]					
1587	Frink Mansfield Smith,	[8]	7-31, 1866	Mt. Vernon, N. Y.		
	Susie Vanderof Gendar,		6-5, 1895			
1588	Clifford Beach,	[8]	1-20, 1868	East Haven.		
1589	Lizzie Frances,	[8]	9-28, 1871	"		
1590	Lois Anna,	[8]	3-10, 1875	"	4-20, 1879	
1591	Olive Eloise,	[8]	6-27, 1880			
	Children of 638 DAVID CLINTON BEACH,[7]					
1592	Millard Fillmore Beach,	[8]	12-11, 1865	Trumbull,	10-2, 1893	L. H. T.
1593	Stephen Youngs,	[8]	7-1, 1868	"	5-7, 1878	
1594	Frederick Youngs,	[8]	8-18, 1874	"		
1595	Fannie Augusta,	[8]	6-, 1876	"	7-1, 1876	L. H. T.
1596	Charles,	[8]	8-21, 1877	"	5-3, 1878	"
1597	David Clinton,	[8]	1878	"		

No.	Name of Wife (or Husband).	Date of Birth.	Date of Marriage.	Residence.	Date of Death.	Place of Burial.
1598	Fannie Sarah, ... 8	2-21, 1879		Trumbull.	8-10, 1880	L. H. T.
1599	Albert, ... 8	6-2, 1880		"		
	Children of 639 GEORGE HENRY CURTIS,7					
1600	Mary Jessie Curtis, . . 8	12-28, 1875		Sumter, S. C.		
1601	Harriet Eva, . . . 8	3-24, 1877		"		
1602	Charles King, . . . 8	10-24, 1879		"		
1603	Minnie Annie, . . . 8	4-24, 1881		"		
1604	George Henry, . . . 8	1-24, 1883		"		
1605	Bertha Eugenia, . . 8	8-18, 1885		"	8-18, 1887	St. Paul's Cem.
1606	Alva Beach, . . . 8	2-24, 1888		"		
1607	Roy Melvin, . . . 8	10-18, 1890		"		
1608	Harold Chappell, . . 8	10-24, 1892		"		
	Children of 640 HORACE BEACH CURTIS,7					
1609	Blanche Charity Curtis, . . 8	12-15, 1884			6-3, 1886	
1610	Dwight, ... 8	12-24, 1886			10-10, 1887	
1611	Betty, ... 8	8-30, 1888			4-30, 1889	
	Children of 642 DAVID M. BEACH,7					
1612	Francelia " Annetta " Beach, . . 8	6-6, 1847	10-6, 1869			
	Cornelius Wasburn (son of Ebenezer) Ruggles,	3-6, 1845	.-7, 1884			
	Charles E. (son of Lyman) Lattin,	3-3, 1844	2-7, 1884			
1613	Mary Elizabeth, . . . 8	8-8, 1849	12-21, 1870	Shelton, Ct.	10-29, 1881	Derby, Ct.
	Frederick G. Perry,	9-29, 1838		Shelton.		
1614	Eli Willard, . . . 8	4-9, 1852	4-25, 1876			
	Lucretia Lord,	5-3, 1849			8-5, 1892	
	Cora Etta Winter (Allyn),	10-19, 1864	6-6, 1893			
1615	William Osborn, . . 8	8-26, 1854	12-1, 1881	Trumbull,		
	Isabella M. Perry,	5-6, 1861				
1616	Marietta Seeley, . . 8	12-20, 1857	9-4, 1878	Hartford.		
	Clarence B. Sherwood,					

Children of 643 JOHN C. BEACH,[7] and 1390.

No.	Name		Born	Married	Where married	Died	Where died
1617	Frederick Morton Beach,	8					d. ae. 18 m.

Children of 645 JOHN S. ADAMS,[7]

No.	Name		Born	Married	Where married	Died	Where died
1618	John Sherwood Adams,	8	9-27, 1840	6- , 1861	Easton, Ct.	12-11, 1890	Easton.
	Mary Hedges,	8	6-1, 1842			5-12, 1856	"
1619	Alice Alosia,	8	3-1, 1855				

Children of 647 MARY ELIZ. ADAMS GILLETTE,[7]

No.	Name		Born	Married	Where married	Died	Where died
1620	Mary Elizabeth Gillette,	8	4-11, 1853	12-3, 1885			
	Rev. Judson Conklin,		4-5, 1856				
1621	George Sherwood,	8	9-28, 1858	3-20, 1884	Easton.		
	Ella L. Sherwood,						
1622	Edward D.,	8	5-1, 1863	10-22, 1887	Easton.		
	Ella J. Wilson,		9-27, 1864				

Children of 650 EMILY J. JACKSON SCARBROUGH,[7]

No.	Name		Born	Married	Where married	Died	Where died
1623	Orrin L. Scarbrough,	8	9-18, 1853	12-27, 1877	Monroe, Ia.		
	Libbie Elrod,		12-28, 1854			4-11, 1881	Monroe.
	Mary Blanch Mason,		4-23, 1859	9-26, 1883		3-15, 1894	"
1624	Edgar S.,	8	9-18, 1853	1-7, 1880	Cumberland, Ia.		
	Sallie M. Churchill,		8-29, 1856				
1625	Clarence Francis,	8	8-22, 1855	10-14, 1880	Minburn, Ia.		
	Belle Coleman,		3-21, 1857			9-2, 1882	Minburn.
	Ellen McCarty,		2-6, 1855	12-17, 1884			
1626	Viola Fidelia,	8	10-17, 1857	3-22, 1882	Fairmount, Ia.		
	Theophilus W. Montgomery,		12-3, 1856				
1627	Ella Delphine,	8	12-29, 1859	12-27, 1888	Searsboro, Ia.		
	Francis Marion Cooper, M. D.,		1-27, 1851				
1628	Hattie May,	8	3-4, 1862			9-28, 1862	Monroe, Ia.
1629	Charles William,	8	5-9, 1864	12-10, 1889	Monroe, Ia.		
	Lulu May Murphy,	8	3-18, 1870				
1630	Adelaide Theodora,	8	10-30, 1862			11-28, 1862	Monroe, Ia.

Children of 651 JOHN WESLEY JACKSON,[7]

No.	Name		Born	Married	Where married	Died	Where died
1631	Roselia Fidelphia Jackson,	8	12-23, 1856			2-25, 1857	

No.	Name of Wife (or Husband).	Date of Birth.	Date of Marriage.	Residence.	Date of Death.	Place of Burial.
1632	Elsie Ann, ... 8	4–5, 1858	} 11–9, 1876	Chillicothe, O.		
	William Orlando Conway,	7–14, 1853				
1633	Sarah Bell, ... 8	4–21, 1861	} 3–10, 1885	Milfordton, O.		
	Harry Graham,	12–29, 1862				
1634	Charles Carban, . . 8	7–27, 1869	} 12–23, 1893	Mount Liberty, O.		
	Minnie Bell Mitchell,	2–21, 1876				
	Children of 632 MARGARET E. JACKSON GLOYD,[7]					
1635	Charles Mordello Gloyd, 8	5–19, 1855	} 9–23, 1880	Monroe. Ia.		
	Laura Shaw,	4–9, 1860				
1636	Mary Ophelia, . . . 8	12–7, 1856	} 9–1, 1879	Canterbury, O.		
	Stephen Burton Lyon,	11–11, 1854				
	Children of 653 JAMES FLETCHER JACKSON,[7]					
1637	Ella M. Jackson, . . 8	. . . .	unm, ...	. . . .	dec.	
	Children of 654 J. SAMANTHA JACKSON ROBERTS,[7]					
1638	Frank Elsworth Roberts, 8	3–9, 1861	} 10–26, 1882	Monroe, Ia.		
	Ada Huddleston,	5–4, 1865				
1639	Frederick Velorus, . . 8	7–31, 1869	} 8–28, 1889	Monroe.		
	Mina Elizabeth Howard,	7–22, 1870				
1640	Charles Verner, . . 8	4–8, 1874	. . . .	Monroe.		
	Children of 655 VICTORINE P. JACKSON WRIGHT,[7]					
1641	Charles Burton Wright, . 8	7–13, 1864	} 2–14, 1889	Monroe, Ia.		
	Mary Custer,	12–25, 1865				
	Children of 661 JERUSHA B. MIDDLEBROOK STOWELL,[7]					
1642	Virginia Theresa Stowell, 8	1–4, 1855	. . . .	Bridgeport, Ct.		

No.	Name		Born		Residence		
	Children of 662 LORINTHA A. MID-DLEBROOK BOOTH,[7]						
	Charles Edward Keith.		6-5, 1848				
1643	Evanah Louisa Booth, ...	8	12-2, 1854	5-6, 1874	Bridgeport, Ct.		
	Children of 663 NATHAN B. MIDDLE-BROOK,[7]						
1644	Sillick Batterson Middlebrook,	8	8-13, 1866				
1645	Emma Augusta, ...	8	11-11, 1868	10-2, 1893	Fawling, N. Y.		
	Reuben M. Olmstead, . . .						
1646	Daisy Louise.	8	3-4, 1871				
1647	Virginia Theresa, ...	8	1-11, 1873				
1648	David Henry, ...	8	11-4, 1875				
1649	William Edward, ...	8	4-19, 1878				
	Children of 664 SARAH L. MIDDLE-BROOK BOGUE,[7]						
1650	Henry Bronson Bogue, . . .	8	7-29, 1865		Brooklyn, N. Y.,		
1651	Lillie May, ...	8	5-14, 1868	12-3, 1891	Glen Cove, N. Y.		
	Joseph Daniel Sayre, D. D. S.,	8	4-, 1864		Brooklyn.	8-16, 1865	M. G. C. B. C.
1652	Nellie Louise, ...	8	11-6, 1871		"		
1653	Charles Alfred, Jr., . . .	8	9-2, 1875		"		
1654	Frederick Fox, ...	8	2-16, 1878		"	2-23, 1879	Greenwood, B'k'l'n.
1655	Leighton Harris, ...	8	9-4, 1881		"		
1656	Mortimer Maddox, ...	8	2-19, 1884		"		
	Children of 665 HENRY B. MIDDLE-BROOK,[7]						
1657	Hattie Middlebrook, ...	8	1876				
1658	Owen Bronson, ...	8	5-13, 1878			5-6, 1876	Alliance, O.
1659	Clara Louise, ...	8	8-26, 1882				
	Children of 667 EMELINE MALLETT COLE,[7]						
1660	George Wilbur Cole, . . .	8	12-14, 1858	11-17, 1881	Bridgeport.		
	Anna Sherwood Burr, . . .		5-22, 1861				
1661	Charles Mallett, ...	8	2-24, 1863	1-11, 1893	Bridgeport.		
	1697 Edith Anna Wheeler,[8]		7-3, 1867		"		
1662	May Emma, ...	8	10-28, 1867				
1663	Jennie Estella, ...	8	12-11, 1871				

No.	Name of Wife (or Husband).	Date of Birth.	Date of Marriage.	Residence.	Date of Death.	Place of Burial.
	Children of 668 MARY E. MALLETT JENNINGS,[7]					
1664	Robert Ross Jennings, ...[8]	12-16, 1855				
1665	Charles Hobert, ...[8]	7-11, 1861				
1666	Howard Skidmore, ...[8]	11-23, 1869				
1667	Sarah Sanford, ...[8]	4-15, 1872				
1668	Mary Sherman, ...[8]	4-15, 1872				
	Children of 670 BRADLEY W. EDWARDS,[7]					
1669	Carrie Louise Edwards, . . .[8]	2-4, 1869				
1670	George Benjamin, ...[8]	5-20, 1873				
	Children of 672 THEODORE A. MALLETT,[7]					
1671	Theodora Augusta Mallett, . . .[8]	11-20, 1858		L. H. Trum.,	8-31, 1872	L. H. Tr.
1672	Caroline Cornelia, ...[8]	3-30, 1861				
1673	Robert Clark, ...[8]	1-30, 1868		Bridgeport.		
	Ella A. Phillips,	. . .	9-30, 1890			
	Children of 673 LORENZO N. MALLETT,[7]					
1674	John Clark Mallett, ...[8]	11-8, 1887				
1675	Grace Nichols, ...[8]	4-1, 1891				
	Children of 674 SARAH A. MALLETT WHEELER,[7]					
1676	Edward Mallett Wheeler, . . .[8]	7-11, 1874		Shelton,	3-26, 1882	Shelton, Ct.
1677	Alice Elizabeth, ...[8]	1-11, 1876		"		
1678	Franklin Lyon, ...[8]	2-1, 1882		"		
	Children of 678 BETSEY A. PLUMB WORDEN,[7]					
1679	Birdseye Plumb Worden, . . .[8]	1-10, 1857		Bridgeport.,	3-8, 1875	M. G. C. B. C.
1680	Edgar Bacon, ...[8]	3-5, 1859		"	8 5, 1859	"

							M. G. C. B. C.
1681	Elizabeth Chappelle,	8	7-15, 1860		Bridgeport,		
	Frederick Joel Lockwood,						
1682	Charles Edward,	8	3-8, 1863	2-14, 1884	"	3-8, 1863	
	Children of 679 CHARLES E. PLUMB,[7]						
1683	Willard Shelton Plumb,	8	7-21, 1857	11-15, 1883	Trumbull.		
	Ida Grace Summers,		10-8, 1858				
1684	Charles Edward,	8	8-24, 1859		Trumbull,	10-29, 1863	Trumbull.
1685	Charles Franklin,	8	1-19, 1863	11-19, 1889	Trumbull, "		
	Elizabeth Clark Tait,		3-23, 1869				
1686	Arthur Edwards,	8	3-1, 1866	11-28, 1889	Trumbull.	5-24, 1894	Trumbull.
	Charlotte Conger Bennett,		8-9, 1867				
1687	Howard E.,	8	1-26, 1870			3-29, 1870	Trumbull.
	Children of 680 FANNIE BRINSMADE MIDDLEBROOK,[7]						
1688	Robert Brinsmade Middlebrook,	8	9-3, 1855	11-15, 1884	Kansas City.		
	Louise E. Rutter,		11-15, 1858				
1689	Louis Frank,	8	5-28, 1866	10-27, 1891	Hartford, Ct.		
	Lillian Willemine Goodale,		12-2, 1872				
	Children of 681 JAMES R. BRINSMADE,[7]						
1690	Alice Caroline Brinsmade,	8	8-1, 1878				
1691	James Beardsley,	8	6-22, 1883				
	Children of 682 DANIEL SEYMOUR BRINSMADE,[7]						
1692	Fannie Louise Brinsmade,	8	9-2, 1872				
1693	Daniel Edwards,	8	8-21, 1874				
1694	Caroline Calhoun,	8	8-21, 1874				
1695	Helen Janette,	8	8-15, 1879				
1696	Wallace Seymour,	8	1-10, 1886				
	Children of 684 HOBART R. WHEELER,[7]						
1697	Edith Anna Wheeler,	8	7-3, 1867	1-11, 1893	Bridgeport, Ct.		
	1661 Charles Mallett Cole,[8]		2-24, 1863		"		
1698	Daniel Fairchild,	8	3-28, 1872		"		

No.	Name of Wife (or Husband).	Date of Birth.	Date of Marriage.	Residence.	Date of Death.	Place of Burial.
	Children of 685 WILMOT C. WHEELER,[7]					
1699	Edward Curtis Wheeler, 8	4–3, 1874	. . . .	L. H. Tr.	9-12, 1874	L. H. Tr.
1700	Lilian Cordelia, 8	6–19, 1876	. . . .	"		
1701	Wilmot Fitch, 8	8–23, 1882	. . . .	"		
	Children of 686 BENNETT SEELEY,[7]					
1702	Caroline Seeley, 8	1–27, 1854	. . . .	Easton, Ct.		
	Children of 693 HARRIET SMITH McELHINNEY,[7]					
1703	Hewlett Henry McElhinney, 8	9–28, 1836	12–14, 1865	Shelbyville, Mo.		
	Charlotte West,	4–27, 1841				
1704	William Walker, 8	5–26, 1838	. . . .	Bethel, Mo.		
1705	Solomon Chambers, 8	5–18, 1840	8–31, 1865	"		
	Lottie Elizabeth Smail,	10–9, 1851				
1706	Robert Tate, 8	2–15, 1843	9–15, 1886	Brookfield, Mo.		
	Effie T. Alexander,	10–27, 1867				
1707	Malissa Esther, 8	3–2, 1845	11–22, 1866	Unionville, Mo.	1-22, 1891	
	Jesse Oldaker West,	1–27, 1845				
1708	Cynthia Eleanor, 8	10–24, 1846	6–9, 1868	Kirby, Mo.		
	Hamilton Wallace McKillip,	9–21, 1837				
1709	John Monroe, 8	8–30, 1848	3–8, 1876	Unionville,		
	Josephine,	6–28, 1859				
1710	Eunice Jane, 8	12–3, 1851	10–21, 1873	Unionville,	9-29, 1881	Unionville.
	Emmett Holt,	8–12, 1851		"		
1711	Clarissa Grace, 8	3–7, 1854	2–26, 1885	Shelbina, Mo.		
	Jerome B. Lowe,	1–1, 1830				
1712	Albert Franklin Pierce, 8	12–31, 1855	9–5, 1880	Unionville.		
	Dora Ann Houston,	3–10, 1861				
1713	Lewis Grant, 8	11–7, 1861	unm., . .	. . . .	8-19, 1892	
	Children of 694 a PATIENCE SMITH LOBAUGH,[7]					
1714	Hulett Smith Lobaugh, 8	. . . .		. . . .		Reymursburgh, Pa.

No.	Name	Gen.	Birth		Place		
1715	Eunice Jane,	8	4-9, 1842	2-23, 1869	Brockport, Pa.		
	Martin Merrian Mohney,		7-28, 1850				
	Children of 694 b DAVID W. SMITH.[7]						
1716	Hewlett Erastus Smith,	8	10-9, 1844			7-20, 1851	Beaver, Pa.
1717	Frances Melissa,	8	9-22, 1846	1-28, 1869	Wilber, Oklahoma.		
	Aaron Meeker Downes,		8-6, 1844				
1718	Philip Clover,	8	8-18, 1848			7-9, 1851	Beaver.
1719	Orin Roundy,	8	2-3, 1851	10-3, 1878	Whitman, Kan.		
	Mary Eliza,		11-28, 1858				
1720	Lowry David,	8	5-26, 1853	11-30 1880	Knox, Pa.		
	Annie Elizabeth Arner,		7-31, 1862				
1721	Eunice "Elizabeth,"	8	11-27, 1855	5-18, 1882	Summerville, Pa.		
	Tom Howard Sovard,		9-28, 1859		Perry, Okla.		
1722	Hila Winifred, M. D.,	8	3-7, 1858		Troy, Pa.		
1723	Hiram Brown,	8	1-1, 1860				
1724	Son,	8	8-24, 1862			9-10, 1865	Beaver, Pa.
1725	Burton Corry,	8	9-20, 1863	8-29, 1888	Ringgold, Pa.	8-24, 1862	Beaver, "
	Bertha Vinnie Brown,		3-3, 1869				
1726	Florence,	8	2-17, 1867				
	Children of 694 c WALKER SMITH.[7]						
1727	Hewlett Edgar Smith,	8	6-26, 1851	10-21, 1875	Heathville, Pa.		
	Lizzie Fleming,		5-1, 1851				
1728	Annis Jane,	8	5-24, 1855	10-3, 1876	Reynoldsville, Pa	1-23, 1882	Smith cem.
	Joseph Curtis Martin,		11-18, 1851				
1729	Maggie Melinda,	8	10-7, 1857	10-3, 1877	Langville, Pa.		
	Walter Scott Bracken,		5-9, 1854				
1730	Viola,	8	8-28, 1860	7-1, 1878	Jefferson co., Pa.	5-29, 1887	Smith cem.
	John Ezekiel Kepler,		1-17, 1859		Patton's Sta., Pa		
1731	Elmer Elsworth,	8	7-4, 1863	7-3, 1889			
	Mary Ellen Myers,		7-2, 1868				
1732	Esther Melissa,	8	10-15, 1865	3-15, 1883	Driftwood, Pa.		
	Joseph Curtis Martin,		11-18, 1851				
1733	Minnie Lockwood,	8	7-11, 1868	1-24, 1894	Dunkirk, N. Y.		
	Robert William Travis,		12-22, 1861		Patton's Station.		
1734	Lillie Eunice,	8	10-3, 1871				
1735	McCurdy Madison,	8	9-14, 1876				

No.	Name of Wife (or Husband).	Date of Birth.	Date of Marriage.	Residence.	Date of Death.	Place of Burial.
	Children of 694 d ABIGAIL SMITH, McFARLAND,[7]					
1736	Eunice McFarland, .8				dec. ae. 3 yrs	
1737	Caroline, .8				" 5	
1738	Clara, .8			California.		
1739	Abigail, .8			"		
1740	Nancy Jane, .8 *Wm. M. Neilson,*					
1741	George Curtis, .8					
1742	Ida, .8 *O. L. Smith,*			Indiana, Pa.	dec. ae. 12 ys	
	Children of 694 e ELIJAH SMITH,[7]					
1743	Hulett Alverson Smith, .8 *Anna C. Crossman,*	10-22, 1851 3-25, 1860	4-24, 1882	Jefferson co., Pa. Indiana co.; Pa		
1744	Philip Elton, .8 *Laura B. Blose,*	5-24, 1854 11-26, 1864	4-17, 1888	Jefferson co., Pa.,	10-14, 1891	Ringgold.
1745	Melvin Lorain, .8 *Mary C. Bond,*	4-23, 1856 5-, 1865	3-27, 1884	" Indiana co., Pa.	6-1, 1892	Jefferson co.
1746	Frances Jane, .8	4-29, 1859		Jefferson co., Fa.	11-2, 1859	Ringgold.
1747	Jasper Clover, .8	8-9, 1860		"	12-13, 1862	"
1748	Eunice Ida, .8 *Orin Means,* *Charley J. Blose,*	10-17, 1862 12-8, 1861	3-24, 1883 12-8, 1887	Jefferson co., Pa.		
	Children of 694 h JOHN CURTIS SMITH,[7]					
1749	Effie May Smith, .8 *Charles W. Ditty,*	1-10, 1873 5-17, 1874	11-27, 1894	Summerville, Pa.		
1750	Maurice Lorain, .8 *Laura Yount,*			Summerville.		
1751	Arthur Otis, .8	10-2, 1876		"		
1752	Firman Riley, .8	8-9, 1879		"		
1753	Ella Lucretia, .8	6-21, 1881				
1754	Ida Marcella, .8	7-13, 1883				

No.	Name	Gen.	Birth	Place	Date	
1755	Sarah P.,	8	3-18, 1885	Summerville.		
1756	Bessie Beatrice,	8	3-15, 1887	"		
1757	Curtis Harl,	8	7-9, 1892	"		
1758	John Harris,	8	7-9, 1892			
	Children of 694 i HENRY SMITH,[7]					
1759	George Luke Smith,	8	6-11, 1863	Shannondale, Pa.,		4-22, 1884
1760	John Melven,	8	2-22, 1865			4-1, 1886
	Ella Yearney,		7- , 1885			
	Ella Lawrence,		11- , 1886			
1761	Emma Luella,	8	5-24, 1867		6-3, 1888	
	Rev. D. B. Stuhlman,					
1762	Clara Abigail,	8	12-28, 1870		6-17, 1891	
	James A. Shafer,		9-29, 1867			
1763	Silas Delbert,	8	12-26, 1872		1894	
	Sadie Simpson,					
	Children of 695 MELISSA PLUMB NICHOLS,[7]					
1764	Horace Plumb Nichols,	8	7-17, 1851		1-11, 1894	
	Bell Curtis,		2-22, 1851			
	Children of 696 EZRA W. PLUMB,[7]					
1765	Luzern Drew Plumb,	8	6-15, 1855	Bridgeport, Ct.		
	Susan (d. of Isaac) Holden,					
1766	Warren Ezra,	8	2-5, 1857	Nichols, Ct.	12-28, 1881	
	Clara Maria Wills,		5-6, 1863			
	Children of 697 ORANGE BEACH PLUMB,[7] *and of 1015,[8]*					
1767	Carrie Burton Plumb,	8	11-3, 1863	Trumbull.	6-21, 1894	
	George William Holmes,		3-25, 1839	Stratford, Ct.		
	Children of 698 MARY E. PLUMB LOCKWOOD,[7]					
1768	Irene A. Lockwood,	8	7 11, 1864	Weston, Ct.,		11-17, 1871 Weston.
1769	William Plumb,	8	12-1, 1867	"		
	Nellie Frances,		11-15, 1869	"	1-7, 1891	

No.	Name of Wife (or Husband).	Date of Birth.	Date of Marriage.	Residence.	Date of Death.	Place of Burial.
	Children of 699 CATHARINE PLUMB NICHOLS,[7]					
1770	John Beach Nichols,[7] . . . .[8]	5-22, 1866	} 1-28, 1894	Nichols.		
	Mable Amelia Murr,					
1771	Katie May, ...[8]	3-5, 1876				
	Children of 702 LYNSON BEARDS-LEY,[7]					
1772	Myron Beardsley, ...[8]	. . . 3-1, 1867			3-14, 1858	Stepney.
1773	Frank, ...[8]					
	Children of 703 MELISSA A. BEARDS-LEY HURD,[7]					
1774	Perry Beardsley Hurd, . . .[8]					
1775	Melissa Ann, ...[8]					
1776	Edwin Arnold, ...[8]					
	Children of 706 MELISSA WHEELER TOMLINSON,[7]					
1777	Walker Sherwood Tomlinson, . .[8]	7-25, 1856	} 10-, 1879	Bridgeport, Ct.		
	Lillie Downs,					
1778	Son, ...[8]	9-10, 1873		Bridgeport, Ct.	9-12, 1873	
1779	William Augustus, Jr., . . .[8]	10-2, 1875		"		
	Children of 707 MARGARET WHEELER BEACH,[7]					
1780	Estelle Melissa Beach, . .[8]	1-11, 1853	} 10-25, 1871			
	George Edward Cleveland, . .	10-25, 1851				
	Children of 708 JOHN MALLETT WHEELER,[7]					
1781	Lillian Isabel Wheeler, . .[8]	4-8, 1868		Bridgeport.		
1782	Anna Rebecca, ...[8]	12-21, 1870		"		
1783	John Walker, ...[8]	4-13, 1872		"		
1784	Harry Augustus, . . .[8]	1-29, 1874				

No.	Name	Gen.	Born	Married		Died / Notes
1785	Jessie Louise,	8	3-4, 1876			
1786	Helen Weed,	8	1-11, 1883			
	Children of 709 MARCUS O. WHEELER,[7]					
1787	Marion Rebecca Wheeler,	8	3-27, 1863			
1788	Sherwood Beardsley,	8	1-25, 1868	4-11, 1891	Bridgeport.	10-6, 1872 — L. H. T.
	Bessie Norman,					
1789	Lizzie May,	8	3-3, 1872			
1790	Arthur Nichols,	8	1-15, 1875			6-21, 1883
	Children of 711 SIDNEY MALLETT[7]					
1791	Alonzo Mallett,	8		unm.		
1792	Eldred,	8		"		dec.
1793	Maria,	8				"
	Rufus E. Glass,					
1794	Theresa,	8				
	Lorenzo Ackerman,					
1795	Marion,	8				
	William Hull,					
1796	Emma,	8				
	Children of 713 S. DeWITT MALLETT.[7]					
1797	Eva Mallett,	8				
	Children of 715 ELIZABETH MALLETT ELDRIDGE,[7]					
1798	Rolland Eldridge,	8				
1799	Cora, ———,	8				
1800	Jenny, ———,	8				
1801	John, ———,	8				
	Children of 716 HELEN MALLETT BILLINGS,[7]					
1802	Helen Billings,	8				
	——— Eddy,					

No.	Name of Wife (or Husband).	Date of Birth.	Date of Marriage.	Residence.	Date of Death.	Place of Burial.
	Children of 719 LEANDER M. HUBBY,[7]					
1803	Louisa Hubby, ... 8					
	—— *Doubleday,*					
1804	Frank, ... 8					
1805	Ella, ... 8					
	Children of 725 MALISSA HALL SHAW,[7]					
1806	Leander Shaw, . . . 8					
	Josephine Pierce.					
	Children of 728 HENRY WILLIAM MALLETT,[7]					
1807	Judson Burr Mallet, . . 8	11-12, 1850	10-4, 1875	Danbury.		
	Helen A. Osborn,	4-13, 1844				
1808	Franklin Pease, . . . 8	12-15, 1852				
1809	William Orrin, . . . 8	7-10, 1858		New Milford.	6-7, 1855	Texas.
	Georgia A. Field,				dec.	
	Henrietta Wickham,	2-28, 1857	10-12, 1879			
	Children of 730 BETSEY SHERMAN FANTON,[7]					
1810	Lemuel Fanton, . . . 8					
1811	Hull, ... 8			Havana.	dec. infancy	
1812	Janet, ——, . . . 8					
1813	Stirling, ... 8				dec. infancy	
1814	Margery, ... 8			Havana.	dec. ae. 14	
	Charles A. Tracey,					
1815	Harriet, ... 8			Catharine.		
	Tracy C. Ford,	10-9, 1850	10-25, 1871	Havana.		
1816	Frank, ... 8	1-18, 1850		Havana.		
	Flora Agard,					

Year	Name		Date	Place	dec.
	Children of 732 ANN SHERMAN UP-DIKE,[7]				dec.
1817	—— Updike,	8			
1818	——,	8			
1819	Janet,	8		Port Byron, N. Y.	
	Oliver B. Tanner,				
	Children of 734 ELI B. SHERMAN,[7]				
1820	—— Sherman,	8			
1821	——,	8			
1822	——,	8			
1823	——,	8			
	Children of 738 DELILAH JONES JUDD,[7] *and* 747.				
1824	Jeannette Elizabeth Judd,	8	8-24, 1840	Bridgeport.	
	Children of 747, REUBEN JUDD,[7] *see* 738,				
	Children of 750 SYLVIA M. JUDD[7]				
1825	Son,	8		Oregon.	
1826	Son,	8		"	
1827	Son,	8		"	
1828	Son,	8		"	
1829	Son,	8		"	
1830	Daughter,	8			
	Children of 753 PAULINE JUDD[7]				
1831	——,	8		California.	
	Children of 754 MARK JUDD,[7]				
1832	—— Judd,	8			
1833	——,	8			
1834	——,	8			
	Children of 755 POLLY BEARDSLEY WHIPPEY,[7]				
1835	Estella Whippey,	8		Hornellsville, N.Y.	
	Ed. Bates,				

No.	Name of Wife (or Husband).	Date of Birth.	Date of Marriage.	Residence.	Date of Death.	Place of Burial.
	Children of 756 OTHNIEL BEADSLEY,[7]					
1836	Ada Beardsley, [8]					
1837	Emma, [8]					
1838	John, [8]					
1839	——, [8]					
	Children of 757 REBECCA BEARDSLEY BUCKLEY,[7]					
1840	Grover Buckley, [8]					
	Children of 761 MARY BEARDSLEY HITCHCOCK,[7]					
1841	George Beardsley Hitchcock, [8]	7-26, 1875		Catharine.		
1842	Fanny Stuart, [8]	11-30, 1876		"		
1843	Milo, [8]	10-31, 1878		"		
1844	Susan Adelia, [8]	7-6, 1882				
	Children of 763 ROSWELL F. BEARDSLEY,[7]					
1845	—— Beardsley, [8]					
1846	——, [8]					
	Children of 766 RHODA BEARDSLEY SMITH,[7]					
1847	Josephine Mahetable Smith, [8]	10-18, 1847	9-4, 1864	Enfield, Ulysses.		
	David A. Wilkin,					
1848	Philo B., [8]	7-22, 1857	12-19, 1877	Ulysses.		
	Ella M. Hosford,					
1849	Jennie L., [8]	8-25, 1864		Ulysses.		
	Children of 767 HENRY BEARDSLEY,[7]					
1850	—— Beardsley, [8]					
1851	——, [8]					

Children of 769 ELIZABETH BEARDSLEY BULKLEY,[7]

Year	Name		Birth		Death	Place		
1852	Louisa A. Bulkley,	8	6-6, 1851					
1853	Merwin D.	8	12-27, 1852	}	1-11, 1874	Catharine.		
	Helen Milspaugh,					"		
1854	William P.,	8	4-24, 1854		4-24, 1878	Ithaca.		
	Nellie Brierly,							
1855	Joseph C.,	8	1-21, 1860		1-17, 1889	Bennetsburg.		
	Emma A. Sharpston,							
1856	Minnie D.	8	2-2, 1862	}	10-26, 1888	Hartford, Pa.		
	Marion W. Hart,							
1857	Aaron E.,	8	3-1, 1864		12-31, 1891	Catharine.		
	Delilah M. Wheeler,							

Children of 771 ALONZO S. BEARDSLEY, [7]

Year	Name		Birth	Death	Place	Extra date	Extra place
1858	Charles Wayland Beardsley,	8	10-19, 1863	. . .	Canandaigua.		
1859	Jennie Day,	8	6-13, 1868	. . .	Catharine.		
1860	Maria Antoinette,	8	1-1, 1874	. . .	"	3-30, 1874	H. Montour, N. Y.
1861	Bruce Sherwood,	8	9-10, 1879	. . .	"		

Children of 772 MARIA BEARDSLEY SHERWOOD, [7]

Year	Name		Birth	Death	Place	Extra date	Extra place
1862	Mary Burr Sherwood,[7]	8	9-15, 1857	10-18, 1888	Southport, Ct.		
	Andrew Burr Huntington,				Bridgeport.		
1863	Antoinette Beardsley,	8	12-1, 1865	. . .	Southport,	11-10, 1866	O. L. C. Southport
1864	Alice Holman,	8	7-13, 1868	. . .	"		

Children of 774 GEORGE R. BEARDSLEY, [7]

Year	Name		Birth	Death	Place	Extra date	Extra place
1865	Fanny E. Beardsley,	8	1-4, 1856	}	Bridgeport,	8-9, 1857	New Boston, Ill.
1866	Fred S., ———,	8	9-22, 1858		Milwaukee.		
1867	John R.,	8	6-16, 1865	. . .	San Diego, Cal.		
1868	Chancy C.,	8	8-7, 1874	. . .	U. S. Navy.		
1869	Edwin W.,	8	3-29, 1877	. . .	"		
1870	Cara A.,	8	4-28, 1881	. . .	St. Helena, Cal.		

No.	Name of Wife (or Husband).	Date of Birth.	Date of Marriage.	Residence.	Date of Death.	Place of Burial.
	Children of 777 FRANCES BEARDSLEY SLOCUM,[7]					
1871	Son, Slocum, ... 8	. . .				
1872	Dau., . Greene, . . . 8	. . .				
	Children of 780 MALLETT SEELEY,[7]					
1873	"George" Munson Seeley, . 8	9-28, 1847	} 3-30, 1865	Bridgeport.		Bridgeport.
	Mary Finemore,	12-, 1847				
	Lydia Frances Curd,	12-20, 1859	11-21, 1883			
1874	Henry Beach, ... 8	12-25, 1850	10-2, 1874	N. Bridgeport..	3-5, 1880	
	Flora Beach,	2 3, 1855				
	Children of 781 CLARK SEELEY,[7]					
1875	Julia Caroline Seeley, . 8	7-21, 1849	6-6, 1872	Stratford, . . .	1893	Stratford.
	Joseph "Henry" Thompson,	3-7, 1847				
1876	Cornelia Justine, . . . 8	4-18, 1851	11- , 1876			
	Dominiques D'Oliver Amello,	. . .				
1877	Lucinda Munson, . . . 8	11-7, 1855	11-10, 1880			
	Bernhard Theodore Burchardi,	. . .				
	Children of 783 JOHN BEARDSLEY, LOVEJOY[7]					
1878	Frank Wilson Beardsley, . 8	9-9, 1856	} 9-7, 1882			
	Emma Edna Reeves,	9-5, 1866				
1879	Fannie F., ... 8	3-1, 1861	} 7-7, 1881			
	John Frank Olmstead,	5-23, 1860				
1880	Seymour Burton, . . . 8	7-13, 1862	} 7-22, 1886		5-12, 1870	Huntington.
	Annie Eliza Wilson,	1-15, 1866				
1881	John W., ... 8	8-8, 1868	. .			
1882	Ethel M., ... 8	1-15, 1878	. .			
	Children of 784 JOHN L. BEARDSLEY,[7]					
1883	Ida Beardsley, ... 8	12-30, 1868				
1884	Howard S., ... 8	1-5, 1871				

dec.ae.10m.

1885	Mary Alice, ...	8	3-25, 1873	
1886	Agnes May, ...	8	2-28, 1875	
1887	Clara Emma, ...	8	8-31, 1876	
1888	Martha, ...	8	4-11, 1879	
1889	Charles Mallett, ...	8	8-9, 1881	
1890	Lester Curtis, ...	8	8-19, 1883	

Children of 785 MARY JANE BEARDSLEY BANKER,[7]

| 1891 | Burt Anthony Banker, . . . | 8 | 2-3, 1859 | Macomb, Ill. 8-6, 1885 |
| | Nellie May Hoffman, . . . | . | 12-3, 1863 | |

Children of 785 a SHERMAN BEARDSLEY,[7]

| 1892 | —— Beardsley, . . . | 8 | . . . . . | |
| | Alonzo Eagan, . . . | . | . . . . . | Bennetsburg, N. Y. |

Children of 785 c MARIA L. BEARDSLEY,[7]

| 1893 | ——, ... | 8 | |
| 1894 | ——, ... | 8 | |

Children of 785 d LUCY A. BEARDSLEY LYON,[7]

1895	Elmer E. Lyon, . . .	8	5-9, 1862	
1896	Joseph I., ...	8	6-18, 1866	2-15, 1893
	Bertha J. Huislander, . . .			
1897	Clara L., ...	8	9-29, 1870	

Children of 785 e D. CURTIS BEARDSLEY,[7]

| 1898 | —— Beardsley, . . . | 8 | |

Children of 787 FRELICH BEARDSLEY,[7]

| 1899 | Lena K. Beardsley, . . . | 8 | 11-30, 1883 | |

Children of 788 SAMUEL AGARD BEARDSLEY,[7]

| 1900 | John Beardsley, . . . | . | 1845 | . . . |

No.	Name of Wife (or Husband).	Date of Birth.	Date of Marriage.	Residence.	Date of Death.	Place of Burial.
1901	Grant, ...8 *Harriet Campbell.*	1846	. . . .	Manson, N. C.		
1902	Harriet A., ...8 *George L. Tram,*	1848	. . . .	Catharine.		
1903	May " Cornelia," . .8 *Samuel Winton,*	. . 1852	. . . .	Catharine.		
	Children of 791 SCIPIO C. BEARDS-LEY,[7]					
1904	Charles I. Beardsley, . .8 *Emma ——,*	6-24, 1856	3-25, 1877	Hoblett, Pa.		
1905	J. Earl, ...8 *Josie E. Noonan,*	7-2, 1861	1-17, 1882	Catharine.		
1906	Lewis, ...8 *Louise Bartlett,*	5-26, 1866	9- , 1888	Watkins, N. Y.		
1907	Hazlitt James, ...8 *Ida May Hall,*	1-21, 1869	5-15, 1890	Danby, N. Y.		
	Children of 792 JAMES E. BEARDS-LEY,[7]					
1908	Menzo Beardsley, . . .8 *Florence Patterson,*	10-5, 1859	10-8, 1884			
1909	Emma, ...8	1860				
1910	Grace C., ...8	4-18, 1867 8 8, 1869				
	Children of 796 JAMES B. BEARDS-LEY,[7]					
1911	Stephen R. Beardsley, . .8					
1912	Sarah, ...8					
	Children of 806 LUCINA BEARDSLEY GIBBS,[7]					
1913	Charles Gibbs, ...8 *Adelia ——,*	9-12, 1845				
1914	Frances, ...8	8-10, 1847	. . . .		6-6, 1858	

No.	Name	Gen.	Date		Place		Date
1915	Nancie L.,	8	4–6, 1852				
1916	Eaton F.,	8	4–6, 1853				
	Julia,						
1917	Manly H.,	8	5–30, 1854				
	Ella,						
	Children of 808 HARRIET A. BEARDSLEY RITTENHOUSE,[7]						
1918	Levi B. Rittenhouse,	8	6–2, 1850				
1919	T. Wilbur,	8	4–25, 1852				
1920	David B.,	8	9–7, 1855				
1921	Horace A.,	8	6–26, 1860				
1922	Arthur,	8	5–9, 1867				
1923	Percy C.,	8	3–27, 1870	11–21, 1890			
	Children of 811 HORACE A. BEARDSLEY,[7]						
1924	Clara E. Beardsley,	8	1–21, 1874				
1925	Ralph W.,	8	11–2, 1878				
1926	Asa,	8	11–20, 1882				
	Children of 813 MARY HOWARD KINGSBURY CAMPBELL,[7]						
1927	Mariette Kingsbury,	8	1844		Caton.		1863
	Seneca Barber,						
1928	Isabel,	8	1848			Millport.	
1929	Bell Campbell,	8	1853	1852			
	William Van Buren				Elmira.	1852	
1930	Lucius M.,	8	1851				
1931	Lucius B.,	8	1858				
	Augusta Stuart,				Jamestown, Tenn.		
1932	John,	8	1861				
	Frances ——,						
1933	James Elmer,	8	1864		Brockton, Mass.		
	Laura Alger,						
	Children of 819 JOSEPHINE HOWARD LATTIN,[7]						
1934	Fred. A. Lattin,	8	1861		Los Gatos, Cal.		1885
	Jessie Cook,						

No.	Name of Wife (or Husband).	Date of Birth.	Date of Marriage.	Residence.	Date of Death.	Place of Burial.
1935	William, ...8	1864	1888	. . .	1883	
	Addie Bowen,					
1936	Joel Couch, ...8	1866				
1937	Ada, ...8	1872				
1938	Ida, ...8	1872	1891	. . .		
	Charles Esterbrook,	. . .		. . .		
	Children of 825 MARY L. RUGGLES COMPTON,[7]					
1939	Anna Dora Compton,[7] . .8	5-13, 1860		Sylvania, Pa.		
1940	Mary Elizabeth, . . .8	9-1, 1861	12-15, 1881	Sylvania. / Troy, Pa.		
	Frank (s. of Orrin F.) Price,					
1941	William Grant, . . .8	10-29, 1864		Sullivan, Pa , .	12-11, 1864	Sullivan.
1942	Fred. Burton, . . .8	1-7, 1870		Troy.		
1943	Henry Walter, . . .8	2-18, 1878		"		
1944	Sarah Louise, . . .8	11-7, 1880				
	Children of 825 MATILDA BEARDSLEY LATTIN,[7]					
1945	James P. Lattin, . . .8	. .		Catharine, . .		
1946	Charles H., ...8	. .			dec.	
	Carrie Conkling.					
1947	Lottie L., ...8	. .			dec.	
	Charles Devoey.					
1948	Dell M., ...8	. .				
	Emmet Brink.					
1949	Beach, ...8	. .			dec.	
1950	Gertie, ...8	. .			dec.	
1951	Ola, ...8	. .				
	George Lovall.					
1952	Fred, ...8	. .				
1953	Cora, ...8	. .				
1954	Arthur, ...8	. .				
1955	Grace, ...8	. .				

No.	Name	Gen.	Date		Place		
	Children of 826 SARAH BEARDSLEY HAWES,[7]						
1956	Orrin F. Hawes,	8	9-15, 1861				
1957	Marilla Levisa,	8					
1958	*Joseph Ritzenthaler,*	8	3-8, 1864				
	Charlotte Eliza,	8					
1959	*Chauncy P. Blessing,*	8	5-7, 1868	1890			
	John Beardsley,	8					
	Pearl Van Huzer,						
	Children of 828 JAMES W. BEARDSLEY,[7]						
1960	James Clarance Beardsley,	8	1873			1877	
1961	Harry,	8	1875			1878	
	Children of 829 CHARLOTTE BEARDSLEY STANLEY,[7]						
1962	La Motte Stanley,	8	4-20, 1868	5-20, 1891	Millport.		Catharine.
	Cora Pratt,						
1963	Gertie May,	8	1-3, 1872		Odessa,	2-6, 1877	
1964	R. DeWitt,	8	3-17, 1874		"		
1965	Myrtle,	8	4-30, 1880		"		
	Children of 830 MARY BEARDSLEY KEYSER LOCKHART,[7]						
1966	Eva Keyser,	8	4-14, 1871	9-, 1888	Odessa.	10-21, 1890	
	Elbert Owen,						
	Children of 832 ALBERT BEARDSLEY,[7]						
1967	Adelbert Beardsley,	8			Catharine.		
1968	John,	8			"		
	Children of 834 JOHN LAMBERT BEARDSLEY[7]						
1969	Glen Beardsley,	8			Catharine.		
1970	Emma,	8			"		
	Children of 839 SARAH BEARDSLEY CLEVELAND,[7]						
1971	Morton George Cleveland,	8	2-11, 1868		Richmond, Pa.		

No.	Name of Wife (or Husband).		Date of Birth.	Date of Marriage.	Residence.	Date of Death.	Place of Burial.
1972	Carl Harvey,	8	5–9, 1872	. . . .	Richmond, Pa.		
	Children of 840 SUSAN BEARDSLEY MAKLEY,[7]						
1973	Addie A. Makley,	8	1–20, 1872	. . . .	Rutland, Pa.		
1974	Archie John,	8	2–12, 1880	. . . .	"		
1975	Gertie Emily,	8	1–21, 1887	. . . .	"		
	Children of 842 HATTIE BEARDSLEY HARVEY,[7]						
1976	Ethel L. Harvey,	8	6–6, 1880	. . . .	Lamb's Creek, Pa.		
1977	Edith,	8	12–8, 1883	. . . .	"		
1978	Harry B.,	8	1–6, 1887	. . . .	"		
1979	Howard Ross,	8	12–27, 1892	. . . .			
	Children of 843a STEPHEN L BEARDSLEY,[7]						
1980	William Beardsley,	8					
	Children of 843b HENRIETTA BEARDSLEY WILLIAMS,[7]						
1981	George Williams,	8					
1982	Carrie,	8					
1983	Roswell,	8					
	Children of 843c ADELIA BEARDSLEY HULL TRIGGS FRANCIS,[7]						
1984	Martha A. Hull,	8	8–9, 1856	. . . .		12–11, 1857	
1985	Charles A.,	8	11–1, 1859	. . . .		1867	
1986	Robert S. Triggs,	8	1–15, 1865	3–9, 1889			
1987	Cora E. Francis,	8	5–15, 1872	9–, 1892			
	I. Peabody,						
1988	Betta M. Francis,	8	1–27, 1875				

Children of 843 d ROSWELL BEARDSLEY,[7]

1989	Cora Beardsley,	[8]	8-20, 1871	
1990	Mary,[7]	[8]	7-21, 1873	
1991	Minnie M.,	[8]	10-29, 1875	Ashby, Minn.
1992	Maude M.,	[8]	1-28, 1877	"
1993	Albert F.,	[8]	11-9, 1878	"
1994	Etta,	[8]	5-20, 1881	"
1995	Edna,	[8]	8-27, 1883	"
1996	Earl B.,	[8]	10-10, 1889	" 12-18, 1889

Children of 843 e WILLIAM H. BEARDSLEY,[7]

1997	George Beardsley,	[8]
	May Sodden,	
1998	Ella,	[8]
1999	Samuel,	[8]
2000	William,	[8]

Children of 843 f MARY BEARDS-LEY INGRAHAM,[7]

2001	Charles Ingraham,	[8]

Children of 843 g ANGELINE BEARDS-LEY HOLMAN CALDWELL ALBRIGHT,[7]

2002	Ida Holman,	[8]
	Thom. Iberson,	
2003	Eugene Caldwell,	[8]
2004	Stella Albright,	[8]

Children of 847 ALBERT H. BEARDSLEY,[7]

2005	Pauline Beardsley,	[8]	1890

Children of 849 GEORGE W. VAN NOTRICK,[7]

2006	Harry R. Van Notrick,	[8]	1875
2007	Edna L.,	[8]	1877
2008	Archie H.,	[8]	1880
2009	William G.,	[8]	1886

No.	Name of Wife (or Husband).	Date of Birth.	Date of Marriage.	Residence.	Date of Death.	Place of Burial.
	Children of 855 LAURA HUBBELL ROLSTON,[7]					
2010	Martha Ann Rolston,[8]	5–13, 1843			9–29, 1844	Damascus, Pa.
2011	William,[8]	3–17, 1846			12–26, 1864	Alabama.
2012	James O.,[8]	12–3, 1847			4–29, 1850	Damascus.
2013	James K.,[8]	8–23, 1850	3–6, 1878			
	Octavia Lewis,					
2014	Katharine L.,[8]	6–24, 1852		New Haven.		
2015	Charles A.,[8]	4–15, 1855	11–1, 1881			
	Leilia Lewis,					
	Children of 856 LEVI HUBBELL,[7] and of 893 b.					
2016	Theodore Hubbell,[8]	7–23, 1850	11– , 1871	New Haven, Ct.		
	Jennie Bronson,	1853				
	Children of 857 CHARLES HUBBELL,[7]					
2017	Charles Hubbell,[8]	1843		New York,	10– , 1885	Bridgeport.
2018	Eugene A.,[8]	11– , 1850		New York.		
	Children of 859 WILLIAM P. KNAPP,[7]					
2019	—— Knapp,[8]					
2020	——,[8]					
2021	——,[8]					
2022	——,[8]					
2023	——,[8]					
	Children of 860 ISAAC M. KNAPP,[7]					
2024	—— Knapp,[8]					
2025	——,[8]					
2026	——,[8]					
2027	——,[8]					
2028	——,[8]					
2029	——,[8]					

No.	Name	Gen.	Born	Married / Died	Place
2030	——,	8			
2031	——,	8			
	Children of *862* ELIZABETH KNAPP CURTIS,[7]				
2032	—— Curtis,	8			
	Children of *863* LUCY A. KNAPP RUDYARD,[7]				
2033	—— Rudyard,	8			
2034	——,	8			
	Children of *869* LEWIS ELISHA CLARK,[7]				
2035	Everard Benjamin Clark,	8	12–24, 1838	6–17, 1874	Milford.
	Princetta M. Pardee,		12–13, 1846		Bethany.
2036	Elisha Beach,	8	6–11, 1841	12–26, 1866	S. Meriden.
	Sarah Louise Williams,		10–14, 1845		
2037	Anna Eliza,	8	7–20, 1843	11–21, 1866	Chicopee, Mass.
	George Willard Bray,		9–28, 1843		
	Children of *870* ALANSON B. CLARK,[7]				
2038	Olin Howard Clark,	8	11–24, 1851	. . .	Hartford, Ct.
	Children of *871* SARAH A. CLARK HUBBARD,[7]				
2039	John Merwin Hubbard,	8	3–12, 1844	10–4, 1871	W. Haven.
	Laura Booth Davis,		11–24, 1860		Oxford, Ct.
2040	Lewis Clark,	8	12–14, 1845	10–23, 1878	W. Haven.
	Fannie A. Smith,		11–16, 1846		Milford.
2041	Edward Eugene,	8	6–10, 1848	11–5, 1877	W. Haven.
	Vara L. Smith,		5–13, 1856		Milford.
2042	Anna Atwater,	8	6–26, 1850	5–29, 1870	W. Haven.
	William Mayhew Cottle,		8–, 1841		Waterbury.
2043	George Henry,	8	1–11, 1855	7–24, 1884	Foo Chow, China.
	Ellen Louise Peete,		7–21, 1859		W. Haven.
2044	Mary Elizabeth,	8	2–17, 1857	6–2, 1880	Waterbury, Ct.
	Charles Reuben Lawrence,		3–30, 1857		"
2045	William Russell,	8	11–18, 1859	. . .	W. Haven.
				3–20, 1871	W. Haven.

No.	Name of Wife (or Husband).	Date of Birth.	Date of Marriage.	Residence.	Date of Death.	Place of Burial.
	Children of 872 AVIS CLARK BUCK-INGHAM,[7]					
2046	Harriett Ann Buckingham, . . . [8]	4-4, 1854	. . .	Milford, . . .	7-6, 1863	Milford.
	Children of 873 NEHEMIAH THOMAS CLARK,[7] *and of 964,*					
2047	Edgar Thomas Clark, . . . [8]	12-14, 1859	8-2, 1888	Milford.	12-8, 1888	
	Anna Lauren Botsford,	4-6, 1864				
2048	Anna Bell, . . . [8]	12-25, 1861	11-1, 1886	. . . .		
	George Andrew Elmer,	1860				
2049	Bertha Amelia, . . . [8]	9-6, 1868		N. Haven.		
	Children of 874 HARRIET CLARK LAW,[7]					
2050	Lizzie Finette Law, . . . [8]	11-10, 1855	12-4, 1878	New Haven.		
	Dennis Albert Blakeslee,	8-11, 1856		"		
2051	Willie Andrew, . . . [8]	12-12, 1859		"	3-7, 1862	
2052	Lyman Thomas, . . . [8]	4-5, 1861	5-16, 1887	"		
	Martha Eldora Blakeslee,	9-6, 1865		"		
2053	George Andrew, . . . [8]	7-15, 1863	11-11, 1886	"		
	Mary Louise Platt,	4-14, 1865				
	Children of 876 HENRY T. WHEELER,[7]					
2054	—— Wheeler, . . . [8]	. . .	. . .	N.Y., . . .	dec.	N.Y.
2055	—— , . . . [8]	. . .	. . .	"	"	"
2056	Mary Ellen, —— , . . . [8]	8-5, 1838	1-7, 1863	"	6-29, 1891	M. G. C. B. C.
	Seymour Whiting Ely,	10-21, 1838		Bridgeport, . . .	10-18, 1890	"
2057	Henry Austin, . . . [8]	5-26, 18	12-26, 18	Bergen, N. J.		
	Mary Eliz. Child,	. . .				
2058	Jennie Griffing, . . . [8]	. . .	. . .	Bridgeport.		
2059	Robert Curtis, . . . [8]	. . .	. . .	"		
	Children of 878 LAURA A. WHEELER HALL,[7]					
2060	Maria Louise Hall, . . . [8]	5-20, 1837	. . .	Bridgeport.		

No.	Name		Born	Married	Residence		M. G. C. B. C.
2061	Frank Howard,	8	1–7, 1841				
2062	Emma Clarissa,	8	5–28, 1848				
2063	George Wheeler,	8	10–25, 1850	10–30, 1871	Bridgeport.	5–4, 1889	
	Alice Lenora Ward,				"		

Children of 882 MARIA WHEELER MERWIN,[7]

No.	Name		Born	Married	Residence		M. G. C. B. C.
2064	Mary Louise Merwin,	8	5–26, 1853		Milford,	9–3, 1856	Milford.
2065	Ida Maria,	8	6–24, 1855		"	7–11, 1889	"
2066	Mary Calina,	8	12–25, 1856		"		
2067	Jane Wheeler,	8	4–3, 1859		"		
2068	Walter Lincoln,	8	10–31, 1860		"		
2069	Laura Hall,	8	11–30, 1862		"		
2070	Sherman Terry,	8	12–8, 1864				

Children of 885 HARRIET BUCKINGHAM LATTIN,[7]

No.	Name		Born	Married	Residence		M. G. C. B. C.
2071	Carrie May Lattin,	8	5–21, 1860	6–8, 1881	Stratford, Ct.	12–14, 1889	Stratford.
	Elmer Beardsley,		8–18, 1856		"		
2072	Willie Valentine,	8	2–14, 1864		"	1–14, 1881	
2073	John Buckingham,	8	9–24, 1870				

Children of 886 FENN MALLETT,[7]

No.	Name		Born	Married	Residence		M. G. C. B. C.
2074	Benjamin Mallett,	8			Southbury, Ct.		
	,						

Children of 887 SALLY MALLETT PEET,[7]

No.	Name		Born	Married	Residence		M. G. C. B. C.
2075	Andred Peet,	8				dec. ae. 13	

Children of 889 THOMAS H. MALLETT,[7]

No.	Name		Born	Married	Residence		M. G. C. B. C.
2076	Lottie R. Mallett,	8					

Children of 895 b CATHARINE MALLETT HUBBELL,[7] *see 856.*

Children of 895 a LUCY ANN HIGBY BALDWIN,[7] *and 958.*

No.	Name		Born	Married	Residence		M. G. C. B. C.
2077	Mary DeWitt Baldwin,	8	7–17, 1844	7–26, 1866			
	Samuel A. Warburton.						

No.	Name of Wife (or Husband).	Date of Birth.	Date of Marriage.	Residence.	Date of Death.	Place of Burial.
	Children of 895 b ELIZABETH HIGBY Y BRISTOL,[7]					
2078	Aristides Bristol, ... 8	8-31, 1849				
	—,					
	Children of 895 c RILEY HIGBY,[7]					
2079	George O. Higby, . . . 8					
2080	Charles, ... 8					
	Children of 895 e MEHETABLE HIGBY DISBROW,[7]					
2081	James G. Disbrow, . . . 8					
	Children of 895 f MARCUS HIGBY,[7]					
2082	— Higby, ... 8				dec.	
2083	—, 8				"	
2084	—, 8				"	
2085	—, 8				"	
2086	—, 8				"	
2087	—, 8				"	
2088	—, 8				"	
	Children of 895 h CHARLOTTE AUGUSTA HIGBY BRIAN,[7]					
2089	Charles Henry Brian, . . 8	2-10, 1868	2-26, 1890			
	Lottie D. Warner,					
2090	Cecile, ... 8	12-7, 1873				
	Children of 902 CHARLES W. PEET,[7]					
2091	Julius Peet, ... 8					
2092	Margaret, ... 8					
2093	—, ... 8					
2094	Florine, ... 8					
2095	Addie, ... 8					
2096	Webster, ... 8					

						M. G. C. B. C.
Children of 904 George A. Hubbell,						
2097	Frank A. Hubbell,	8	. . .	Bridgeport.	. . .	
	Mary Dunning,					
2098	Samuel W.	8	. . .	Bridgeport.	. . .	
	Carrie Turney,					
2099	Freddie,	8	. . .		. . .	
Children of 905 Clarissa Hubbell Corbusier,						
2100	Samuel W. Corbusier,	8	12–30, 1851	Bridgeport,	. . .	1–16, 1862 M.
2101	Nebbie C.,	8	9–24, 1854	"	. . .	5–20, 1855 G.
2102	Alfred B.,	8	9–20, 1857	"	. . .	12–8, 1861 C.
2103	Lilly A.,	8	6–1, 1860	"	. . .	11–6, 1861 B.
2104	Alfred C.,	8	11–15, 1862	"	. . .	5–14, 1868 C.
2105	Laura B.,	8	11–10, 1864	"	. . .	
	J. Buckingham Marsh,				3–29, 1893	
2106	Clara B.	8	6–26, 1869		. . .	
Children of 906 William W. Wheeler,						
2107	—— Wheeler,	8				
2108	——	8				
2109	——,	8				
Children of 907 Elizabeth Wheeler Hubbell,						
2110	Henry Hubbell,	8	. . .		. . .	
Children of 913 Frances Mallett Rich,						
2111	Sarah Frances Rich,	8	1–30, 1843	Bridgeport	. . .	
	Wheeler Hawley,				9–1, 1864	
Children of 919 a Sarah Mallett Beach,						
2112	—— Beach,	8				
2113	——,	8				

No.	Name of Wife (or Husband).	Date of Birth.	Date of Marriage.	Residence.	Date of Death.	Place of Burial.
2114	*Children of 919 b Z. TAYLOR MAL-* *LETT,*[7] Julia Mallett,					
2115	*Children of 921 CAROLINE MALLETT* BLAKEMAN,[7] Alfred Augustus Blakeman,[8] *Emma Louisa (d. of Orville) Curtis,*	7-19, 1850 8-7, 1851	1-7, 1872	Stratford, Ct. " "		
2116	*Children of 922 MARK S. MALLETT,*[7] Sherman B. Mallett.[8]	2-9, 1853			3-10, 1859	
2117	Harriet D.,[8]	12-15, 1855			4-27, 1857	
2118	Sherman Benjamin,[8] *Mary E. (d. of Theo.) Judson.*	11-12, 1859 9-28, 1865	10-24, 1888	Hartford, Ct. Stratford.		
2119	Susan Catharine,[8] *Harrison S. Bennett,*	4-8, 1862 9-23, 1861	11-18, 1888		4-26, 1891	
2120	*Children of 923 HENRY C. MAL-* *LETT,*[7] Carrie Mallett,[8] *Wm. Wilberforce Tibbals,*	1-30, 1856 1-15, 1852	12-23, 1880			
2121	William Somers,[8]	9-8, 1858			4-6, 1862	
2122	Henry Curtis,[8]	6-30, 1861			4-5, 1862	
2123	James A.,[8]	1-14, 1863		Stratford. "		
2124	Sarah Curtis,[8] *G. Carlton Russell,*	1-28, 1865	10-27, 1891	Boston, Mass. Stratford.		
2125	Grace Elizabeth,[8] *Maynard T. Smith,*	10-30, 1867	2-10, 1890	Bridgeport.		
2126	*Children of 924 ALFRED B. MAL-* *LETT,*[7] William Stannard Mallett,[8]	3-22, 1565		Newport News, Va.		
2127	Amelia Jones,[8] *Louis Upshur.*	10-30, 1868	12-19, 1888			
2128	Arthur Tibbals.	8-31, 1876				

	Children of 926 CHARLOTTE MALLETT HYDE,[7]				
2129	Annie Louisa Hyde,	8	1-6, 1877		
2130	Eleanor May,	8	5-13, 1879		
	Children of 931 b MARGARET MALLETT MILES,[7]				
2131	Son, Miles,	8			
2132	Son,	8			
	Children of 935 RICHARD L. BALDWIN,[7]				
2133	Mary Dewitt Baldwin,	8		} Boston.	
	George Stearns,				
2134	Emma Louise,	8			
2135	Susan D.,	8			
2136	Edward Lewis,	8			
2137	Wilson Leslie,	8			
	Children of 936 MARTHA BALDWIN MILES,[7]				
2138	Edward G. Miles,	8	2-2, 1846	} 10-12, 1870	Milford.
	Mary (d. of Wm.) Brooks,		2-14, 1847		
	Children of 940 ADAM P. BALDWIN,[7]				
2139	Arthur Pond Baldwin,	8	8-22, 1856	} 8-18, 1881	N. Y. Milford.
	Caroline G. (d. of John H.) Wingfield,				
	Children of 942 CHARLES S. BALDWIN,[7]				
2140	Frederick Hickson Baldwin,	8			
2141	Lizzie Jaffrey,	8			
2142	Grace Dewitt,	8			
2143	Alice,	8			
2144	Martha Pond,	8			
	Children of 943 CHARLOTTE BALDWIN NETTLETON,[7]				
2145	Anna Nettleton,	8			
2146	David Lewis,	8			

No.	Name of Wife (or Husband).	Date of Birth.	Date of Marriage.	Residence.	Date of Death.	Place of Burial.
2147	Dewitt Baldwin, ...8					
2148	Alfred, ...8					
2149	Son, ...8					
	Children of 945 MARY MILES SPERRY,[7]					
2150	—— Sperry, ...8					
2151	——, ...8					
2152	——, ...8					
2153	——, ...8					
2154	——, ...8					
2155	——, ...8					
	Children of 947 SARAH MILES ——,[7]					
2156	——, ...8					
2157	——, ...8					
	Children of 949 SAMUEL A. MILES,[7]					
2158	Norman S. Miles, ...8	2-16, 1840	} 1-16, 1867	College Sp'gs, Ill.		
	Mary E. McConnell,	1-21, 1847				
2159	Lucy D., ...8	. . . .	. . . .	Milford.		
2160	Ernest Strong, ...8	. . . .	. . . .	¨		
	Children of 952 SAMUEL BURTON BALDWIN,[7] *see 895 a.*					
	Children of 954 JAMES B. BALDWIN,[7]					
2161	Helen Irving Baldwin, ...8	6-1, 1851	. . . .	Milford.		
2162	Herbert L., ...8	4-2, 1860	. . . .			
	Children of 956 ALBERT A. BALD-WIN,[7]					
2163	Susan A. Baldwin, ...8	3-4, 1863	. . . .	. . . .		
2164	Benjamin P., ...8	5-21, 1867			6-14. 1872	

No.	Name	Born	Married / Died	Place	
	Children of 957 NATHAN A. BALDWIN,[7]				
2165	Nathalie Baldwin,[8]	12-27, 1864	5-13, 1886	N. Y.	
	Morton (s. of Geo.) Grinnell, M. D.,				
	Children of 958 LAURA BALDWIN CORNWALL,[7]				
2166	Adolphus Cornwall,[8]	8-9, 1849	1-25, 1872	Milford,	9-1, 1878
	Kate McCorkendale,				9-, 1878
2167	Laura Grove,[8]	11-3, 1851	10-, 1870		Brooklyn.
	Duncan McCorkendale,		11-12, 1874	Brooklyn, N. Y.,	
	James B. Muir,			"	2-, 1871
2168	George Rockwell,[8]	3-16, 1855			
2169	Henry Clay,[8]	4-2, 1859			
	Children of 959 TIMOTHY H. BALDWIN,[7]				
2170	Caroline Atwater Baldwin.[8]	9-30, 1849	7-27, 1876		3-30, 1877
	Miguel A. Alvares, M. D.,				3-, 1853
2171	David Smith,[8]	8-9, 1851			
2172	Lucy Higgins,[8]	10-5, 1854			9-30, 1883
2173	Elizabeth Wheeler,[8]	6-27, 1856			
	Arthur E. Walradt,				
2174	Emily Lockwood,[8]	4-28, 1860	12-23, 1884		
	Children of 962 LUCY BALDWIN STEVENS,[7]				
2175	Nathan Baldwin Stevens,[8]	11-2, 1859			
2176	Bertha,[8]	3-7, 1862			
2177	John Bright,[8]	11-3, 1864			
2178	Lucy Beatrice,[8]	9-4, 1876			
	Children of 963 HENRY CLAY BALDWIN,[7]				
2179	Emma Blauvelt Baldwin,[8]	1-5, 1864		Brooklyn.	
2180	Henrietta Clay,[8]	9-23, 1865			
2181	Harry Clay,[8]	12-1, 1867			
2182	Jessie,[8]	10-26, 1869			
2183	Nathan Adolphus,[8]	8-27, 1871			
2184	Mary Vanderhoef,[8]	1-22, 1875			

No.	Name of Wife (or Husband).	Date of Birth.	Date of Marriage.	Residence.	Date of Death.	Place of Burial.
	Children of 964 ABIGAIL P. BALDWIN CLARK,[7] *see 873,*					
	Children of 965 CALVIN D. BALDWIN,[7]					
2185	Mary Baldwin, [8]	11-7, 1860	} 1-12, 1882	Milford.		
	Arthur L. Judson,	...		Stratford.		
	Children of 966 EDWIN BALDWIN,[7]					
2186	Evaline S. Baldwin, [8]	1866				
2187	Anna Minor, [8]	3- , 1870				
2188	(Susan Peck)? [8]	1874				
	Children of 968 WILLIAM R. HIGBY,[7]					
2189	Martha Louise Higby, [8]	1-14, 1848	} 10-14, 1880			
2190	Helen Augusta, [8]	5-23, 1860				
	George Manson Eames,	1-19, 1859				
	Children of 975 SARAH BALDWIN CROCKETT,[7]					
2191	Charles W. Crockett, [8]	8-5, 1852				
2192	Carrie S., [8]	5-2, 1855				
	Children of 976 ELIZA BALDWIN WELTON,[7]					
2193	Oliver Welton, [8]	7-8, 1853	} 11-25, 1877			
	Carrie Holland,	...				
2194	Andrew N., [8]	12-27, 1857				
2195	Walter S., [8]	2-3, 1860	} 6-18, 1879			
	Hattie Lindsley,	...				
2196	Esther L., [8]	3-5, 1863				

No.	Name	Born		Died	Place		Notes
	Children of 977 WILLIAM P. BALDWIN,[7]						
2197	Joseph R. Baldwin, ...8	1-17, 1858	}				
	Savilla Livingston, ...	. . . .					
	Children of 980 SAMUEL BEACH, M. D.,[7]						
2198	Fannie Beach, ...8	1836	}	11-4 1879			
	— *Ely,*	1838		1869			
2199	Samuel Swift, ...8	10-15, 1842	}	10-20, 1868	Oberlin, Ohio.	7-22, 1874	M. G. C. B. C.
	Bena Cushing, ...	1849					
	Children of 981 CORNELIA BEACH CURTIS,[7]						
2200	John Beach Curtis, ...8	12-15, 1830		unm.	. . . .	2-26, 1859	M. G. C. B. C
2201	Cornelia Mary, ...8	8-20, 1832	}	12-2, 1863	. . . .	1-1, 1885	M. G. C. B. C
	Edwin Banks, ...	8- , 1825					
	Children of 982 SHELDON BEACH,[7] see 411.						
	Children of 985 LOUISA BEACH FAIRCHILD,[7]						
2202	Henry Charles Fairchild, . . .8	7-17, 1842	}	9-30, 1863	Bridgeport, Conn.		
	1287 Mary L. (d. of Joel) Shelton,[7]	2-18, 1842			Huntington, "		
2203	Alfred Beach, ...8	7-13, 1845	}	6-18, 1873	Bridgeport, "		
	Eliza Mills (d. of Gideon) Tomlinson,	10-7, 1847			Stratford, "		
	Children of 986 ELIZABETH BEACH UFFORD,[7]						
2204	William Ufford, ...8	12-15, 1831	}	1-5, 1870	. . . .	4-21, 1891	
2205	Daniel, ...8						
	Annie Mandeville, ...	. . . .					
	Children of 987 WILLIAM BEACH,[7]						
2206	Katharine Elizabeth Beach. . .8	9-1, 1840	}	6-21, 1866	Elmira.		
	Timothy Smith Pratt,	1-16, 1836					
2207	Mary Emily, ...8	3-3, 1842	}	9-19, 1856	Elmira, N. Y., . .	4-17, 1891	
	J. Leslie Gregg, ...	. . . .					

No.	Name of Wife (or Husband).	Date of Birth.	Date of Marriage.	Residence.	Date of Death.	Place of Burial.
2208	*Children of 988 MARY BEACH LYON,*[7]					
	Roger Horace Lyon, ...[8]			N. Y.		
	Katharine J. Luther,	9-20, 1837	1-31, 1888			
2209	Mary W.; . . . .[8]	1-21, 1840	10-10, 1866	Bridgeport, Ct.		
	John S. Lindsley, M. D.,	1-19, 1838		N. Y. City.		
2210	*Children of 989 JAMES W. BEACH,*[7]					
	Wilbur Augustus Beach, . . .[8]		1-22, 1874	Elmira, N. Y.		
	Jennie W. Garner,					
2211	Frederick Silliman, ...[8]	6-15, 1853	11-16, 1878	Bridgeport,	dec.	M. G. C. B. C.
	Emily E. Upson,	5-31, 1850				
2212	Robert James, (Rev.), . . .[8]	5-9, 1864		"		
2213	*Children of 991 REV. ISAAC JENNINGS,*[7]					
	Isaac Jennings, D. D., . . .[8]	4-30, 1848	12-13, 1871			
	Mary E. (d. of Rev.Stephen B.) Leonard,					
2214	Walter Loomis, ...[8]	7-6, 1850	. . . .		10-16, 1850	Stamford, Ct.
22 5	Sophia Day, ...[8]	8-4, 1851	. . . .		1-11, 1861	Bennington, Vt.
2216	Frederick Beach, ...[8]	8-6, 1853	7-27, 1880			
	Laura Hall (d. of T. W.) Park,					
2217	Matthias Day, ...[8]	1-8, 1857	9-8, 1885		12-25, 1860	Bennington.
2218	Chas. Green Rockwood, . . .[8]	11-17, 1859				
	Mary Jeannette (d. of A. B. Gardner),					
2219	Robert Gould, ...[8]	3-28, 1862	. . . .			
2220	Philip Burton, ...[8]	12-7, 1865	6-25, 1891			
	Edith T. (d. of Dan'l) Robinson,					
2221	William Bigelow, ...[8]	7-20, 1871				
2222	*Children of 993 ELIZABETH JEN-* *NINGS HOSFORD,*[7]					
	William Beach Hosford,[7] . . .[8]	8-9, 1842	1866			
2223	Catharine Jennings, ...[8]	6-18, 1845				
	George Clark,					

No.	Name		Birth		Residence	
	Children of 994 CATHARINE JEN-NINGS PARSONS,[7]					
2224	Electa Clark Parsons,	8	8-25, 1851	8-18, 1886		
	Chas. Wilson Riggs,					
2225	Louise Shepherd,	8	6-10, 1854			
	Rev. Albert Whiting,			9- , 1873		3- , 1878
	Rev. Robert Abbey,			1-2, 1882		10-8, 1890
2226	Frederick Jennings,	8	12-3, 1861			
2227	Elizabeth Cornelia,	8	1-17, 1864			
	Children of 995 JOHN GILES JEN-NINGS,[7]					
2228	John Gould Jennings,	8	9-28, 1856	1-23, 1884		
	Lillian May Lampson,					
2229	Caroline Hubbell,	8	9-28, 1856	8-14, 1884		
	Newton Sherwood Calhoun,					
2230	George Conkling,	8	12-21, 1861			
	Children of 997 WILLIAM S. ED-WARDS,[7]					
2231	William Beebe Edwards,	8	3-12, 1866		Brooklyn.	
2232	Martha (Sister M. Benedicite),	8	9-4, 1867		San Francisco.	
2233	Lucy Breeze,	8	2-7, 1869		Bridgeport.	
2234	Georgiana Beebe,	8	12-28, 1870		Oakland, Cal.	
	Channing Howard Cook,					
2235	David Sannds,	8	3-20, 1873	3-31, 1891		
2236	Joseph Paulding,	8	5-5, 1880			
	Children of 998 HARRIET EDWARDS WALLER,[7]					
2237	William Edwards Waller,	8	12-17, 1861	6-7, 1894	Trumbull, Ct.,	
	Susan Gilman (d. of James) Ludlum.		11-11, 1863			
2238	Mary Gordon,	8	2-13, 1864	2-17, 1887	Trumbull,	5-29, 1890
	Geo. Anson Starkweather, Lieut. U.S.A.					10-21, 1891
2239	Harriet Henry,	8	5-27, 1867		Trumbull.	
	Children of 1000 WILLIAM S. WHEELER,[7]					
2240	Mary Wheeler,	8	9-21, 1869			
2241	Jennie Alice,	8				dec.

No.	Name of Wife (or Husband).	Date of Birth.	Date of Marriage.	Residence.	Date of Death.	Place of Burial.
2242	Charles Augustus, ... 8	8-15, 1871			dec.	
2243	William Albert, ... 8	3-27, 1881				
2244	Theodore Beardsley, ... 8	3-17, 1883				
2245	Laura Josephine, ... 8					
	Children of 1002 THEODORE W. BEACH,[7]					
2246	Anna Beach, ... 8	10-22, 1873				
2247	Florence, ... 8	6-19, 1878				
	Children of 1008 STILES B. NICHOLS,[7]					
2248	George Drew Nichols, ... 8	12-3, 1859	10-7, 1885	Huntington, Ct.		
	Fanny A. Rowley.					
2249	Stiles Alonzo, ... 8	7-30, 1862	10-2, 1889			
	Jessie Booth Judson,	11-9, 1865				
	Children of 1011 VIRGINIA BURTON HOLMES,[7]					
2250	Elias Burton Holmes, ... 8	1-8, 1870		Chicago.	i-11, 1881	Rose Hill, Chi.
2251	Louise, ... 8	8-13, 1871		"		
2252	Ira Germain, ... 8	4-8, 1876		"		
	Children of 1012 LEGRAND STERLING BURTON,[7]					
2253	Legrand Sterling Burton, . . 8	3-4, 1878		Chicago.		
	Children of 1014 STEPHEN L. BURTON,[7]					
2254	Stiles Burton, ... 8	3-25, 1877		Chicago,	5-8, 1891	Chicago.
2255	Sophia, ... 8	10-12, 1879		"		
2256	Robert Clarkson, ... 8	9- , 1881				
	Children of 1015 CAROLINE BURTON PLUMB,[7] *see 697.*					

No.	Name	Born	Died	Residence	Married	Place
	Children of 1016 ELI PLUMB BURTON,[7]					
2257	Alice Carrie Burton, .8	9-24, 1871		Trumbull.		
2258	Rollin Eli, .8	4-15, 1877		"		
2259	Carrol Elbert, .8	3-23, 1879				
	Children of 1018 LORENA BURTON BRADLEY,[7]					
2260	Jennie Lorena Bradley, .8	4-7, 1867				8-23, 1876 Riverhead, N. Y.
2261	Lorena Jennie, .8	6-27, 1870	11-1, 1892	Hemptstead, L. l.		
	Mortimer Howell.	9-17, 1869				
2262	Hattie Emma, .8	4-14, 1878				
	Children of 1019 ORVILLE B. BURTON,[7]					
2263	Melissa Bell Burton, .8	2-13, 1886		Trumbull.		
	Children of 1022 EMILY JONES REYNOLDS,[7]					
2264	Wilmot Summers Reynolds, .8	1-11, 1863	11-10, 1886	Bridgeport.		9-20, 1890
	Grace L. Beebe, .	8-22, 1863				
	Susan E. Hubbell, .	8-11, 1862	10-18, 1892			
	Children of 1023 FANNIE SEELEY BECKWITH,[7]					
2265	Martha A. Beckwith, .8	5-16, 1863				
2266	Emily H., .8	6-3, 1869				
2267	Alfred L., .8	3-4, 1858				
	Children of 1024 SHELDENA A. BEACH MACRAE,[7]					
2268	Euphan Washington Macrae, .8	10-9, 1862		Fauquier co., Va.		
2269	Susan Amelia, .8	8-29, 1864	9-30, 1889	Garden City, Mo.		
2270	*James Richards Macrae,* .8	8-25, 1866	9-20, 1893	N. Y. City.		
	John,					
	Katharine Green,					
2271	Martha Beach, .8	8-2, 1868		Delaplane, Va.		
2272	Ellen Douglas, .8	5-12, 1870				1-12, 1871 Abingdon, Va.
2273	Edgar Elliott, .8	12-18, 1871		Delaplane, Va.		
2274	Sheldena Amanda, .8	7-1, 1874		"		10-27, 1879 Elmwood, Va.
2275	Richard Moncure, .8	2-17, 1877				

No.	Name of Wife (or Husband).		Date of Birth.	Date of Marriage.	Residence.	Date of Death.	Place of Burial.
	Children of 1026 ELLIOTT E. BEACH,[7]						
2276	Lilly Heach,	8	10-11, 1872		Philadelphia,	11-19, 1872	
2277	Martha Edwards,	8	4-4, 1874		"		
2278	Edgar Elliott,	8	11-3, 1875		"		
2279	Charles Edward,	8	9-23, 1881		"	1-27, 1882	
2280	Elizabeth Harned,	8	4-10, 1884		"	3-, 1885	
	Children of 1027 GEORGE E. SUMMERS,[7]						
2281	—— Summers,	8					
2282	——,	8					
	Children of 1032 EMELINE BOOTH ESTABROOK,[7]						
2283	William Booth Estabrook,	8	1-27, 1856		Ithaca.		
2284	Frances Asenath,	8	2-22, 1858		Catharine,	2-25, 1861	
	Children of 1035 IVAH A. BOOTH HORTON,[7]						
2285	Harry Booth Horton,	8	10-29, 1868				
2286	Emeline Estabrook,	8	3-29, 1872			6-3, 1884	
	Children of 1039 HENRIETTA BOOTH STULL,[7]						
2287	James Winthrop Stull,	8	3-14, 1877		Valley City, N. D.		
	Children of 1043 EBEN. WARD FARRINGTON,[7]						
2288	Susan Fanny Farrington,	8	7-22, 1887				
	Children of 1044 MARY FARRINGTON CUSHING,[7]						
2289	Herman Cushing.	8	9-17, 1888				
2290	Gertrude,	8	8-24, 1891				

Children of *1047* WILLIAM W. HOOPER,[7]

No.	Name	gen	Born	Married	Place	Died	Residence
2291	William Edward Hooper,	8					
2292	Louisa Renchor,	8					
	William Cotlin Daughtry,						
2293	James Havelock,	8					
2294	Charlotte Elizabeth,	8					
	Benjamin Crowell Alston,						

Children of *1048* EDWARD JONES HOOPER,[7]

No.	Name	gen	Born	Married	Place	Died	Residence
2295	William Edward Hooper,	8	12-9, 1845	12-22, 1869	Birmingham, Ala.		
	Mattie P. Meriwether,						
2296	Theresa V.,	8	6-28, 1848	8-12, 1869	Birmingham.		
	Capt. Joseph Forney Johnston,						
2297	Mary Louisa,	8				dec. inf.	Montgomery, Ala.

Children of *1049* MARY HOOPER HOOPER,[7]

No.	Name	gen	Born	Married	Place	Died	Residence
2298	Helen de Berniere Hooper,	8					
	James Wills,						
2299	Frances de Berniere,	8			Raleigh, N. C.	dec.	
	Hon. Spier (s. Att. Gen. Spier) Whitaker,						
2300	Henry de Berniere,	8			Edenton, N. C.		
	Jessie Wright,				Norfolk, Va.		
2301	Julia Charlotte,	8			Chapel Hill, N. C.	dec.	
	Prof. Ralph H. Graves,						

Children of *1050* JOSEPH HOOPER,[7] and *1055*,

No.	Name	gen	Born	Married	Place	Died	Residence
2302	John Eccles Hooper,	8	3-1, 1861		Jacksonville, Fla.		
2303	William Francis,	8				dec. inf.	
2304	Francis Edward Joseph,	8				" "	

Children of *1052* THOMAS C. HOOPER,[7]

No.	Name	gen	Born	Married	Place	Died	Residence
2305	Daughter,	8	10-15, 1850			10-15, 1850	Fayetteville.
2306	Susan Taylor Hooper,	8	4-30, 1852	12-17, 1874	Fayetteville, N. C.	2-28, 1878	Chester, S. C.
	Charles Strong Brice,		10-19, 1881		Wilmington, N. C.	1854	Fayetteville,
2307	Son,	8	1854				
2308	Margaret Broadfoot,	8	7-28, 1855	unm,	Fayetteville,	6-19, 1889	Wilmington.

No.	Name of Wife (or Husband).	Date of Birth.	Date of Marriage.	Residence.	Date of Death.	Place of Burial.
2309	Joseph Caldwell, 8	5-24, 1857	1-15, 1893	Zanesville, O.		
	Louise Cunningham,					
2310	Sarah Jerkins, 8	8-26, 1859	1-28, 1880	Gadsboro, S. C.,		
	William W. Weston,	12-12, 1853		Fayetteville,		Fayetteville.
2311	Annie Bryan, 8	8-26, 1859		"	10-12, 1860	"
2312	George Stevenson, 8	2-12, 1861			6-3, 1861	
2313	Amelia Jones, 8	5-13, 1862	5-20, 1882	Talladega, Ala.		
	Winborn Lawton Mellichampe,	8-8, 1858				
2314	James Stevenson, 8	8-13, 1865		Wilmington.		
2315	Clara Hughes, 8	8-29, 1867		"		

Children of 1055 MARY ECCLES HOOPER,[7] see 1050.

Children of 1056 FRANCES ECCLES LANNEAU,[7]

No.	Name of Wife (or Husband).	Date of Birth.	Date of Marriage.	Residence.	Date of Death.	Place of Burial.
2316	Bazile Lanneau, 8	1859			1860	

Children of 1058 ELIZABETH ECCLES McLAURIN,[7]

No.	Name of Wife (or Husband).	Date of Birth.	Date of Marriage.	Residence.	Date of Death.	Place of Burial.
2317	Edward Jones Eccles McLaurin, 8	1854	1890	Jacksonville, Fla.		
	Mary Ella Ives,	4-13, 1855		Lake City, Fla.	1871	Lake City.
2318	Duncan, 8	1856				
2319	Elizabeth Eccles, 8	1859	1890	Jacksonville.	1876	Lake City.
	Edward Everett Cleaveland,	11-30, 1844				
2320	John D., 8	1861				
2321	Bazile L., 8	1862				
2322	Mary, 8	1864				
2323	Francis, 8	1866				
2324	Joseph H., 8	1868				
2325	Janet, 8	1870			1870	

No.		Name	Born	Birthplace	Died	Death place
		Children of 1659 EDWARD JONES HARDIN,[7]				
2326	8	George Hardin,		Tyler, Tex.		
2327	8	Mary,		"		
2328	8	Sophie,		"		
		Children of 1664 SARAH RENCHOR ANDERSON,[7]				
2329	8	Mary Louisa Anderson,				
		Children of 1675 PETER MALLETT HALE,[7]				
2330	8	Ellen Williams Hale,	8-6, 1876	Winston, N. C.		
		Peter M. Wilson,				
2331	8	Edward,	9-7, 1858	Baltimore.	1865	Fayetteville.
2332	8	Janet,	12-1, 1862			
2333	8	Henry Whiting,	4-, 1865	Raleigh.	11- , 1868	
2334	8	Kate,	2-12, 1869			
2335	8	Mabel,	2-21, 1871			
2336	8	Thomas,	2-14, 1876		8-12, 1881	Fayetteville.
2337	8	Joseph Herndon,	4-28, 1881			
		Children of 1676 SARAH C. HALE HAIGH.[7]				
2338	8	Sarah Hale Haigh.	1856		1875	Fayetteville.
2339	8	Edward Hale,	1868		dec.	"
2340	8	Alice Stone,				
		Clement Huske.				
2341	8	Susan Edwards,	1870	Waycross, Ga.		
		Children of 1677 EDWARD J. HALE,[7]				
2342	8	Joseph Hill Hale,	1863	Fayetteville,	dec.	Fayetteville.
2343	8	Edward Jones,	1868	"		
2344	8	Louis,	1871	"		
2345	8	Frederick,	1874	"		
2346	8	Thomas,		"		
		Children of 1678 WILLIAM GILMER ADAMS,[7]				
2347	8	William Jackson Adams,	10-5, 1872			

No.	Name of Wife (or Husband).	Date of Birth.	Date of Marriage.	Residence.	Date of Death.	Place of Burial.
2348	Carlton Walker, [8]	5-6, 1875				
2349	John Greene, [8]	10-20, 1877				
2350	Francis De Berniere, [8]	6-24, 1883				
	Children of 1085 JOHN MOSELEY WALKER,[7]					
2351	William Lippitt Walker, [8]	4-14, 1884		Wilmington.		
2352	Margaret Lane, [8]	3-11, 1887		Fayetteville.		
	Children of 1086 JOHN WALKER WEBER,[7]					
2353	Cara Carlton Weber, [8]	11-30, 1880		Nashville, Tenn.		
2354	Willie Harris, [8]	2-7, 1886		Sewanee, Tenn.,	2-13, 1886	Sewanee.
2355	Margaret Isabella, [8]	5-18, 1888		Nashville, Tenn.		
2356	Maude Graves, [8]	12-24, 1890		"		
2357	John Walker, [8]	12-24, 1890		"	6- , 1891	Sewanee.
2358	Leroy Ellis, [8]	3-11, 1893		"		
	Children of 1087 HENRI CARLTON WEBER,[7]					
2359	Beulah Beaumont Weber, [8]	2-28, 1885		Nashville.		
2360	Charles Beaumon, [8]	6-6, 1887		"	6-22, 1888	Nashville.
2361	Louise, [8]	12-22, 1888		"		
	Children of 1102 GEORGE WILLIAM HOOPER,[7]					
2362	Elizabeth Fleming Hooper, [8]				6-15, 1884	
2363	Emma Thurston, [8]					
	A. S. Hough,					
2364	Charlotte Isabella, [8]					
	B. K. Colliere,					
2365	Charles Mallett, [8]					
2366	Caro Mallett, [8]				7- , 1890	
2367	Juliet de Berniere, [8]					
2368	George Beattie, [8]					

Children of 1103 CHARLES MALLETT HOOPER,[7]

No.	Name	Gen.	Born	Place	Died	Death place
2369	Walter Yonge Hooper,	8				dec.
2370	Callie,	8				
	Robin Monkhead,					
2371	Louisa,	8				
2372	Nellie,	8				
2373	Edward,	8				

Children of 1110 JOHN W. MALLETT,[7]

No.	Name	Gen.	Born	Place	Died	Death place
2374	Mary Hyman Mallett,	8	9-1, 1874	Leighton. Ga.		
2375	Charles Mercer,	8	4-11, 1876			
2376	James Strange,	8	7-4, 1879	Leighton.	10 15, 1879	Fayettville.
2377	Nannie Strange,	8	12-15, 1883			

Children of 1111 CHARLES PETER MALLETT,[7]

No.	Name	Gen.	Born	Place	Died	Death place
2378	Margaret Wright Mallett.	8	1868	Wilmington, N. C.	1-17, 1893	
	Robert Lee Holmes,		1-17, 1866			
2379	Wilson Aiken,	8	1870	Montgomery, Ala.	4 24, 1894	
	Pauline Burdine,		1872			
2380	Jane Carter.	8	1872			
2381	Marion Alexander,	8	1874			

Children of 1119 SOPHIA B. MALLETT McNIDER,[7]

No.	Name	Gen.	Born	Place	Died	Death place
2382	William de Berniere McNider,	8	6-25, 1882			
2383	George St. Claire,	8	11-22, 1885			

Children of 1125 SUSAN MALLETT HOLMES,[7]

No.	Name	Gen.	Born	Place	Died	Death place
2384	Pierre Mallett Holmes,	8	5-11, 1883	Wilmington, N. C.		
2385	Owen,	8	1889	Wilmington, N. C.		

Children of 1126 CHARLES E. MALLETT,[7]

No.	Name	Gen.	Born	Place	Died	Death place
2386	Caroline Louisa Mallett,	8	4- , 1891			
2387	Pierre,	8	1893			
2388	Dorothy,	8	7- , 1894			

No.	Name of Wife (or Husband).	Date of Birth.	Date of Marriage.	Residence.	Date of Death.	Place of Burial.
	Children of 1149 DE BERNIERE SMITH,[7]					
2389	Bruce Ford Smith, [8]	10-22, 1881				
2390	Mary Mallett, [8]	5-16, 1883				
2391	Mallett de Berniere, [8]					
2392	Lothrop Lewis de Berniere, [8]					
	Children of 1150 PERCY H. MALLETT,[7]					
2393	Percy Webb Mallett, [8]	7-14, 1888		Brooklyn,	3-13, 1891	Bk'ln.
2394	Marguerite Isabel, [8]	4-21, 1892		Bay Ridge, N. Y.		
2395	Guy Chandler, [8]	5-24, 1894		"		
	Children of 1153 JAMES FENNER LEE,[7]					
2396	Mary Cornelia Lee, [8]	7-8, 1867		Baltimore,		
2397	Arthur Fenner, [8]	6-28, 1869		"	1875	
2398	Sarah Fenner, [8]	12-17, 1870		"		
2399	James Fenner, [8]	6-9, 1872		"	2-3, 1892	
2400	Emily Harper, [8]					
2401	Sophia Howard, [8]	1-21, 1876			1876	
	Children of 1154 J. HENRY LEE,[7]					
2402	Elizabeth Tyson Lee, [8]	4-18, 1874		Baltimore, Md.		
2403	Stephen States, [8]	3-4, 1876		"		
2404	Guilielma Poultney, [8]	8-18, 1878		"		
2405	Amabel, [8]	4-15, 1880		"		
	Children of 1156 AMABEL LEE GEORGE,[7]					
2406	Stephen "Lee" George, [8]	8-26, 1882		Baltimore.		
2407	Amabel Lee, [8]	7-27, 1885		"		
2408	Henrietta Cowman, [8]	12-5, 1887		"		
2409	Sarah Fenner, [8]	11-11, 1889		"		

Children of 1157 JAMES FENNER MALLETT, Jr.,[7]

No.	Name	Gen.	Born	Married	Residence	Died	Place
2410	Hugh Mallett,	8					
2411	Mary,	8					

Children of 1162 ELLEN MALLETT ELLIOTT,[7]

No.	Name	Gen.	Born	Married	Residence	Died	Place
2412	—— Elliott,	8					

Children of 1184 ADELINE M. WYCKOFF FOULKE,[7]

No.	Name	Gen.	Born	Married	Residence	Died	Place
2413	Joseph Mallett Foulke,	8	9-11, 1886		Denver.	6-12, 1889	Denver, Col.
2414	Harry Mallett,	8	7-21, 1890				

Children of 1186 ELIZABETH WYCKOFF FOULKE,[7]

No.	Name	Gen.	Born	Married	Residence	Died	Place
2415	Adeline Mallett Foulke,	8	5-20, 1890			7-20, 1890	Denver, Col.

Children of 1188 MINERVA STUART GOODWIN,[7]

No.	Name	Gen.	Born	Married	Residence	Died	Place
2416	Mary E. Goodwin,	8	7-19, 1851	1-18, 1884	Millport, N. Y.		
	Ezra Davenport,		9– , 1851				
2417	Sophia,	8	8-24, 1853	11-18, 1877	Elmira.		
	William Stanton,		3-31, 1841				
2418	William Curtis,	8				1857	
2419	Matthew Christian,	8	7-26, 1859	7-4, 1888	Horseheads.		
	Mary Jane Davenport (Taylor),						
2420	John "Franklin,"	8	1-24, 1862	12-2, 1888	Syracuse.		
	Eva Burris,						
2421	"Charles" Porter,	8	3-8, 1865		Millport.		
2422	"Ida" May,	8	8-16, 1868	10-18, 1892	Watkins.		
	Lewis Messig,						
2423	Nathan B.,	8	10-24, 1870		Watkins.	12– ,1880	
2424	"Burr" Wellington,	8	9-5, 1873	1– , 1892	Watkins.		
	Emma Wilbor,						

Children of 1189 GEORGE STUART,[7]

No.	Name	Gen.	Born	Married	Residence	Died	Place
2425	Charles Stuart,	8	8-2, 1860	12-10, 1854	Millport.		
	Jennie Rebecca Moore,		9-19, 1866				

No.	Name of Wife (or Husband).	Date of Birth.	Date of Marriage.	Residence.	Date of Death.	Place of Burial.
2426	Mahlon J., . . . 8	1-26, 1863	10-29, 1890	Syracuse.		
	Jennie F. Cross,			"		
2427	William C., . . . 8	9-25, 1866	8-28, 1888	"		
	Shirley Belle Kendal,	1870				
2428	Ulysses Grant, . . 8	11-21, 1874	. . .	Millport.		
	Children of 1190 ELIZABETH STUART GOODWIN,[7]					
2429	William C. Goodwin,[7] 8	5-1, 1858	10-8, 1882	Elmira, N. Y.		
	Rachel Blanchard,	11-2, 1848				
2430	" Flora " Lorena, 8	4-26, 1866	12-20, 1885	Monterey, N. Y.		
	Marshall Mowry,	5-1, 1861				
2431	John, . . 8	4-26, 1869	12-7, 1892			
	Emma Brandt,	2-15, 1873				
2432	" James " Elmer, 8	10-12, 1873	unm., . .	Millport.	10– , 1893	Millport.
2433	" Dora " Bell, 8	9-22, 1878	. .			
	Children of 1196 MARY COUCH CHAPMAN,[7]					
2434	Josephine Chapman, 8					
	—— King,					
2435	*Lestina,* 8					
	S. Beardsley,					
	Children of 1197 EDWARD J. COUCH,[7]					
2436	George Couch, 8					
2437	Frank, 8					
2438	——, 8					
2439	——, 8					
	Children of 1198 ESTHER COUCH CARPENTER,[7]					
2440	Edward Carpenter, 8					
	Kate Ford,					

No.	Name		Birth	Date	Place
2441	Emma,	8			
	Clarence Grant,				
	Children of *1200* **SAMUEL T. COUCH,**[7]				
2442	Vinton "Myron" Couch,	8	8-22, 1863		
2443	William L.,	8	9-30, 1865		
2444	Harriet,	8	6-15, 1869	2-22, 1889	Odessa.
	Samuel Jones,		1868		Odessa, N. Y.
2445	"Joel" Sanford,	8	5-3, 1872		
2446	George,	8	8-24, 1881		
	Children of *1202* **EUNICE MALLETT STERLING,**[7]				
2447	John Sterling,	8	11-18, 1869	6-, 1892	Mosherville, Pa.
	Alma Brewer,				
	Children of *1204* **EPHRAIM MALLETT,**[7]				
2448	"Charlotte" Louisa Mallett,	8	4-14, 1866	11-5, 1887	Millport.
	Walter Evarts,				Odessa, N. Y.
2449	"Olin" Alanson,	8	9-26, 1869	3-4, 1893	"
	Dora Eunice Bowers,				"
	Children of *1206* **SYLVESTER F. MALLETT,**[7]				
2450	Isaac Mallett,	8	1869		
2451	Willie,	8	1873		
2452	Daughter,	8			
	Children of *1210* **MARY MALLETT KINNAMAN FERGUSON,**[7]				
2453	Louisa Sereptia Kinnaman,	8	4-, 1858		
2454	Frank Ferguson,	8			
2455	Wells,	8			
2456	Adelia,	8			
2457	Sarah,	8			
2458	Carrie T.,	8			
2459	Jacob,	8			
2460	Elmer,	8			
2461	Charles,	8			
2462	John,	8			

No.	Name of Wife (or Husband).	Date of Birth.	Date of Marriage.	Residence.	Date of Death.	Place of Burial.
2463	George, ... 8					
2464	Mary, ... 8					
	Children of 1211 ABRAM W. MAL-					
	LETT,[7]					
2465	Eliza Mallett, ... 8	1856				
2466	James, ... 8	1859				
2467	Perry, ... 8	1863				
2468	Rebecca, ... 8	1866				
2469	Charles, ... 8	1873				
2470	Lottie, ... 8	1875				
2471	Elton, ... 8	1876			1–5, 1876	
2472	Mattie, ... 8	1878				
2473	William, ... 8	1880				
2474	Eddie, ... 8	1882				
2475	Ira, ... 8	1886				
2476	May, ... 8	1892			8–3, 1893	
2477	Mauddie, ... 8	1894				
	Children of 1219 WESLEY MAL-					
	LETTE,[7]					
2478	John Mallette, ... 8			Bennettsburg, N. Y.		
	Children of 1220 REBECCA MALLETTE					
	LATTIN,[7]					
2479	Annie E. Lattin, ... 8	12–12, 1866	12–12, 1886	Millport.		
2480	Byrd Lattin, ... 8	12–, 1865				
	"Martha" Jane, ... 8	8–4, 1872				
2481	U. S. Grant, ... 8	9–28, 1874				
	Children of 1222 SMITH MALETTE,[7]					
2482	Frederica Malette, ... 8	2–5, 1871		Elmira.		
2483	George Albert, ... 8	2–28, 1873			1–21, 1874	Millport.

No.	Name	Born	Married	Residence	Died / N. Haven.
	Children of 1228 ARRON H. MALLETT,[7] [8]				
2484	Effie Barnum Mallett, [8]	3-5, 1890			
	Children of 1229 LIZZIE MALLETT JUDSON,[7]				
2485	—— Judson, [8]	1883			N. Haven. 1885
	Children of 1230 SAMUEL S. MALLETT,[7] [8]				
2486	Charlie Merritt Mallett, [8]				
2487	——, [8]				
	Children of 1234 HARRIET SMITH CRAMER,[7]				
2488	Florence Cramer, [8]	1878?			
2489	Marvin, [8]	1880?			
2490	Marguerite, [8]	1883?			
2491	Ruth, [8]	1887?			
	Children of 1240 JAMES B. MALLETTE,[7] [8]				
2492	Frederick A. Mallette, [8]	2-8, 1857	2-14, 1884	Geneva.	
	Florence A. Moore, [8]	12-17, 1858		Phelps, N. Y.	
2493	James Franklin, [8]	1-4, 1864		Jersey City.	
2494	Elizabeth, [8]	11-8, 1868		Binghampton.	10-4, 1873
	Children of 1242 CHARLOTTE MALLETTE GRIFFITH,[7]				
2495	Fred W. Griffith, [8]	12-17, 1858	10-1, 1889	Palmyra, N. Y.	
	Mary E. Adams, [8]	11-10, 1865			
2496	J. Cuyler, [8]	11-16, 1863			
2497	James Malette, [8]	3-25, 1865	11- , 1890		
	Dora Pulver, [8]	10-13, 1871			
2498	Willie, [8]	5-18, 1867			
2499	Mary E., [8]	7-12, 1871			
2500	Frank A., [8]	8-17, 1873	1-16, 1894		5- , 1871
	Christine Beuchenstein, [8]	8-2, 1873			
2501	Lena May, [8]	5-3, 1880			

No.	Name of Wife (or Husband).		Date of Birth.	Date of Marriage.	Residence.	Date of Death.	Place of Burial.
	Children of 1243 SARAH J. MALLETTE GARLOCK,[7]						
2502	Olin J. Garlock,	8	7–5, 1861				
	Nina V. Crandell,		7–10, 1867	12–23, 1885	Palmyra.		
2503	Hattie Bell,	8	1–2, 1869				
	Oscar D. Tiffany,		9–6, 1868	2–7, 1890	Palmyra.		
2504	Charlotte E.,	8	11–21, 1871				
2505	Rachel May,	8	8–29, 1874				
	Children of 1246 ELIZABETH BACON STUART,[7]						
2506	Eva Stuart,	8	5–9, 1870			6–16, 1892	Catharine.
	Bradley Coon,		9–13, 1866	6–18, 1890			
2507	Roscoe,	8	5–12, 1872	unm,			
2508	Olin D.,	8	1–1, 1875				
2509	Jay B.,	8	6–10, 1879				
2510	Clarence,	8 Scott,	1–11, 1881				
	Children of 1247 HARRIET MALLETT SCOTT,[7]						
2511	Frank Scott,	8	11–19, 1871		Horseheads, N. Y.		
2512	Willis Malette,	8	9–8, 1876				
	Children of 1251 EMMA MALLETT COCHRAN,[7]						
2513	Walter Cochran,	8	2– , 1879			1865	
2514	Arthur,	8	2– , 1882				
	Children of 1268 BEACH HALL,[7]						
2515	Charles Edward Hall,	8	10–23, 1854	8–18, 1880			
2516	"Idalette" Louisa,	8	7–17, 1856		Perth Amboy, N. J.		
	Edward W. Barnes,						
2517	Cora Pauline,	8	3–27, 1858				
2518	Frances "Isabel,"	8	9–2, 1863	10–20, 1892	Des Moines, Ia.		
	—— Bentley.						

No.	Name		Birth	Place		M. G. C. B. C.
	Children of 1275 SYLVIA NICHOLS NORTHROP.[7]					
2519	Mary "Elizabeth" Northrop,	8	11-18, 1853		1-7, 1871	
2520	Emily "Jane,"	8	10-27, 1855			
2521	"Lydia" Augusta,	8	10-1, 1857			
2522	"Clara" Louisa,	8	4-25, 1860			
2523	William Nichols,	8	10-7, 1863			
	Children of 1278 AUGUSTA NICHOLS HURD.[7]					
2524	Wilson Nichols Hurd,	8	1-24, 1868			
2525	John Shelton,	8	6-12, 1872			
2526	Edward Legrand,	8	5-1, 1874			
	Children of 1282 CATHARINE JACKSON MALLETT,[7] see 537.					
	Children of 1286 CHARLES J. JACKSON.[7]					
2527	"Lorenzo" Sterling Jackson,	8	1878	Stepney, Ct.		
2528	Chester Arthur,	8	1882	"		
2529	Percy,	8	1890	"		
	Children of 1287 MARY L. SHELTON FAIRCHILD,[7] and 2202.					
2530	Frederick Shelton Fairchild,	8	10-19, 1864			
	Children of 1288 JOHN C. SHELTON.[7]					
2531	John Consider Shelton,	8	1-8, 1882	Bridgeport,	1-16, 1893	M. G. C. B. C.
2532	Jean Louisa,	8	3-10, 1884			
2533	Mary Agnes,	8	5-15, 1887		6-4, 1889	M. G. C. B. C.
2534	Anna Gertrude,	8	1-8, 1890			
2535	Ruth Clare,	8	12-29, 1892			
	Children of 1289 ISAAC E. SHERMAN.[7]					
2536	William Sherwood Sherman,	8	3-4, 1873		8-14, 1874	M. G. C. B. C.
2537	Cora,	8				
2538	John Consider,	8				
2539	Sally Shelton,	8				

No.	Name of Wife (or Husband).	Date of Birth.	Date of Marriage.	Residence.	Date of Death.	Place of Burial.
	Children of 1290 ADELAIDE MALLETT HARROD,[7]					
2540	Mary Alma Harrod, [8]	10-7, 1864	3-26, 1884	Norwalk, O.		
	Albert Squire Mead,	1-25, 1863		Toledo, O.		
2541	George Henry, [8]	11-19, 1867		Norwalk.		
2542	Emma Louisa, [8]	5-16, 1874		"		
2543	Frederick William, [8]	9-20, 1878		"		
	Children of 1291 ISABELLA MALLETT SQUIRE,[7]					
2544	Edna Gertrude Squire, [8]	11-27, 1873	1- , 1894	Hudson, Mich.		
	—,			Hudson.		
2545	Mary Amanda, [8]	3-13, 1876		"		
2546	Willis Burrett Durand, [8]	11-30, 1878		"		
2547	Clarence Elmore, [8]	8-14, 1880		"		
2548	Frank C., [8]	4-3, 1887				
	Children of 1293 STEPHEN E. MALLETT,[7]					
2549	Wallace Cole Mallett, [8]	12-19, 1884		Concordia, Kan.		
2550	Olive, [8]	8-6, 1887		"		
	Children of 1295 BETSEY MALLETT GRISWOLD,[7]					
2551	Henry Griswold, [8]				dec.	
	Children of 1297 ISAAC MALLETT,[7]					
2552	Maud Elizabeth Mallett, [8]	11-18, 1880		Garden Grove, Ia.		
2553	Mabel Amelia, [8]	11-21, 1882				
2554	James Isaac, [8]	5-3, 1885				
2555	Addie Iola, [8]	1-5, 1891				
	Children of 1298 CHARLES D. MALLETT,[7]					
2556	Francis Griswold Mallett, [8]	11-12, 1884		Plymouth, Wis.		

Children of *1306* CHARLES S. MALLETT,[7]					
2557	Verona Mallett,	8	6-25, 1892		
2558	Ethel Jane,	8	2-26, 1894		
Children of *1307* ELIZABETH MALLETT NORTHROP,[7]					
2559	Edith Northrop,	8	12-16, 1892		
Children of *1312* GEORGE D. MALLETT,[7]					
2560	Dwight Sterling Mallett,	8	1-27, 1884		Tashua.
2561	Ruth Harriet,	8	7-22, 1889		"
2562	Dorothy,	8	2-1, 1892		"
2563	Son,	8	6-7, 1894	6-7, 1894	Tashua.
Children of *1314* IDA MALLETT BEARDSLEY,[7]					
2564	Theodore Jerome Beardsley,	8	11-30, 1888		
Children of *1315* BELL LEAVITT SHULTUS,[7]					
2565	Walter A. Shultus,	8	1875		Gr. Rapids, Mich.
2566	——,	8			dec.
2567	——,	8			dec.
Children of *1316* SYLVIA LEAVITT HIZER,[7]					
2568	Ernest Henry Hizer,	8	8-27, 1867		Lyons, Mich.
2569	George Wilbur,	8	11-30, 1870		"
2570	Herbert Elmer,	8	12-31, 1876		"
Children of *1318* SHELDON LEAVITT,[7] M. D.,					
2571	Cyrus "Franklin" Leavitt,	8	6-20, 1873 }	10-20, 1893	Chicago, Ill.
	Mae Bell Kerns,		10-2, 1873 }		
2572	Florence,	8	8-10, 1886		"

No.	Name of Wife (or Husband).	Date of Birth.	Date of Marriage.	Residence.	Date of Death.	Place of Burial.
	Children of 1319 MARTHA LEAVITT, COGSHALL,[7]					
2573	Grace Augusta Cogshall, ...8	3-16, 1872	. . . .	Michigan.		
2574	Wilbur Adelman, ...8	2-8, 1874	. . . .	"		
2575	Fred. Charles, ...8	10-18, 1875	. . . .	"	9-12, 1882	Buchanan, Mich.
2576	Nellie Bell, ...8	3-21, 1877	. . . .	"		
2577	Mattie Elmira, ...8	4-17, 1879	. . . .	"		
	Children of 1322 FRED. E. LEAVITT, [7]					
2578	Hazel Viola Leavitt, ...8	5-16, 1883	. . . .	Gr. Rapids, Mich.		
2579	Edith Martha, ...8	12-23, 1886	. . . .	Fargo, N. Dak.		
2580	Sheldon Avery, ...8	10-30, 1891	. . . .	St. Paul, Minn.		
	Children of 1323 DAVID S. LEAVITT,[7]					
2581	Lillian Gertrude Leavitt, ...8	7-30, 1891				
	Children of 1327 MARY LEAVITT HOAG,[7]					
2582	Daughter, Hoag, ...8	3-2, 1885	. . . .	Gr. Rapids,	3-2, 1885	Gr. Rapids.
2583	Daughter, ...8	9-6, 1886	. . . .	"	9-6, 1886	"
2584	Son, ...8	12-17, 1887	. . . .	"	12-17, 1887	"
2585	Maurice Leavitt, ...8	7-21, 1892	. . . .			
	Children of 1335 SARAH MALLETT TREADWELL,[7]					
2586	John Walter Treadwell, . . .8	5-18, 1859	10-25, 1882			
1345	Annie L. (d. of David) *Wakeley,*	7-14, 1863				
	Children of 1336 MARY WAKELEY THOMPSON,[7]					
2587	Emma Louise Thompson, ...8	2-25, 1866	11-1, 1888	Stamford, Ct.	6-23, 1894	Stamford .
	Bradley Thorp, .	11-16, 1867		"		

Children of *1339* SARAH HALL HAUGH,[7]

No.	Name	Gen.	Born	Birthplace	Married	Died	Died place
2588	Frances Irene Haugh,	8	12–5, 1887	Newtown, C.			
2589	Sarah Agnes,	8	7–5, 1892	"			

Children of *1340* CORNELIA HALL JENNINGS,[7]

No.	Name	Gen.	Born	Birthplace	Married	Died	Died place
2590	George Mallett Jennings,	8	10–24, 1879				
2591	Harry Austin,	8	9–29, 1885				
2592	Ada,	8	7–18, 1887				
2593	Lewis Wakeley,	8	1–12, 1891				

Children of *1341* CHARLES A. HALL,[7]

No.	Name	Gen.	Born	Birthplace	Married	Died	Died place
2594	Marjorie Hall,	8	3–24, 1890	L. H. Tr.		8–14, 1893	L. H. Tr.
2595	Mildred,	8	7–10, 1892	"			

Children of *1343* MELVIN A. WAKELEY,[7]

No.	Name	Gen.	Born	Birthplace	Married	Died	Died place
2596	Miles Bradley Wakely,	8	12–12, 1872				
2597	Irene Melinda,	8	3–23, 1874				
2598	David Lewis,	8	1–13, 1877				
2599	Eva,	8	7–29, 1881				

Children of *1345* ANNIE WAKELEY TREADWELL,[7] and of *2556*,

No.	Name	Gen.	Born	Birthplace	Married	Died	Died place
2600	Daughter, Treadwell,	8	3–8, 1889			3–8, 1889	Tashua.

Children of *1346* FRANCES MALLETT KENNEDY,[7]

No.	Name	Gen.	Born	Birthplace	Married	Died	Died place
2601	Frank Mallett Kennedy,	8	2–15, 1875				

Children of *1347* AMANDA HALL CURTIS,[8]

No.	Name	Gen.	Born	Birthplace	Married	Died	Died place
2602	Charles Gould Curtis,	9	9–17, 1854		5–20, 1875	12–2, 1876	
2603	*Mary H. Botsford,*	9	9–29, 1862				
	George Washington,	9	5–11, 1862			2–2, 1863	
2604	Grace Isabel,	9	10–29, 1864				

No.	Name of Wife (or Husband).	Date of Birth.	Date of Marriage.	Residence.	Date of Death.	Place of Burial.
	Children of 1348 DANIEL M. HALL,[8]					
2605	Esther Ann Hall, [9]	6-26, 1853	4-16, 1890			
	Rev. Abram Herbert Manee, [9]					
2606	David M., [9]	5-17, 1855	12-24, 1879			
	Ella E. Clark.					
2607	Francis, [9]	11-15, 1857			dec.	Stepney, Ct.
2608	Arthur, [9]	12-11, 1860			"	"
2609	Sarah Frances. [9]	5-23, 1864				
	Children of 1352 REV. BENJAMIN T. HALL,[8]					
2610	May Hall, [9]	6-9, 1861				
	Children of 1353 SARAH MALLETT MORRIS,[8]					
2611	Gertrude Elizabeth Morris, [9]	7-18, 1858				
2612	Mary E., [9]	2-6, 1861	6-4, 1889			
2613	S. Eugenia, [9]	10-28, 1866				
	Burton E. Canfield,					
	Children of 1354 BURR MALLETT,[8]					
2614	Mary Emilia Mallett, [9]	11-8, 1861	12-24, 1888			
	Charles M. Hatch,	11-20, 1863				
2615	Marcus Burr, [9]	11-16, 1865				
2616	Henry Montville, [9]	10-6, 1867				
2617	Sara J., [9]	7-11, 1874				
	Children of 1355 ALVIRA MALLETT WARNER,[8]					
2618	Reuben Mallett Warner, [9]	10-13, 1862				
	Alice E. Randall.	1-11, 1861				
2619	Marcus L., [9]	2-21, 1864			2-21, 1864	Bridgewater.
2620	S. Emma, [9]	10-16, 1868				

No.	Name		Born	Married	Died	Residence
	Children of 1359 ARRESTA BURCH SELLECK,[8]					
2621	Elosia Ann Selleck,	9				
	Children of 1362 WILLIAM ISBELL,[8]					
2622	Lizzie Isbell,	9				
2623	———,	9				
	Children of 1363 GEORGE ISBELL,[8]					
2624	Mary Isbell,	9				
2625	Son,	9				
2626	Son,	9				
2627	Daughter,	9				
	Children of 1364 ALBERT BEACH MALLETT,[8]					
2628	Anna Maryetta Mallett.	9	5-1, 1870			
	Alfred Carson,					
2629	Lillie Frances,	9	5-26, 1872			
	Frank Beach,			10-11, 1893		Bridgeport, Conn.
2630	Bessie Amelia,	9	5-18, 1882			
	Children of 1368 ISABELLA ISBELL KNOX,[8]					
2631	Lena Knox,	9				
	Burton Merrill,			9-14, 1892		12-14, 1892
	Children of 1370 SARAH MINOR WARNER,[8]					
2632	George W. Warner,	9	1-7, 1867			
	Minnie L. Hine,		6-21, 1869	11-7, 1888		New Milford, Ct.
2633	Franklin,	9	8-21, 1870			New Milford, Ct.
	Carrie A. Corbin,		7-20, 1888	6-9, 1892		New Milford, Ct.
2634	Bertha A.,	9	1-9, 1873			
2635	Eunice A.,	9	4-24, 1875			"
	Children of 1371 CHARLES E. MINOR,[8]					
2636	Clarence A. Minor,	9	11-29, 1869			
2637	Sarah B.,	9	2-27, 1871			

No.	Name of Wife (or Husband).	Date of Birth.	Date of Marriage.	Residence.	Date of Death.	Place of Burial.
2638	Alvin W., ... 9	7-31, 1872	} 10-7, 1893			
2639	Wilfred C., ——, .. 9	5-11, 1877				
2640	Edith S., ... 9	9-16, 1878				
2641	Susan A., ... 9	8-7, 1882				
	Children of 1374 ADELIA MINOR PARTRIDGE,[8]					
2642	Alice E. Partridge, . 9	5-2, 1879		Newtown, Ct.		
2643	John W., ——, ... 9	2-9, 1881		"		
2644	Arthur E., ... 9	8-29, 1884		"		
2645	Bessie I., ... 9	7-21, 1886		"	2-12, 1890	
2646	Ernest M., ... 9	4-1, 1888		"		
2647	——, ... 9	5-28, 1894		"		
	Children of 1376 LIZZIE MINOR BOOTH,[8]					
2648	Louis Booth, ... 9	2-1, 1882				
2649	Edna, ... 9	8-21, 1883				
2650	Ethel, ... 9	7-28, 1889				
	Children of 1378 HATTIE McKINNEY BALL,[8]					
2651	Harry Ball, ... 9	1877?		Danbury.		
2652	Kittie, ——, ... 9	1881?		"		
2653	Jessie, ... 9	1886?		"		
2654	Bessie, ... 9	1886?		"		
2655	Daughter, ... 9	1890?				
	Children of 1383 GEORGE H. MALLETT,[8]					
2656	Charles Mallett, . 9					
2657	Henry, ... 9					
2658	Deborah, ... 9					

No.	Name	Born	Married
	Children of 1385 Harriet Foote Van Orden,[8]		
2659	Norman Van Orden, ...9		
	Children of 1390 Jane Gilbert Beach,[8] *see 643.*		
	Children of 1394 Edward Woodin,[8]		
	—— Woodin, ...9		
	Children of 1396 Helen Wayland Burr,[8]		
2661	Clarence Burton Burr, ...9	2–21, 1876	9–11, 1872 Stepney.
	Children of 1401 Harriet Banks Curtis,[8]		
2662	Lillie G. Curtis, ...9	7–7, 1872	
2663	Royal Banks, ...9	2–17, 1874	
2664	Arthur Barnum, ...9	7–19, 1875	
	Children of 1404 George W. Mallette,[8]		
2665	Mattie B. Mallette, ...9	5–1, 1886	10–18, 1891
2666	George E., ...9	11–28, 1887	
2667	E. Burd Grubb, ...9	9–21, 1889	
2668	Walter, ...9	10–15, 1891	
2669	Randolph D., ...9	12–28, 1892	
	Children of 1410 Sarah Sanford Tyler,[8]		
2670	John Lacey Tyler, ...9	7–17, 1875	
2671	Yula May, ...9	5–22, 1880	
	Children of 1411 Yula Sanford Osborn,[8]		
2672	Charles Herbut Osborn, ...9	11–15, 1885	
2673	George Walter, ...9	2–16, 1888	
2674	Grace Ann, ...9	6–4, 1891	

No.	Name of Wife (or Husband).	Date of Birth.	Date of Marriage.	Residence.	Date of Death.	Place of Burial.
	Children of 1412 FRANKLIN T. DAVIS,[8]					
2675	Arthur Burr Davis, [9]	5-12, 1877			2-26, 1879	Woodlawn, N. Y.
2676	Edward Burr, [9]	3-26, 1880				
	Children of 1415 EDWARD M. DAVIS,[8]					
2677	Walter Vernon Davis, [9]	10-21, 1884				
2678	Mary Mallette, [9]	7-2, 1887				
	Children of 1419 IRVING SANFORD MALLETTE,[8]					
2679	George Alfred Mallette, [9]	5-5, 1889				
	Children of 1422 STANLEY A. MALLETTE,[8]					
2680	Dorothy J. Mallette, [9]	8-12, 1893				
	Children of 1425 WILLIAM O. DAVIS,[8]					
2681	Frances Mallette Davis, [9]	10-1, 1880				
	Children of 1432 SARAH GRIFFIN RAINOUS,[8]					
2682	Stanley Atwood Rainous, [9]	10-25, 1890				
2683	Jennette Mallette, [9]	12-11, 1892				
	Children of 1433 FANNY MALLETT BROWN,[8]					
2684	Amelia Brown, [9]	11-7, 1848				
	Lewis H. Mansfield,	10-10, 1827	4-20, 1868	Bethel, Ct.	5-7, 1882	Bethel.
	George W. Platt,	4-9, 1853	6-7, 1883		7-10, 1891	

Children of 1434 SYLVIA MALLETT JENKINS WARDNER,[8]

No.	Name		Birth	Marr.	Place	Date	Place
2685	Mary Augusta Jenkins,	9	1-24, 1848	2-8, 1865	Danbury, Ct.		
	Leander Haynes,		11-27, 1837		Springfield, Ill.		
2686	William Burr,	9	6-14, 1857	6-5, 1892	Benton, Mo.		
	Pearl Cloar,		9-20, 1873		Union Cy;, Tenn.		
2687	Alice Philip Wardner,	9	8-27, 1864	5-28, 1882	Springfield, Ill.		
	Frederick Martin Slack,		3-14, 1857		Chicago.		
2688	Cora Ella,	9	8-10, 1866	5-5, 1885	Springfield,	10-16, 1893	La Porte, Ind.
	Jayson Cook Cox.		5-21, 1853		Cleveland, O.		

Children of 1435 JOHN WELSEY MALLETT,[8]

No.	Name		Birth	Marr.	Place	Date	Place
2689	Laura Evelyne Mallett,	9	8-8, 1860	5-13, 1883	Bridgeport.	2-5, 1884	Tashua.
	John Vincent Eyre,		3-25, 1862				
2690	Ida Jane "Bessie,"	9	2-20, 1869	5-19, 1887	Bridgeport.	11-4, 1887	M. G. C. B. C.
	Geo. E. Eightme, D. D. S.,						

Children of 1436 A. BURR MALLETT.[8]

No.	Name		Birth	Marr.	Place	Date	Place
2691	William Burr Mallett,	9	5-24, 1868	7-25, 1893	Chicago.		
	Lillian May McCutcheon,		5-7, 1872				

Children of 1437 HARRIET P. MALLETT JONES,[8]

No.	Name		Birth	Marr.	Place	Date	Place
2692	Howard Lane Jones,	9	8-30, 1871		Cecil, Kas.		

Children of 1438 ANTHA JANE MALLETTE BURR EDWARDS,[8]

No.	Name		Birth	Marr.	Place	Date	Place
2693	Lester Burr Edwards,	9	7-8, 1865			8-5, 1878	L. H. T.

Children of 1439 CHARLES SHERMAN MALLETTE,[8]

No.	Name		Birth	Marr.	Place	Date	Place
2694	Harry D. Mallette,	9	12-17, 1871			8-3, 1872	Paris, Ill.
2695	Charles Ernest,	9	8-24, 1873				
2696	Edward Lee,	9	7-21, 1877				
2697	Frank Harris,	9	10-17, 1878			1-10, 1878	
2698	George Arthur,	9	7-23, 1880			12-14, 1878	
2699	Sylvia Irene,	9	7-15, 1883				
2700	Ona May,	9	1-16, 1885			12-4, 1883	Decatur, Ill.
2701	Chester Earl,	9	10-22, 1886			11-4, 1890	"

No.	Name of Wife (or Husband).		Date of Birth.	Date of Marriage.	Residence.	Date of Death.	Place of Burial.
	Children of 1440 MARY E. MALLETT DOWNS,[8]						
2702	Abertha Downs,	9					
	Children of 1442 SARAH A. MALLETT PLUMB,[8]						
2703	Maud Nannette Plumb,	9	11–24, 1878				
	Children of 1443 AMARIAH MALLETT, Jr.,[8]						
2704	Sadie Augusta Mallett,	9	5–5, 1881				
2705	Bessie May,	9	9–13, 1883				
2706	Minnie Bell,	9	1–13, 1889				
2707	John Wesley,	9	1–9, 1893				
2708	Yula,	9	10–4, 1894				
	Children of 1445 EMILY D. BENNETT DeFOREST,[8]						
2709	Sarah Elizabeth DeForest,	9	1–2, 1851			1–5, 1851	Tashua.
2710	Evylin Clarissa,	9	7–17, 1854			7–17, 1854	
2711	Mary Frances,	9	2–22, 1858	10–13, 1881	Milford, Ct.	8–4, 1894	Milford, Ct.
	William Otis Spencer,		9–13, 1857				
2712	James Henry,	9	7–5, 1863			7–19, 1863	
2713	Ella May,	9	5–12, 1867				
	Children of 1448 MARY J. BENNETT GLEASON,[8]						
2714	Thomas P. Gleason,	9				7–19, 1868	Tashua.
2715	Wilbur Frank,	9	9–1, 1872				
	Children of 1450 ALEX. JEROME BENNETT,[8]						
2716	Franklyn Alexander Bennett,	9	9–15, 1866				
2717	Florence Isabella,	9	2–22, 1870				
2718	Edward Jerome,	9	8–18, 1871				

No.	Name	Gen.	Born	Married	Place	Died	
2719	Sarah Clarissa,	9	11-8, 1873			11-20, 1873	
2720	Ella W.,	9	11-13, 1875				
2721	Lewis Winton,	9	2-26, 1877			8-9, 1877	
2722	Theodora,	9	4-30, 1878			8-9, 1878	
2723	Grace,	9	9-22, 1879				

Children of 1452 MARTHA A. BENNETT FOWLER,[8]

2724	Wilbur Gleason Fowler,	9	2-1, 1867	1-21, 1892			
	Mable Cora Farnsworth,		9-20, 1874				
2725	Edward Daniel,	9	12-30, 1869			4-30, 1870	L. H. T.
2726	Clarence Sturges,	9	9-14, 1874			1-14, 1878	"

Children of 1453 FRANK C. BENNETT,[8]

| 2727 | Ruby Bennett, | 9 | 12-14, 1876 | | | | |
| 2728 | Berenice, | 9 | 11-5, 1880 | | | 7-18, 1891 | M. G. C. |

Children of 1455 CASSIUS M. MALLETT,[8]

2729	Allie Harning Mallett.	9	4-8, 1874				
2730	Willie Bronson,	9	3-29, 1876				
2731	Gurtie,	9	8-16, 1878				

Children of 1464 SARAH MALLETTE ANGLE,[8]

| 2732 | Fraka Angle, | 9 | 8-20, 1883 | | | | |
| 2733 | Gey Walter, | 9 | 4-3, 1886 | | Cobelskill, N. Y. | | |

Children of 1466 CHARLES G. MALLETTE,[8]

| 2734 | Edith Mallette, | 9 | 11-8, 1882 | | | | |
| 2735 | Frederick, | 9 | 5-2, 1887 | | " | | |

Children of 1470 JENNIE L. MALLETTE NICHOLS,[8]

| 2736 | David Howard Nichols, | 9 | 2-7, 1886 | | | 12-2, 1892 | M. G. C. B. C. |

No.	Name of Wife (or Husband).		Date of Birth.	Date of Marriage.	Residence.	Date of Death.	Place of Burial.
	Children of 1471 HELEN LOUCKS FLOWER,[8]						
2737	Ann "Isadore" Flower,	9	4-11, 1852	3-6, 1877		2-14, 1890	
	Erwin Barney Ruddock,	9	12-29, 1852				
2738	Mary Elizabeth,	9	12-18, 1853	12-16, 1880		11-12, 1884	
	Lewis Allen Scott,	9	9-, 1857				
2739	Albert "Herman,"	9	6-1, 1856	7-6, 1877			
	Addie Bean,						
2740	Don Ruric,	9	3-2, 1859	9-22, 1891			
	Mary Chase,	9					
2741	Frank Zephon,	9	5-4, 1861	11-15, 1888			
	Katie Maria Reycraft,	9	3-22, 1871				
2742	John Arthur,	9	2-23, 1863	1-8, 1888		7-7, 1889	
	Clara Adeline Burton,		1-8, 1871	8-7, 1892			
	Elizabeth Beaumont,	9					
2743	Ella May,	9	4-25, 1865	2-22, 1883			
	Llewellyn Smith Richmond,		9-25, 1848				
2744	Helen Ilura,	9	12-24, 1867	2-26, 1889			
	John Reycraft,	9	4-8, 1867				
2745	Claude Lincoln,	9	6-30, 1870				
2746	Maude Lena,	9	11-18, 1872				
2747	Jennie Caroline,	9	5-24, 1875				
2748	Bertie Erwin,	9	9-21, 1877			9-28, 1877	
2749	Agnes Lorena,	9	3-14, 1880				
	Children of 1472 WILLIAM P. LOUCKS,[8]						
2750	Fay Albert Loucks,	9	2-21, 1867		Lakin, Kas.,	4-13, 1886	
2751	Charles Alton,	9	6-12, 1873		"		
	Children of 1473 JANE LOUCKS GATES,[8]						
2752	Ruric R. Gates,	9	7-2, 1859	8-9, 1883	Dorset, O.		
	Jessie Ritter,		9-28, 1864				

No.	Name	Gen.	Born	Married	Place	Date	Residence
2753	Walter William, ...	9	12-16, 1867	} 2-8 1891	Dorset, O.		
	Minnie Leonard,		10-15, 1869				
	Children of 1474 MILES LOUCKS,[8]						
2754	Frank E. Loucks, . . .	9	7-29, 1870	} 8-25, 1892	Chicago.	5-29, 1879	Crawford, Pa.
	Ruth Irene Andrews,		1-1, 1871				
2755	Bernie, . . .	9	9-20, 1875	. . .			
	Children of 1476 GEORGE B. **LOUCKS,[8]**						
2756	Una Loucks, . . .	9	9-20, 1874	} 9-17, 1892			
	George Berton Bartlett,		8-30, 1871				
2757	Lyman, . . .	9	3-6, 1879				
2758	John Russell, . . .	9	5-14, 1887				
2759	Ora Gates, . . .	9	4-14, 1889				
2760	Iva Ruth, . . .	9	5-24, 1893				
	Children of 1477 MARY E. LOUCKS HAVENS,[8]						
2761	Eunice Isadore Havens, .	9	9-22, 1868	. . .	Springboro, Pa.	12-12,1872	Springboro.
2762	Ralph Bowman, . . .	9	4-15, 1870				
	Kate W. Woodbury,		12-23, 1874	3-30, 1891			
	Children of 1478 JAY ALBERT **LOUCKS,[8]**						
2763	Neva Minta Loucks, . .	9	7-13, 1887				
2764	Noel John, . . .	9	9-4, 1890				
	Children of 1479 JOHN ZEE LOUCKS,[8]						
2765	Flossie Prudence Loucks,	9	4-23, 1882				
2766	Lottie Pearl, . . .	9	12-22, 1884				
2767	Ernest Wilbert . . .	9	4-17, 1887				
2768	Mertie Eva, . . .	9	10-29, 1889				
2769	Carl Willard, . . .	9	10-21, 1891				
2770	Daughter, . . .	9	4-1, 1894				
	Children of 1480 DAYTON R. **LOUCKS,[8]**						
2771	Maud Eleanora Loucks, .	9	11-20, 1891				
2772	Claud Alexander, . . .	9	12-27, 1893				

No.	Name of Wife (or Husband).	Date of Birth.	Date of Marriage.	Residence.	Date of Death.	Place of Burial.
	Children of 1481 David E. Esmey,[8]					
2773	Claude Henry Esmey, ... 9	1-14, 1867		New York.		
2774	Maynard Jerome, ... 9	11-22, 1869		"		
2775	Dwight E., ... 9	12-26, 1874		"		
	Children of 1489 Elizabeth Mallett McEwen,[8]					
2776	Charlie Roy McEwen, . . . 9	1-14, 1894				
	Children of 1490 Helen Mallett Hess Wickoff,[8]					
2777	Berton Livingston Hess, . . . 9	12-13, 1878				
2778	Willie James Wickoff, . . . 9	2-18, 1891				
2779	Dorothy Katie, ... 9	4-13, 1893				
	Children of 1497 Emma Mallette Bennett,[8]					
2780	Lena Bennett, ... 9	11-4, 1869	} 5-11, 1887	Otego, N. Y.		
	William H. Richards, . . .	10-8, 1864				
2781	Charles, ... 9	5-1, 1871		Otego.		
2782	Della, ... 9	10-11, 1872				
2783	Fred, ... 9	2-13, 1876				
	Children of 1498 Estella Mallett Shumway,[8]					
2784	Frednethia Shumway, . . . 9	1-1, 1878				
	Children of 1499 Charles Ansel Mallette.[8]					
2785	Leroy Heath Mallette. . . . 9	5-30, 1884				
2786	Edna Gordon, ... 9	4-7, 1888				
2787	George Ansel, ... 9	3-12, 1892				
2788	Frank Luverne, ... 9	8-6, 1893				

No.	Name	Gen.				
	Children of 1500 WILLIAM JAMES MALLETTE,[8]					
2789	Clinton Artleus Mallette,	9	4–23, 1888			
2790	Harry L. Keaggy,	9	10–7, 1889			
2791	Clarence Elmer,	9	3–4, 1891			
2792	Gaven Spellington,	9	7–8, 1893			
	Children of 1501 JEROME RUFUS MALLETTE,[8]					
2793	Ethel May Mallette,	9	9–19, 1890			9–26, 1890
2794	Jerome Kenneth,	9	9–2, 1891			
	Children of 1503 FLORENCE MALLETT FARQUHARSON,[8]					
2795	Lloyd J. Farquharson,	9	2–22, 1883			
2796	Charles,	9	2–7, 1888			
	Children of 1504 ANN G. MALLETT JOHNSON,[8]					
2797	Carrie Johnson,	9	9–15, 1885			
2798	Flossie,	9	8–19, 1887			
	Children of 1511 JAMES DEY MALLETT,[8]					
2799	Mary L. Mallett,	9	4–10, 1879			1–5, 1892
	Children of 1512 ALVARO MALLETT,[8]					
2800	Charles S. Mallott,	9	11–11, 1888	Fultonville, N. Y.		
	Children of 1513 ARIVA MALLETT LATHERS,[8]					
2801	Cora V. Lathers,	9	1–30, 1880	Amsterdam, N. Y.		
2802	Newell G.,	9	12–5, 1882	"		
2803	Minnie M.,	9	9–7, 1885	"		11–18, 1885	Amsterdam.
2804	Emmett A.,	9	10–5, 1886	"		
2805	Lela E.,	9	4–27, 1889	"		
2806	Dora B.,	9	3–13, 1891	"		9–12, 1892	Amsterdam.

No.	Name of Wife (or Husband).	Date of Birth.	Date of Marriage.	Residence.	Date of Death.	Place of Burial.
	Children of 1514 ARMENIA MALLETT ROBERTS,[8]					
2807	Schuyler Roberts, 9	11-6, 1884				
2808	Ethel Bell, 9	1-16, 1890				
2809	Clarence D., 9	11-22, 1894				
	Children of 1515 SANFORD MALLETT,[8]					
2810	Hazel Mallett, 9	11-13, 1891		Lykens, N. Y.		
2811	Burt, 9	11-21, 1892		"		
2812	Jennie, 9	11-8, 1894		"		
	Children of 1525 MARVIN MALLETT,[8]					
2813	Jennie Secor Mallett, 9	2-14, 1882				
2814	Myrtle, 9	7-22, 1883				
2815	Nellie, 9	10-2, 1885				
2816	Leon G., 9	4-26, 1893				
	Children of 1527 CORA MALLETT PELTON,[8]					
2817	Bernice Almira Pelton, 9	7-7, 1893		Auburndale, O.,	6-9, 1894	
2818	Clifford Elias, 9	7-7, 1894		"		
	Children of 1529 FLORENCE MALLETT GOVE,[8]					
2819	Maud Mallett Gove, 9	9-26, 1874		Petersburg, Mich.		
2820	Nellie C., 9	5-15, 1876		"		
2821	Charles J., 9	2-12, 1878		"		
2822	Harry Collins, 9	11-30, 1884		"		
2823	Ned, 9	4-19, 1890		"		
	Children of 1530 VIOLA MALLETT HALL,[8]					
2824	Edna Earle Hall, 9	2-22, 1872	11-26, 1891	Erie, Mich.		
	Boyd Orin Bristoll,	9-13, 1867				
2825	Fay, 9	8-28, 1875		Erie.		

No.	Name	Gen.	Born	Married	Place	Died	Residence
2826	Clarence Elihu,	9	9-3, 1878		Erie,		
2827	Stephen S.,	9	1-23, 1884		"	8-31, 1882	
	Children of 1533 EARL GRANDISON MALLETT,[8]						
2828	Malvina Dorothea Mallett,	9	5-22, 1885		Toledo, O.		
2829	Maud May,	9	2-6, 1887		"		
2830	Manley Martin,	9	7-6, 1889		"		
2831	Dorothea Ruth,	9	9-14, 1891		"		
2832	Mabel Myra,	9	4-23, 1893		"		
	Children of 1534 JAMES SPENCER MALLETT,[8]						
2833	Clarence Birt Mallett,	9	1-16, 1891		Wolsey, S. D.		
2834	Clifford Stephen,	9	1-29, 1893		Toledo, O.		
	Children of 1543 MARIA LEWIS HARWOOD,[8]						
2885	Flora Harwood,	9					
	Amos Butler,						
	Charles Grover,						
2886	Charles, ——,	9					
	Children of 1544 DAVID LEWIS,[8]						
2837	Alferetta Maria Lewis,	9	9-20, 1859			3-20, 1860	
2838	Estella Melvina,	9	4-7, 1861	6-30, 1892			
	Benjamin Meyer.		4-7, 1860		Toledo.		
2839	Arthur David,	9	11-25, 1863			4-10, 1871	Auburndale, O.
2840	John,	9	10-21, 1866			11-1, 1866	Menomine, Mich.
2841	Fanny Jane,	9	4-30, 1868	10-29, 1888	Auburndale,	1-18, 1895	Auburndale, O.
	Frank Mitchell,				Bowling Green. O.		
	Robert J. Garbutt.				Milton, W. Can.		
2842	Claude Roy,	9	5-30, 1870	5-21, 1892			
	Fila Miller.		10-22, 1873				
2843	Jessie Ida.	9	10-21, 1873			10-13, 1875	Auburndale.
2844	Boyd C.,	9	1-1, 1876		Toledo.		
2845	Nellie B.,	9	4-29, 1879		"	10-6, 1878	
2846	Lucretia Belle,	9	10-18, 1881				
2847	Roscoe Dawson,	9	12-14, 1883				

No.	Name of Wife (or Husband).	Date of Birth.	Date of Marriage.	Residence.	Date of Death.	Place of Burial.
	Children of 1547 ELIZABETH LEWIS BENTON,[8]					
2848	Ella Benton, ... 9	4-22, 1859	12-25, 1883	Toledo, O.		
	Freeman Orr;	4-10, 1857				
	Children of 1549 ADELBERT LEWIS,[8]					
2849	Ellen Lewis, . . 9	9-26, 1868	12-19, 1888	Toledo, O.	11-12, 1894	Forest Cem. T.
	Robert G. Hull.	7-7, 1854		"	10-12, 1869	Nannocken, Mich.
2850	Martin, ... 9	10-11, 1869				
2851	Sarah Ann, . . 9	8-30, 1870	1892	Fremont, O.		
	Fred McFunn,	1860		Toledo.		
2852	Hattie, . . . 9	11-25, 1872	9-30, 1891	"		
	Frank Trumpy,	10-16, 1871				
2853	Dora, . . . 9	12-4, 1874		Toledo.	12-5, 1874	Nannocken.
2854	Edna Cora, . . 9	9-16, 1876				
2855	George, . . . 9	6-13, 1881		Toledo.	6-14, 1881	Nannocken.
2856	Emily, . . . 9	11-22, 1882		Toledo.		
	Children of 1550 BENJAMIN F. MALLETT,[8]					
2857	Eugene Battenburg Mallett, . 9	1-30, 1871	10-16, 1890	W. Toledo, O.		
	Mary Herk,	11-30, 1866				
2858	Franklin Benjamin, . 9	8-25, 1873		Toledo.		
2859	George William, . . 9	1-8, 1876		"		
2860	Sherman, . . . 9	2-20, 1881		"	7-30, 1881	W. Toledo.
2861	Freddie, . . . 9	9-19, 1883		"	10-5, 1886	"
2862	Julia Anna, . . 9	8-23, 1886				
2863	Harry Edwin, . . 9	8-1, 1891				
	Children of 1551 ANNA MALLETT DORR,[8]					
2864	Charles A. Dorr, ... 9	9-29, 1870				

No.	Name		Birth		Place		Place
	Children of 1558 MARY MALLETT PEASE,[8]						
2865	Maurice Elmer Pease,	9	5-19, 1871		Scitico, Ct.		Somers
	Mary Elizabeth Sykes,			7-28, 1894	England.		
2866	Harold Eugene,	9	4-24, 1874		Somers, Ct,	12-31, 1877	"
2867	Helen Sophia,	9	12-31, 1877		Scitico,	10-31, 1885	"
2868	Bertram Everett,	9	3-28, 1889		"	7-2, 1889	
	Children of 1562 AMANDA MALLETT SPENCER,[8]						
2869	Florence Spencer,	9	9-22, 1886		Scitico, Ct.	12-12, 1886	Somers, Ct.
2870	Bessie,	9	7-23, 1888		E. Pepperell, Mass.	8-27, 1888	"
2871	Ruth Viola,	9	5-21, 1890				
2872	Hazel Belle,	9	12-4, 1893		W. Fitchburg, Mass.		
	Children of 1563 FRANCES MALLETT BROCK,[8]						
2873	Florence Eliza Brock,	9	7-31, 1863	1-7, 1881	Toledo, O.		
	Thomas Lattin,						
2874	Samuel Light,	9	10-21, 1865	3-4, 1890			
	Lutie Blalock,						
2875	Edward William,	9	3-28, 1868	9-23, 1894			
	Bessie Jackman,						
2876	John Allison,	9	4-2, 1870				
2877	Milford Mallett,	9	6-8, 1872				
2878	Nelson Henry,	9	2-7, 1875				
2879	Alice Gertrude,	9	4-28, 1877				
	Children of 1564 ELLEN MALLETT EFF,[8]						
2880	Della Eff,	9					
2881	Bessie,	9					
2882	Caroline,	9					
2883	Nellie,	9					
2884	Jessie,	9					
2885	Clifford,	9					
	Children of 1565 ALVIN HARTWELL.[8]						
2886	Delora Angelia Hartwell,	9	2-3, 1853	12-30, 1869	Gilbertsville, N. Y.		
	Charles Valson Daniels,		10-15, 1849				

No.	Name of Wife (or Husband).	Date of Birth.	Date of Marriage.	Residence.	Date of Death.	Place of Burial.
2887	Warren T., ——, [9]			Candor, N. Y.		
	Children of 1570 DANIEL L. WELCH,[8] Welch, [9]					
2888	——, [9]					
2889	——, [9]				dec. inf.	
2890	——, [9]	3-1, 1873			"	
					10-25, 1882	
	Children of 1571 EMMA ANTHONY ANTHONY,[8]					
2891	Adaline Lavinia Anthony, [9]	4-25, 1870			8-4, 1870	Forest Lawn C., [Buffalo.
	Children of 1572 EDWARD L. AN-THONY,[8]					
2892	Edith Adaline Anthony, [9]	1-11, 1879				
2893	Cora Williams, [9]	5-29, 1880				
2894	Norman Hume, [9]	5-11, 1889				
	Children of 1573 BERTHA CLARK FERRIS,[8]					
2895	Estella Clark Ferris, [9]	2-15, 1891				
2896	Herbert Curtis, [9]	4-20, 1892				
2897	——, [9]	3-25, 1893				
	Children of 1580 BERTHA BRADLEY JONES,[8]					
2898	Flora Sherman Jones, [9]	12-23, 1890				
2899	Rose Elizabeth, [9]	1-31, 1893				
	Children of 1587 FRINK MANSFIELD SMITH,[8]					
2900	Susie Gendar Smith, [9]	5-15, 1894		Mt. Vernon, N. Y.		

No.	Name		Born		Residence	Married
	Children of 1612 ANNETTA BEACH RUGGLES LATTIN,[8]					
2901	Alice Washburn Ruggles,	9	8-11, 1871			
2902	Nellie Beach,	9	1-5, 1874			
2903	Robert Lyman Lattin,	9	1-23, 1885		Shelton, Ct. "	1-20, 1874
	Children of 1613 MARY BEACH PERRY,[8]					
2904	Jessie Bennett Perry,	9	4-21, 1872			8-22, 1872
2905	Emily Blackman,	9	7-19, 1874			
2906	Fanny Elizabeth,	9	1-23, 1884			
	Children of 1614 ELI W. BEACH,[8]					
2907	Willard Buckingham Beach,	9	5-16, 1877			9-8, 1892
	Children of 1615 WILLIAM O. BEACH,[8]					
2908	Ernest Perry Beach,	9	4-24, 1883		Trumbull,	5-10, 1883
2909	Daughter,	9	10-12, 1886			10-12, 1886
2910	Georgia Susan,	9	8-20, 1890			
	Children of 1616 MARIETTA S. BEACH SHERWOOD,[8]					
2911	Edith Alida Sherwood,	9	7-15, 1879		Hartford.	
2912	Walter Beach,	9	2-28, 1882		"	
2913	Lester Booth,	9	2-24, 1883		"	
2914	Wilbur Seeley,	9	7-4, 1886		"	
2915	Clarice,	9	7-5, 1889		"	
2916	Carrie Etta,	9	8-5, 1891			
2917	Son,	9	8-16, 1894			9-22, 1889
	Children of 1618 JOHN S. ADAMS, Jr.,[8]					
2918	Alice Alosia Adams,	9	3-1, 1855		Easton,	5-12, 1856 Easton.
2919	Grace Hedges,	9	1866		"	
	Lorenzo Clark,			1887			
	Children of 1621 GEORGE S. GILLETTE,[8]					
2920	Willard Sherwood Gillette,	9	2-9, 1886			

No.	Name of Wife (or Husband).		Date of Birth.	Date of Marriage.	Residence.	Date of Death.	Place of Burial.
	Children of 1622 EDWARD D. GIL-						
	LETTE,[8]						
2921	Clifford W. Gillette,	9	11–10, 1888				
2922	Mary A.,	9	1–5, 1891				
	Children of 1623 ORRIN L. SCAR-						
	BROUGH,[8]						
2923	Mabel Elrod Scarbrough,	9	3–20, 1881		Monroe, Ia.		
2924	Sanford Clark,	9	6–23, 1884		"		
2925	Ira Mason,	9	5–13, 1885		"		
2926	Anna Florence,	9	8–26, 1888		"		
2927	Fred Raymond,	9	1–21, 1891		"		
	Children of 1624 EDGAR SCAR-						
	BROUGH,[8]						
2928	Harry Edgar Scarbrough,	9	7–11, 1882		Cumberland, O.		
2929	Levi Jackson,	9	5–30, 1886		"		
2930	Katharine B ,	9	2–16, 1889		"		
2931	Ada Ola,	9	2–10, 1892				
	Children of 1625 CLARENCE SCAR-						
	BROUGH,[8]						
2932	Birdie Bell Scarbrough,	9	9–1, 1882		Minburn, Ia.		
2933	Emily Esther,	9	5–5, 1888		"		
2934	Gale,	9	12–9, 1889		"		
2935	Vernon,	9	7–24, 1892		"		
	Children of 1626 VIOLA SCARBROUGH						
	MONTGOMERY,[8]						
2936	Myrtle Adelaide Montgomery,	9	11–14, 1883		Fairmount, Ia.		
2937	Charles Edgar,	9	7–13, 1885		"		
2938	Alvaro Roy,	9	7–5, 1893				

No.	Name	Gen.	Born	Place	
	Children of 1627 ELLA SCARBROUGH COOPER,[8]				
2939	Nellie May Cooper,	9	11-11, 1889	Searsboro', Ia.	
2940	Clara Beatrice,	9	5-28, 1891	"	
	Children of 1629 CHARLES W. SCARBROUGH,[8]				
2941	Hugh Andrew Scarbrough,	9	11-12, 1893	Monroe, Ia.	
	Children of 1632 ELSIE ANN JACKSON CONWAY,[8]				
2942	Eugene Conway.	9	2-2, 1878	Chilicothe, O.	
2943	Frank McKendry,	9	5-2, 1881	"	
2944	Harry,	9	10-29, 1884	"	
2945	Verner,	9	11-10, 1887	"	3-5, 1888
2946	Hazel,	9	6-15, 1891	"	
2947	Chuley,	9	7-8, 1894	"	8-18, 1894
	Children of 1635 CHARLES M. GLOYD,[8]				
2948	Ralph Bliss Gloyd,	9	5-20, 1893		
	Children of 1636 MARY GLOYD LYON,[8]				
2949	Maude Olive Lyon,	9	7-27, 1880	Canterbury, O.	
	Children of 1638 FRANK E. ROBERTS,[8]				
2950	Minnie Ethel Roberts,	9	3-1, 1886	Monroe, Ia.	
2951	Bernice Evangeline,	9	8-17, 1890	"	
	Children of 1639 FREDERICK ROBERTS,[8]				
2952	Howard Ezekiel Roberts,	9	2-1, 1891	Monroe, Ia.,	
	Children of 1643 E. LOUISE BOOTH KEITH.[8]				
2953	Una Eva Keith,	9	5-2, 1875		
2954	Harry Dana,	9	2-25, 1877		
2955	Arthur Sturges,	9	4-20, 1882		
2956	Harrison Dana,	9	5-4, 1888		12-13, 1886

No.	Name of Wife (or Husband).	Date of Birth.	Date of Marriage.	Residence.	Date of Death.	Place of Burial.
	Children of 1660 GEORGE W. COLE,[8]					
2957	Aimee Burr Cole, ...9	2-7, 1885				
2958	Clifford Mallett, ...9	5-22, 1888				
2959	Mabelle Sherwood, ...9	1-29, 1890				
	Children of 1685 CHARLES F. PLUMB,[8]					
2960	Ethel Frances Plumb, ...9	6-17, 1890		Trumbull.		
	Children of 1686 ARTHUR E. PLUMB,[8]					
2961	Daughter Plumb, ...9	4-10, 1894				
	Children of 1688 ROBERT B. MIDDLEBROOK,[8]					
2962	Robert Middlebrook, ...9	7-10, 1885				
2963	Frances Hannah, ...9	12-8, 1886				
2964	Nettie Brinsmade, ...9	11-9, 1888				
2965	Ruth Augusta, ...9	6-16, 1891				
	Children of 1689 LOUIS F. MIDDLEBROOK,[8]					
2966	Mary Beach Middlebrook, . . .9	9-8, 1894				
	Children of 1703 HEWLETT H. MCELHINNEY,[8]					
2967	John Samuel McElhinney, ...9	9-29, 1866	6-4, 1893	Shelbyville, Mo.,	12-15, 1873	
	Lillie Bell Gilbert, ...	10-2, 1876				
2968	Nelson Preston, ...9	3-1, 1870		"		
2969	Edwin Solomon, ...9	6-17, 1872		"		
2970	Albert Denwiddie, ...9	4-1, 1875				
	Children of 1705 SOLOMON C. MCELHINNEY,[8]					
2971	John Delos McElhinney, ...9	6-1, 1866		Bethel, Mo.		
2972	Sarah Harriet, ...9	10-18, 1867		"		

No.	Name		Born	Married	Place	Died
2973	Ella Elen,	9	8-26, 1869			
2974	David Henry,	9	6-20, 1871		Bethel, Mo.	8-2, 1871
2975	Robert Ernest,	9	10-20, 1872		"	7-22, 1874
2976	James Edgar,	9	4-18, 1875		"	5-8, 1876
2977	Albert Ira,	9	1-16, 1878		"	
2978	Solomon Snail,	9	9-17, 1880		"	
2979	Edna Grace,	9	10-16, 1882		"	
2980	Willie Pearl,	9	7-23, 1884		"	9-1, 1884
2981	Percy Earl,	9	8-15, 1885		"	
2982	Benjamin Harrison,	9	5-23, 1888		"	
2983	Effie Jewell,	9	10-14, 1890		"	
2984	Gertrude May,	9	7-4, 1893		"	

Children of 1706 ROBERT T. McEl-
HINNEY,[8]

No.	Name		Born	Married	Place	Died
2985	Lee Stewart McElhinney,	9	9-21, 1890		Brookfield, Mo.	

Children of 1707 MALISSA McEl-
HINNEY WEST,[8]

No.	Name		Born	Married	Place	Died
2986	Lillie Isabel West,	9	8-25, 1867	3-29, 1891		
	I. L. Miller,					
2987	Hattie Eunice,	9	11-8, 1870			
2988	Jessie Abner Monroe,	9	10-13, 1872	3-13, 1892		
	Mary Bell Mills,					
2989	Melissa Clara,	9	11-22, 1876			
2990	Gracie Abigail,	9	6-24, 1884			

Children of 1708 CYNTHIA McEl-
HINNEY McKILLIP,[8]

No.	Name		Born	Married	Place	Died
2991	Minta Harriet McKillip,	9	2-22, 1869	9-11, 1892		1892
	J. W. Wren,					
2992	Bertie Lee,	9	7-17, 1870			
2993	Ernest William,	9	2-1, 1872			
2994	Eva Eunice,	9	10-6, 1873	6-25, 1894		
	Fred. Tarr,					
2995	Clara Elizabeth,	9	9-23, 1875			
2996	Frank Hamilton,	9	9-10, 1877			
2997	Ella May,	9	9-12, 1879			
2998	Goldie Hila Maud,	9	7-3, 1883		Forest Grove, Mo.	1-4, 1890
2999	Bessie Malvern,	9	10-24, 1887			

No.	Name of Wife (or Husband).	Date of Birth.	Date of Marriage.	Residence.	Date of Death.	Place of Burial.
	Children of 1709 JOHN M. McELHINNEY,[8]					
3000	Lewis Everett McElhinney, [9]	3-2, 1877		Queen Cy., Mo.		
3001	Irving Monroe, [9]	11-29, 1878				
3002	Josephine Maud, [9]	1-10, 1881				
3003	Harvey Clyde, [9]	5-6, 1883				
3004	Haschal, [9]	1-31, 1886			2-4, 1886	
3005	Lena Pearl, [9]	1-31, 1887				
3006	Henry Guy, [9]	10-26, 1889				
3007	Lucinda Ivie, [9]	6-12, 1892				
	Children of 1710 EUNICE McELHINNEY HOLT,[8]					
3008	Charles Emmett Holt,[8]	9-7, 1874		Bethel, Mo.		
3009	Henry Orville, [9]	12-22, 1875		Shelby co., Mo.		
3010	Noah B., [9]	2-16, 1878		Putnam co., Mo.		
3011	F. Lee, [9]	5-5, 1880		Unionville, Mo.		
	Children of 1711 CLARA McELHINNEY LOWE,[8]					
3012	Cessna Irvine Lowe, [9]	2-22, 1887		Kansas.		
3013	Coral Inez, [9]	8-16, 1889		Missouri.		
3014	———, [9]	3-18, 1891		"		
	Children of 1712 ALBERT F. P. McELHINNEY,[8]					
3015	Alvah Hewlett McElhinney, [9]	11-9, 1882		Unionville, Mo.		
	Children of 1715 EUNICE LOBAUGH MOHNEY,[8]					
3016	David Franklin Mohney, [9]	12-26, 1869				
3017	Marvin Merrian, [9]	5-19, 1876				
3018	William Lester, [9]	1-2, 1880			3-29, 1881	Ringgold, Pa.
3019	Benjamin Lyle, [9]	8-8, 1881			9-9, 1881	"
3020	John Curtice, [9]	11-9, 1883				

No.	Name	Gen.	Born	Residence	Died	Death place
	Children of 1717 FRANCES SMITH DOWNES,[8]					
3021	Clifford Lanoir Downes,	9	11-18, 1869	Kansas.		
3022	Edwin Orton,	9	12-15, 1870	Oklahoma.		
3023	Bertha,	9	7-25, 1872	Beaver, Pa.		
3024	Mora Elizabeth,	9	12-28, 1873	"		
3025	Estella Abby,	9	12-18, 1875	"		
3026	Jennie Winifred,	9	4-15, 1879	"		
3027	Frances,	9	6-19, 1882	"	12-28, 1886	Beaver
3028	Anna,	9	6-19, 1882	"	12-21, 1886	"
3029	David Lowry,	9	8-8, 1884	"	1-1, 1887	"
3030	Son,	9	5-28, 1886	"	2-11, 1887	Beaver.
	Children of 1719 ORIN R. SMITH,[8]					
3031	Lizzie May Smith,	9	5-15, 1886			
	Children of 1720 LOWRY D. SMITH,[8]					
3032	Margaret Elizabeth Smith,	9	6-9, 1882			
3033	Hila Florence,	9	7-18, 1884			
3034	Sarah Frances,	9	7-22, 1886			
3035	Annie Amelia,	9	6-20, 1891			
	Children of 1721 ELIZABETH SMITH SOWARD,[8]					
3036	Tom Wheeler Soward,	9	5-8, 1883	Winfield	9-28, 1884	Winfield.
3037	Arthur Lee,	9	1-19, 1886	"		
3038	Nella D.,	9	7-17, 1888	"		
	Children of 1725 BURTON CORRY SMITH,[8]					
3039	Sidney Ralph Smith,	9	5-26, 1889	Ringgold, Pa.		
3040	Grant Wheeler,	9	9-13, 1892	"		
3041	Elizabeth,	9	3-29, 1894	"		
	Children of 1727 HEWLETT E. SMITH,[8]					
3042	Mamie Rebecca Smith,	9	1-16, 1877	Heathville, Pa.		
3043	Kossie McCurdy,	9	4-26, 1878	"		
3044	Eddie Alvin,	9	10-31, 1879	"		
3045	Anderson William,	9	2-27, 1883	"		
3046	Guy Roscoe,	9	1-10, 1888	"		

No.	Name of Wife (or Husband).		Date of Birth.	Date of Marriage.	Residence.	Date of Death.	Place of Burial.
3047	Wilbur Byers, ...	9	3-13, 1894	. . . .	Heathville, Pa.		
	Children of 1728 ANNIS J. SMITH MARTIN,[8]						
3048	Nellie Blanche Martin, . . .	9	5-24, 1878	. . . .	Reynoldsville, Pa.		
	Children of 1729 MAGGIE SMITH BRACKEN,[8]						
3049	Cora Lee Bracken,	9	8-6, 1878	. . . .	Langville, Pa.		
3050	Benton Blair,	9	6-1, 1881	. . . .	"		
3051	Nettie Andra,	9	1-24, 1885				
3052	James Alexander,	9	11-14, 1887				
3053	Tacy May,	9	4-18, 1890				
3054	Walker Smith,	9	9-21, 1892				
	Children of 1730 VIOLA SMITH KEPLER,[8]						
3055	Alta Kepler,	9	4-9, 1879	. . . .	Jefferson Co., Pa.		
3056	Albert, "	9	12-17, 1881	. . . .	"		
3057	Mary Myrtle,	9	12-24, 1883	. . . .	"		
3058	Grace Pearl,	9	1-25, 1886	. . . .	"		
	Children of 1731 ELMER E. SMITH,[8]						
3059	Claude Meyers Smith,	9	12-28, 1890	. . . .	Patton's Sta., Pa.		
3060	Grace Esther,	9	7-28, 1893	. . . .	"		
	Children of 1732 ESTHER SMITH MARTIN,[8]						
3061	Joseph Clyde Martin,	9	2-5, 1884	. . . .	Driftwood, Pa.		
3062	Eugene Earl,	9	2-7, 1891				
	Children of 1743 HULETT A. SMITH,[8]						
3063	Jasper Asa Lorain Smith,	9	12-24, 1883	. . . .	Oliver twp., Jeff. co., Pa.		
3064	Burtin Clyde,	9	12-10, 1885		" "		
3065	Bertha Clair,	9	12-10, 1885		" "		

No.	Name	Gen.	Birth	Residence	Death	Death place
3066	Mary Etta,	9	6-20, 1887	Macalmont tp.,Jeff.co.,Pa		
3067	Earl Alverson,	9	11-15, 1888	Oliver twp., Jeff. co., Pa.		
3068	Bleakney,	9	12-9, 1890	" "		
	Children of 1744 PHILIP E. SMITH,[8]					
3069	Mearl D. Smith,	9	4-10, 1889	Oliver twp.,Jeff.co., Pa.,		
3070	Elton Blain,	9	11-16, 1890	" "		
	Children of 1745 MELVIN L. SMITH,[8]					
3071	Beatrice Smith,	9	5-14, 1885	Young twp., Jeff. co., Pa.,	1-20, 1888	Jeff. co.
	Children of 1748 EUNICE SMITH MEANS BLOSE,[8]					
3072	Cora May Means,	9	2-15, 1884	Oliver twp., Jeff. co., Pa.	8-18, 1884	Ringgold, Pa.
3073	Mary Ethel Blose,	9	9-14, 1888	" "	3-30, 1890	
3074	Melvin Smith,	9	8-10, 1892	" "		
3075	Son,	9	8-10, 1892	" "	dec.	Ringgold.
3076	Lulu Mazzie,	9	3-30, 1895	" "		
	Children of 1760 JOHN M. SMITH.[8]					
3077	Merrill E. Smith,	9	3-22, 1886			
3078	Son,	9				
3079	Son,	9				
3080	Daughter,	9				
	Children of 1762 CLARA SMITH SHAFER,[8]					
3081	Ethel Shafer,	9	12-13, 1892			
	Children of 1765 LUZERN DREW PLUMB,[8]					
3082	Marian Plumb,	9	1-29, 1890			
3083	Helen Holden,	9	9-18, 1891			
	Children of 1766 WARREN EZRA PLUMB,[8]					
3084	Frederick Henry Plumb,	9	10-23, 1882			
3085	Rubie Maria,	9	6-30, 1884			
3086	Julia Adeline,	9	10-18, 1886			

No.	Name of Wife (or Husband).	Date of Birth.	Date of Marriage.	Residence.	Date of Death.	Place of Burial.
3087	Edith May, ... 9	5-8, 1889				
3088	Allen Warren, ... 9	10-14, 1892				
	Children of 1780 ESTELLE BEACH CLEVELAND,[8]					
3089	Grace Maud Cleveland. . . . 9	9-30, 1877				
	Children of 1793 MARIA MALLETT GLASS,[8]					
3090	Harry Glass, ... 9					
3091	Mary E., ... 9					
	Harry Robinson,					
	Children of 1794 THERESA MALLETT ACKERMAN,[8]					
3092	Grace Ackerman, ... 9					
	Children of 1802 HELEN BILLINGS EDDY,[8]					
3093	Son Eddy, ... 9					
	Children of 1807 JUDSON B. MALLETT,[8]					
3094	Henry Alonzo Mallett. . . . 9	7-17, 1877		Danbury, Ct., . .	10-30, 1884	
3095	Edna Jane, ... 9	3-29, 1879				
3096	Grace Estella, ... 9	10-6, 1884			11-1, 1885	
	Children of 1809 WM. ORRIN MALLETT,[8]					
3097	Son Mallett, ... 9	10-12, 1880		N. Milford, Ct.		
3098	John Andrew, ... 9	10-9, 1882		"		
3099	Floyd Elsworth, ... 9	3-9, 1884		"		
3100	Wesley Perry. 9	4-11, 1885		"		
3101	Mabel Agnes, ... 9	8-31, 1886		"		
3102	Ruth Elinor, ... 9	7-23, 1890		"		
3103	Florence Anah, ... 9					

No.	Name		Date		Place		
3104	*Children of 1811* HULL FANTON,[8]	9	.	.	Havana, N. Y.		
	— Fanton,	9	.	.	Havana.		
	Children of 1816 FRANK FANTON,[8]						
3105	Florence B. Fanton,	9	10–5, 1872	.	Havana.	1–12,1894	
3106	Eaton Agard,	9	11–9, 1876	.	"		
3107	Grace L.,	9	10–27, 1878	.	"		
3108	Thomas Langley,	9	2–26, 1882	.	"		
3109	Frank, Jr.,	9	3–12, 1883	.	"		
	Children of 1835 ESTELLA WHIPPEY BATES,[8]						
3110	— Bates,	9					
3111	—,	9					
	Children of 1847 JOSEPHINE SMITH WILKIN,[8]						
3112	Helen A. Wilkin,	9	7–16, 1865	.	Enꜰeld.		
3113	Harry,	9	7–9, 1866	.	"		
3114	Homer,	9	5–12, 1869	.	"		
3115	Harvey,	9	11–30, 1875	.	"		
	Children of 1848 PHILO B. SMITH,[8]						
3116	Ira H. Smith,	9	12–13, 1879	.	Ulysses.		
3117	Cora R.,	9	10–6, 1884	.	"		
3118	Arthur B.,	9	3–15, 1891	.	"		
	Children of 1862 MARY SHERWOOD HUNTINGTON,[5]						
3119	Andrew Sherwood Huntington,	9	3–15, 1891	.	Springfield, Mass.		
3120	David Hull Sherwood,	9	10–26, 1892	.	Bridgeport, Ct.		
	Children of 1866 FRED. S. BEARDSLEY,[8]						
3121	— Beardsley,	9	.	.	Milwaukee.		
	Children of 1873 GEORGE M. SEELY,[8]						
3122	Lulu Effie Seeley,	9	6–6, 1867 }	4–16, 1890	Bridgeport,	5–6, 1893	N. Bridgeport.
	William Jones,	9	7–, 1867		"		
3123	Flora Card,	9	9–3, 1884	.	"	6–14, 1886	M. G. C. B. C.

No.	Name of Wife (or Husband).	Date of Birth.	Date of Marriage.	Residence.	Date of Death.	Place of Burial.
3124	Mallett, [9]	2-18, 1886		Bridgeport,	2-18, 1886	M. G. C. B. C.
3125	Alice Beach, [9]	12-30, 1887		"		
3126	Florence Glover, [9]	9-18, 1891		"		
	Children of 1875 Julia Seeley Thompson,[8]					
3127	Harriet Kirtland Thompson, [9]	4-29, 1874		Stratford, Ct.		
3128	Julia Seeley, Jr., [9]	3-7, 1876		"		
3129	Joseph Henry, Jr., [9]	3-11, 1879		"		
3130	Jesse Cornelius, [9]	6-24, 1887				
	Children of 1878 Frank W. Beardsley,[8]					
3131	Emma Edna Beardsley, [9]	1-14, 1891				
	Children of 1879 Fannie Beardsley Olmstead,[8]					
3132	Harold J. Olmstead, [9]	8-28, 1882				
	Children of 1880 Seymour B. Beardsley,[8]					
3133	Alice Gladys Beardsley, [9]	12-7, 1887				
	Children of 1891 Burt A. Banker,[8]					
3134	Glenn Beardsley Banker, [9]	12-4, 1888		Manson, N. C.		
3135	Mary Maurice, [9]	1-28, 1893				
	Children of 1901 Grant Beardsley,[8]					
3136	May Beardsley, [9]	5-6, 1874				
3137	Ida, [9]	8-4, 1876		"		
3138	Edith, [9]	5-22, 1878		"		
3139	Ada, [9]	6-15, 1881		"		
3140	Nellie, [9]	4-8, 1884		"		
3141	Catharine, [9]	5-6, 1886		"		
3142	Samuel Agard, [9]	6-1, 1889		"		

Children of *1902* HARRIET BEARDS-LEY TUM,[8]

3143	Addie Tum,	9	11-24, 1875	. . . . .	Catharine, N. Y.
3144	Bert,	9	8-7, 1878	. . . . .	"
3145	Legrand Fr st,	9	11-6, 1880	. . . . .	"
3146	Frank,	9	10-25, 1887	. . . . .	"

Children of *1505* CORNELIA BEARDS-LEY WINTON,[8]

3147	Georgiana Winton,	9	2-10, 1874	. . . . .	Catharine.
3148	Ernest,	9	3-6, 1876	. . . . .	"
3149	Ralph,	9	10-14, 1878	. . . . .	"
3150	Nellie,	9	11-4, 1880	. . . . .	"
3151	Arabella,	9	5-27, 1883	. . . . .	"

Children of *1904* CHARLES I. BEARDS-LEY,[8]

3152	Anna Beardsley,	9	1878

Children of *1905* J. Earl BEARDS-LEY,[8]

3153	Edna Belle Beardsley,	9	4-21, 1890

Children of *1906* LEWIS BEARDS-LEY,[8]

3154	George Beardsley,	9	5-25, 1890

Children of *1907* HAZLITT J. BEARDS-LEY,[8]

3155	Herman Beardsley,	9	4-27, 1891
3156	Chester,	9	6-27, 1892

Children of *1908* MENZO BEARDS-LEY,[8]

3157	Leda Beardsley,	9	10-8, 1885
3158	Bessie,	9	1-2, 1889

Children of *1927* MARIETTA KINGS-BURY BARBER,[8]

3159	John Barber,	9	. . . . .	Caton.

No.	Name of Wife (or Husband).	Date of Birth.	Date of Marriage.	Residence.	Date of Death.	Place of Burial.
3160	Myrtie,[9]			Caton		
3161	Euphemia,[9]			"		
	Children of 1929 BELL CAMPBELL VAN BUREN,[8]					
3162	Lily Van Buren,[9]			Elmira.		
3163	Amy,[9]			"		
3164	Cora,[9]			"		
	Children of 1931 LUCIUS B. CAMPBELL,[8]					
3165	Elmer Kendal Campbell,[9]	1881			1885	
	Children of 1932 JOHN CAMPBELL,[8]					
3166	Robert Campbell,[9]					
3167	Mary Bell,[9]					
3168	Lucius Elmer,[9]					
	Children of 1933 JAMES E. CAMPBELL,[8]					
3169	Lelia Campbell,[9]					
	Children of 1934 FRED A. LATTIN,[8]					
3170	Leon Lattin,[9]	1887				
3171	George,[9]	1890				
	Children of 1935 WILLIAM LATTIN,[8]					
3172	Harry Lattin,[9]	1892				
	Children of 1938 IDA LATTIN ESTERBROOK,[6]					
3173	Daughter Esterbrook,[9]	1892			1894	
3174	Fred,[9]	1893				

Children of 1940 MARY COMPTON PRICE,[8]

No.	Name	Born	Residence	Died	Place
3175	George Ransom Price,[9]	7-19, 1884	Troy, Pa.		
3176	Willard B.,[9]	4-27, 1887	Troy, Pa.		

Children of 1947 LOTTIE LATTIN DEWEY,[8]

| 3177 | —— Dewey,[9] | | | | |

Children of 1948 DELL LATTIN BRINK,[8]

| 3178 | —— Brink,[9] | | | | |
| 3179 | —— ,[9] | | | | |

Children of 1951 OLA LATTIN LOVALL,[8]

3180	—— Lovall,[9]				
3181	—— ,[9]				
3182	—— ,[9]				
3183	—— ,[9]				

Children of 1957 MARILLA HAWES RITZENTHALER,[8]

| 3184 | —— Ritzenthaler,[9] | | | | |

Children of 1959 JOHN B. HAWES,[8]

| 3185 | —— Hawes,[9] | | | | |

Children of 1962 LA MOTTE STANLEY,[8]

| 3186 | Don Stanley,[9] | 4-11, 1892 | Millport. | | |

Children of 1966 EVA KEYSER OWEN,[8]

| 3187 | Cecil Owen,[9] | 12-21, 1889 | Mecklenburg. | | |

Children of 2013 JAMES K. ROLSTON,[8]

3188	Rosa L. Rolston,[9]	7-7, 1879	Damascus, Pa.		
3189	Charles B.,[9]	3-16, 1881	"		
3190	Fanny L.,[9]	3-21, 1882	"		
319	Bennie H.,[9]	10-9, 1883	"		
3192	Eugene K.,[9]	7-26, 1885	"	4-23, 1881	Damascus.
3193	Earl E.,[9]	3-31, 1887	"	6-, 1887	Damascus.

No.	Name of Wife (or Husband).	Date of Birth.	Date of Marriage.	Residence.	Date of Death.	Place of Burial.
3194	Arthur B.,[9]	1-26, 1889		Damascus, Pa.		
3195	Laura A.,[9]	3-16, 1891		"		
	Children of 2015 CHARLES A. ROLSTON,[8]					
3196	Gertie A. Rolston,[9]	4-21, 1883				
3197	Ethel J.,[9]	10-31, 1885				
3198	Floyd O.,[9]	6-4, 1891				
3199	Clifford W.,[9]	11-1, 1893				
	Children of 2016 THEODORE HUBBELL,[8]					
3200	Henry L. Hubbell,[9]	9-13, 1872		New Haven, Ct.		
3201	William,[9]	9-13, 1874		"		
3202	Mary M.,[9]	12-25, 1875		"		
	Children of 2017 CHARLES HUBBELL,[8]					
3203	—— Hubbell,[9]					
	Children of 2086 ELISHA B. CLARK,[8]					
3204	Lewis Evans Clark,[9]	10-20, 1868	10-17, 1893	S. Meriden, Ct.		
	Minnie Bell Watrous,	10-19, 1871		Tracy.		
3205	Emily Louise,[9]	1-5, 1871	11-1, 1888	S. Meriden, Ct.		
	Charles H. Holland.	9-14, 1861				
3206	Ida May,[9]	7-1, 1874				
3207	Lucy Etta,[9]	1-23, 1876				
3208	Hattie Mabel,[9]	11-23, 1878				
3209	Olin Griffith,[9]	4-5, 1884				
	Children of 2087 ANNA CLARK BRAY,[8]					
3210	Arthur Ensign Bray,[9]	11-17, 1868		Chicopee, Mass.,	6-28, 1878	Chicopee.
3211	Frank Clayton,[9]	6-22, 1874		"	7-2, 1878	"
3212	Charles Willard,[9]	8-27, 1879		"		
3213	Maud Luella,[9]	11-27, 1882				

No.	Name		Birth		Birthplace	Marriage	Place
	Children of 2039 JOHN M. HUBBARD,[8]						
3214	Stella L Hubbard,	[9]	8-26, 1876	.	W. Haven, Ct.,	10-12, 1892	
	Children of 2040 LEWIS C. HUBBARD,[8]						
3215	John Brace Hubbard,	[9]	12-25, 1879	.	W. Haven.		
3216	Kathiebel May,	[9]	11-2, 1883	.	"		
3217	Harry B.,	[9]	9-2, 1885	.	"		
	Children of 2041 EDWARD E. HUBBARD,[8]						
3218	Minnie Vara Hubbard,	[9]	3-15, 1878	.	W. Haven.		
3219	Bertha May,	[9]	11-12, 1880	.	"		
3220	William Eugene,	[9]	5-25, 1883	.	"		
3221	Nellie Louise,	[9]	9-23, 1884	.	"	8-9, 1885	W. Haven.
3222	Florence Eunice,	[9]	6-28, 1889	.	"		
	Children of 2043 GEORGE HENRY HUBBARD,[8]						
3223	Daisy Fenn Hubbard,	[9]	1-7, 1887	.	China.		
3224	Winifred May,	[9]	2-7, 1889	.	"		
3225	George Graham,	[9]	11-3, 1890	.	"		
3226	Norman Squires,	[9]	9-7, 1892	.	"		
3227	Neela Louise,	[9]	9-12, 1885	.			
	Children of 2044 MARY HUBBARD LAWRENCE,[8]						
3228	George Hubbard Lawrence,	[9]	4-19, 1883	.	Waterbury, Ct.		
3229	Anna Louise,	[9]	9-12, 1886	.	"		
3230	William Cottle,	[9]	4-18, 1888	.	"	11- , 1889	Waterbury.
	Children of 2048 ANNA BELL CLARK ELMER,[8]						
3231	Marion Beatrice Elmer,	[9]	5-11, 1890	.	New Haven, Ct.	5-19, 1894	Milford, Ct.
3232	George Edgar,	[9]	7-9, 1893	.	"		
	Children of 2050 LIZZIE LAW BLAKESLEE,[8]						
3233	Harriett Finette Blakeslee,	[9]	7-2, 1880	.			
3234	Martha,	[9]	9-16, 1882	.			
3235	Albert Dennis,	[9]	6-7, 1884	.			

No.	Name of Wife (or Husband).	Date of Birth.	Date of Marriage.	Residence.	Date of Death.	Place of Burial.
3236	Harold Law, ... 9	1-8, 1886				
3237	Miles Grant, ... 9	1-20, 1888				
3238	Dorothy, ... 9	9-15, 1891				
	Children of 2052 LYMAN T. LAW,[8]					
3239	Helen Marjorie Law, ... 9	10-11, 1889				
	Children of 2056 MARY E. WHEELER ELY[8]					
3240	Seymour Whiting Ely, . . 9	7-6, 1864	. . . . .	Bridgeport, . . .	8-23, 1867	M. G. C. B. C.
3241	Cornelia Maria, ... 9	3-27, 1866	6-17, 1891		11-8, 1892	Hartford.
	Clarence W. Church,					
3242	Henry Wheeler, ... 9	5-3, 1868	. . . . .	Bergen, N. J.	5-1, 1889	M. G. C. B. C.
3243	Mary Ellen, ... 9	11-14, 1870		Bridgeport, . . .		
3244	Edith Griffing, ... 9	3-29, 1873	9-26, 1894	"		
	George Sherman Hawley,					
3245	Alfred Brockway, . . . 9	11-7, 1875	. . . . .	Bergen.	11-8, 1875	M. G. C. B. C.
3246	Edgar Brodhead, . . . 9	6-10, 1877	. . . . .	"		
3247	Clara Louise, ... 9	10-30, 1879	. . . . .	"		
3248	Frances Griscelle, . . . 9	8-15, 1882	. . . . .	"		
	Children of 2057 HENRY A. WHEELER.[8]					
3249	Minnie Wheeler, . . . 9	. . . . .	. . . . .	Bridgeport, . . .	dec.	M. G. C. B. C.
3250	Jessie Odell, ... 9	. . . . .	. . . . .	Bergen.		
3251	Charles, ... 9	. . . . .	. . . . .			
	Children of 2063 GEORGE W. HALL,[8]					
3252	Laura May Hall, ... 9	8-29, 1872	8-29, 1891			
	John Lewis Green,	. . . . .				
	Children of 2074 BENJAMIN MALLETT.[8]					
3253	Wilbur Mallett, ... 9					

No.	Name	Gen.	Birth	Death	Residence	M. G. C.
	Children of 2077 MARY D. BALDWIN WARBURTON,[8]					
3254	Lucy May Warburton,	9	6-19, 1867			
3255	Jessie Ella,	9	9-7, 1870			
3256	Carrie Amelia,	9	6-27, 1872			
3257	Elizabeth Stowe,	9	10-30, 1875			
3258	Susie Alice,	9	2-14, 1877			
3259	Samuel A.,	9	9-12, 1879			
3260	Edward H.,	9	5-1, 1881			
3261	Walter Louis,	9	2-23, 1884			
	Children of 2078 ARISTIDES BRISTOL,[8]					
3262	Clarence Page Bristol,	9	2-23, 1874			
3263	Clifford S.,	9	2-2, 1875			
3264	Gracie,	9	12-3, 1878	6—, 1881		
	Children of 2089 CHARLES HENRY BRIAN,[8]					
3265	Richard Lewis Brian,	9	5-1, 1891			
	Children of 2097 FRANK A. HUBBELL,[8]					
3266	Frederick Hubbell,	9			Bridgeport.	
3267	Howard,	9			"	
3268	Mable,	9			"	
	Children of 2098 SAMUEL W. HUBBELL,[8]					
3269	Walter Hubbell,	9			Bridgeport.	2-10, 1886
	Children of 2111 SARAH F. RICH HAWLEY,[8]					
3270	Frank Wheeler Hawley,	9	9-25, 1865		Bridgeport.	
3271	Edwin Westfield,	9	2-16, 1868		"	
3272	Harry Waterbury,	9	5-3, 1871		"	
3273	Nettie Laurena,	9	12-11, 1872		"	
3274	Wheeler,	9	5-23, 1875		"	

No.	Name of Wife (or Husband).	Date of Birth.	Date of Marriage.	Residence.	Date of Death.	Place of Burial.
	Children of 2115 ALFRED A. BLAKEMAN.[8]					
3275	Robert Sylvester Blakeman, ...9	2-5, 1873		Stratford.		
3276	Frederick Orville, ...9	8-22, 1874		"	7-27, 1891	
3277	Alfred Augustus, ...9	4-24, 1880		"		
	Children of 2118 SHERMAN B. MALLETT.[8]					
3278	Howard Mallett, ...9	2-22, 1892				
	Children of 2119 SUSAN C. MALLETT BENNETT.[8]					
3279	Charles Harrison Bennett. 9	10-9, 1888			11-12, 1889	
3280	Esther S., ...9	4-4, 1891				
	Children of 2125 GRACE MALLETT SMITH.[8]					
3281	Elsie Mallett Smith, ...9	3-26, 1891				
3282	Helen Grace, ...9	12-15, 1892				
	Children of 2133 MARY D. BALDWIN STEARNS.[8]					
3283	Son Stearns, ...9					
	Children of 2158 NORMAN S. MILES.[8]					
3284	Carrie S. Miles, ...9	10-7, 1868			11-4, 1875	
3285	Louie, ...9	4-2, 1872				
3286	Willie, ...9	2-1, 1876				
3287	Theodore S., ...9	2-9, 1878				
	Children of 2166 ADOLPHUS CORNWALL.[8]					
3288	George Archibald Cornwall, ...9	1-20, 1873		Brooklyn.		
3289	Isabel K., ...9	12-16, 1874		Plainfield, N.J.		
3290	Adolphus Duncan, ...9	10- , 1876		Garden Cy., N.Y.		

No.	Name		Place		
	Children of 2167 LAURA CORNWALL MUIR,[8]		Garden City.		
3291	Lina Muir,[9]	9–, 1875	Garden City.		
3292	Laura,[9]	9–, 1877	Chicago.		
	Children of 2173 ELIZABETH BALDWIN WALRADT,[8]				
3293	Lucy Baldwin Walradt,[9]	3-29, 1886			
	Children of 2190 HELEN HIGBY EAMES,[8]				
3294	Charlotte Marie Eames,[9]	10-12, 1883	Bridgeport.	8-12, 1888	M. G. C.
3295	Helen,[9]	10-30, 1886	"		
3296	Martha Louise,[9]	10-30, 1886	"		
3297	William Higby,[9]	10-18, 1892	"		
	Children of 2193 OLIVER WELTON,[8]				
3298	Herbert N. Welton,[9]	5-18, 1879			
3299	Le Roy,[9]	1-2, 1882			
	Children of 2195 WALTER S. WELTON,[8]				
3300	Walter J. Welton,[9]	4-22, 1881			
	Children of 2197 JOSEPH R. BALDWIN,[8]				
3301	William L. Baldwin,[9]	1-12, 1881			
	Children of 2198 FANNIE BEACH ELY,[8]				
3302	Mary Cushing Ely,[9]	8-1, 1871	Oberlin, O.	9-15, 1872	
3303	Katharine Ely,[9]	1872			
	Children of 2199 SAMUEL SWIFT BEACH,[8]				
3304	Samuel Cushing Beach, M. D. [9]	1870			
3305	——— ,[9]				
	Children of 2201 CORNELIA CURTIS BANKS,[8]				
3305	Daniel Curtis Banks,[9]	10-11, 1867	Bridgeport,	12-23, 1884	M. G. C.

No.	Name of Wife (or Husband).	Date of Birth.	Date of Marriage.	Residence.	Date of Death.	Place of Burial.
	Children of 2202 HENRY C. FAIRCHILD,[8] *see 1287.*					
	Children of 2203 ALFRED B. FAIRCHILD,[8]					
3306	Eva Louisa Fairchild,[9]	1-8, 1878		Bridgeport,	5-18, 1878	Nichols, Ct.
3307	Ralph Tomlinson,[9]	1-24, 1882		"		
3308	Alfred Huntington,[9]	5-26, 1886		"		
	Children of 2205 DANIEL UFFORD,[8]					
3309	William M. Ufford,[9]					
3310	Charles,[9]					
	Children of 2206 KATHARINE BEACH PRATT,[8]					
3311	Anna Beach Pratt,[9]	6-5, 1867				
3312	Olive Margaret,[9]	9-11, 1869				
3313	William Beach,[9]	10-22, 1872				
	Children of 2207 MARY E. BEACH GREGG,[8]					
3314	William Walker Gregg,[9]	9-8, 1870			12-3, 1881	
3315	Edward Lewis,[9]	10-21, 1873				
	Children of 2208 ROGER H. LYON,[8]					
3316	Roger Luther Lyon,[9]	8-20, 1889				
	Children of 2209 MARY W. LYON LINSLEY,[8]					
3317	Mary Linsley,[9]	10-14, 1867	11-20, 1889	N.Y.		
	Cornelius J. Horton,			White Plains, N.Y.		
3318	Lilian,[9]	10-8, 1870		N.Y.		
3319	Edith,[9]	3-23, 1873		"		
3320	Gertrude,[9]	1-22, 1875			1-22, 1878	

No.	Name	Gen.	Born	Died	Residence
	Children of 2216 FREDERICK B. JENNINGS,[8]				
3321	Percy Hall Jennings,	9	5-16, 1881		
3322	Elizabeth,	9	6-28, 1887		
3323	Frederick B.,	9	2-19, 1891		
	Children of 2218 CHAS. G. R. JENNINGS,[8]				
3324	Margaret Jennings,	9	8-1, 1889		
	Children of 2223 CATHARINE HOSFORD CLARK,[8]				
3325	Edward Clark,	9	2-, 1868	7-, 1875	
	Children of 2224 ELECTA PARSONS RIGGS,[8]				
3326	Robert Jennings Riggs,	9	1-3, 1888		
3327	Edith Clara,	9	9-11, 1889		
3328	Charles Henry,	9	2-, 1892		
	Children of 2225 LOUISE PARSONS ABBEY,[8]				
3329	Robert Parsons Abbey,	9	10-5, 1882		
3330	Henry McCracken,	9	, 1886	9-, 1887	Nanking, China.
3331	Catharine Jennings,	9	7-26, 1888		
3332	Marion Grace,	9	3-2, 1891		
	Children of 2228 JOHN G. JENNINGS,[8]				
3333	Isaac Lampson Jennings,	9	1-14, 1885		
	Children of 2229 CAROLINE JENNINGS CALHOUN,[8]				
3334	Tracy Jennings Calhoun,	9	7-11, 1885		
3335	Caroline Conkling,	9	4-22, 1887		
	Children of 2238 MAY WALLER STARKWEATHER,[8]				
3336	George Gordon Starkweather,	9	2-12, 1888		Washington, D. C.
3337	Walter Hallett,	9	10-6, 1889		Milwaukee, Wis.

No.	Name of Wife (or Husband).	Date of Birth.	Date of Marriage.	Residence.	Date of Death.	Place of Burial.
	Children of 2248 GEORGE DREW NICHOLS,[8]					
3338	Ina Frances Nichols, ... 9	12-16, 1889				
3339	Cora Drew, ... 9	8-12, 1891				
	Children of 2249 STILES A. NICHOLS,[8]					
3340	Charles Judson Nichols, . . . 9	8- , 1892				
	Children of 2264 WILMOT S. REYNOLDS,[8]					
3341	Laura Summers Reynolds, . . 9	7-24, 1887				
	Children of 2269 MINNIE MACRAE MACRAE,[8]					
3342	Hannah Sheldena Macrae, . . . 9	7-17, 1892		Garden City, Mo.		
3343	James Richards, ... 9	3-8, 1894				
	Children of 2287 a FRANCY BOOTH MYERS,[8]					
3344	Henry Ray Myers, ... 9	1-28, 1892			2- , 1892	
	Children of 2287 d ELLEN BOOTH BAKER,[8]					
3345	Francis Baker, ... 9	3-1, 1888				
3346	Sarah, ... 9	1- , 1892				
	Children of 2287 f CARRIE BOOTH PARKS,[8]					
3347	Jay Parks, ... 9	9-16, 1890				
3348	Eva, ... 9	8-31, 1892				
3349	Infant, ... 9	7-30, 1894				
	Children of 2287 o CORA E. BOOTH WAKEMAN,[8]					
3350	Lew Elizabeth Wakeman, . . 9	12-29, 1890			9-1, 1892	Stewarts Corners.

3351	Edna M., ...	9	1-13, 1892	
	Children of 2287 q ADENAH BOOTH BANKS,[8]			
3352	Harold A. Banks, . . .	9	6-1, 1892	
	Children of 2287 v HENRIETTA BOOTH MOREY,[8]			
3353	Florence Morey, . . .	9	9-17, 1882	
3354	Raymond, ...	9	6-3, 1884	
3355	Howard, ...	9	3-31, 1886	
3356	Infant, ...	9	1-11, 1891	
	Children of 2287 w ALVIN BOOTH,[8]			
3357	Russell Booth, . . .	9	12-8, 1888	
3358	Robert, ...	9	10-13, 1890	
	Children of 2287 x EMMET R. BOOTH,[8]			
3359	Wayne E. Booth, . . .	9	7-11, 1892	
	Children of 2287 z MARY PERRIGO CONGER,[8]			
3360	George Perrigo Conger, .	9	5-18, 1884	Geneva, N. Y.
3361	Walter, ...	9	8-16, 1890	"
	Children of 2292 LOUISA HOOPER DAUGHTRY,[8]			
3362	William Wilberforce Daughtry,	9		
3363	Spier Whitaker, . . .	9		
3364	Henry Lawrence, . . .	9		
3365	Ernest Moore, . . .	9		
3366	Florence Moore, . . .	9		
3367	Joseph, ...	9		
3368	Venie Kearney, . . .	9		
	Children of 2293 JAMES H. HOOPER,[8]			
3369	—— Hooper, . . .	9		
3370	——, ...	9		

No.	Name of Wife (or Husband).	Date of Birth.	Date of Marriage.	Residence.	Date of Death.	Place of Burial.
	Children of *2294* CHARLOTTE HOOPER ALSTON,[8]					
3371	Bettie Robert Alston,	9				
3372	Charlie Cook,	9				
3373	Lilian Mayfields,	9				
3374	Malcohn L. E.,	9				
3375	{John Crowell,	9				
3376	{Robert Mumford,	9				
3377	Bernadine,	9				
	Children of *2295* WILLIAM E. HOOPER,[8]					
3378	Theresa V. Hooper, *Smith Morehead Evans,*	9 10-11, 1870	10-7, 1890	Birmingham, Ala.		
3379	Mary D.,	9 6-25, 1873				
3380	Kathleen,	9 2-19, 1875				
3381	William E.,	9 4-5, 1877				
3382	Ethel Knox,	9 8-27, 1879			6-19, 1878	Selma, Ala.
3383	Henry Johnston,	9 8-7, 1881			1-30, 1894	Birmingham.
3384	William,	9 10-7, 1892			5-26, 1898	Birmingham.
	Children of *2296* THERESA HOOPER JOHNSTON,[8]					
3385	Kate Hardee Johnston,	9 5-16, 1870		Birmingham.		
3386	William Hooper,	9 2-15, 1872		"	6-23, 1871	
3387	Edward Douglas,	9 8-7, 1875		"		
3388	Forney,	9 9-9, 1880				
3389	Joseph C.,	9 6-11, 1885			11-11, 1889	Birmingham.
	Children of *2298* HELEN DEB. HOOPER WILLS,[8]					
3390	Harry C. Wills,	9				
3391	George Blount,	9				

No.	Name	Gen.	b.	birthplace	d.	place
	Children of *2299* FANNY DEB. HOOPER WHITAKER,[8]					
3392	DeBerniere Hooper Whitaker,	9				
3393	Bessie Lewis,	9				
3394	Percy du Ponceau,	9				
3395	David Spier,	9				
3396	Vernon Edelen,	9				
	Children of *2300* HENRY DEB. HOOPER,[8]					
3397	Henry deB. Hooper,	9				
3398	Louise Maclaine,	9				
	Children of *2301* JULIA HOOPER GRAVES,[8]					
3399	Ralph H. Graves,	9				
3400	Ernest,	9				
3401	Louis,	9				
3402	Mary deB.,	9				
	Children of *2306* SUSAN HOOPER BRICE,[8]					
3403	William Robert Brice,	9	9-16, 1875	Wilmington, N. C.		
3404	Susan Annette,	9	8-22, 1877	"		
	Children of *2310* SARAH HOOPER WESTON,[8]					
3405	Thomas Isaac Weston,	9	4-15, 1881	Grovewood, S. C.		
3406	William Stevenson,	9	7-27, 1883	"		
3407	John Tillinghast,	9	10-11, 1887	Sand Hills.	5-27, 1886	Gadsden.
3408	Joseph Hooper,	9	7-8, 1885	Gadsden, S. C.,	5-29, 1886	"
3409	Mary Elizabeth,	9	11-12, 1891	"		
3410	Christian Tucker,	9	12-28, 1893	"		
3411	Sarah Hooper,	9				
	Children of *2313* AMELIA HOOPER MELLICHAMPE,[8]					
3412	Edward Winborn Mellichampe,	9	7-25, 1881	Talladega, Ala.		
3413	Thomas Hooper,	9	6-4, 1883	"	1-25, 1884	Florence, S. C.
3414	James Hooper,	9	9-27, 1885	"		

No.	Name of Wife (or Husband).	Date of Birth.	Date of Marriage.	Residence.	Date of Death.	Place of Burial.
3415	Joseph Stanley, ... 9	1-28, 1888	. . . . . .	Talladega, Ala.	5-31, 1889	Edenton, S C.
3416	Augustus Chavasse, ... 9	5-7, 1890				
3417	DeBerniere, ... 9	2-7, 1893				
	Children of 2317 Edward Mc- Laurin,[8]					
3418	Duncan McLaurin, ... 9	1891				
	Children of 2319 Elizabeth Mc- Laurin Cleaveland,[8]					
3419	Kathleen Cleaveland, . . . 9	1893				
	Children of 2378 Margaret Mal- lett Holmes,[8]					
3420	Caroline Wright Holmes, . . 9	10-29, 1893				
	Children of 2416 Mary Goodwin Davenport,[8]					
3421	Jennie B. Davenport, . . . 9	4-1, 1885				
3422	Grace, ... 9	3-23, 1892				
	Children of 2417 Sophia Goodwin Stanton,[8]					
3423	Frank Stanton 9	2-27, 1879				
3424	Louis Nathan, ... 9	4-10, 1884				
	Children of 2420 J. Franklin Goodwin,[8]					
3425	Ida Goodwin, ... 9	8-29, 1890	. . .	Syracuse, . .	9-2, 1891	
3426	Florence Ruth, ... 9	7-22, 1892	. . .	"		
	Children of 2424 Burr W. Good- win,[8]					
3427	Wilbor Nathaniel Goodwin, . . 9	9- , 1893	. . . .	Watkins, N. Y.		

	Children of 2444 HATTIE COUCH JONES,[8]		
3428	Mary Eveline Jones, ... 9	6–, 1892	
3429	———, ... 9	8–11, 1894	
	Children of 2492 FREDERICK A. MALETTE,[8]		
3430	Emma Rachel Malette, . . . 9	5–3, 1885	Geneva, N. Y.
3431	James, ... 9	2–14, 1890	
	Children of 2495 FRED. W. GRIFFITH,[8]		
3432	Frederick Adams Griffith, . . 9	9–7, 1894	Palmyra, N. Y.
	Children of 2502 OLIN J. GARLOCK,[8]		
3433	Nelson J. Garlock, . . . 9	12–10, 1887	Palmyra, N. Y.
3434	Wilton J., ... 9	9–14, 1889	" "
	Children of 2503 HATTIE GARLOCK TIFFANY,[8]		
3435	Olin Dewitt Tiffany, . . . 9	6–26, 1891	Palmyra.
3436	Ruth Elizabeth, ... 9	10–12, 1893	"
	Children of 2506 EVA STUART COON,[8]		
3437	Cornelia Coon, ... 9	9–27, 1894	
	Children of 2516 LETTIE HALL BARNES,[8]		
3438	Son Barnes, ... 9		
3439	Daughter, ... 9		
3440	Son, ... 9		
3441	Son, ... 9		
3442	Son, ... 9		
	Children of 2518 ISABEL HALL BENTLEY,[8]		
3443	Son Bentley, ... 9		
	Children of 2540 MARY HARROD MEAD,[8]		
3444	Ellen Adelaide Mead, . . . 9	12–21, 1886	

No.	Name of Wife (or Husband).		Date of Birth.	Date of Marriage.	Residence.	Date of Death.	Place of Burial.
3445	Royal Albert, ...	9	12–2, 1888				
	Children of 2586 John W. Tread- *well,[8] see 1345.*						
	Children of 2587 Emma Thompson *Thorp,[8]*						
3446	Bessie May Thorp, . . .	9	7–10, 1889	. . . .	Stamford, Ct.		
3447	Georgianna, ...	9	2–28, 1891	. . . .	"		
3448	Frances Mildred, . . .	9	12–9, 1893	. . . .	"		
	Children of 2602 Charles Gould *Curtis,[9]*						
3449	Charles Botsford Curtis, .	10	1–22, 1876	. . . .	. . . .	6–2, 1878	
	Children of 2605 Etta Hall *Manee,[9]*						
3450	Herbert Abram Manee, . .	10	4–17, 1892				
	Children of 2606 David M. *Hall,[9]*						
3451	May Bell Hall, ...	10	10–14, 1883				
3452	Raymond Clark, ...	10	3–28, 1888				
3453	Lena Beatrice, ...	10	2–26, 1890				
	Children of 2618 Eugenia Morris *Canfield,[9]*						
3454	Morris Canfield, . . .	10	4–1, 1891				
	Children of 2618 Reuben M. *Warner,[9]*						
3455	Reuben Grandison Warner, .	10	1883				
3456	Levi Mallett, ...	10	3–6, 1885				
3457	Howard, ...	10					
3458	———, ...	10					

Children of *2628* ANNA MALLETT CARSON,[9]

No.	Name		Born	Place	Event	Event Place
3459	—— Carson,	10				
3460	——,	10				

Children of *2631* LENA KNOX MERRILL,[9]

No.	Name		Born	Place	Event	Event Place
3461	Son Merrill,	10	6- , 1893			

Children of *2632* GEORGE W. WARNER,[9]

No.	Name		Born	Place	Event	Event Place
3462	Frederick G. Warner,	10	8-16, 1889			
3463	William H.,	10	2-14, 1893			
3464	Mabel,	10	7-14, 1894			

Children of *2684* AMELIA BROWN PLATT,[9]

No.	Name		Born	Place	Event	Event Place
3465	Granville A. Platt,	10	6-29, 1884	Bethel, Ct.,		
3466	Grace E.,	10	2-27, 1888	"	5-16, 1885	Bethel,

Children of *2685* MARY JENKINS HAYNES,[9]

No.	Name		Born	Place	Event	Event Place
3467	Leila May Haynes,	10	6-4, 1866	Springfield, Ill.	4-28, 1887	
	Allen Dow Jacobus,		5-2, 1862	Edgerton, Wis.		
3468	Georgia Luella,	10	9-26, 1871	Fairmount, Ill.		

Children of *2688* CORA WARDNER COX,[9]

No.	Name		Born	Place	Event	Event Place
3469	Jennie Louisa Cox,	10	3-21, 1886	Cleveland, O.		
3470	Alice Mildred,	10	1-14, 1888	"		

Children of *2691* WILLIAM BURR MALLETT,[9]

No.	Name		Born	Place	Event	Event Place
3471	Weldon Ainstie Mallett,	10	10-14, 1894			Chicago.

Children of *2711* MARY DE FOREST SPENCER,[9]

No.	Name		Born	Place	Event	Event Place
3472	William Henry Spencer,	10	1-24, 1888	Milford, Ct.		
3473	Russell De Forest,	10	3-4, 1889			

No.	Name of Wife (or Husband).	Date of Birth.	Date of Marriage.	Residence.	Date of Death.	Place of Burial.
	Children of 2724 WILBUR GLEASON FOWLER,[9]					
3474	Clarence Bennett Fowler, . . . [10]	3-14, 1893				
	Children of 2737 DORA FLOWER RUDDOCK,[9]					
3475	Fannie Elizabeth Ruddock, . . [10]	2-24, 1879				
	Children of 2739 HERMAN FLOWER,[9]					
3476	Albert Henry Clay Flower, . . [10]	4-, 1878				
3477	Mary Helen, ... [10]	1881				
3478	Emma, ... [10]	3-, 1890				
	Children of 2741 FRANK Z. FLOWER,[9]					
3479	Lloyd Edwin Flower, . . . [10]	8-18, 1890				
3480	Ray Sydney, ... [10]	7-29 1892				
	Children of 2742 JOHN A. FLOWER[9]					
3481	Audrey Flower, ... [10]	6-15, 1893				
	Children of 2743 ELLA FLOWER RICHMOND,[9]					
3482	Pearle Arthur Richmond, . . [10]	3-16, 1886				
3483	Frank Almond, ... [10]	4-9, 1888				
3484	Helen Hannah, ... [10]	10-21, 1889				
3485	Albert Llewellyn, ... [10]	5-6, 1891				
3486	Maud Charlotte, . . . [10]	8-7, 1892				
	Children of 2744 HELEN FLOWER REYCRAFT,[9]					
3487	Harold Raymond Reycraft, . . [10]	4-27, 1890	. . . . .			
	Children of 2752 RURIC R. GATES,[9]					
3488	Lloyd Gates, ... [10]	9-12, 1885	. . . . .	Dorset, O.		

No.	Name		Date	Place	Date	Place
	Children of 2753 WALTER W. GATES,⁹					
3489	Leonard Gates,	10	1-14, 1892	Dorset, O.		
3490	Ruth,	10	7-17, 1893	"		
	Children of 2754 FRANK E. LOUCKS,⁹					
3491	Milford Err Loucks,	10	8-23, 1893			
	Children of 2762 RALPH B. HAVENS,⁹					
3492	Nelson Woodbury Havens,	10	10-23, 1892			
	Children of 2780 LENA BENNETT RICHARDS,⁹					
3493	Fred Reuben Richards,	10	10-7, 1891			
	Children of 2824 EDNA HALL BRISTOL,⁹					
3494	Blaine Josiah Bristol,	10	8-30, 1892			
	Children of 2835 FLORA HARWOOD BUTLER GROVER,⁹					
3495	Arthur Butler,	10				
3496	Daughter Grover,	10				
3497	Daughter Grover,	10				
	Children of 2836 CHARLES HARWOOD,⁹					
3498	Daughter Harwood,	10				
3499	Daughter	10				
	Children of 2841 FANNY LEWIS MITCHELL GARBUTT,⁹					
3500	Judson Roy Mitchell,	10	10-8, 1889	Auburndale.	9-12, 1893	Auburndale, O.
3501	Charles Garbutt,	10	1892	"	1893	"
3502	———,	10	1893	"	2-3, 1895	
3503	———,	10	1-18, 1895			
	Children of 2849 ELLEN LEWIS HALL,⁹					
3504	Hazell May Hall,	10	5-26, 1890	Toledo, O.		
3505	Alma Bernard,	10	11-20, 1893	"		

No.	Name of Wife (or Husband).	Date of Birth.	Date of Marriage.	Residence.	Date of Death.	Place of Burial.
	Children of 2852 HATTIE LEWIS TRUMPY,[9]					
3506	Earl Trumpy, ... 10	4-10, 1892	. . . .	Toledo,	9-22, 1892	Forest Cem., T., O.
3507	Bertie Edwin, ... 10	6-3, 1893	. . . .	"		
	Children of 2857 EUGENE MALLETT,[9]					
3508	Clarence Edward Mallett, . . 10	2-3, 1892				
	Children of 2873 FLORENCE BROCK LATTIN,[9]					
3509	Ernest William Lattin, . . 10	2-10, 1882				
3510	Fred, ... 10	8-1, 1884				
3511	Thomas Edward, ... 10	7-13, 1887				
3512	Agnes Marion, ... 10	8-18, 1890			10-4, 1890	
3513	Maynard James, ... 10	8-1, 1892				
	Children of 2874 SAMUEL L. BROCK,[9]					
3514	George Brock, ... 10	10-10, 1891				
3515	Clifford, ... 10	12-11, 1893				
	Children of 2886 DELORA HARTWELL DANIELS,[9]					
3516	Charles Alvin Daniels, . . . 10	12-26, 1871				
3517	Frederick, ... 10	6-23, 1873			12-6, 1874	
3518	Francis Ralph, ... 10	10-29, 1877				
	Children of 2919 GRACE ADAMS CLARK,[9]					
3519	Lora Clark, ... 10	2– , 1888				
	Children of 2986 LILLIE WEST MILLER,[9]					
3520	Jesse Oliver Miller, ... 10	1-19, 1892				
3521	Abner William, ... 10	7– , 1894				

3522	*Children of 2988* JESSE A. M. WEST,[9] Noah Billie West, ...10	7–21, 1893	
3523	*Children of 3091* MARY GLASS ROLINSON,[9] Richard Rolinson, ...10		
3524 3525	*Children of 3205* EMMA CLARK HOLLAND,[9] Mabel E. Holland, ...10 Charles A., ...10	2–10, 1889 3–3, 1892	
3526	*Children of 3241* CORNELIA ELY CHURCH,[9] Lela Adelaide Church, . . .10	10–13, 1892	Hartford, Ct.
3527	*Children of 3317* MARY LINSLEY HORTON,[9] Herbert Linsley Horton, . . .10	3–11, 1893	
3528 3529	*Children of 3378* THERESA HOOPER EVANS,[9] Wm. Hooper Evans, ...10 Johnsie, ...10	9–3, 1891 9–2, 1893	Birmingham, Ala.
3530	*Children of 3467* LEILA HAYNES JACOBUS,[10] Clyde Earl Jacobus, ...11	12–8, 1888	Edgerton, Wis.

ADDENDA.

No.	Name of Wife (or Husband).	Date of Birth.	Date of Marriage.	Residence.	Date of Death.	Place of Burial.
56	Philo Mallett, / *Eunice Wheeler,*	4-2, 1760 / 4-10, 1762				
68	Elijah Mallett, / *Sarah Stanford,*		12-1, 1794			Episcopal Church Records, Stratford, Ct.
71	Ebenezer Wheeler, / *Naomi (d. Nath'l and Rachel Lewis) Wheeler,*		9-1, 1792			
77	Salmon Mallett,	1761				
94	*w. Hannah (d. Stephen and Rhoda Middlebrook) Hubbell.*					
96	Luke Beardsley, / *Sarah Laborie (Lane),*		1-9, 1791			
99	*w. Amy Somers,*	1778				
	Children of 25 LEWIS MALLETT.[4]					
112	Lucy Mallett, / *John (s. of John) Fowler,*	10-7, 1769	1785	Milford.	10-13, 1790	Milford.
108	Lewis, / *Anna (d. Landa) Beach,*	5-5, 1758 / 1759		Milford.		
109	John, / *Mehitable (d. Duncan) Weir,*	6-12, 1767 / 1761	1789	Milford, / "	1-1, 1835 / 1834 / 1837	Milford. / "
110	Eunice, / *Wm. (s. Wm.) Coggeshall,*	6-3, 1758 / 1762	3-9, 1779	Orange,	1800	Orange.
111	Miles, / *Mary Ann (d. Sam'l) Miles,*	1766	1-2, 1788	Orange.	6-25, 1844 / 1803	"
115	Peter, / *Eliza (d. Sam'l) Terrell.*	1772		Orange.	1828	
113	Nancy, / *Sam'l Worden,*	1774		Stratford.	1846	

No.	Name	Gen.	Born	Married	Birthplace	Died	Where died
114	Mary,	5	11–, 1794	. . . .	. . . .	11–, 1799	
	Daniel (s. John) Miles,		10–, 1747	. . . .	. . . .	9–, 1808	
116	Avis,	5		5–29, 1793	. . . .	1802	Lost at sea.
	Henry Turner,				. . . .		
117	Isaac,	5		6–12, 1796	. . . .		
	Sarah Brintnall,				. . . .		

Children of 26 EUNICE MALLETT BALDWIN,⁴

No.	Name	Gen.	Born	Married	Birthplace	Died	Where died
117a	*Eunice Baldwin,	5	5–5, 1753	11–30, 1775	Milford,	5–15, 1776	Milford.
	Capt. Wm. Davison,						
121	Nathan,	5	1–8, 1755	2–16, 1784	. . . .	1803	
	Avis (d. Sam'l) Durand,		11–, 1765				
119	Content,	5	1763	3–25, 1792	. . . .	1801	
	Elias (s. Elias) Currington,		2–19, 1764			1829	
120	Mary, (s. John) Durand,	5	1769	2–18, 1791	. . . .	1850	
	Wm. (s. John) Durand,		4–27, 1760			1841	
126	Elihu Baldwin, m. 1st, Abigail Gunn, no ch.; 2d, Phebe Gunn.						
127	Elizabeth Baldwin, was the second wife of Garrett (s. Garrett) De Witt, b. 1763.						
143	Naomia Summers,⁵ and Ely Burton,	5		. . . .	. . . .	. . . .	
159	Elijah Booth,	5	12–28, 1771	. . . .	Born in Conn.,	7–14, 1841	Catharine, N. Y.
	Rachel Beardsley,				. . . .	10–4, 1841	

Children of 56 PHILO MALLETT,⁵

No.	Name	Gen.	Born	Married	Birthplace	Died	Where died
218	Delason Mallett,	6	2–14, 1798	. . . .	. . . .	3–21, 1881	Argusville, N. Y.
	Anna Mariah Davis,		2–7, 1801				"
219	Charles Grandison,	6	. . . .	. . . .	Washington, O.,	2–, 1878	W. Toledo, O.
	Keziah,				. . . .		"
220	Benjamin,	6	5–15, 1784	. . . .	. . . .	5–11, 1859	"
	Betsey Dego,						
	Mary Jones,						
222	Lois,	6	2–8, 1802	. . . .	Roseburn, N. Y.	12–25, 1886	W. Toledo.
	Marlyn Hoyt Stevens,		1813			4–21, 1888	Roseburn.
			1810			10–24, 1886	"

Children of 63 HULDAH MALLETT WHEELER,⁵

No.	Name	Gen.
236a	George Wheeler,	6

[1] This from inscription on grave-mark in cemetery, Milford, Ct.

No.	Name of Wife (or Husband).	Date of Birth.	Date of Marriage.	Residence.	Date of Death.	Place of Burial.
236b	William, [6]					
236c	James, [6]					
236d	Henry, [6]					
236e	Sally, . George Smith, [6]			N. Y.		
236f	Caroline, *Thomas.* [6]					
236g	Harriet, *Henry Hall.* [6]					
236h	Sophia, *Jesup,* [6]					
239	Elizabeth Middlebrook, [6]	2–, 1811	} 2-21, 1855	Stamford, Ct.		
	Hiram Beardsley,	4-30, 1811				
	Children of 72 David Wheeler,[5]					
261	Eunice Wheeler, [6]	12 5, 1793	} 3-7, 1815	Beaver Tp., Pa..	6-6, 1869	Beaver.
	Hulett Smith,	8-1, 1792			2-11, 1879	"
263	Abigail, [6]	12-9, 1801		Long Hill, Tr.,	10-28, 1889	"
312	Lewis Beardsley, [6]	3-4, 1796	} 3-11, 1821	Catharine,	3-27, 1885	Catharine.
	Nancy Lewis,	10-3, 1801			6-19, 1867	"
	Elizabeth Lyon,	5-2, 1804			2-12, 1873	"
315	w.,	1817				
	Children of 110 Eunice Mallett Coggeshall.[5]					
354a	William Coggeshall, [6]	12-27, 1780	} 7-4, 1802		1810	At sea.
	Julia (d. Wm.) Atwater,	1780				
354b	John, [6]	9-26, 1782			1828	Abroad.
354c	George, [6]	1784			1807	
	Eliza Pierp nt.					
354d	Charles, [6]	5-28, 1793	unm.,		1820	At sea.
354e	James, [6]	2–, 1795	"		1817	Porto Rico.

No.	Name		Born	Married	Residence	Died	Remarks
354f	Francis,		1797	unm.,		1825	At sea.
358	Mary Ann Mallett,			3-2, 1820			
359	Lewis,	6				11-22, 1816	Drowned at Niagara Falls
360	Miles,	6		unm.,		4-, 1817	Drowned.
364	Lucy,	6				3-23, 1881	Milford.
362	Phebe,	6	9-2, 1808			11-3, 1810	
366	Fowler,	6			Orange.		

Children of 112 LUCY MALLETT FOWLER.[5]

No.	Name		Born	Married	Residence	Died	Remarks
366a	John Fowler,	6	5-15, 1786		Milford,	7-28, 1810	At sea.
	Elizabeth Curtis,		2-8, 1791				
366b	Luke,	6	11-14, 1787		Milford,	1856	
366c	Susannah,	6	1790		"	8-13, 1820	At sea.

Children of 114 MARY MALLETT MILES.[5]

No.	Name		Born	Married	Residence	Died	Remarks
372a	Daniel Miles,	6	1778	10-12, 1800		1812	
	Martha (d. of Clement) Northrop,						
372b	Polly,	6	1778			1782	
372c	Betsey,	6	1780			1844	
	Isaac Treat,		11-30, 1780	9-14, 1800			
372d	Jared,	6	1782				
	———,						
372e	Polly,	6	1785	9-3, 1806		1825	
	Reuben Whitehead,				Atlanta, Ga.,		
372f	Eunice,	6	1791				
	——— Smith,						
372g	Diana,	6	1795	9-16, 1818	Georgia.		
	Joel (s. Noah) Kelsey,						
375	*w.* Dianna,	6		unm.,			
377	Eliza,	6	12-19, 1869			2-11, 1895	Milford, Ct.
378	Horace,	6	7-3, 1813	1-15, 1884		8-2, 1894	Milford.
	Julia Ann (d. of Jedidah) Stowe,						
379	Mary,	6	1810			1844	
	Nathan (s. of Nathan & Avis) Fenn,					1862	

No.	Name of Wife (or Husband).	Date of Birth.	Date of Marriage.	Residence.	Date of Death.	Place of Burial.
	Children of 116 AVIS MALLETT TUR-NER,[5]					
380a	Eliza Turner, 6					
	—— Oviatt,					
	Children of 119 CONTENT BALDWIN CARRINGTON,[5]					
382a	Esther Carrington, 6		9-2, 1810	Westville, Ct.		
	Newell Johnson,					
382b	Elizabeth. 6					
	Deuzill Hitchcock (Hotchkiss?),					
382c	Albert, 6			Seymour, Ct.		
	Betsey Brown.					
	Olive Merriman.					
382d	Content, 6	10-19, 1799	1-18, 1824			
	Curtis (s. Abel) Oviatt,	1- , 1800				
382e	Nelson, 6	10- , 1812	5-9, 1837			
	Mary (d. John) Carrington,	5- , 1808				
382f	Calvin, 6					
	Sarah Smith,					
382g	Elias, 6	6- , 1814		Harwinton, Ct.		
	Nancy Crook,			New Canaan, Ct.		
	Children of 120 MARY BALDWIN DURAND,[3]					
382h	William Durand, 6	2-22, 1792	2-4, 1811		11-12, 1812	
	Nancy (d. of Isaac) Buckingham,	5- , 1795				
382i	Mason Andrew, 6	9-26, 1798	8-22, 1824		1832	
	Charlotte E. Bradley,	7-28, 1797				
382k	Charlotte, 6		unm, . . .		1834	
382l	Calvin, 6	2-1, 1802	4-27, 1847		1884	
	Mary Cecil Hunter,					
382m	Mary, 6	12-4, 1803	1840		1888	
	Francis Trowbridge,					
382n	David H., 6	1-19, 1810	1840		1843	
	Mary (d. Elijah) Brian,	6- , 1816				

No.	Name	6	Born	unm., / married	Place	1885	Manilla.
382o	Nathan,	6	11-14, 1812				
383	David Lewis Baldwin,	6				1-2, 1877	
384	Eunice,	6	1790	1-10, 1805			
	Sam'l (s. Theophilus) Miles,						
385	Marcus,	6		1-6, 1820			
	Jerusha (d. Sam'l) Parsons,						
386	Martha,	6	1796			11-22, 1878	M. G. C. B. C.
387	w. Lucy (d. Timothy) Higgins,		4-23, 1805			1879	
388	w. Susan (d. Michael) Peck,		3-14, 1799				
389	Charlotte,	6	1-27, 1801	10-14, 1824	Bridgeport,	9-25, 1891	M. G. C. B. C. "
	Harvey (s. Sam'l) Higby,			8-1, 1824		5-29, 1875	
390	w. Esther (d. Anthony) Stowe,			10-26, 1825			
	(Another record gives),						
	Children of 126 ELIHU BALDWIN [5]						
390a	Abigail Gunn Baldwin,	6	8-2, 1785 / 10-3, 1785	9-20, 1809		1844	
390b	Spencer (s. of Wm.) Stowe,	6	7-10, 1791		Middlebury, Ct.	1870	
	Samuel,	6	bap.				
	Maria Baldwin,						
390c	Elihu,	6	bap. 6-20, 1792	4-4, 1816			
	Mary (d. Sam'l & Jane) Clark,						
390d	Elizabeth,	6	bap. 3-12, 1794	9-23, 1829			
	Joseph (s. Richard) Platt,						
390e	Phoebe,	6	bap. 7-1, 1798 / 12-20, 1799	12-10, 1820		1838	
	Geo. R. (s. David B.) Ingersoll,					1854	
390f	Mary Ann,	6	bap. 10-12, 1800	11-26, 1820			
	Richard (s. Fisk) Platt,						
	Children of 127 ELIZABETH BALD- *WIN DEWITT, [5]*						
390g	Elizabeth Dewitt,	6			Sparta, Ga.		
	—— Wylie,						
390h	Katharine,	6			N. Haven.		
	Cyprian Wilcox,						
390i	Avis,	6					
	Rev. —— Beaman,						
390k	Maria,	6			Litchfield, Ct.		
	Amos Smith,						

No.	Name of Wife (or Husband).	Date of Birth.	Date of Marriage.	Residence.	Date of Death.	Place of Burial.
3901	Cornelia, [6]					
	Eli B. Clark,			Watertown, Ct.		
390m	Margaret, [6]	1810	unm.,		1826	
390n	William, [6]		"	N. Orleans, La.		
390o	David, [6]		"	Havana.		
390p	Garret, [6]		"	New York.		
390q	John, [6]		"	Georgia.		
394	Hosea Edwards, [6]	7-27, 1802				
395	David S., [6]	6-22, 1794	12-22, 1880			
	Harriet,	9-16, 1808				
	Children of 159 Elijah Booth,[5]					
418	Catharine Booth, [6]	1796			5-18, 1862	Catharine.
	Mason Jones,					"
419	Ransom Eben, [6]	5-8, 1796	1-1, 1818	Catharine, N. Y.,	1-13, 1870	"
	Sally McClure,	3-30, 1801			3-18, 1839	
420	Solomon Smith, [6]	3-11, 1798	2-6, 1826		10-14, 1864	Watkins.
	Fanny Goodspeed Evans.	4-29, 1798		Nichols, N. Y.,	9-30, 1841	"
421	Winthrop Elijah, M. D, [6]	1-1, 1802	1-1, 1842	Watkins, N. Y.,	11-7, 1875	
	Harriet M. Thayer,	7-13, 1818		Ithaca, N. Y.,	9-26, 1865	
422	John Isaac, [6]	11-16, 1804	1832	Catharine, N. Y.,	5-9, 1863	Groton.
	Hannah Thompson,	10-13, 1814			6-20, 1842	Catharine.
	Mary Hurley,	4-6, 1823	9-7, 1843	Townsend, N. Y.		
428	Charlotte Catharine Jones, [6]					
499	George B. Mallett, [6]				12-19, 1894	Millport, N. Y.
563	h. *Edwin Dayton*,				10-23, 1894	Peyton, Col.
588	A. Merilla Mallett Bennett, [7]				2-8, 1895	Tashua, Ct.
594	Maria D. Mallett, [7]	1840			1-22, 1841	

No.	Name		Born	Married	Place	Died	Residence
601	w. Catharine H.,					1867	Argusville, N. Y.
614	Erasmus Darwin Mallett,	7	1852	3-, 1872	Bath, N. Y.,	1-, 1892	
	Mary Decker,						
615b	Giles Fonda Mallett,	7	10-9, 1825	4-18, 1847	Auburndale, O.	10-4, 1852	
	Adaline Haughton,		3-17, 1835	11-21, 1854			
	Laura Jane Doud,						
615c	*w. C. Maria.*	7					
615d	George Washington Mallett,	7	11-20, 1831	11-22, 1862	Huron, S. Dak.	11-13, 1876	Washington, O.
	Malvina Blackman,		12-31, 1834	8-15, 1878	Plymouth, Mich.		
	Fannie Comstock,		11-7, 1839		Westford, N. Y.		
615e	Mary M.,	7	11-15, 1853	5-22, 1862	Toledo, O.		W. Toledo.
	Oscar Smith DeWolf, M. D.,	7	4-14, 1832				
615f	James E.,	7	11-21, 1831	unm.,		1854	W. Toledo, O.
615g	Valorous Lake,	7	4-1, 1837	2-22, 1858	Whiteford, Mich.,	4-9, 1875	"
	6150 Clementine Mallett,[7]		4-23, 1841				
615i	Sally Anne Mallett,	7	2-5, 1809			1-24, 1892	W. Toledo, O.
	William Lewis,		2-15, 1807			8-30, 1884	
615k	*w. Mrs. Benjamin Mallett,*	7					
615l	Montiere,	7	2-15, 1834	12-25, 1857	Toledo.	9-7, 1887	Alabama.
	Mary Jane Hynes,		9-20, 1831		W. Toledo.		
616m	Voltaire,	7	1-, 1843	1861?		During Civil War. 1868	Sylvania. O.
	Olive Benton,						
615n	James Salmon,	7	12-12, 1824	8-18, 1846	Scitico, Conn	2-6, 1893	Somers, Ct.
	Fidelia Pease,		1-8, 1822			2-9, 1893	"
615o	Clementine,	7	4-23, 1841	2-22, 1858	Whiteford, Mich,	4-9, 1875	W. Toledo.
	615g Valorous Luke Mallett,[7]		4-1, 1837	1-28, 1885	Temperance, Mich.		
	Chas. Lyman Clary.		4-28, 1841		W. Toledo,		
615oo	Nathan Dego,	7				9-10, 1870	W. Toledo.
	Eliza Thompson.						
616	Sarah Stevens,	7	1837			8-, 1848	Sharon Spr.
618	Caroline Welch,	7					
619	Lyman Wakeman,	7	3-22, 1818		Schodack, N. Y.,	1836	Canajoharie, N. Y.
	Judith Stansell,		11-28, 1820			1840	"
620	Abram Gandeson,	7	12-8, 1829	10-14, 1856			
	Eliza Könskern,						

No.	Name of Wife (or Husband).	Date of Birth.	Date of Marriage.	Residence.	Date of Death.	Place of Burial.
623	Adaline V.; Jacob C. Anthony, 7	3-7, 18 / 8-24, 1813	8- , 1847	Buffalo, N. Y. "	8-10, 1890	F. L. Buffalo.
624	Roswell C., 7 / Harriet Augusta Bartlett,	11-1, 1830 / 2-3, 1826	1-1, 1857	Redwood, Cal. / Jamaica Plains, Mass.,	9-30, 1889	Redwood.
642	w. Emily,	3-2, 1818				
649	h. Nathan Harris,	3 15, 1824				Monroe, Ia.
650	Emily J. Jackson, / Andrew Jackson Scarbrough, 7		11-2, 1852			Monroe, Ia.
652	h. Morgan B. Gloyd, 7			Monroe, Ia.,		"
653	James F. Jackson, 7					"
654	Julia S.; / E. Roberts, 7			Monroe, Ia.,		
659	4th w. Elizabeth Johnson.	5-30, 1827				
660	h. Arthur McLane,			Erie, Ill.		
675	h. Austin A. (s. Philo) Hall.					
679	Charles E. Plumb, 7 / Susan Ann Hall,	6-12, 1832 / 1-23, 1832			2-11, 1895	Trumbull, Ct.
	*Children of 261 EUNICE WHEELER SMITH,*6					
693	Harriet Grace Smith, 7 / John McElhaney,	1-14, 1816 / 4-7, 1807	3-24, 1884	Bethel, Mo., / Brookfield, Mo.	1-29, 1891	Shiloh Cem., Mo.
694	Esther; 7 / Samuel M. Milliren,	2-14, 1818 / 1-31, 1810	5-16, 1837	Pepin, Wis. "		Pepin, Wis.
694a	Patience, 7 / Peter Lobaugh,	1-14, 1820			6-7, 1870 / 4-1, 1845	Reymursburgh, Pa.
694b	David Wheeler, 7 / Elizabeth Clover,	1-14, 1822 / 8-27, 1824	11-2, 1843	Ringgold, Pa. / Beaver Tp., Pa.,	1-9, 1890	Beaver.
694c	Walker; 7 / Mary Simpson,	3-9, 1824 / 2-12, 1830	7-4, 1849	Patton's Sta., Pa.		

No.	Name		Born		Married	Residence	Died	Residence
694d	Abigail,	7	12-18, 1825		...	...	5-30, 1860	Maysville, Pa.
	Irvin McFarland,							
694e	Elijah,	7	5-22, 1828		1-1, 1850	Ringgold, Pa., ..	3-9, 1863	Ringgold.
	Mary Jane Clover,		5-1, 1831			Sprankle Mills, Pa.		
694f	Malissa,	7	3-28, 1830				1-20, 1834	Beaver twp.
694g	Caroline,	7	4-12, 1832		...	Jacksonville, Fla.		
	Irvin McFarland,					Indiana, Pa.		
694h	John Curtis,	7	8-22, 1883		...	Summerville, Pa.	4- , 1872	
	Sarah Kunselman,		4-2, 1854					
694i	Henry,	7	4-3, 1885		9-30, 1862	Shannondale, Pa.		
	Jane Simpson,		4-12, 1839					
695	Abigail Plumb Nichols,	7	...		...		11-26, 1894	Nichols.
702	*w. 1st Alsada Drew*,	7	...		...		11-29, 1867	Stepney.
757	Rebecca Beardsley,	7	...					
	George Buckley.							
	Children of 312 LEWIS BEARDSLEY,[6]							
785a	Sherman Beardsley.	7	1823					
785b	Francis Schuyler,	7	5-14, 1825		1862			
	Elizabeth Kennedy,		1837					
785c	Maria Louise,	7	12-2, 1827					
785d	Lucy Ann,	7	7-28, 1829		10-14, 1857	Catharine, N. Y.,	10-28, 1886	Catharine.
	Joseph Lyon,		6-30, 1832				4-10, 1892	"
785e	David Curtis,	7	8-28, 1887					
785f	John L. , .		8-28, 1886		1860		1888	Catharine.
	Roxena Bacon,							
	Children of 315 LUCIUS BEARDSLEY,[6]							
786	Delphine Beardsley,	7	7-15, 1845		9-10, 1865	Catharine.		
	Eli Stanley,		5-29, 1845					
787	D. Freeling,	7	6-19, 1849		9- , 1870			
	Lucretia Kendall,		3- , 1850					
852	Susan Hubbell,	7	7-5, 1800		...		11-13, 1856	
853	Ira,	7	1802		...			
854	William,	7	1806		...		8-1, 1835	

No.	Name of Wife (or Husband).	Date of Birth.	Date of Marriage.	Residence.	Date of Death.	Place of Burial.
855	Laura, ... 7	4–15, 1813	9–9, 1841			
856	Levi B., ... 7	9–29, 1816				
857	Charles, ... 7					
949	Samuel A. Miles, ... 7	10–11, 1819				
980	Samuel Beach, M. D.,	1808	1829			
982	Sheldon, Miranda Emmeline,		4–24, 1837			
1000	*w. Rebecca F. Parks.*					

Children of 418 CATHARINE BOOTH JONES,[6]

No.	Name of Wife (or Husband).	Date of Birth.	Date of Marriage.	Residence.	Date of Death.	Place of Burial.
1028a	Lorenzo Jones, ... 7				dec.	
1028b	Elijah, ... 7	1824 or 5			1–4, 1843	
1028c	Menander, ... 7	1826			11–11, 1849	
1028d	Rachel Ann, ... 7					
	Miles Benson.					

Children of 419 RANSOM E. BOOTH,[6]

No.	Name of Wife (or Husband).	Date of Birth.	Date of Marriage.	Residence.	Date of Death.	Place of Burial.
1028e	Chancy I. Booth, ... 7	5–24, 1819			2–22, 1869	Van Ettonville.
1?28f	Sally Ann, ———, ... 7 *Norman Thompson,*	10–12, 1820				
1028g	Ransom, ———, ... 7	10–10, 1827		Burdette. Catharine,	5–12, 1875	Owego.
1028h	Matilda, ... 7	2–1, 1832			2–4, 1832	

Children of 422 JOHN ISAAC BOOTH,[6]

No.	Name of Wife (or Husband).	Date of Birth.	Date of Marriage.	Residence.	Date of Death.	Place of Burial.
1041a	Winthrop E. Booth, ... 7 *Sarah M. Babcock,*	2–21, 1833 4–29, 1836	2–16, 1859	Venice, N. Y.		

No.	Name	Gen.	Born	Married	Residence	Died	Death place
1041b	Smith,	7		10-15, 1862	Auburn, N. Y.		
	Annie Smith,	7	5-27, 1884		Catharine.		
1041c	Mary Elizabeth,	7	5-7, 1887	11-12, 1856	Searsburg, N. Y.		
	James Allen,	7	9-8, 1835		Scipio, N. Y.	8-31, 1882	Stewart's Cor., N. Y.
1041d	Jerome T.,	7	5-2, 1832	6-4, 1861			
	Ellen E. Griswold,	7	3-11, 1837	6-6, 1883			
	Anna D. Murray,	7	5-4, 1844				
1041e	John I.,	7	11-3, 1860	10-16, 1860	Groton, N. Y.	10-25, 1882	Groton.
	Sarah Hard,	7	11-9, 1838			3-18, 1846	Catharine.
1041f	Cornelia Hannah,	7	10-11, 1840	7-16, 1856	Geneva, N. Y.		
	William Perrigo,	7	6-2, 1840				
1041g	Louisa P.,	7	7-7, 1825		Catharine. N. Y.		
1041h	*Morgan B. Becker,*	7	4-4, 1842	9-30, 1869	Towsend, N. Y.		
1041i	Adella M.,	7	7-16, 1844		Venice, N. Y.		
	Frank N. Tracy,	7	10-2, 1846	8-11, 1875	Kankakee, Ill.		
			3-31, 1852				
1050	Joseph C. Hooper,	7		3-23, 1859			
1097	Joseph H. Seawell,	7			Baltimore.	3-1, 1895	Baltimore.
	Florence Hamilton,	7				2-4, 1895	"
1156	Amabel Lee,	7					
	John C. George,	7					
1203	*h. John Sterling,*		5-4, 1817				
1207	*h. James Woodward,*		1830	1867			
1209	Francis A. Mallett,	7		1-26, 1870			
1354	Burr Mallett,	7			Bridgewater, Ct.,	3-8, 1895	Bridgewater, Ct.
1379	Charles E. Dayton,	7		11-21, 1894			
	Clara Hasleton,	7					
	*Children of 520 ABRAM G. WELCH,*7						
1570a	Grace Gertrude Welch,	8	7-15, 1857		San Francisco, Cal.		
1570b	Charles Jay,	8	2-28, 1859		"		
1570c	Emma Dell,	8	8-12, 1861		Oakland, Cal.		
1570d	Annie Dexter,	8	5-14, 1865		"	4-26, 1892	Oakland.

No.	Name of Wife (or Husband).	Date of Birth.	Date of Marriage.	Residence.	Date of Death.	Place of Burial.
	Children of 624 ROSWELL C. WELCH.[7]					
1572a	Walter Roswell Welch, 8	12-12, 1862	12-21, 1887	Redwood, Cal.		
	Lizzie Bonilla,					
1572b	Lillian Florence, 8		11-1, 1888	Redwood, Cal.		
	George W. Eikerenkotte,					
	Children of 694 ESTHER SMITH MILLIREN,[7]					
1713a	Melissa Ann Milliren, 8	3-9, 1888	7-7, 1857	Clover Tp., Pa.,	10-11, 1893	Brookville, Pa.
	Silas Richard Anderson,	6-10, 1833		Brookville, Pa.		
1713b	Hulett Jonathan, 8	2-14, 1840	3-31, 1862	Pepin, Wis.		
	Phidelia Charlotte Goss,	2-1, 1842		"		
1713c	Eunice, 8	2-12, 1842		Clover Tp., Pa.,	5-2, 1844	Troy, Jeff. co., Pa.
1713d	Wesley Walker, 8	7-12, 1844		" "	9-28, 1846	" "
1713e	Irvin Henry, 8	5-1, 1847	10-30, 1877	Pepin, Wis.		
	Emma L. Holden,	10-3, 1855				
1713f	Caroline Patience, 8	5-2, 1849	2-28, 1869	Owatonna, Minn	3-12, 1873	Wabasha, Minn.
	Evan Crum,	11-23, 1835		Wabasha, Minn.,		
1713g	Mary Henrietta, 8	6-2, 1851	2-28, 1869	Clover Tp., Pa.		
	Eli Minder,	10-5, 1888		Ella, Wis.		
1713h	Silas Augustus, 8	7-9, 1853		Clover Tp., Pa.		
1713i	Barton Leander, 8	5-2, 1855	2-1, 1880	Pepin, Wis.		
	Carrie A. Plummer,	11-2, 1862				
1713k	Milo Carlton, 8	4-9, 1857	5-25, 1880	Verdi, Minn.		
	Hannah E. Little,	11-18, 1859		Pepin, Wis.		
1713l	Milton Samuel, 8	4-27, 1858	12-5, 1880	"		
	Clara Jane Whitmarsh,	8-15, 1864		"		
1781	Lillian I. Wheeler,				5-8, 1895	M. G. C. B. C.
	Children of 1028d RACHEL JONES BENSON,[7]					
2282a	Son Benson, 8					

Children of 1041 a WINTHROP E. BOOTH,[7]

No.	Name		Born	Residence	Married	Place	Died
2287a	Franey E. Booth,	8	6-29, 1860	Venice, N. Y.	11-23, 1889	Stewarts Corners, N. Y.	1-20, 1894
	John R. Myers,						
2287b	Mary E.,	8	2-3, 1862		8-21, 1879		
	John Taylor,		8-10, 1863				
2287c	Lorena E.,	8	7-8, 1865		5-29, 1891		
	George E. Bustato,						
2287d	Ellen,	8	6-5, 1868		7-18, 1886		
	George E. Baker,						
2287e	William H.,	8	2-4, 1870				
2287f	Carrie C.,	8	5-6, 1872				
	Seymour Parks,		8-1, 1862		6-6, 1888		
2287g	Edna A.,	8	4-26, 1878				

Children of 1041 b SMITH BOOTH,[7]

No.	Name		Born	Residence	Married	Died
2287h	Mattie E. Booth,	8	3-19, 1864	Trumansburg, N. Y.	6-18, 1890	
	Elbert Lemoyne Hickok,		11-28, 1867	Auburn, Cayuga co., N. Y.		
2287i	Fred Elbert,	8	12-6, 1865	Owego, Tioga co., N. Y.	4-14, 1892	
	Katherine Cook Steele,		12-14, 1870			
2287k	Charlotte H.,	8	7-29, 1870	Groton, N. Y.	6-21, 1893	
	Homer Cornell Stevens,		11-6, 1868	Syracuse, N. Y.		
2287l	George S.,	8	9-28, 1875	Auburn.		

Children of 1041 c MARY E. BOOTH ALLEN,[7]

No.	Name		Born	Married	Place	Died
2287m	Jennie Ellen,	8	7-15, 1859	11-23, 1879	6-23, 1885, Trumansburgh, N. Y.	
	Chas. E. Thompson.					
2287n	Edna M.,	8	11-7, 1861	9-20, 1882		
	Chas. D. Uhl,		9-2, 1853			
2287o	Cora Estelle,	8	1-31, 1868	2-6, 1889		
	David Dumont Wakeman,					
2287p	James Stephen,	8	3-10, 1870	8-4, 1892		
	Jennie Clara Mosher,					

Children of 1041 d JEROME T. BOOTH,[7]

No.	Name		Born	Married
2287q	Adenah Booth,	8	11-17, 1864	10-28, 1885
	Alton E. Banks,		7-22, 1860	
2287r	Minnie E.,	8	6-30, 1872	
2287s	Clark G.,	8	7-12, 1876	

No.	Name of Wife (or Husband).	Date of Birth.	Date of Marriage.	Residence.	Date of Death.	Place of Burial.
2287t	Nina M., [8]	3-16, 1884				
2287u	Delos T., [8]	6-26, 1887				
	Children of 1041 e JOHN I. BOOTH,[7]					
2287v	Henrietta Booth, [8]	1-6, 1862	12-8, 1880			
	D. L. Morey,					
2287w	Alvin, [8]	3-24, 1863	9-15, 1886			
	Fannie M. Perrigo,					
2287x	Emmet R., [8]	4-15, 1866	4-9, 1890			
	Flora Eastwood,					
2287y	Bertha B., [8]	11-3, 1869	8-24, 1892			
	Gurnsey Williams,					
	Children of 1041 f CAROLINE BOOTH PERRIGO,[7]					
2287z	Mary Estelle Perrigo, [8]	10-25, 1858	9-15, 1880			
	Nathaniel Parker Willis Conger,	1-1, 1858				
	Children of 1041 h LOUISA BOOTH BECKER,[7]					
3531	Shirley M. Becker, [8]	11-14, 1870	10-18, 1893			
	Wilmer Young,	3-20, 1865				
3532	Beulah L., [8]	5-17, 1875				
3533	Mable R., [8]	11-27, 1883				
3534	Elizabeth, [8]	9-6, 1885				
	Children of 1572 a WALTER R. WELCH,[8]					
3535	Roswell Carlton Welch, [9]	1888				
3636	Harriet Bartlett, [9]	1893				
	Children of 1572 b LILIAN WELCH EIKERENKOTTE,[8]					
3537	George Carlton Eikerenkotte, [9]	9-30, 1889		Searsville, Cal.,	8-28, 1890	Redwood, Cal.
3588	Earle, [9]	9- , 1893		Redwood.		
3539	Florence Augusta, [9]	1-17, 1895				

No.	Name	9	Birth	Marr./Death	Place	Date	Place
	Children of 1713a MELISSA MILLIREN ANDERSON,[8]						
3540	Albion Lee Anderson,	9	5–6, 1858		Brookville, Jeff. co., Pa.	12–14, 1860	Brookville.
3541	Otis Edgar,	9	1–20, 1860		" "	10–12, 1865	Brookville.
3542	Mark Elmer,	9	6–13, 1862		" "		
3543	Samuel Clyde,	9	9–11, 1864				
3544	Robert Nicholson,	9	12–2, 1868				
3545	Frank Elson,	9	12–9, 1870				
3546	Gertrude Lavilla,	9	12–10, 1877				
	Children of 1713b HULETT J. MILLIREN,[8]						
3547	Samuel Wesley Milliren,	9	3–31, 1863	1–19, 1888	Mondovi, Wis.		
	Mary Ramharter,		6–30, 1870		Durand, Wis.		
3548	Philip Goss,	9	7–1, 1864		Pepin, Wis.		
3549	Frank Anderson,	9	7–12, 1866	9–19, 1893	Pepin, "		
	Barbara Francis De Frang,		12–28, 1871				
3550	Harry Winter,	9	2–28, 1869		Pepin, Wis.		
3551	Clarence Hulett,	9	1–13, 1873		Pepin, "		
	Children of 1713e IRVIN H. MILLIREN,[8]						
3552	Clyde E. Milliren,	9	3–5, 1879		Pepin, Wis.		
3553	Mabel,	9	2–1, 1885		"		
	Children of 1713f CAROLINE MILLIREN CRUM,[8]						
3554	Frank Milliren Crum,	9	9–28, 1870	2–28, 1892	Owatonna, Wis.		
	Minnie M. Giebel,		12–4, 1866		Nelson, Wis.		
3555	Arthur Evan,	9	8–13, 1872				
	Children of 1713g MARY MILLIREN MINDER,[8]						
3556	Jessie Esther Minder,	9	12–7, 1872		Pepin, Wis.		
3557	Nellie Blanche,	9	7–29, 1877		"		
3558	Delbert Barton,	9	1–16, 1879		"		
	Children of 1713i BURTON L. MILLIREN,[8]						
3559	Leroy Milliren,	9	11–6, 1880		Pepin, Wis.		

No.	Name of Wife (or Husband).	Date of Birth.	Date of Marriage.	Residence.	Date of Death.	Place of Burial.
3560	Arthur, ... 9	3-22, 1883	. . .	Pepin, Wis., . . .	dec.	
3561	Eunice, ... 9	3-22, 1883	. . .	"	"	
3562	Bertha M., ... 9	12-26, 1886				
3563	Blossom, ... 9	2-2, 1893				
	Children of 1718k MILO C. MILLIREN,[8]					
3564	Esther Maud Milliren, . 9	3-18, 1881	. . .	Verdi, Minn.		
3565	Jennie Edna, ... 9	7-18, 1882	. . .	"		
3566	Mary Ethel, ... 9	7-29, 1884		"		
3567	Jessie Little, ... 9	2-28, 1886		"		
3568	Cecil Milo, ... 9	6-9, 1889		"		
3569	Myrtle Edith, . . . 9	7-29, 1891		"		
3570	Lois Grace, ... 9	6-26, 1893		"		
	Children of 1718l MILTON S. MILLIREN,[8]					
3571	Iola Milliren, ... 9	12-15, 1882				
3572	Byron Monroe, . . . 9	5-20, 1890				
3573	Walter Donald, . . . 9	7-20, 1893				
	Children of 3547 SAMUEL W. MILLIREN,[9]					
3574	George Samuel Milliren, . 10	12-14, 1890	. . .	Pepin, Wis.		
3575	Ferdinand Alfred, . . . 10	6-24, 1893	. . .	"		
	Children of 3549 FRANK A. MILLIREN,[9]					
3576	Dwight Milliren, . . . 10	12-15, 1894	. . .	Pepin, Wis.		
	Children of 3554 FRANK M. CRUM,[9]					
3577	Romeo Earl Crum, . . . 10	9-10, 1894	. . .	Owatonna, Minn.		
2524	Wilson N. Hurd, . . .		5-29, 1895	Shelton, Ct.		
	Bertha Violet (d. Thom. J.) Northrop,			Naugatuck, Ct.		

BEARDSLEY FAMILY.

No.	Name of Wife (or Husband).	Date of Birth.	Date of Marriage.	Residence.	Date of Death.	Place of Burial.
	Abraham Beardsley, ...	3-6, 1696	4-17, 1723	Stratford.		
	Esther Jeanes, a descendant of Wm. Jeanes, Warden of Christ ch., Stratford, Ct., . .			Stratford.	about 1776	
	Children of ABRAHAM BEARDSLEY,					
	Geo. Beardsley, . .	bap. 12- , 1723				
	Ruth Sherman.					
	Abraham, ...	bap. 11-6, 1725				
	Martha, . . . *Stout.*	bap. 4-28, 1728				
	Abigail, . . .	bap. 5-3, 1730				
	—— *Nichols.*					
	William, ...	bap. 4-9, 1732			1821	Huntington, Ct.
	Priscilla ——.					
	Isaac, . . .	bap. 3-4, 1734			4-16, 1826	
	(16) *Mehitable Mallett,*[4] .	1737			3-25, 1820	
	John, . . .	bap. 1-18, 1738	7-14, 1762			
	Rachel Smith.					
	Sarah, ...	bap. 1-1, 1738				
	Michael, . . .	bap. 9-14, 1740	4-7, 1768		3-25, 1820	
	(19) *Eunice Mallett,*[4] .	1744				
	Esther.					
	Benjamin Beach.					

(Continued on next page.)

Children of GEORGE and RUTH BEARDSLEY,
   Ann, Charity and Philip Beardsley.

Children of WILLIAM and PRISCILLA BEARDSLEY,
   Philo, Elijah, Abram (unm.), David S. Beardsley.

Children of ISAAC and MEHITABLE BEARDSLEY,
   See page 48, 49.

Children of JOHN and RACHEL BEARDSLEY,
   Elisha, born 1763; Sarah, 1765; Martha, 1767; John, 1769 (died at Lansing, N. Y.); Rachel, 1771 (married Col. Booth); Andrew, 1774; John, 1776; Jennie, 1779; Katharine, 1783; Mary Beardsley, 1786.

William Beardsley's son Philo, married and lived in Newtown, Ct.; a weaver; one of his sons, Charles Beardsley, was a physician of good reputation.

Wm. B.'s second son Elijah, married Joanna, daughter of Isaac Lyon. Their children were, Philander, Rachel and John Beardsley.

Wm. B.'s fourth son, David S., married Sarah Lovell; they had one son, David S. Beardsley.

The foregoing brief history of the Beardsley family is taken from the record of Elam Beardsley (p. 59), and may be of interest to the descendants of Mehetable and Eunice Mallett Beardsley.

PROBATE RECORDS, FAIRFIELD, CT.

Book, 1775–1778; pages 56 and 57.

Here followeth an Inventory of ye Estate of Mr. John Mallet Late of Stratford Dec'd as prosented to be apprized by us the Subscribers being under Oath as the Law directs as followeth (viz) August 27th 1776.

To wearing Apparel, ... £1 : 7 : 6

9 lb. old pewter, o | 6.   2 earthen plates & trenchers, 1 | 0,   1 : 6

1 Case Draws 1 | 16.   Old Round Table 3 | 0, ... 1 : 19 : 0

1 Small Looking Glass 5 | 0.   Iron pot 4 | 6.   1 pail 2 | 6,   12 : 0

2 wooden bowls 1 | .   old churn 1 | .   1 cheese press 6d, .   2 : 6

Cream pot 6d.   1 Corn Casket 1 | , ... 1 : 6

Tongs & peal 4 | .   Old Iron 2 | 6.   old Copper Kittle 30 | ,   1 : 16 : 6

2 gallon Bottles 4 | .   Old Oil Can 1 | .   half bushel 2 | ,   .   7 : 0

1 old Sieve 4d.   1 Candle Stick 2d.   9 baggs 12 | , ...   12 : 6

Small Steelyards 2 | 6.   6 Case bottles 5 | , ...   7 : 6

1 Chest & Tools 5 | .   5 sheets 20 | .   1 bed 45 | .   4 old
  coverlids 8 | , ... 3 : 18 : 0

2 pillow cases 2 | .   8 old chairs 4 | .   1 great chair 3 | , .   9 : 0

old chest 1 | 6.   7¼ lb. of White Lead 5 | 6.   1 Trammel
  2 | 6, ...   9 : 6

1 Brass Kittle 20 | .   old Hammer 6d.   1 flax Hetchel 10 | ,   1 : 10 : 6

28½ lb. Sheeps Wool, ... 2 : 7 : 6

2 Augers 2 | 6.   hand Saw 2 | .   1 Iron Square 2 | .   1
  plow 1 | , ...   7 : 6

Drawing knife & 2 gimblets 2 | 6.   5 old Chizzels 2 | 6, . .   5 : 0

1 Adze 2 | .   old broad Ax 3 | 6.   Beattle & one wedge 2 | 3,   7 : 9

an ax 2 | .   Iron Shovel 3 | 6.   2 hoes 4 | .   Steel Trap 8 | ,   17 : 6

3 Bridles 4 | 3.   Corn fan 5 | .   1 Sythe & Cradle 4 | , . .   13 : 3

1 Horse Collar & part of Geers 4 | 6.   1 Clevis & pins 3 | 6,   7 : 6

Stone hammer 1 | .   1 pitch fork 2 | .   Small do 1 | , . . .   4 : 6

Yoke Irons 2 | 6.   1 B—& h—Ring 8d.   1 chain 5 | 6, . .   8 : 8

plow & Irons 6 | .   ferrel for a fork—Old Gouge 4d, . .   6 : 4

1 Grind Stone 7 | .   1 post ax 1 | .   1 wash Tub 2 | 6, . .   10 : 6

7 old hogsheads 16 | .   11½ bushels of Rie 1 : 12 : 9, . . . 2 : 8 : 9

17 Swine all, ... 6 : 13 : 0

1 Coopers Adze 3 | . Crowbar 5 | . 1 Churn 7 | . 1 Gun 40 | ,   2 : 15 : 0

1 pr of Oxen £12.   3 two yr old Heifers £6, ... 18 : 0 : 0

1 pr of young Oxen £10.   1 pr. of Steers £8.   3 yr olds

£4.4 | , ... 22 : 4 : 0

1 yellow Cow 2.18 | 1 Red white face Cow 2.15 | , ... 5 : 13 : 0

1 Red Cow same price 3.0 | . 1 Red Cow 3.0 | , ... 6 : 0 : 0

1 Dark Red Cow 2.13 | . 12 yr Old Bull 2. 2 Calves 1.10 | , 6 : 3 : 0

30 Bushels of Wheat 6.15 | .   36 Bushels of Oats 2.8 | , . . 9 : 3 : 0

23 Bushels Meslin 4.   1 Black Mare & yearling Colt 11, . . 15 : 0 : 0

28 sheep 7.14 | . 1 Cart & Wheels 5, ... 12 : 14 : 0

100 acres of Land West of ye Highway, ... 425 : 0 : 0

1 shop on said Land, ... 10 : 0 : 0

78 acres East of ye Highway, ... 390 : 0 : 0

2 acres of Orchard 20.   12 acres Bogg Meadow 6, ... 26 : 0 : 0

The house on said Orchard 40.   Old Barn 4, ... 44 : 0 : 0

SAM'L ADAMS   } *Apprizers*
JEREMIAH HUBBELL }

At a Court of Probate Held in Fairfield September ye 2d 1776 Then ye above and foregoing Inventory was proved in Common forms may appear by ye Orig'el on file and was by said Court approved and Ordered to be Recorded.

Test.   HEZEKIAH SILLIMAN, *Clerk.*

An addition to the Inventory of Mr. John Mallet, Dec'd:

To 70 Bushel of Indian Corn, ... £8 : 15 : 0

165 lb of flax a 6d per pound, ... 4 : 2 : 0

6 Bushels of flax seed 18 | . 20 lb of Tanned Leather

1.3 | 4, ... 2 : 1 : 4

SAM'L ADAMS   } *Apprizers*
JEREMIAH HUBBELL }

FROM PROBATE RECORDS, FAIRFIELD, CT.

To the Worshipful Court of Probate for ye East District of Fairfield County. An exact acct. of the apprized of the Estate of Peter Mallet Late of Stratford Decd.

	£	s	d
To 1 Pr Oxen £15. Do 1 pr £12, ...	27	0	0
Do 1 pr. £10. 1 Dun white-faced Cow £3. Do. Red white-			
faced, £3 : 10, ...	16	10	0
Do blk ox £2.15. Do farrow one £2–10. Do brown, 55 | .,	8	0	0
Do pide one 60 | . Do red pide 60 | . Do Red white faced			
65 | , ...	9	11	0
Do red young cow £3.10. Do Dun farrow, 50 | . Do			
Red do 50 | , ...	8	10	0
Do 3 four yr Old Steers £9. Do 4 three yr. old steers £10,	19	0	0
Do 6, 2 year olds £13.4. Do 8, yr old £9, ...	22	4	0
Do 1 old mare 50 | . Do young mare £5. Do 1 Colt £1, .	8	10	0
Do 1 Rone mare £9. Do 1 Horse £8. Do Stallion Horse, £5,	22	0	0
Do 1 blk Horse £5. Do 70 sheep £24, ...	29	0	0
Do 8 Swine £6.4. Do 14 Swine £7.10. Do Negro Girl			
Peg £16, ...	29	0	0
Do 1 Negro man Simon £70. Do Negro man Fortune £70,	140	0	0
Do 1 Negro man Cesar £55. Do Negro woman Molatto			
Ann £40, ...	95	0	0
Do 68 acres Land over agt House East highway at £5.10, .	374	0	0
Do homestead 45 acres and ½ at £6, ...	273	0	0
Do Sherman Lot 30 acres at £4–10, ...	135	0	0
Do up'r farme 230 acres at £4.10, ...	1035	0	0
Do house, barns & buildings on homestead, ...	95	0	0
Do Barn and Old house on up'r farme, ...	27	0	0
Do Rye & Wheat on Ground, ...	45	0	0
Do 164 bushels wheat at 5 | 3, ...	42	18	8
Do bus'el Indian corn at, ...			
Do of flax in the Barn, ...		0	0

Lawful money, ... £2475 : 7 : 8

BONDS, NOTES ALL YORK MONEY.

Do on note of hand due from Mr. Beebee, N. Y. money, . . 39 : 3 : 0
Do on note from Eph'm Peet, £11 : 2. Do from Samuel
    Beardslee, £10 : 4, ... 31 : 6 : 0
Do Math'w Hawley, £12 : 9. Do Eln'th Sherman, £9 : 10 : 8, 26 : 15 : 8
Do Dav'd Mallet, £52 : 10 : 6. Do Sol. Burton, £46 : 8 : 6, 98 : 19 : 0
Do Jesse Bankes, £14 : 18 : 14. Do Eben booth, £64 : 3 : 5, 79 : 1 : 9
Do Sam'l Jackson & Gersham Hubble, £64 : 14 : 4. Do Sol-
    omon Palmer, £70 : 7 : 7, ... 135 : 1 : 11
Do William Lampher, £10. Thos. Benedict, 105 : 10 . . 115 : 10 : 0
Do Will'm Tanner & Samuel Canfield, £104 : 10 : 0. Do
    David Wheeler, 120 : 15 : 0, ... 225 : 0 : 0
Do Will'm Lampier & Moses Wheeler and Math'w Hawley, 269 : 0 : 0
Do Solomon Palmer, £231. Do Sam. Averel & Daton,
    £218 : 16, ... 449 : 16 : 0
Do Curtiss Fairchild & Birdseye, £105 : 10. Do James
    Hard, £105 : 10, ... 211 : 0 : 0
Do Thad'es Burr, £315. Do Roger Sherman, £79 : 11, . . 394 : 11 : 0
Do 3 notes from Mr. Dan'el Booth, ... 147 : 13 : 0
Do Dan'el Bradley, £15 : 9. Do Isaac Pitkin & Duncane,
    £116 : 18, ... 132 : 7 : 0
Do Sam'l Hall, ... 4 : 0 : 0
Do Jos. Phelps, £29 : 10. Do Dav'd, £200 : 16, ... 230 : 6 : 0
Do James Davison & Smith, £103 : 10. Do Ozias Goodwin
    & Gilman, £35, ... 138 : 10 : 0
Do Jos. Phelps, £29 : 8. Do Dan'el Fulsome, £29 : 8, . . 58 : 16 : 0
Do Ozias Goodwin & Gilman, £420. Do Jos. Phelps and
    Ann, £543 : 7, ... 963 : 7 : 0
Do Jos. Osmer & Turlson, £419. Do Dav'd Hubbard,
    £135 : 15, ... 739 : 15 : 0
David Hubbard, £376 : 4. Do Dan'el Hayden & Phelps,
    338 : 8, ... 714 : 12 : 0
Do Dav'd Hubbard, 271 : 16 : 0. Do Dan'el Hayden &
    Avery, 128 : 7, ... 400 : 3 : 0
Do Tho's Burr, £5 : 12 : 10. Do Jos. Phelps & Tilotson, £420, 932 : 10 : 0

      York money, ... £4461 : 19 : 0

To 1 Coat 20 | . Do —— 10 | . flanel Coat 10 | . Do
  great Coat 6 | . 1 hat 10 | , ...   2 : 16 : 0
pr Breeches 10 | . Shirt 6 | . pr boots 13 | . 3 pr stock'gs
  7 | . Sword 8 | . 3 Shirts 7 | , ...   2 : 11 : 0
blue vest 10 | . Gun 35 | . 17 y'd flan'el, 2 : 2 : 0. 40 yd
  tow cloth 5 : 3 | 4., ...   7 : 0 : 7
Sadle 25 | . Do old Sadle 5 | . Sa'd baggs 14 | . Side Sa'd
  35 | . 2 brid'l 5 | 6., ...   4 : 4 : 6
27 lb Lin. yarn 54 | . Do 13 ; tow 17. 47 lb. Pewter 58 | .
  brass kettle 54 | , ...   9 : 3 : 0
Brass kettle £1 : 2. Do 1 at 4 | . Iron Pot 10 | . Do 5 | .
  Do 6 | . kettle 5 | . Frying pan 4 | , ...   2 : 16 : 0
1 Tea kettle 5 | . 1 warming pan 5 | . tin oven 12 | . 2
  Canisters 2 | 2. Coffee pot, Pan, tun'l and Dipper 5 | , .   1 : 9 : 0
1 Tea-pot 3 | . 9 knives and Forks 7 | . 5 Candlesticks 4 | .
  2 pr sheers 1 | . pr sheep sheers 2 | . pr. Steely'd 3 | , .   1 : 0 : 0
Great steely'd 13 | . water pot 2 | . box & heater 6 | .
  Peel & tongs 6 | . Trivet and Tost Iron 4 | , ...   1 : 11 : 0
Grid Iron 2 | . Rung Iron 8 | . Scimmers 2 | . Lamp &
  fork 1 | 6. pr. hand Irons 8 | . ham'r 2 | , ...   16 : 2
2 tram'el 7 | 2. Raisors 3 | . Earth. Ware 10 | . Jug 4 | .
  Case & 8 bottles 14 | . 9 Glass bottles 5 | , ...   2 : 3 : 0
bed, Pillows & bolster 66 | 6, wt. 51, at 34 | . Do 8 | . Do
  post bed 30 | , ...   6 : 18 : 0
1 Cov'd ¦ 2 blanket & quilt 44 | . Do 5 | . Cov'd 38 | . 2
  blankets 16 | , ...   4 : 18 : 0
15 sheets £3 : 15. 8 Pillow cases 8 | . 3 table Clothes, 5 | .
  a Thacher and 10 Towels 7 | , ...   4 : 15 : 0
negro beds 22 | . Chest Draws 15 | . Chest 21 | . Drop
  table 8 | . Stand 2 | 4. bedstead 12 | , ...   3 : 3 : 0
4 bed Cords 8 | . look. Glass 6 | . Chest 5 | . 3 tables
  12 | . pr knee Buckles Silver 7 | , ...   1 : 18 : 0
1 Silk hand kf 3 | , and 3 hol'd Caps 3 | . 15 Chains 30 | .
  Cheese Press, Great wheel and Reel 13 | , ...   2 : 9 : 0
Dutch wheel 9 | . Chop knife 2 | . 5 Pails 7 | 6. 2 Chains
  10 | . 2 butter Tubs 4 | , ...   1 : 12 : 6
3 woodn Bottles 6 | . table 4 | 12. Dry Cask 24 | . hatchet
  8 | . 10 Trays & bols 17 | 6, ...   2 : 19 :

3——Dishes 4 | . Do wood Dishes 7 | . little wheel 2 | .
  beatle & weg's 3 | , ...   16 : 0
Curry comb | 2. Saw, Gimlet, Aug'r & Sq'r 9 | . 10 bags
  10 | . 3 bu. Salt 12 | , ...   1 : 11 : 0
2 Shovels 5 | . Grindstone 6 | . 20 bus Rye 50 | . 30 Bus'el
  Oats 37 | . Clav'el 6 | , ...   5 : 4 : 0
5½ lb nails 3 | 8. bible 15 | . 3 small bibles 7 | . Watts
  verse book 1 | , ...   1 : 6 : 8
Testament 2 | . 10 old Books 10 | . adds 3 | . 4 Sickles 6 | .
  5 bells 5 | . 52 lb Old Iron 13 | , ...   1 : 19 : 0
2 set plow Irons 20 | . 3 Chains 22 | 9. 2 pr Clav's 4 | .
  Set plough Irons 15 | . Do 15 | , ...   3 : 16 : 9
pr Iron band Cart wheels 3 | 5. 2 Syths 2 | . pr horse
  Geers 8 | . 4 yokes & Irons 18 | , ...   4 : 13 : 0
4 bbls pork £12. Do 1 bbl beef £1 : 15 : 18. bbl Syd'r 7 | 4.
  6 Empty hogsh'd 1 | 10, ...   22 : 9 : 0
11 Empty bbl 36 | . Beer & meat Casks 10 | . 26 lbs flaxe
  13 | , ...   2 : 19 : 0
4 lb Lead & 1 lb powder 5 | . 2 Flasks 5 | , ...   0 : 10 : 0
                                                        ———————
                                                        109 : 7 : 11

The above worke completed June 25th, 1760.

Theoph's Nichols, ⎫
Samuel Gregory, ⎬ *apps.*
James Walker, ⎭

INDEX.

INDEX.

MALLET.

OTHER NAMES THAN MALLET.

9 780788 415890